The Inner Work of Age

"This is a profound book. Take your time with it. You will find a broad range of ideas, interviews, and spiritual practices pointing to the inner work that we need to undertake for ourselves, our families, our communities, and our planet. Choose from among the vast array of insights and practices that Connie makes available to you and get to work."

THOMAS R. COLE, PH.D., McGOVERN CHAIR IN
MEDICAL HUMANITIES AT THE UNIVERSITY OF TEXAS
HEALTH SCIENCE CENTER AT HOUSTON AND
AUTHOR OF *THE JOURNEY OF LIFE* AND *OLD MAN COUNTRY*

"*The Inner Work of Age* is an inspiring roadmap to uncover our motivations for what we do with our precious long lives. Even after many years of teaching positive aging and activism, this book has me questioning and exploring my inner self to consider my future choices."

LYNNE ISER, PRESIDENT OF ELDERS ACTION NETWORK,
FOUNDING EXECUTIVE DIRECTOR OF
SPIRITUAL ELDERING INSTITUTE,
AND CERTIFIED SAGE-ING LEADER

"We need stories of possibility. This is a rare book distilled from Connie's deep and broad experience studying the leap from adulthood to elderhood. When I read it, I knew I was in the presence of a wise guide."

RICHARD LEIDER,
FOUNDER OF INVENTURE—THE PURPOSE COMPANY AND
AUTHOR OF *THE POWER OF PURPOSE*

"Connie Zweig expands on my invitation to 'refirement.' *The Inner Work of Age* offers us a veritable resource book on healthy aging and refiring of the soul that honors the rite of passage that eldership is and that our society neglects to its peril. I highly recommended her diligent and insightful contributions!"

MATTHEW FOX, SPIRITUAL THEOLOGIAN,
FOUNDER OF CREATION SPIRITUALITY, AND
AUTHOR OF *THE HIDDEN SPIRITUALITY OF MEN*
AND *JULIAN OF NORWICH*

Also by Connie Zweig, Ph.D.

Nonfiction

To Be a Woman: The Birth of the Conscious Feminine

Meeting the Shadow: The Hidden Power of the Dark Side of Human Nature with Jeremiah Abrams

Romancing the Shadow: A Guide to Soul Work for a Vital, Authentic Life with Steve Wolf, Ph.D.

Meeting the Shadow of Spirituality: The Hidden Power of Darkness on the Path (formerly *The Holy Longing*)

Fiction

A Moth to the Flame: The Life of the Sufi Poet Rumi

The Inner Work of Age

Shifting from ROLE to SOUL

CONNIE ZWEIG, PH.D.

Park Street Press
Rochester, Vermont

Park Street Press
One Park Street
Rochester, Vermont 05767
www.ParkStPress.com

Text stock is SFI certified

Park Street Press is a division of Inner Traditions International

Cataloging-in-Publication Data for this title is available from the Library of Congress

ISBN 978-1-64411-340-0 (print)
ISBN 978-1-64411-341-7 (ebook)

Printed and bound in the United States by Lake Book Manufacturing, Inc.
The text stock is SFI certified. The Sustainable Forestry Initiative® program
promotes sustainable forest management.

10   9   8   7

Text design by Priscilla H. Baker and layout by Virginia Scott Bowman
This book was typeset in Garamond Premier Pro, Legacy Sans, Avenir, and Gill Sans
with Museo Sans and Hermann used as display typefaces

To send correspondence to the author of this book, mail a first-class letter to the
author c/o Inner Traditions • Bear & Company, One Park Street, Rochester, VT
05767, and we will forward the communication, or contact the author directly at
conniezweig.com.

To Neil

who wears the face of the Beloved for me

☙

To the grandchildren

who are the future

Contents

FOREWORD

Meeting the Shadow of Age   xiii
by Harry R. Moody, Ph.D.

PROLOGUE

A Letter to My Fellow Travelers in Late Life   xvii

INTRODUCTION

Age Is Our Curriculum   1

PART I

The Divine Messengers

1   Aging from the Inside Out   14

     The Buddha's Divine Messengers   16

     Rites of Passage   19

     What Is "Old?" Telling the Whole Truth   25

     When Do We Become "Old"?   32

     Aging as Fate   34

2   The Three Portals of Age   38

     Shadow Awareness: Portal to Depth   40

     Pure Awareness: Portal to Silent Vastness   49

     An Interview with Rabbi Rami Shapiro   54

     An Interview with Kirtan Chant Leader Krishna Das   56

     Mortality Awareness: Portal to Presence   59

3 Meeting Ageism from the Inside Out
and the Outside In   68

    Meeting Your Inner Ageist: From the Inside Out   70

    The Dramatic Consequences of the Inner Ageist   75

    Meeting the Collective Shadow of Ageism:
      From the Outside In   78

    *An Interview with Ageism Crusader Ashton
      Applewhite*   84

4 Retirement as a Divine Messenger   89

    To Retire or Not to Retire?   92

    Retirement from the Outside In   96

    Retirement as Reinvention: Encore Careers   100

    Shadow-Work for Retirement: From the Inside Out   104

    Retirement from Clinical Practice: My Story
      as a Helping Professional   110

    Retirement as Spiritual Practice: From Role to Soul   116

5 Life-Changing Illness as a Divine Messenger   121

    From Terrible Wound to Sacred Wound   123

    Closing the Mind/Body Split   125

    Illness of the Body: Cancer as an Answer   127

    Shadow-Work for Illness: From the Inside Out   135

    Caregiving from the Inside Out   140

    Illness of the Mind: Depression or Disillusionment   145

    Illness of the Brain: Memory Loss as Epidemic   148

    Delaying Memory Loss and Enhancing Plasticity   153

    *An Interview with Buddhist Psychologist
      Rick Hanson*   156

    Illness as Spiritual Practice: From Role to Soul   158

PART 2

Life Review and Life Repair

6 A Review of Your Lived and Unlived Life   164

Physician Rachel Naomi Remen on Seeing Her
Life with New Eyes   170

The Ego's Life Review: What Was Expressed   172

The Shadow's Life Review: What Was Repressed   181

*An Interview with Father Thomas Keating,
Founder of Centering Prayer*   185

**7 Emotional and Creative Repair to
Release the Past and Live in the Present**   190

Emotional Repair: Reinventing Relationships
from Role to Soul   194

An Interview with Jungian Analyst James Hollis   199

An Interview with Psychiatrist Roger Walsh   208

Lost Creativity Found: The Gold in the Dark Side   209

**8 Spiritual Repair to Reimagine
Our Beliefs and Reclaim Our Practices**   218

Shadow-Work for Spiritual Disillusionment   219

Spiritual Work: Reclaiming Our Practices   231

PART 3

From Hero to Elder

9 Elder with a Thousand Faces   242

What Is an Elder?   245

Becoming an Elder: A Rite of Passage   255

*An Interview with Ron Pevny, Founder of the
Center for Conscious Eldering*   257

Letting Go: Inner Work for Resistant Heroes   259

Meeting the Inner Elder: An Initiation   266

New Beginnings: Reimagining the Elder from
    the Inside Out   269

An Interview with Mythologist and Storyteller
    Michael Meade   271

An Interview with Poet, Novelist, Activist
    Deena Metzger   273

An Interview with Jungian Analyst Lionel Corbett   276

Honoring One of My Elders: Jungian Analyst
    Marion Woodman   277

**10   Elder Wisdom and the Call
to Age into Awakening**   **281**

The Final Divine Messenger: The Monk's
    Call to Awaken   283

Awakening into Higher Stages of Awareness   285

What Is Wisdom?   291

Transmitting Wisdom to Future Generations   297

An Interview with Integral Philosopher Ken Wilber   299

An Interview with Mystic Robert Atchley   300

An Interview with Buddhist Teacher
    Anna Douglas   301

**11   Elder Activism and the Call to Serve
Something Larger than Ourselves**   **308**

The Call to Sacred Service and Elder Activism   310

The Shadow Side of Service   313

Heeding the Call or Denying the Call: Inner Work
    for Resistant Elders   318

An Interview with John Sorensen, Founder of
    Elders Action Network   322

An Interview with Roshi Wendy Egyoku Nakao,
    Former Abbot of the Zen Center of Los Angeles   323

Conscious Grandparenting: Caring for the Souls
    of Our Young Ones   326

Climate Change: Collective Mortality Awareness   330

PART 4

Life Completion

12 Moving toward a Completed Life 338

An Interview with Altered States
Pioneer Stanislav Grof **344**

An Interview with Transpersonal Psychologist
Frances Vaughan **345**

13 Reimagining Death as the Last Rite 348

The Shadow Knows: Its Secret Preparation for
the End **351**

An Interview with Spiritual Teacher
Mirabai Bush, Coauthor with Ram Dass **356**

EPILOGUE

A Legacy Letter to the Grandchildren 361

Acknowledgments 366

APPENDIX

A Shadow-Work Handbook for
Aging Consciously 369

Bibliography 371

Index 384

Meeting the Shadow of Age

By Harry R. Moody, Ph.D.

However much I fled, my shadow did not leave me. . . .
Only the sun has the power to drive away shadows, the sun
* increases and diminishes them;*
seek this from the sun.
      MYSTICAL POEMS OF RŪMĪ (TRANS. A. J. ARBERRY)

During many decades as a gerontologist, executive, speaker, and writer in the positive aging and conscious aging communities, I waited and watched for a depth psychologist to bring the inner world into our field. I frequently left conferences disappointed that we didn't hear the voices, the subjective experiences, of the older people we were studying. I eagerly hoped that someone eventually would build bridges between the crucial objective social, institutional, economic, and political issues and the equally crucial subjective psychological, emotional, and spiritual issues of our aging population.

For example: What does someone experience who finds renewed purpose after ending a long career? How can that renewal be supported by institutions and community? What is the subjective experience of making amends with someone who betrayed us in an effort to feel forgiveness at the end of life? What is it like internally to make a shift from unconscious senior, living in denial, to conscious Elder, living with deep awareness and sharing her gifts? And how can society enable more people to make this psychological shift?

Conversely, what is the inner lived experience of a woman whose self-image is rooted in her work but who loses her career to ageism? What happens to a man's self-respect when he can no longer be a provider? What is the internal experience of a woman who becomes critically ill, facing her mortality for the first time, and is unable to care for her family? How can society and families support aging transitions that involve not just changes in roles but profound internal changes in identity, meaning, and purpose?

Then *The Inner Work of Age* arrived on my desk, as if in answer to my plea. In stories and interviews, it uncovers a realm of aging that is unexplored territory: the unconscious, or Shadow, as Carl Jung called it. The Shadow is that part of us that lies beneath or behind the light of awareness. It contains our rejected, unacceptable traits and feelings. It also contains our hidden gifts and talents that have remained unexpressed or unlived. As Jung put it, the essence of the Shadow is pure gold.

As Rumi said above, only the sun, the light of awareness, can expose those dark, unknown recesses within us and eventually diminish them. The brighter the sun, the fainter the shadow. And Connie Zweig, well-known author of bestsellers on this topic, is the ideal explorer to go where no author has gone before—into the shadows of age.

Her book is organized around the unconscious inner obstacles that block our capacity to fulfill the extraordinary possibilities of late life. But more than that, it offers the tools—her method of shadow-work and spiritual practices from many traditions—to overcome those obstacles. Let me give you one example.

I believe that our dreams show us what we already know but cannot see. Jung developed dream work to explore the Shadow for that reason. Years ago, I had this dream: I applied to medical school at the age of seventy and felt distressed because I was rejected. Upon waking up, I realized that ageism is in me, not just outside of me in social institutions.

There are many books about the ravages of cultural ageism. But Connie writes about the "inner ageist"—that part of me that rejected myself in the dream. And that part of you, dear reader, that rejects yourself by hanging on to youth, self-image, success, control, and denial of death at all costs. In other words, she explores ageism from the inside out, guiding us to become aware of the inner ageist and to allow it out of the shadow and into the light.

Connie advocates for a combination of inner work and social justice work to resolve other critical issues of our time as well, from the global aging population to climate change, political activism, service and legacy, the cancer epidemic, family caregiving, repairing relationships, and spiritual awakening. In each case, she includes the dimension of the Shadow, broadening and deepening the inner landscape of the issue.

In the end, this book is a call to awaken emotionally, spiritually, and culturally to live fully who we are.

To extend Rumi's metaphor, as the day draws to an end, shadows build. At twilight, when the sun goes down, it becomes harder to see. When night falls, and there is no light, we make our way blindly, feeling for the path. So it is with old age. Only the sun—the light of awareness—has the power to drive away shadows. And this book and its tools promise to shed light on your fulfilling and surprising path ahead.

Harry R. Moody, Ph.D., former vice president and director of academic affairs for AARP, former director of the Brookdale Center for Healthy Aging at Hunter College, and former chair of Elderhostel (now Road Scholar), is currently faculty at the Fielding Graduate University and editor of the *Human Values in Aging* newsletter. He is coauthor of *Aging: Concepts and Controversies* and author of *The Five Stages of the Soul: Charting the Spiritual Passages That Shape Our Lives.* He is a recipient of the Lifetime Achievement Award from the American Society on Aging.

In my beginning is my end . . .

T. S. ELIOT

A Letter to My Fellow Travelers in Late Life

If you feel lost or disoriented, unable to see what's next for you;

If you feel isolated and don't know how to find your tribe;

If you feel regret about a past action and it keeps gnawing at you;

If you wish to give forgiveness or to be forgiven;

If you seek a new contemplative practice for this stage of life;

Or if you simply long for something more, such as more self-knowledge or gratitude, more meaning or contribution, then you can find it here.

You can discover how to reorient by turning within, attuning to your soul's longing and cultivating a deeper shift in awareness. You can discover how to move through the passage of late life as a rite, releasing past forms, facing the unknown, and emerging renewed as an Elder filled with vitality and purpose.

And if you have a loved one who is a traveler in late life, or if you are a therapist or caregiver to one, then you can find precious guidance to assist him or her in this book. You can open doors that will offer your loved one fresh insight and, perhaps, lead him or her in a new direction.

The simple fact of a birthday, of putting one more year behind us, does not bring about this transition from adult to Elder. The path onto this stage of life is filled with inner obstacles. So, it must be walked with intention. It requires specific tools to uncover those obstacles and to learn how to move past them. It also requires us to bring forward those traits and gifts that served us in earlier stages of life—our self-awareness, sense of social justice, deep empathy, embeddedness in nature, consensus-building skills, creative know-how, and spiritual thirst. As we gather these fruits of our labors within us, we prepare to begin the inner work of age.

Whatever age you are, fellow traveler—Baby Boomer, Generation X, Gen Y (Millennial), or Gen Z—if you have opened this book, then you have heard the call. Every generation has a tale, a myth, that is rooted in its cultural moment, the need and the promise of the era—a controversial war, a booming or stumbling economy, a breakthrough innovation, a political swing of the pendulum, a demand for social justice, a public health crisis, an ongoing climate crisis, even a collective mood of hope or despair. As a result, aging from the outside in—retirement security, food and housing security, workplace ageism, race equity, social services, health care options—looks different for different generations. But aging from the inside out, my focus here, is the same for all generations, for all human beings in any era.

For this reason, we all have the opportunity to radically reinvent and reimagine the process of aging for ourselves. And I don't mean merely doing more or doing differently. I don't use "reinvention" in the way that many experts do—from the outside in. That's the topic of most books about aging.

Rather, our emphasis here is on the internal, less familiar terrain of soul—those subtle yearnings that appear in images and fantasies, the ways we respond or fear to respond to those messengers, and the symbolic meanings we glean from them. As we learn the psychological and spiritual practices that are offered in this book, we discover how to orient to our inner worlds in this way. We deepen our self-knowledge and become able to reimagine age for ourselves, eventually shifting from denial to awareness, from self-rejection to self-acceptance, from obligation to flow, from holding on to letting go. Even from distraction to presence.

The result: a newfound freedom from the constraints of past roles and identities, an emerging sense of becoming who you were always meant to be, and a profound gratitude for the way that your life unfolded. As we make this internal shift in awareness, a natural generosity arises within us, and we seek to share our gifts of love and wisdom as a lasting legacy.

This is the deeper dimension of age, the universal inner journey of human development or expanded awareness, which includes the extraordinary potentiality of this stage of life, the unfolding of our psychological and spiritual authenticity and authority, and even the unfolding of advanced stages of human development, which are described in every religious and spiritual tradition as the purpose of late life.

This process is not about what we do or don't do: more work and more volunteering or less work and less volunteering. Rather, it's about *how* we do it: the internal state of mind that can arise as we do this inner work of age. This deep work is a unique journey for each of us. But the hunger for it is universal.

When I began to research this book, I offered workshops to hundreds of people over the age of fifty, and they all, to a person, expressed this hunger. Most participants described it as feeling disoriented, without direction, groping in the dark. They reported that they felt marginalized, invisible, and unimportant. Others spoke about the loss of purpose that came with the loss of work roles or family roles. Many could not let go of the past to be fully present now. Some spoke openly about their fear of illness and death. But each one also told me that he or she sensed, intuitively, that there was something more to life, something hidden that had been missing, a mystery that remained unexamined.

As I listened to many people for several years, I began to hear a pattern: People entering late life suffer another identity crisis, a return of the questions *Who am I? What are my values? What do I believe? What matters most to me? How can I give back to the common good?*

We typically ask these questions during a midlife crisis, too. But at that stage of life, the response tends to be a change in roles, a change in career or spouse or geographical location. However, in late life, a change in role is not sufficient. There is no romantic or geographic solution to our longing.

As I began to share the framework of this book with my workshop participants—the idea that late life is a call to another rite of passage—and teach them the practices outlined here, they told me they discovered how to center themselves and find a new orientation in space and time. As one woman said, "Oh, I've had an identity crisis before. I've heeded a call to change. I know how to do this. What was frightening before is familiar now with this framework to orient me."

One man told me, "In midlife, I was always striving to progress, to move forward. It doesn't feel right to say that I'm moving forward now. It's more like I'm moving further, still growing but in a totally different way at a different pace."

Another woman reported that when she turned seventy, she couldn't find what she called an "internal GPS" for this period. She had no navigator and no destination until she learned, with the inner work of age, how to orient toward soul.

On the other hand, many people strive to be young or "ageless," pushing themselves to do more so that they can feel relevant or successful, using anti-aging products to uphold their image, and denying the deeper call of late life. Typically, they are not aware that they are in denial of age, that they are struggling with internal, unconscious obstacles that block their development and the flow of their lives.

These "shadow characters," which we will explore in this book, resist transition and impede us from discovering the hidden power of late life. They reinforce the walls of denial out of fear of change or loss, keeping us stuck in archaic roles and identities for years, which leads to an absence of aliveness and stagnation, even depression. So, in the clutches of an internal shadow character, we fail to cross over and enter a new stage of development. We fail to fulfill our destiny.

This leads us to the purpose of this book: to guide you past denial to the inner work that allows you to investigate your resistance to life as it is. When we examine life consciously, in the context of impending death, we can fully respond to the messengers of age. We can repair the past to fully inhabit the present. And we can be free to make the transitions in late life as meaningful and rewarding as they can be. As a result, we can age from the inside out.

For many of us, this stage of life can be challenging. Our lifelong ideals and high expectations crash up against limits of all kinds—the limits of an aging brain/mind/body, the limits of a fraying financial safety net, the limits of discrimination against age, race, and gender, even the limits of love. Certainly, the limits of time.

The vibrant promise of our youth may seem dreamlike, a sweet song lost in the noisy, chaotic air of this moment. Perhaps we have suffered immense wounding and loss; we may feel weakened and discouraged both with ourselves and with society. We may need guides even now to complete our quest, to hand on our gifts to future generations. My hope is that this book can be such a guide for you.

As longevity expands for many of us, it opens the opportunity to expand our awareness as well. I invite you to do the inner work of age so that you make the shift from role to soul. This is the work of life completion for every generation. This is the last line of the song.

Age Is Our Curriculum

Clearly, every older generation no longer lives in the world in which it grew up. With the dizzying speed of change, we travelers in late life may feel exhausted or left behind. Our democracy, once taken for granted, has been hacked. Bookstores are as extinct as mastodons. Customer-service jobs have been replaced by robots. Phones now act as prosthetics. Digital platforms are the kids' playgrounds. And the grandkids are talking to Alexa as if she's a wish-granting genie in the walls of their homes.

As we watch today's massive scientific and technological breakthroughs unfold, we also watch widespread social and cultural breakdown. We are living in a time of simultaneous, interconnected crises: a rapidly warming climate that's creating extreme weather events, the risk of future pandemics, a backlash against globalization and liberal democracy, an ever-expanding concentration of power in multinational corporations and social media platforms, and a growing awareness of racial inequity in every domain of life. So, why read (or write!) about aging? At first glance, it may seem mistaken to focus on this issue, given the urgency of others. But age—by the numbers—tells a startling story. And that story is not merely about increasing longevity but about the changing form and meaning of human life and its course of development in families and communities.

Age is a lens through which we can view other crises. This lens enables us to see the intersectionality of issues that appear to be separate.

It also exposes the strengths, weaknesses, and inherent responsibilities of society for young and old alike. The statistics in the following box describe the larger story in which our personal stories are unfolding.

Age by the Numbers

- *Demographics:* In 2017, the United Nations Department of Economic and Social Affairs predicted that by 2050 the world's population over sixty years old will reach two billion. In the United States, a 2017 Census Bureau report predicted that by 2050 the population over age sixty will be greater than eighty-three million. And, it said, by 2035, for the first time, there will be more older adults than children. These statistics have multiple implications for the labor force, health care, social security, housing, transportation, consumerism, education, and family patterns.

- *Income inequality and age:* Income inequality and longevity inequality (inequality in the number of years lived) are correlated. A 2016 study by Eric Neumayer and Thomas Plümper found that governments could reduce differences in life span among diverse groups with policies that increased wealth in low-income communities.

- *Gender inequality and age:* Gender and age intersected in a 2001 study reported by Michael Anzick and David Weaver of the Social Security Office of Policy. The poverty rate for older women is 11.8 percent, compared with 6.9 percent for men in the same age group. And for unmarried women it's 17 percent.

- *Racial inequality and age:* The poverty rate for older people of color is more than twice as high as the rate for all older people. In 2019, Sabrina Terry reported, for the National Community Reinvestment Coalition, that 83 percent of African American senior households and 90 percent of Hispanic senior households have insufficient money to live out their years, compared with 53 percent of Whites. Racial health disparities also result in lower life expectancy. For example, Black women appear to be aging faster than White women. A 2010 study led by Arline Geronimus, published in *Human Nature,* found that Black women between the ages of forty-nine and fifty-five are seven and a half years biologically older than White peers due to chronic stress. The evidence: shorter chromosome telomeres, indicating cell death and poor survival.

- *Sexual orientation inequality and age:* In a large study of gender identity and age, reported by Karen Fredriksen-Goldsen et al., in *The Gerontologist,* researchers found dramatic health disparities between LGBTQ people over fifty and their heterosexual counterparts. For example, older gay men and women were more likely to have chronic disease and depression. Same-sex couples faced higher poverty rates than their heterosexual peers.

- *Voting and age:* According to a report by Joy Intriago on the website SeniorsMatter.com, a 2012 study on voting and age revealed that 90 percent of people over sixty are registered to vote, while only 75 percent of those between eighteen and thirty are registered. As the older demographic grows, so does their impact.

- *Immigration and age:* There is a surprising link between age and immigration. Mauro Guillen, professor at the Wharton School, suggested that there is one proven way to rebalance our low birth rate with our growing older population: immigration. Contrary to conventional wisdom, most immigrants are of working age. In the United States in 2017, their average age was thirty-one. Guillen proposes encouraging the immigration of health care workers, such as doctors, nurses, and home health aides, who are needed to address the increasing needs of those in late life.

- *Mental health/gun policy and age:* The intersection of age, guns, poverty, and isolation has created an epidemic of suicide among White men over fifty. According to a 2016 report from the

U.S. Centers for Disease Control and Prevention, 3,291 men over age seventy-five committed suicide, compared with 510 women of the same age. The causes: deteriorating physical health, cognitive impairment, emotional pain, and guns in the home. Kim Soffer reported, in the *Washington Post,* that higher rates of gun owner-ship among older adults mean higher rates of suicide.

- *Addiction and age:* The face of addiction is growing older. According to the National Institute on Drug Abuse, the U.S. pop-ulation over fifty-five increased 6 percent from 2013–2015, while the proportion of that population seeking treatment for opi-oid abuse increased 54 percent. And the proportion of those using heroin more than doubled during that period. In addition, 65 percent of people over sixty-five reported high-risk alcohol use, and more than one-tenth of them reported binge drinking. Clearly, addiction in older adults intersects with chronic pain, loss, financial stress, isolation, and mental illness.

- *Climate change and age:* Finally, those of us in late life are more susceptible to the widespread effects of climate change than younger people. A 2016 Environmental Protection Agency fact sheet listed the risks: Extreme heat events increase dangers for those with heart disease, lung disease, and diabetes. Evacuations due to fires or floods may not be possible due to personal or institutional mobility limitations. Poorer air quality due to warming, pollution, and dust worsens preexisting respiratory conditions. Contaminated water exacerbates gastrointestinal problems.

Baby Boomers were the first generation to wake up to the interconnectedness of ecosystems and the impact of our lifestyle choices on our habitat. We were the first to observe the changes in climate patterns due to increasing CO_2 in our atmosphere from fossil fuels. Climate change didn't start with us, but 85 percent of the carbon that's been poured into the atmosphere in all of history has been emitted during the past thirty years. It is a huge part of our legacy, and it's our sacred obligation to do whatever we can to protect future generations from its consequences.

We can see from this short list of issues that age is a lynchpin for action on our social and economic problems. But if we deny our age and its value because we buy into collective ageist norms, how will any of these profound issues be addressed in the context of age? How will we, as individuals, find the moral voice of the Elder and support younger generations to take the path forward to a better quality of life for everyone? We can see, through this lens, that it's time for an age justice movement.

But there is a deeper, more intimate reason to explore age, too.

The Promise of
the Inner Work of Age

In 2018, as I was working on this book, I interviewed many people, some renowned and some unknown—but none I would call ordinary. We spoke openly about their inner experiences of aging, their trials and triumphs, their fears and hard-won wisdom. I learned, especially, about their inner obstacles on the spiritual journey of aging, and how they worked through those obstacles in order to uncover the treasures of late life. I found myself moved to tears and felt a profound affinity with them.

Through that work, combined with many years of research, investigation, and practice, I found that this inner work of age can free us from internal obstacles and allow change (which is inevitable) to change us (which is not inevitable). The psychological and spiritual practices that are offered here eventually lead us to discover an advanced stage of human development that is hidden in plain sight—*the shift from role to soul.* This phrase was coined by spiritual teacher Ram Dass, a Harvard psychologist who returned from India in the 1960s and became a renowned guide and bestselling author. He describes this shift in identity from the active roles that we have fulfilled during our lives to something deeper, something connected to a spiritual essence that has inherent value and does not depend on our productivity, accomplishments, or self-image. Ram Dass calls this spiritual essence loving awareness. Whether we call it soul, Spirit, Higher Self, or God, when we begin to identify with That, we begin to become who we really are. With this next stage of development, we can unearth the treasures of late life.

Treasures of Late Life

- Releasing the past so that it no longer controls how we feel or act now
- Releasing our hurt, anger, resentment, and regret by using emotional repair to reframe relationships
- Cultivating a genuine self-acceptance of who we are now, which liberates us from our inner critic and empowers us to feel and act with full authenticity
- Finding a broader and deeper view of our life stories, which reveals our soul's mission
- Reclaiming our lost creativity and exploring its joyous value today
- Creating a quieter mind, which gives us space from negative emotions about aging
- Experiencing a deeper identity, which offers freedom from our past roles and responsibilities
- Discovering a revitalized energy that opens us to play, beauty, and gratitude
- Reconnecting with activism and service, which ends isolation and connects us to a kinship community
- Choosing a spiritual practice that fits our stage of life and

brings rewards to our mental health, brain health, and emotional health

- Living with a renewed orientation toward the future that includes our evolutionary purpose and legacy
- Ultimately, feeling a sense of peace in the face of death

You may look at these shiny treasures and believe they would be impossible for you to find. They may seem aspirational to you, but not within your reach. So, let me suggest another way to think about them: These are the traits of an Elder.

As we release our midlife heroic efforts and values, our wounds and regrets, and start to see our lives from a higher vantage point—as we discover renewed purpose and meaning in late life—we begin to cross a threshold from Hero to Elder. This archetypal shift in awareness, much like the shift from role to soul, does not occur spontaneously. It requires conscious intention and inner work to cultivate the emerging Elder, to become free of the past, grounded in presence, aware of the shadow, and in service to the common good.

In the interviews, several key life transitions came up again and again. These transitions allow for the shift from role to soul and Hero to Elder—if we know how to move through them. So, the book focuses on those transitional thresholds and, critically, those internal obstacles that stop us from crossing these thresholds and therefore stop the evolution of the soul.

Obstacles to Finding the Treasures

- If we identify with youth and deny age, we are unaware of our ageism against ourselves and unknowingly support institutional ageism in our culture. (We'll explore this in chapters 1 and 3.)
- If we identify with ego, self-image, success, or other midlife values in late life, we miss the opportunities to connect with shadow and soul. (We'll explore this in the first four chapters.)

- If we identify with doing and deny our need to slow down to self-reflect, we keep doing what we've always done, rather than experiencing aging as spiritual practice. (We'll explore this in chapter 4.)
- If we identify with a healthy body/mind and ignore physical or cognitive symptoms, we miss the possibilities of self-care. As a result, we don't experience illness as a spiritual practice. (We'll explore this in chapter 5.)
- If we identify with a narrow band of time, without a 360-degree view of our past, present, and future journey, we remain stuck in denial of the past and fear of the future. (We'll explore this in chapter 6.)
- If we identify with regret about the past or feel like a victim of our history, we miss the opportunity to let go of the past, give and receive forgiveness, and live and die in peace. (We'll explore this in chapters 6 and 7.)
- If we identify with past religious or spiritual beliefs and don't reexamine them so that they are congruent with who we are now, we won't repair our relationship to Spirit or to our place in the greater universe. (We'll explore this in chapter 8.)
- If we deny and resist the inner work of age because the ego cannot let go of control, we lose the chance to become an Elder. (We'll explore this in chapters 2 and 9.)
- If we identify with a narrow, separate sense of self, we lose the opportunity to cultivate our connection to something larger than ourselves and move into higher stages of awareness. (We'll explore this in chapter 10.)
- If we identify with feelings of isolation and powerlessness, we deny the call to serve the common good. (We'll explore this in chapter 11.)
- If our evolution is blocked by any of the obstacles listed above, we cannot consciously do the work of life completion. (We'll explore this in chapter 12.)

- If we identify with the body and deny death, we cannot receive the gifts of mortality awareness to consciously prepare for death. (We'll explore this in chapter 13.)

How to Use This Book

Each chapter offers practices from shadow-work and spiritual contemplative traditions to help us break through denial, become aware of these inner obstacles, and overcome them. These practices ask us to slow down, turn within, and self-reflect.

Personal shadow is a term coined by renowned Swiss psychiatrist Carl Jung, who served as an Elder to me while I was writing this book. The shadow develops in each of us as children as we inevitably identify with socially acceptable traits (politeness, generosity, caretaking, and so on) to form a conscious ego and banish their opposites (rudeness, stinginess, self-centeredness, and so on) into the unconscious shadow. These unacceptable feelings, images, and desires lie dormant in the shadow but may erupt abruptly in hurtful or self-destructive behavior, addiction, and projections of all kinds.

With shadow-work, we learn how to listen to the inner voices of the shadow that lead us to do the same things we have always done without the results we want. Instead, we can detect these voices as shadow characters and work with them in a specific way. In these pages, we will meet the shadows of age together, in particular those images, fantasies, and fears about late life that are influencing us outside of awareness and stopping us from finding the treasures.

When you come to a section on shadow-work practices, please stop and reflect on one question at a time. These contemplative questions may move your attention into unfamiliar, even uncomfortable territory, so you may find yourself resisting or distracting your mind. You may feel restless or agitated. Simply take a deep breath and return to the question, let it simmer, and see what arises. This is your private space, so no one else needs to know what comes up. You can make notes in your journal and return to any question at a later time. (The appendix in the back of the book also outlines the steps of shadow-work for continued practice.)

I love the poet Rainer Maria Rilke's instruction to *live* our questions now. If one of the questions you encounter in this book seems particularly rich for you, carry it with you like a bud until it opens.

You may notice that the names of shadow figures (Critic, Doer, Provider, Victim, Inner Ageist, and so on) and other terms (Elder, Inner Elder, Hero, and so on) are often capitalized to highlight that they are not being used in common parlance but, rather, as archetypes to represent a symbolic and universal quality, in addition to a personal, individual one.

With spiritual practice, you learn how your mind operates. Eventually, we can observe our shadow characters, rather than obey them. With deeper practice, we can let go of our past roles and beliefs about ourselves, expand our identity to something larger, and move into a new stage of awareness. You can select those practices that intuitively feel right for you and practice them consistently. You will notice your heart opening, your mind relaxing, and your sense of self enlarging to include more and more parts of yourself, as well as other individuals and groups you did not previously include in your circle of self.

When you come to a section on spiritual practices, please stop and be still. If you are an experienced meditator, you may find new ways to practice that are specifically oriented to age. If you are not familiar with meditation, find those practices that seem accessible and attractive to you, and be patient with yourself. For instance, you may simply follow your breath before moving into practices that seem too unfamiliar. Belly breathing is an excellent preparation for shadow-work.

With this combined inner work, we can make the shift of identity from role to soul, dropping our conditioned personas, habitual fears, and automatic reactions and choosing, instead, to be fully real, transparent, and free, perhaps for the first time. Age is our curriculum.

Before becoming a therapist, I believed that self-reflection was a natural, innate tendency in people. But I have since learned that it's an
acquired skill that can be difficult to learn, especially for those who
have a loud inner Critic, heavy guilt about the past, or deep anxiety
about the future. So, I have tried to make the reflective practices in this
book simple and directly connected to each person's own experience.

The inner work of age is not homework but soul work. Read slowly.
Watch your resistance as it comes up; observe the fears and the skepticism. Beware of an inner voice that is like a young student who fears
disapproval: "I can't do this right." "I'm not smart enough." Beware of
the inner Rebel: "Don't tell me what to do." "I've done it my way all
along."

Please don't obey these voices. Instead, try to open to the possibility
that these practices are some of the tools you need, right here, right now.
They are based on your own life experience, not theory or concepts that
you need to study. And you can contemplate them at your own pace.

This book does not provide you with the contents of the meaning
that you will discover; that is an individual exploration. My hope is that
with this inner work you will be released to move forward and find
direction, even vision, for your own late life.

A note on language: The terminology used in this book reflects my
own history and meditative experience. If it doesn't reflect your own
beliefs, please don't let that stop you. Both of my spiritual lineages,
Vedanta and depth psychology, teach that there is an essence within
sentient beings that is eternal and connects us to something greater
than ourselves. I refer to it as soul. But, again, this book is not about
beliefs. It's about your own internal experience.

I use the term *pure awareness* to refer to what Buddhists call emptiness, *sunyata,* or, in meditation, *rigpa.* It is essentially awareness without an object. Buddhist teacher Joan Halifax describes it as vastness.
Sunyata translates as "unobstructed." In this context, the obstructions
are the unconscious internal obstacles that appear as repeating thoughts

and emotional attachments. They are the objects of attention that obscure pure awareness and that we focus on here.

However, this book is meant to present an inclusive, nondenominational approach to direct spiritual experience. I have included interviews with teachers of many traditions about their experience of aging and spiritual practice. Each speaks within his or her framework, and my hope is that everyone will find an affinity here. So please, as you read, feel free to replace my term *pure awareness* with *emptiness, God, Self, the Divine, Higher Power,* or any other term that, for you, refers to the ultimate reality.

I am not dismissing the important distinctions of belief in these traditions. But, as you will see, this book is not about beliefs. It is about the foundational spiritual experience that is at the root of religious and spiritual beliefs in all perennial traditions.

If you remain open to the message in this book, it can be a guide for you to heed the call to step onto the path of late life with your gains and losses, gifts and limitations all gathered within you now as the wisdom of a lifetime. It can be a summons to trade the image of youth for the depth of age, to trade distraction for self-knowledge, to trade reaction for reflection, to trade information for wisdom, and to trade a tight grip for an open hand.

Clearly, science has extended human life by leaps and bounds, but, at the same time, human life has been emptied of meaning for many. We have added years to life, but not life to years. Yet here we are, with decades of life remaining to us after our reproductive years and even after retirement—more than any generation before us. Yes, we need institutional innovation and policy support across a wide range of issues. But if we don't learn to age from the inside out, we won't fulfill the promise of our souls.

Aging is our next frontier—a physical, emotional, moral, cognitive, and spiritual frontier. Its mysteries and its terrors need to be faced consciously and mindfully, and this book offers the inner tools we need to do just that. We can only truly reinvent late life from the inside out.

PART I

The Divine Messengers

Part I explores the identity crisis that often accompanies entry into late life. It may be triggered when we encounter the divine messengers that were witnessed by Siddhartha Gautama, the Buddha—illness, old age, and death. Today it also may be triggered by retirement, which can act like a divine messenger to help us see reality as it is.

In this section I also offer three portals to age consciously and move through this identity crisis: pure awareness, shadow awareness, and mortality awareness. Like the Buddha, we may be led to aging as a spiritual journey.

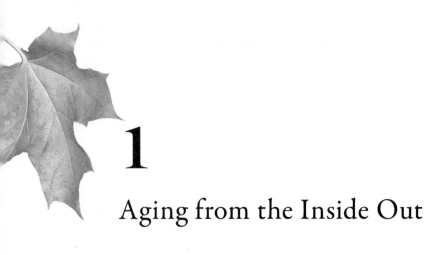

1

Aging from the Inside Out

A Late-Life Identity Crisis:
My Story

As my sixty-eighth birthday approached, I had the following dream: I'm put-
ting my purse into the backseat of a car, and a woman comes and grabs it,
running off with it. I chase her, calling out and following her into a house.
The living room is sparse and messy. I look through everything, then go into
the bedroom and even look under the mattress. I can't find it. She turns and
says, "Okay," then opens a drawer, takes out the purse, and gives it to me.
I recognize her as Paula T. from high school. I see that there's no phone or
wallet in the bag; I had changed purses the night before.

I hadn't thought of sixty-eight as a significant birthday, but apparently
the inching toward late life had triggered another identity crisis—the
loss of my ID, or identity, as symbolized by the driver's license in my
wallet. I knew all about midlife crisis, but I hadn't heard much about
late-life identity crisis.

When I contemplated the dream and realized that the thief was
someone who had gone to high school with me, I paid attention. I had
rejected my past in profound ways in order to separate from my overly

close and controlling family. Now, a woman from my past was trying to steal me back.

How does the past move through us in the present day, haunting our dreams, fueling our desires, driving our deepest needs? Which invisible figures of the past are here now, hidden deep within? Which ancestors are shaping us, critics sabotaging us, lovers seducing us, and peers competing with us? Why would a high-school acquaintance, whom I had not known well and had not seen in fifty years, show up to steal my purse?

Paula was Other to me, even back then—image-conscious, popular, comfortable in her body, confident with boys, and disinterested in learning. I identified with none of those traits. I was an academic, loved learning, and didn't much care about appearance. But beneath all that, I felt awkward and inadequate when trying to connect with boys.

In the dream, I'm compelled to get back the bag and its contents, to reclaim it from the past. This is a key task of late life—to recognize early self-concepts and rejected parts, begin to repair them, and cultivate a broader, deeper sense of identity. With her tricky action, Paula had pulled me back into my adolescent world, only to find that my real identity was not what I thought it was back then and is not what I think it is now.

When I hold the purse again, it's empty. My ID was not really stolen; the purse was just an empty vehicle for identity.

Identity is complex, formed of endless generations of genetic streams running through us, family narratives filled with memory, pride, and shame, and socially constructed stories of gender, race, and class, which are constantly reinforced by the tribal subcultures in which we live. Yet, even as we encourage and advocate for people to stand up for their racial and gender identities today, we are learning that these are not fixed; race, gender, and sexual orientation are proving to be more complex, even more fluid, than we knew.

Similarly, within us, we are not fixed, singular selves. Our alter egos or part selves unconsciously identify with certain traits and reject others, forming our conscious identities ("I'm like this, not like that"). But we may discover that one identity ("I'm a strong, independent woman") contradicts another ("I don't know what I'll do if he leaves me"). That realization may leave us wondering who we really are.

Our stage of life—that aspect of identity that concerns us here—also shapes who we think we are ("still young," "not yet old," "really old"). A late-life identity crisis can be triggered when we lose our loved ones, roles, appearance, health, independence, contribution, and relevance—and our sense of having unlimited time. We suffer these losses with ongoing grief and disorientation. And the deepest spiritual question arises again and again: Who am I? Who am I without X? Who am I if X happens?

In the dream, my purse is like my body—it's been robbed. The thief of age has stolen my ID and forced me to contemplate again where my identity is truly located. It's not in a possession; it's not in my body; it's not in my beliefs; it's not in my relationships; it's not in my race or gender. These merely comprise the vehicle for the journey of the soul.

As the vehicle declines in late life, what does the soul ask of us? Are we stuck in a past identity that no longer serves this stage of life? Are we unknowingly living a worn-out personal story or myth that we no longer believe? Or are we fighting an old fight, such as the one against parental values, that no longer matters?

The high-school acquaintance in my dream was a messenger from the hidden world, reminding me that I no longer need to reject the past of my youth, that I no longer need to fight for an identity of my own. That task belongs to an earlier stage of the journey. I am in a new moment now, a new stage of life, trying to reorient to become an Elder.

The Buddha's Divine Messengers

The dream messenger reminded me of a famous Buddhist tale of divine messengers, a tale of waking up to the truths of human life. It is said that more than two thousand years ago, in the north of India, there was a prince, Siddhartha, who lived in a palace with beautiful gardens filled with the sounds of bells, music, fountains, and songbirds. The king, his father, made sure that Siddhartha was surrounded only by strong men and beautiful women. The king was determined that his son would grow up to succeed him without ever knowing fear, suffering, or sadness.

But curiosity snared the prince. When he was twenty-nine, he ordered his charioteer to take him outside the palace gates. At the edge of a crowd, he saw a woman and man, both bent and gaunt. Their skin was cracked, their teeth chattered, gray hair hung to their shoulders, and their hands shook.

The prince asked his charioteer, "What are these? Has nature made them like this?"

"Sire, these creatures are like all others who live into the twilight of their years. They are old. They were once children nursing at their mother's breasts; they grew to have strength and beauty; they married and raised families. Now they are near the end of life. They suffer from the press of time that mars beauty, ruins vigor, kills pleasure, weakens memory, and destroys the senses. They are a ruin of what they were."

The prince asked, "Will this also be my fate?"

"My lord, no one who lives can escape this fate."

The prince shuddered, uttered a deep sigh, and shook his head. His eyes wandered to the happy crowds. "And yet the world is not frantic with terror! How can they ignore our common fate?"

For an instant, the prince saw through the surface of his existence as if seeing through a painted screen. Meeting old age, he encountered the first divine messenger—and his first glimpse of the truth. So began his journey to become the Buddha.

I, too, was in denial, sheltered from the storm of the phenomenal world. My father, too, overprotected me, surrounding me with the hum of beauty, music, and love, determined that I would succeed him in material achievement. And when I left his palace garden at eighteen, I was, like many young people, under a spell: oblivious of the stark realities of human suffering, heedless of old age, sickness, and death. This spell of youth leads us to feel immortal and to live as if life has no limits.

After Siddhartha saw the frail old man and woman, he saw two more messengers: someone ill and someone dead. But, walking farther, he saw a wandering monk and imagined, in an instant, a life beyond suffering, a life of higher purpose dedicated to spiritual awakening. His soul awakened to a longing for that life, to go beyond his own suffering and to liberate others.

If we have been in denial, the emergence of these divine messengers—old age, illness, death—triggers a profound identity crisis in us. They are gods or archetypal forces that carry the power to shock us out of the spell. They also carry the power to awaken in us an awareness of the fragile nature of our bodies, the fleeting quality of time, and the end to come. Potentially, they awaken in us a profound yearning to shift our priorities, to turn our attention and energies away from the trivial and toward what is essential in life, away from distraction and toward the inner life. This yearning stirs our souls with a deep restlessness, a divine discontent with conventional life, and a need for something more, which I call the "holy longing." If we pay attention, the holy longing may lead us onto a spiritual path.

If we live long enough, we will always observe divine messengers. Certainly, we will have been ill, or observed someone else ill, struggling with terrible pain, and perhaps losing control of their body. We will have seen our own grandparents and parents grow old and frail, and perhaps lose control of their mind. We will have seen death, even up close, the cessation of breath, the cooling and hardening of the body, perhaps the brief sensation of something wispy leaving the room.

But to what degree do we allow ourselves to look, clear-eyed, at the whole truth about age? Do we allow these experiences to penetrate us, to break the spell and alter our lived reality? How many of us have walked away from our comfortable lives, as the Buddha did, toward what matters most to us? How many of us have followed the whisper of the soul, its restless longing to go beyond ego, to transcend our current perspective or stage of awareness?

Let's imagine, for a moment, that the Buddha did not heed the calls of the messengers. Perhaps he denied their meaning or importance and returned to the palace, becoming just another king. Or perhaps he entered the street and joined the fray, becoming just another hedonist or nihilist. Following the path of denial, he would not have followed his fate and fulfilled his destiny. Siddhartha would not have crossed the threshold to become the Buddha.

There is something in each of us that resists the summons of the messengers and longs to stay asleep, complacent in our ways, pushing away the reality of our aging and, therefore, our spiritual development. There is something in us that wants only to return to the palace of denial again and again, to remain young and naive, or strong and in control, or productive and heroic, something that wants things to be as we wish them to be. This identification with youth and denial of age is the first obstacle to overcome in reinventing ourselves.

Rites of Passage

Today the divine messengers of age go unheralded. Though they are inevitable, they go unwelcomed. We celebrate a christening, a toddler's first steps, a bar mitzvah, a graduation, a wedding. We may throw a party to celebrate a retirement. But afterward? Most of us tend to view our final years, which may last decades, merely as a slow decline, a series of disconnected, meaningless events and impairments eventually leading to death.

No one teaches us how to heed the messengers. No one models for us how to retire, become a grandparent, recover from illness, or lose a loved one as a sacred passage into a new stage of awareness. Or how to complete a life review in order to distill the wisdom of our unique experience. Or how to repair relationship wounds so that we can forgive ourselves and others. Or how to engage the moral voice of the Elder so that we can become activists and serve the larger world. Or how to find the contemplative practice that fits us now, in this stage of life, in order to move beyond ego and become a Spiritual Elder. No one teaches us how to shift from role to soul.

We have no guides for moving through the transitions of our older years and for becoming Elders ourselves. We are aging without a map. So, how can we find the treasures of this stage? Fortunately, there are models and guides from other cultures and extensive study of life transitions as potential rites of passage. Ron Pevny, author of *Conscious Living, Conscious Aging,* wrote that for life transitions to become successful rites of passage, they require three steps: letting go, liminal time, and new beginnings. *Letting go* refers to leaving behind past roles, attitudes, regrets, and identities that no longer serve our development so that we can move forward. *Liminal time,* or the neutral zone, refers to the fallow period between identities in which we feel lost, formless, empty, and afraid. It's a bit like a chrysalis—no longer caterpillar, not yet butterfly. And it may include deep grieving for all that has been lost. *New beginnings* refers to the emergence of a new sense of self, passion, purpose, and vision—and, I would add, a potential next stage of awareness.

During the passages of late life—retirement from paid work, completing emotional unfinished business, experiencing illness and caregiving, becoming an Elder, engaging in service for the common good, and cultivating spiritual development—these three steps of transition are key. In fact, they describe the evolution of the soul as we move through these passages, shedding skins and emerging anew. Ken Wilber, the prolific founder of Integral Institute, whose work on higher stages of awareness informs this book, describes this evolutionary process as one in which we "transcend and include," that is, transcending one stage of awareness while including the previous stages.

For instance, as we transcend midlife, letting go of the roles and responsibilities of this time, we may enter a neutral zone in which we feel not young/not old. We are between clear-cut roles and identities, still active and engaged, but not quite sure who we are anymore. We are no longer primarily parents or primarily defined by our job. With its uncertainty and absence of labels, and with its built-in loss of the past, this neutral zone carries a fundamental anxiety.

Eventually, with inner work, we move beyond midlife and cross a threshold into late life, emerging as an Elder. We let go of the striving and pushing; we let go of the "shoulds." We release our past identities but carry all that we've learned, all that we love, always, within us. In this way, we are evolving from role to soul.

The words *transition* and *transcend* both have the prefix *trans-*, meaning to cross over or go beyond. A transition is a passage to a next stage of life, both internal and external, such as from child to adolescent, from single to married adult, from senior to Elder. Traditionally, such transitions were marked by sacred rites. The stages of life themselves, as we know them, are social constructs that enable us to name and support these transitions. For instance, the term *adolescence*, coined in 1904 to describe the stage between childhood and adulthood, helped to focus society on the needs of people at this stage. But our time of life today, between retirement and frail old age, remains unnamed and therefore unserved. And, because of this conceptual deficit, our vision of this stage of life is deficient, too. As renowned gerontologist Bill Thomas says, "We suffer from aging illiteracy."

On the other hand, transcendence is an internal shift to another level of awareness, or a change in stage, not age. When we complete the developmental tasks described in this book for each arena of life, when we move through them consciously, releasing the past, stepping into the unknown, and emerging on the other side, we can transcend the ego's past identity and begin to live from a different center of gravity, shifting from, for example, hero to Elder.

If we continue to transcend past roles and identities, eventually transcending ego and awakening into higher stages of awareness, we can become Spiritual Elders. That is, our ego development includes inner work leading to adult maturity (Ken Wilber calls this Growing Up), then our spiritual development, beyond ego, includes inner work leading to awakening (Wilber calls this Waking Up).

This vision of aging as a spiritual journey is not a new idea. Most of the world's spiritual traditions envision late life as a time for retreat from the world, contemplation, and ego transcendence. More recently, Carl Jung pointed out that the root of his patients' post-midlife problems was lack of a spiritual outlook.

Rabbi Zalman Schachter-Shalomi, whose book, *From Age-ing to Sage-ing* (with Ronald S. Miller), and organization, Sage-ing International, inspired me to write this book, said it this way: "Without envisioning old age as the culminating stage of spiritual development, we short-circuit this process and put brakes on the evolutionary imperative for growth that can be unleashed by our increased longevity. We are driven by this instinct for life completion as an individual and as a species still evolving."

I believe this instinct for life completion is the manifestation of our spiritual yearning, or holy longing, that appears in late life. It's the evolutionary force within us that seeks the shift from role to soul.

Of course, there are those who stare directly at their age in late life, accepting their entrance into this new stage with pride. Perhaps they have welcomed transitions throughout their lives, felt unafraid of crossing thresholds at different stages, and embraced transformation. Perhaps in childhood they had positive models of Elders, whom they cherished, so they can now envision themselves like those people. Perhaps they feel the purpose of service or spirituality, which orients them now with meaning and direction.

Carol Orsborn, author and blogger, wrote in her book *Older, Wiser, Fiercer*, "By the time we are old, we have lived long enough to know what we and the world are capable of: the heights to which we can rise, and the depths to which we can sink. . . . Perhaps evolution has given us old age," she continued, "because it takes so long to get beyond denying, defending, and storytelling to live life in its intended intensity. . . . Few of us become willing to take on the potential for the pain of awakening before we have tried every apparent shortcut—and there are many. . . . At long last, we run out of options, panting across the boundary to this new land, inhabited by a handful of others like us: old, brave souls who are struggling to become not only older and wiser, but fiercer."

Carol told me in a private conversation, "At sixty-three, I wasn't who I used to be—and I needed to pick up the spiritual practice I had begun in my twenties to be able to see things and accept things as they are." She spent a period sitting in uncertainty, shedding her previous life, heeding an inner call to step out of the whirlwind and walk along the riverbank near her home—and not worry about what anyone else thought.

Her advice: "Don't wait to start your spiritual practice until it's too late. We need that clear, quiet awareness to center us in the midst of the hits that keep coming with age."

But most of us, aging in an anti-aging culture, are not fierce with reality; we want to look away and forget for a while, pushing the messenger back into the darkness of the unconscious, until it shows up again in some inexplicable symptom or repeating forgetfulness or sudden loss of vitality. And we find ourselves being dragged into it, protesting, crying out against the inevitable.

Even if we admit that it's happening, we may compartmentalize this awareness, delaying it for a while: "I can't slow down now, maybe in three years." Or we may attempt to bargain with it, cutting a deal to reduce our fear: "I'll exercise harder and longer, and I'll be okay." Or we simply project it, unconsciously attributing it outside of ourselves to *them*: "I'm still in my sixties, not old yet. But those people are." In all of these denials, we miss out on the greatest opportunity of this time: to reinvent ourselves from the inside out and become who we were meant to be.

In any case, the encounter with age continues to occur, in small ways, happening often, sometimes as a gentle nudge, sometimes as an all-out assault. When we feel humiliated by the unrecognizable face in the mirror and ask, "Who is *that*?" When we feel ashamed by our loss of ambition or sex drive and ask, "Who am I without *that*?" When we are not resilient enough to recover from an injury and ask, "When can I get back to normal?" With each of these encounters, we may feel shame, or even betrayed by our bodies. Our surprise reveals a lack of awareness that aging is occurring. A tension emerges between our denial, or our belief that we can control aging, and our reality as we are living it.

An eighty-five-year-old female client once told me that someone at the gym asked her age. "You look good," the stranger told her.

"You mean, good for my age?" she quipped. "How old do you think I am?"

The stranger responded, "Seventy-seven."

"No, I'm sixty-two."

The stranger raised his eyebrows.

"You don't believe me," she stated. "I'm not an age, I'm a person."

Is this denial—or successful aging? Is this rejecting the stereotype, and the projection that goes with it, that older people carry? Is it identifying with something other than the body? Or is it a failure to accept herself as she is and face the reality of the limits of her body and her time?

As I explored these issues with her, she called me an ageist because I was trying to help her accept her reality. I suggested that she was reactive because she was not at peace with her age. If she didn't begin to examine the unconscious issues beneath her feelings—which blocked her ability to let go of her ego's self-image and release midlife values of success and productivity—then she would lose the opportunity to contemplate and complete the tasks for late life. She would lose the chance to hear the messengers and cross the threshold.

For those of us who explored consciousness in earlier years, late life is a call to return. Our emotional and spiritual development does not stop here; it continues in every moment, in every day. And our aging can be a vehicle for slowing down, reorienting to the inner world, watching the breath, being fully present, and learning to witness the internal obstacles as they arise. Aging is our grist for the mill, as spiritual teacher Ram Dass put it. It's our material for turning experience into insight.

For those who heard the call and denied it earlier, late life is a call to begin. If not now, when?

What Is "Old"?

Telling the Whole Truth

I spoke with a friend while writing this page. At eighty-nine, she told me, "I walked six miles today. The Fitbit said that I did my steps."

"How did you feel?" I asked.

"Tired," she replied. "But then Bill wanted to have sex, so I did that, too."

Grinning, I thought to myself, "This is not my mother's old age!"

For some of us, an extended health span is catching up to an extended life span. In the past, this was not the case: Many years of decline, with chronic illness and loss of capacities, preceded the end of life. But today many of us experience decades of good health extending into late life, with a sudden decline before death.

So, our fearful images of age—slow drivers who shouldn't be behind the wheel; people suffering from dementia and left behind in nursing homes; shuffling shoppers pushing their walkers through the grocery store—stem from stereotypes that mask another kind of aging that's happening all around us. Just think: In 2016, a ninety-five-year-old Finnish woman set the record for the world's oldest woman to complete a 500-foot bungee jump. In early 2019, a 103-year-old woman was sworn in as a junior ranger at the Grand Canyon.

But, clearly, this is not everyone's experience. Late life is neither the dreaded stereotype nor the rare exception. We cannot buy into the anti-aging message that is pitched, packaged, and sold to us relentlessly, which idealizes aging while ignoring the suffering of decline. But we also cannot buy into the stereotypes of decline—old people are frail, useless, miserable, and a drain on our resources. That story has led to ageist institutions and a picture of older people as "Other," an unconscious attribution onto others of what we fear in ourselves, which only contributes to the suffering of those in late life.

Rather, let's tell the whole truth—no denial *and* no romanticizing. As Ram Dass put it, "Don't feed the drama or deny it." In this way, we can move into late life consciously, with eyes and heart open.

Our quality of late life is lived individually, not as a group. It can be more than accommodation of change. It can mean overcoming past fears, developing fresh aptitudes, cleaning up toxic relationships, living more in the present moment, and transcending the ego, allowing it to take a backseat so that life opens to an intuitive flow. It can be a time of mining the gold from the dark side, reclaiming unfulfilled dreams and expressing unrealized talents.

But it also can be lonely, frightening, vulnerable, uncertain, and disorienting, another dark night of the soul. And this is especially the case for those without a guide, financial resources, or a contemplative practice.

Late life is defined and confined by many forces. Certainly, there are genetic predispositions and variations that affect aging. So, our bodies—our health, illness, and resilience—define and confine our experience of aging. Acute and chronic physical health issues may take our time and attention, leaving little energy for inner work, unless it's already a deep habit.

Those of us who have financial resources and a felt sense of affluence also will have "time affluence," which allows us the space to devote to inner work. For those who struggle with survival needs, however, evolutionary needs can seem like a luxury. So, class differences inform our experience of late life, and racial differences do, too (as we saw in the statistics provided in the introduction). In addition, the support we get from our families and social networks and our beliefs about meaning and purpose all contribute to our capacity to do the inner work of age.

We all hold conscious and unconscious attitudes that support or undermine our health and resilience. For example, if our identity is rooted in our image, we may struggle to adjust to the incremental changes that occur in our appearance, losing confidence and motivation. My friend Jackie told me that her wrinkles are a curse. "I never liked my body," she said. "But over the years I had come to accept my shape, even though it doesn't look anything like supermodels. But now—those hideous wrinkles. They just brought back all of those feelings of self-hate."

My friend's lifelong negative gaze onto her own body had moved to her aging face, which she judged and rejected, believing she could never accept those lined and sagging cheeks. When I pointed out that an inner part of her was buying into an ageist prejudice that compared her face to a youthful ideal, Jackie looked startled. "I just assumed everyone saw it that way. Old is ugly," she replied.

There is a resistance rising to that equation. The glorious grandmas of Instagram are modeling underwear, swimwear, and colorful, high-style clothing in unfettered self-expression, their silver hair shining in the sunlight. Dorrie Jacobson, eighty-three, former Playboy bunny, great-grandma, has redesigned herself as a style blogger and has 35,000 followers. Baddie Winkle, eighty-nine, in tie-dye and face paint, has millions of followers. Their chant: Age no longer dictates the way we live.

Others, whose identity is rooted in a role at work or in financial status, may have more difficulty maintaining self-esteem as those sources of identity change. One man told me, "Who am I if I'm not a psychologist, helping others all day?" Another said, "I built this company from the ground up—and now they want me out. What is the meaning of my life without my company?"

People who have explored their own psychologies and come to understand themselves deeply may have a different experience. They may know what triggers their anxiety, what they need if depression arises, and how to ask for support. They may be better able to tolerate loss and uncertainty, and their emotional resilience may give them more flexibility to adapt to the changes that occur with aging.

Extroverts and introverts will age differently, too. The former will tend to move toward more interaction through service, community work, and family and social relationships. They gain energy in groups and feel more purposeful in stable marriages and family intimacy. Introverts will tend to move toward more quiet settings where solitary time and inner work can be done. This helps them conserve energy and tap into internal resources.

Our religious and spiritual beliefs and experiences also define and confine aging. For members of organized religions, church and synagogue communities can be a source of social support and a venue to serve others. Clergy can confirm faith and provide ritual space for transitions. But most churches and synagogues, though they welcome youth, provide no rituals to celebrate seniors becoming elders. And, of course, the exoteric or public forms of these traditions offer no spiritual practices to gain access to mystical states or higher stages of development.

For those of us who have taken a more individual path as unaffiliated seekers, our practices become essential. During the interviews for this book, I found people using a wide range of contemplative techniques for centering, quieting the mind, releasing the noise of the day, and opening to a deeper source. Some applied their practices primarily for relaxation; others attained higher stages of awareness over decades of practice. But in each case, meditation was a refuge and a buffer against the losses and disorientation of age.

Our cultures also define and confine aging. We age in contexts, such as families, communities, groups, and nations, that communicate possibilities and limits about everything, including age. They shape what goes into the shadow and remains unexpressed, as well as what is consciously lived out and fully expressed in our late life.

For example, the movement for "positive aging" or "successful aging" emerged a decade ago to counter the consequences of long-term negative views of "old." Proponents urged people over fifty to maintain productivity, engagement, contribution, physical and mental health, sexuality, and autonomy. It's an ideal that's appealing and increasingly possible for many of us for decades. And it's correlated with high degrees of life satisfaction.

However, the concept of successful aging also has a shadow side: Ideals quickly become "shoulds." Productivity—as an ideal—sets up lack of productivity as a failure and privileges doing over being, and action over contemplation, thereby reinforcing collective values of work, money, and heroic individualism, which may lead people to feel shame when they lose their capacities.

Contribution—as an ideal—sets up lack of contribution as selfish or being a burden. Those who have raised families, completed careers, and served others may no longer feel called to do so. And introverts naturally may wish to slow down, stop earning their self-worth, and start simply being it.

Physical health—as an ideal—sets up loss of health as a personal failure. But in late life some physical limitation inevitably will emerge, even if it is only near the time of death.

Autonomy and self-reliance—as an ideal—set up dependency and vulnerability as failure. Yet we will inevitably face painful limits to our autonomy in late life.

In addition, these ideals create unconscious images in us, like stock photos in the recesses of our minds: the attractive older White couple walking on the beach; the handsome older White man cutting the ribbon at the opening of a new business venture; the well-dressed older White woman who makes a commercial for intimacy products.

These ideals and images obscure the complex, idiosyncratic reality of aging. What if the viewer cannot see him- or herself in these successful agers? What if the "shoulds" that we internalize as the ideals of successful aging are not accessible or even desirable to us? What if we lack financial resources to fulfill them? What if we lack access to health care or social support? What if we are people of color? Gay? Differently abled? Caregivers? Homebodies? Chronically ill? Clearly, if almost any of us compare ourselves to these standards, we will see ourselves as failing to age well.

Finally, cultural messaging about successful aging emphasizes an outer orientation over an inner one and, as a result, more ego reinforcement. Aging from the inside out requires, instead, a shift from productivity to contemplation, from money to meaning, from role to soul. In effect, late life compels inner development and connecting to something larger than ourselves, not more empire building. We are at risk of losing the meaning of late life if we define it by the standards of an earlier stage of life.

The vision of "successful aging" has had enormous positive impact on raising awareness about the many possibilities of reimagining late life. But it sets up a false dichotomy. The full truth is that, beneath the many physical, emotional, cognitive, and social diminishments of late life, most of us experience a quality of youthfulness or even change-lessness. Many of us continue to be productive, however we define it, throughout our seventies and later. Others choose to slow down, change gears, and turn toward a more private life of grandparenting, creativity, and spirituality. And, at some point, we all grapple with diminishments and loss of control in the face of larger forces.

At that time, we don't want to be measured against the cultural expectations of agency, independent self-control, and productivity. We don't want to be compared to the standards of other stages of life. Rather, we need to align with change and deepen our self-acceptance to create the life that reflects who we are now.

In summary, to try to encapsulate the meaning of "old" in a three-letter word simply reduces it. All the nuance is lost in the naming. The Latin root of the word old, alere, means "nourish." Somehow, in our postmodern, youth-oriented society, the precious, ancient meaning of old, whether it's "nourished" or "nourishing," has vanished. My prayer would be that Elders are both.

My client Bob, at the age of seventy-five, put it this way: "I feel old. I don't want to do anything. But I'm afraid to do nothing."

When I pointed out that he was finally free of obligation, he said, "But I'm obligated to do something. Who am I when I do nothing?"

Clearly, his identity is tied to doing, as it is for most of us in the West. When doing slows or stops, a late-life identity crisis roars to the surface. With our self-worth linked to our accomplishment, we feel at sea without a rudder.

A friend, William, age seventy-three, who was a bodybuilder, needed several back surgeries and told me that he felt betrayed by his body. He could no longer go horseback riding or get an endorphin high at the gym. He shut down emotionally and became unavailable to his friends and family. But as he explored his emotional response to his new limits, he understood that he was rejecting help and fearing dependency. His biggest fear—to lose his independence and need others to care for him—had emerged from the shadow.

As he opened to his wife and adult children and allowed their roles to be reversed, permitting them to care for him in a new way, William felt freed of the lifelong pattern of heroic self-reliance. Slowly, he found a mature kind of dependency. His connections with his loved ones deepened, and he began to accept the new reality more calmly, finding its gifts. There is both success and failure in his story, endings and beginnings.

The whole truth is this: Aging is not one-dimensional. It's full of opposites:

- Being and doing
- Freedom and dependency
- Purpose and disorientation
- Vitality and fatigue
- Holding on and letting go
- Extroversion and introversion
- Pleasure and pain
- Gains and losses
- Beginnings and endings

When we inquire into late life, we need to be mindful of where we put our attention: on growth or decline, gains or losses, holding on or letting go. And we need to remember that neither concept, on its own, tells the full, nuanced truth. Instead, we benefit from holding the tension of these opposites, exploring both the light side and the dark side of late life, its gifts and its struggles, its developmental possibilities and its very real challenges. We must stop splitting the good and the bad in aging, which pushes one side into our blind spot. If, from here on, we teach only positive visions of late life—reinvention, freedom, purpose, creativity—then the reality of decline—pain, loss, and endings—is denied. We don't want to deny either the promises or the perils of this stage of life.

Rather, let's reclaim the power of definition over the concept of "old" in all its complex nuances and bring them to the light of awareness. Let's talk about progress *and* decline, gain *and* diminishment, beginnings *and* endings—and stretch ourselves to hold these opposites together in our awareness for ourselves and for the culture at large.

Perhaps, as Carl Jung suggested, if we hold the tension of opposites and let them simmer for a while, rather than choosing one side and banishing the other into denial, a novel third possibility will emerge: the capacity to become a true Elder, who does not think in black-and-white terms, splitting good and bad, projecting one or the other, but who holds the tension of shadow and light—who is both nourished and nourishing.

When Do We Become "Old"?

The concept of "old" has different meanings in the eye—or age—of the beholder. When do we pass from young to old? Do we undergo a phase transition, like the shift from water to ice? Is the shift triggered by a chronological change, a social acknowledgment of senior status, a diminishment of capacity, an alteration of appearance, or an internal, subjective experience?

I asked a nineteen-year-old client, Sue, a college freshman, what aging means to her and when it begins. She replied, "It means that the body breaks down and probably starts around forty." She associated aging with losing her ability to run marathons and having her blond hair turn gray. When asked what she would want to be doing at seventy, she said, "I hope I'm not too wrinkled or too needy and can still do what I want to do."

Like many young people, Sue could not envision herself in positive ways in later years, despite an intimate, supportive relationship with her grandmother. Clearly, her unconscious stereotypes were more powerful than that actual relationship.

There's a large gap between young people's perceptions of "old" and the lived experiences of older people. As reported by Shelley Emling of AARP, a 2017 study by U.S. Trust found that perceptions of the onset of old age vary widely among different generations. Millennials, for example, say that you are old once you turn 59. Gen Xers, on the other hand, hold a slightly more generous view, saying that old age begins at 65. When it comes to older baby boomers and even older members of the silent generation, both agree that you're not really old until you hit age 73.

So I ask again: What is age? How much is biology and health? How much is mind and attitude? And how much is cultural construction and stereotyping?

A client, Kit, age seventy-two, told me that he had two very differing cultural contexts and sets of messages about late life. In his family, there was not one single positive model of an Elder in any grandparent, friend, or teacher who was wise, safe, and sheltering. When his mother was in her sixties, she grew very depressed, stopped doing pottery, and lost her vitality. When his father retired in his fifties, he lost all desire to create or produce anything. In his eighties, he grew kinder but also developed Alzheimer's, and Kit and his brother cared for him. So Kit's personal history didn't offer him any model of growing old with intention, awareness, creativity, or service. Instead, it left him fearful about the future.

But there was another image of "old" embedded in his psyche. When he was twenty, Kit had begun meditation. His first teacher, an

Indian yogi, was a divine messenger for him, like the monk observed by the Buddha. From the moment he saw this yogi sitting cross-legged, in white robes, eyes closed, Kit had another vision of aging as an inner journey whose aim is the evolution of soul.

He saw his future self as a contemplative, not a doing machine—a soul, not a body. He recognized that late life comes with a freedom from doing, from obligatory roles, financial concerns, and even family duties. It could be a time, rather, to let go of the small stuff, turn within, and focus on life completion and spiritual development. At the age of seventy-three, Kit picked up his spiritual practices and found his way back to inner silence. He did not become a monk but deepened his meditation, opened his heart, and let go of his to-do list. Gradually, his identity began to shift from his ego's role in society to his soul's deeper yearning.

Aging as Fate

As we've seen, our experience of aging is structured not only by our genes but also in part by culture as a social construct. However, while aging may look and feel different in various bodies and various cultures, it remains the certain fate of every human being. No matter who we are, how we've lived, and what we've learned, eventually, our individuality—that is, my Connie-ness and your you-ness—will end its corporeal existence.

The meanings we give to the construct of age—When do you become old? How does age define who you are? What is age-appropriate dress or behavior? What does it mean that you're too old to do *that*?—are rooted in our early and ongoing life experiences and in the gestures, glances, and jokes that we internalize about late life, whether from family, friends, or media. If we internalize negative messages about growing old, then we will never find the treasures that lie beneath our feet.

But there is something more behind the familial and cultural messages about late life: the archetype of age. The fairy tales we heard while growing up, which we then read to our children and grandchildren, introduce us to the "wise old man," "good witch," "magician," "sage," or "mentor." The Harry Potter books introduced millions of children to Professor Dumbledore, headmaster, Elder, and adversary of the man who embodies evil. The Lord of the Rings series brought us Gandalf, and the Star Wars series brought us Yoda and Obi Wan Kenobi, all timeless, wise, memorable figures.

Other cultures throughout history have been aware of this blueprint. In Hinduism, Kali, the divine mother who is imagined as dark-skinned, many-armed, and wearing a necklace of skulls, is the goddess of birth, death, and transformation. She contains the opposites of creation and destruction; they are paired within her, not divided, as they are in the West, weaving time in a mythic cycle, rather than a straight line.

In ancient Greece, the spirit of age was embodied in Geras, a shriveled old man with a cane, who appears on ancient pottery. For the Greeks, the more Geras, or the more years and gravitas one acquired, the more virtue and excellence one gained.

The gods of age are often personifications of time and fate. For example, the ancient Roman god Saturn, known as Chronos, or Father Time, is envisioned as an elderly bearded man with wings. He carries a scythe, like the Grim Reaper, and an hourglass, to show time fleeting. He reveals the lie of endless life and the truth of mortality.

But today the archetype of age has been reduced to a stereotype, its timeless value and radiant beauty vanished.

Age and death are always already present; they are given, decreed, woven into the web of life from the beginning for every living thing. How do we relate to these larger forces? Are they in us, or are we in them? The tree doesn't resist when its leaves begin to brown and fall to the soil. But we, on the other hand, are aware of the changing seasons. Aging is a moment-to-moment encounter with forces beyond our control. As these forces manifest in our lives, whether as a diminishment of our capacities, chronic pain, illness, or grief for lost loved ones, we have only one choice: how we relate to our fate. Do we cling to the blossoms of spring or let go to flow with the larger forces of nature?

Consciously or unconsciously, we live in this tension between our ego's desires for immortality, safety, and unconditional love and this certain fate. What if, in late life, we could surrender to the forces at work in our aging? Is the decline of the body an opening for the arising of something else? What does the aging body reveal of the soul? How do we become simply who we are now?

Shadow-Work Practices

Please take some time to reflect deeply and write in your journal.

Your Divine Messengers
- In what form did the summons come to you?
- How did you respond?
- What part of you resists and stops you from responding?
- What are the consequences of resistance?

Your Perception of "Old"
- In childhood, how did you view old people?
- In midlife, how did you view old people?
- How do you view them now?
- What are your deepest fears about aging?
- What are your greatest pleasures in aging?

Spiritual Practices

Begin to practice a deep acceptance and authentic appreciation of every season of life. Begin to see birth and death, young and old, as two aspects of the same rhythmic cycle of life.

In *The Blooming of a Lotus*, a book of mindfulness practices, Zen master Thich Nhat Hanh offers the following practice on the divine messengers to help us move past denial and come face-to-face with our fears. He says that, as we welcome our fears into awareness, they lose energy, and their impact on us lessens.

༺∞༻

"Knowing I will get old, I breathe in. Knowing I can't escape old age, I breathe out.

Knowing I will get sick, I breathe in. Knowing I can't escape sickness, I breathe out.

Knowing I will die, I breathe in. Knowing I can't escape death, I breathe out.

. . . .

Determined to live my days deeply in mindfulness, I breathe in. Seeing the joy and benefit of living mindfully, I breathe out."

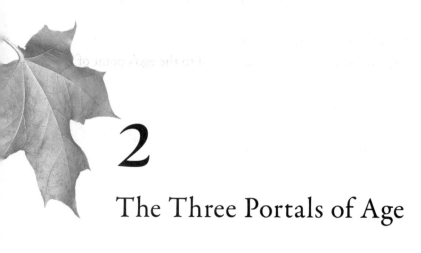

2

The Three Portals of Age

A Key in the Darkness: A Sufi Tale

A Sufi man comes to visit his friend and finds him on his hands and knees, crawling on the sidewalk beneath a streetlamp, searching for something.

The man asks, "What are you looking for?"

"I'm looking for the key to my house, but I can't find it."

"Let me help," says the man, and he gets down under the streetlamp to look.

But neither can find the key. The man asks his friend to recall his steps and think about where he lost it.

"I lost it in my house," his friend responds.

Astonished, the man asks, "Then why look out here on the sidewalk?"

"There's more light here."

Like the friend in this story, we all tend to look for answers to problems in the light of awareness, among those beliefs or strategies that we already know. But the keys hide in the darkness, beneath the boundary of awareness, in the invisible world.

Most psychologies or self-help programs focus on the light, attempting to repair our self-esteem, to change our dysfunctional behaviors,

38

thinking patterns, and communication styles, or to rewrite the stories we tell ourselves about our lives. If they are limited to the ego's point of view, then they seek the ego's objectives: looking good, feeling in control, getting things done. This identification with ego and self-image is a key obstacle to overcome in aging from the inside out. The ego's goals are not the real tasks of late life. Our tasks now require us to move our attention from the exterior world to the interior one, from the ego's role in society to the soul's deeper purpose.

Every spiritual tradition teaches that the ego is a construct of the mind that serves us well during our midlife heyday but eclipses our deeper identity, whether that is called our Christ nature, Buddha nature, Atman, Self, or Spirit. I use the word *soul* to refer to this essence, the aspect of every human being that is not a small, separate entity, like ego, but connects us to the universal, spiritual nature of everything.

As Ram Dass puts it, "The ego is a tiny room. But the soul can merge into the One."

And this is what I mean by "aging from the inside out." If we merely move around our internal furniture, redesigning our roles and maintaining high gear, we do not see through the ego's charade. Instead, we permit it to continue its endless efforts at control. And this does not carry us deeper into our spiritual center, beyond ego.

On the other hand, if we practice breaking our identification with limited, ever-changing aspects of ourselves, like physical appearance or productivity, and move our attention more and more toward soul, we can diminish the ego's grip and attune to a deeper call: What does the soul ask of us now?

In late life, we can pose this question internally no matter what activity we are engaged in, whether we are quietly drinking a cup of tea, sitting in a noisy meeting, cooking a festive family dinner, or running a marathon. Our identity or self-sense at any moment can be rooted in ego or rooted in soul. It's not what we're doing but *how* we're doing—our state of mind—that makes the difference.

As we reorient to the depth of the inner world and this shift in identity from role to soul continues, we focus more and more on nourishing the soul and its priorities. As a result, we feel less fear and more trust; we feel less bound and more free.

This shift requires three qualities of awareness, like three keys hiding in the dark:

- Shadow awareness: portal to depth
- Pure awareness: portal to silent vastness
- Mortality awareness: portal to presence

Many of us have done psychotherapy, gained great insight, changed our behaviors, and even uncovered unconscious family patterns and shadow issues. But, no doubt, we also discovered that psychological work has its limits; it does not go beyond ego to connect us with the spiritual domain.

At the same time, many of us have explored yoga, meditation, and psychedelics to quiet the mind, expand our awareness, and enter altered states. But, no doubt, we also discovered that contemplative practice has its limits; it does not bring emotional healing or repair from trauma.

For this reason, as we move through this promising stage of late life, we need the three keys: We need to break through denial with shadowwork, activate the next stage of our soul's development with a contemplative practice, and maintain mortality awareness to be fully present and use our time well. Let's explore them in sequence.

Shadow Awareness
Portal to Depth

The shadow is our personal unconscious, that part of our mind that is behind or beneath our conscious awareness. We can't gaze at it directly. It's like a blind spot in our field of vision. Because it is hidden, we need to learn how to seek it. To do so, we need to be able to see in the dark.

Why? The shadow holds the key to removing the inner obstacles that block us from finding the treasures of late life.

When we are children, the conscious ego and the unconscious shadow develop in tandem. Each is reinforced by the messages, even the glances, of parents, teachers, clergy, siblings, and friends when we try to gain love and approval. If our sadness is shamed, it is exiled into the shadow. If our anger is punished, it is pushed into the shadow. Our ego develops to accommodate the loss of those authentic feelings.

The shadow is like a darkroom in which our feelings, dreams, and images lie dormant. Shadow-work is like the process of development in which our feelings, dreams, and images come back to life.

In the context of age, most of us learn that being independent, quick, productive, and strong are highly valued and result in rewards of approval and status. On the other hand, we learn that their opposite traits—dependent, slow, unproductive, and weak—are devalued and result in disapproval and shame. Naturally, we dread the loss of these socially acceptable traits as we age, slow down, do less, and need others more.

If our images of and associations with aging remain outside of our awareness, dormant in the darkroom, then we are blind to them. We don't even notice that we fail to notice them. Like my eighty-nine-year-old friend, who told me that he didn't want to be with "old people" because he wasn't like them, we deny our reality and reject a part of ourselves. Our physical, cognitive, and emotional changes carry a heavy burden of shame. But without that awareness, our opportunities are lost.

When we learn how to establish a conscious relationship with those parts of ourselves that are outside of awareness, we can attune to our many inner voices and detect which can be guides for us now—and which can sabotage our dreams. We can learn to slow down, turn within with curiosity, and open to what's calling to us without dismissing it—and without being taken over by it. That's what I call "romancing" the shadow.

For example, we might hear a whisper: "I need more time alone." "I need less time alone." "I want to write that memoir, but I'm afraid." "I need to slow down, but I don't want to feel useless." "I need to find a new purpose, but I'm tired most of the time." "I need to be forgiven, but it will never happen." "I want to learn meditation, but I can't quiet my mind." "I want to teach young children, but what can I teach?"

These conflicting inner voices make it difficult to hear the signal through the noise, the inner guidance that speaks a deeper truth. Which voices do we follow? Which do we disregard?

When we learn to attune to this internal guidance, we have the potential to resolve our late-life identity crisis and reorient in another direction. Whatever the call, we can heed it and align with it, rather than resist it. We can allow it, rather than become possessed by it. We drop the past, step into uncertainty, and emerge in a new stage of awareness.

By learning to orient toward the unconscious and meet the shadows of age more consciously, we add a new dimension to the inner work of age: We expand our awareness and deepen our self-knowledge to include that which has been excluded for so long—a deferred dream, a secret desire, a hidden talent. Now, when the ego no longer reigns supreme, we can open ourselves and allow these banished feelings and fantasies to be heard.

In *A Little Book on the Human Shadow,* the eloquent poet Robert Bly, now an Elder, put it this way: When we are young, we carry behind us an invisible bag, into which we stuff any feelings, thoughts, or behaviors that bring disapproval or loss of love—anger, tears, neediness, laziness. By the time we go to school, our bags are already a mile long. In high school, our peer groups pressure us to stuff the bags with even more—individuality, sexuality, spontaneity, different opinions.

"We spend our life until we're twenty deciding which parts of ourselves to put into the bag," Bly said, "and we spend the rest of our lives trying to get them out again." That is a CliffsNotes definition of shadow-work: trying to get the material out of the bag.

The feelings and capacities that were rejected by the ego and exiled into the shadow contain the hidden treasures of late life. If the ego strives for strong, then weak goes into the shadow. If the ego strives for progress, then decline goes into the shadow. If the ego strives for vitality, then fatigue goes into the shadow. If the ego strives for speed, then slowness goes into the shadow. And if the ego strives for power, then powerlessness goes into the shadow. And these opposite qualities are split into "good" and "bad."

When one of those "bad" traits from the shadow manifests in late life, the inner critic can get loud ("You're weak . . . unproductive . . . tired all the time . . . just a victim"). Our self-talk becomes dark, comparing us to others, finding us lacking, pushing us to do more. Our inner critic sabotages our self-acceptance and our capacity for presence. It sabotages our acceptance of others and the river of life that moves through us. And it sabotages the flow of our wisdom out into the world. The result: shame, self-hate, depression, and isolation.

The nature of the shadow is to hide, to remain outside of awareness. It acts out indirectly, in a sarcastic remark ("I can't believe she wore that at her age") or a sour mood ("I feel defeated and invisible"). Or it sneaks out compulsively in an addictive behavior ("I can't stop myself"). Or it shows up in a projection, such as when we feel an immediate dislike of a stranger ("Who does he think he is?") or when we feel humiliated and ashamed ("I'm so embarrassed to be treated like I'm helpless").

Therefore, we need to learn to catch a glimpse of it when it appears; we must sharpen our senses so that we are awake enough to notice when it erupts. Then we can romance it, or coax it out into awareness. Like a coy lover, it will tend to recede back behind the curtain. With patience, we can invite it out into the light.

This process of slowly bringing the shadow into awareness, shedding light on the darkness, forgetting and remembering it again, is the nature of shadow-work. Eventually, we can learn to create a conscious relationship with our shadow and reduce its power to unconsciously sabotage us.

In the context of age, shadow-work helps us reduce the magnetic pull of inner and outer ageism and break the spell of youth that keeps us in denial so that we can ripen into the full truth of who we are now. If we apply Bly's metaphor to the shadows of age: What about "old" is stuffed into the bag that you drag around behind you? What stereotypes, fantasies, and images about aging are you carrying, unknowingly, into your late life? What creative or spiritual aspirations are hiding there, suspended in time?

Fear can be a silent companion on the journey of age. We may fear pain, loneliness, and becoming irrelevant and invisible. We may be frightened of losing a loved one, losing control of our bodies, losing the meaning of our lives. Some of us carry a fear of failure to live fully, to make a real contribution, or to share real love. We fear that we will fail to tell our real truth. We fear dying with regrets.

We also carry positive talents or traits in the shadow: a creative or spiritual dream that was sacrificed for the responsibilities of adulthood. Perhaps it was a dream to paint or sing or an aspiration for spiritual development. These fantasies and longings, lying dormant in the bag, await our attention in late life.

If we heed the summons, then, like Siddhartha, we will need to choose how to respond, how to follow it and find the narrow path to its meaning. We will need to allow ourselves to align with *what is,* cross the threshold, and become deeply changed.

Of course, we cannot simply wish to age consciously or overcome denial by intention or willpower. But we have a choice to look toward a rejected or denied part of ourselves—deepening wrinkles, a slower gait, a pending retirement, or a recurring dream of death—or to turn away from it. And we have a choice to look toward a dormant desire or long-buried dream—that novel that's been gestating for decades, that fantasy of swimming in the warm Caribbean, that charity work that's been pulling at our heart—or to turn away from it.

In his essay "The Stages of Life" (1931), Carl Jung put it this way: "A human being would certainly not grow to be seventy or eighty years old if this longevity had no meaning for the species. The afternoon of human life also must have a significance of its own and cannot be merely a pitiful appendage to life's morning. . . . Whoever carries over into the afternoon the law of the morning . . . must pay for it with damage to his soul."

In other words, if we deny the inner summons by striving to remain young, if we allow the ego and its drives to retain control when late life is calling, then the soul will suffer. The ambition of the ego for power will sabotage the ambition of the soul for evolution. And our deepest purpose will fail.

Approaching the age of sixty-five, my client Joseph had been a youthful, idealistic baby boomer whose dream of succeeding as a novelist had carried him through midlife. When he came to see me, he had a younger wife, two small children, and a heavy debt and dreaded getting out of bed in the morning. He worked strictly because he needed the money, while his novel languished. This was not how he had imagined his sixties: a young wife who would soon see him as old, two kids to put through college, and no time for himself or his creativity. So, he had come to feel unease about the future and had a pessimistic view about aging.

Joseph was trapped by two inner obstacles: He remained unconsciously identified with youth and with his ego's self-image.

"If only I had built a different career," Joseph opined. "If only I hadn't had two kids this late." But he wasn't wrestling with his disillusionment in an effort to digest it, and he wasn't wrestling with his choices in an effort to affirm them. Rather, he felt himself to be a victim of his fate.

As I listened week after week, I began to hear the same mechanical, repetitive statements, which are a sign that a shadow character is appearing. "I'm trapped," he would say. "I live in obligation—big house, private school, nanny. I'll never get out alive."

I asked Joseph which specific bodily sensations arose with these thoughts. He said that he experienced a heavy, sinking feeling in his chest and his shoulders tended to slouch.

Then I inquired into which feelings came up at the same time. Helplessness, futility, and despair, he said.

Each of these—repeating thoughts, feelings, or sensations—is a cue to be on alert for a shadow.

Some people (thinking types) are better able to access a shadow character by detecting their inner dialogue. It typically has a critical, negative tone. So, when you are romancing a shadow, you might ask yourself, "What am I saying to myself over and over again?"

Others (feeling types) are more in touch with their emotional shifts. You might ask yourself, "Which feelings accompany the voice of this shadow character?"

And others (sensation types) are more naturally aware of their physical sensations. You might ask, "Which parts of my body feel tight or constricted, numb or empty, tingling and alive, when this voice appears?"

As a shadow character emerges, it can take on a shape or a personality. Then we visually personify this internal character to make it more conscious. Perhaps there is an image that emerges with it. You might ask yourself, "Who in me believes and feels this way? How old is this shadow character? Is it male or female?" You ask these questions to invite an unknown stranger to come out into the light of awareness and make itself available for a conscious relationship.

During our exploration, I asked Joseph whether he was seeing an image or figure inside his imagination. He quickly said, "Sisyphus—rolling that damn stone up the hill for all eternity." And he sighed deeply.

Next, we trace the roots of this shadow character by recalling a recent time when we fell into the same pattern. My client saw instantly that, only days before, he had been longing to write, but his wife asked him to watch the kids. "I felt so obligated," he said, as his shoulders slouched.

Now we work to uncover the character's history so that we can see that our reaction in the present moment is really a reaction from the past. We are time-traveling when a shadow character emerges.

To go further back and trace the history of his shadow character, I asked Joseph to close his eyes and recall an earlier time in his life when he had experienced the same inner messages, emotions, or sensations. He recalled a long-forgotten memory of his brother bullying other kids and getting kicked out of elementary school, bringing shame on his parents. He remembered vowing to himself at age seven: "I will be a good boy. I will make them proud."

In this way, Sisyphus was born within him. For decades, this character protected Joseph from feeling like a "bad boy" and urged him on as a hard worker and provider. But now, as he entered his later years and longed for more freedom, aliveness, and creativity, Sisyphus was sabotaging him. Joseph saw, too, that he was much like his father, who had sacrificed his musical talent to provide for a family and ended his life in deep resentment.

Joseph's personal shadow, like everyone's, is embedded in family shadow, such as intergenerational secrets or taboos. It, in turn, is embedded in cultural shadow, such as religious groups or national identities. As our society faces its history of racism and White privilege, we are meeting a collective shadow.

For many of us, the relentless Provider, in the image of Sisyphus, supporting the family, is handed down unconsciously, like brown eyes. So is the Caregiver, the Doer, the Nurturer, the Helper. So many of these patterns arise from the internalization of productivity and duty as core values. And though we all need open-ended time for self-reflection in order to engage with our shadow, the workaholic, materialistic values of our culture make this unconventional option difficult for everyone. So, it's vitally important to become aware that there is often a shadow character within who is driving our ambition and sense of obligation (one of my clients calls it "the Driver"). As we enter late life, that figure can sabotage the evolution of soul.

As these shadow patterns recur repeatedly and you identify the image, thoughts, and feelings as a character, they can take on a shape, a personality, even a name. In this way, they are differentiated from the general mass of unconscious material. By naming our shadow characters, locating them in the body, and hearing their messages, we can loosen their hypnotic grip over our life and make other choices. If we meditate and use self-observation to slow down and identify the pattern the next time it occurs, we may have a nanosecond to catch it—and choose not to respond automatically.

For example, Joseph can say to himself, "There's Sisyphus now. Do I need to fulfill this obligation in this moment, or can I make a different choice, perhaps taking some time to be playful or to write?"

In the beginning of shadow-work, we simply observe the pattern and learn to watch it, to be with the shadow rather than stuff it back into the bag. Down the road, with practice and self-reflection, we meet our shadow characters and feel a greater freedom of choice; we are able to reject its message, rather than believe it and act it out. In Joseph's case, he will be able to set down the stone and follow his own flow.

Eventually, with deep practice, we can break our unconscious identification with a character. This thought, feeling, or sensation, which always sounds and feels the same, is not who we are; it's not our real identity as a soul. Rather, it's a character that has taken over for the moment with its own agenda.

With his new shadow awareness, Joseph faced some difficult challenges. The idealistic dreamer in him didn't want to acknowledge any limits or give up any options. His younger sister had died, then his father. But these personal losses did not lead him to reflect on his own mortality. He was gripping his idealism as if it were a life raft.

"I have lots of time," he said. "I can still follow my dream later."

But, at the age of sixty-five, natural limits are coming forward. If we deny them, we are at risk of remaining in the clutches of a shadow character and triggering a late-life identity crisis.

The Sisyphus shadow drove Joseph to maintain his responsibilities at a reckless pace. But it seemed to me that he needed to take a different kind of responsibility: to be internally accountable for the choices he had made—to work for pay, marry a younger woman, have two kids, live a comfortable lifestyle—so that he could stop feeling like a victim of his story. He needed to choose his wife and children again—or not. If he continued to push relentlessly and unconsciously obey Sisyphus, his life would not change, and like his father, he would die with regret.

Joseph also needed to act on his own behalf, not act out unconsciously by having an affair or by quitting his job on a lark to get out from under the stone. Such options may look like an exit, but they are both simply reactions to Sisyphus. They don't stem from deeper internal guidance.

After several months of romancing Sisyphus, Joseph could detect when it was trying to control his behavior. He began to meditate and catch the inner dialogue of this shadow character more quickly and clearly. Eventually, he could even admit to himself that his time remaining was limited. He was ready to change his life.

Pure Awareness

Portal to Silent Vastness

I always teach shadow-work in conjunction with meditation. Over the years, many people have asked me what one has to do with the other. The answer: If we are to allow into conscious awareness that which we most fear and dread—such as dependency, degeneration, and death—we need to be grounded in something larger than our personality, something beyond ego, which lies within each of us.

The term *pure awareness* refers to a state in which the mind, having gone beyond itself, is silent, open, resting, and simply aware of awareness. We might also call it *transcendence, emptiness, sunyata,* or *turiya,* which means pure consciousness in the Hindu tradition. Pure awareness is a portal to silence, which is already always there. Every mystical tradition has a name for it—and a Way to it. It's the universal state of transcendence that the founder of every religion experienced. And it's within each of us—between each thought, between each breath.

Pure awareness is not another object of awareness, like a thought or sensation. It's the subject, the knower of all the objects. Whether we refer to it as emptiness or fullness, as Self or no-Self, it's awareness itself, or as Ram Dass called it, loving awareness.

As we cultivate and dwell in the silence of pure awareness as a regular practice, a dispassionate inner observer, or witness, unfolds. We experience the witness as an objective inner spaciousness, a silent distance from the contents of our mind. When we feel overwhelmed by a shadow character and its loud, repetitive thought pattern, eventually, with the practice of pure awareness, we can simply witness that shadow, while sitting in our silent center. This is a key stage in the evolution of the soul.

Linda, a colleague, described it this way: "After raising three kids and completing a full-time career, I'm so grateful that I have time to just be. I can sit in this impersonal witness awareness, beyond the noise of my mind, and I'm fulfilled. I don't need to march in the streets or try to fix anything. I notice that the peace I exude is my influence on others. It affects everyone around me, and that's enough now."

As we age, we need to cultivate this awareness preventively, not when we're in the midst of a physical or emotional crisis, grasping for solutions. We need to build a life raft now by cultivating a practice that brings us back to our center every day, not when the tidal wave is on the horizon.

Of course, that does not mean that a wave of health crises and losses won't come; it does not mean that our grief will be any easier to bear. But it means that we will have more internal calm from which to relate to the crises that come into our lives. When we learn to silence the noise of the mind and to witness our fleeting thoughts, we can slowly break our identification with these thoughts. We may even glimpse something in us that does not change or age but is timeless.

People ask me, "Why sit still in these chaotic, dangerous times? Shouldn't we be doing more, not closing our eyes? Shouldn't we be paying attention to the news to stay informed? Shouldn't we be marching in the streets?"

As more people grow irritated, outraged, and frightened by the world outside—the climate crisis, uprisings of racism and hate, global pandemics, and rampant misinformation—we need a daily refuge where we can recover and rejuvenate. We need more than ever a way to silence our noisy mind and go beyond our shadowy thoughts, in this way aligning with something deeper than the day's headlines.

But meditation is not only for ourselves. Our sitting practices prepare us to serve the common good with a clear mind and open heart. Because we're all interconnected, when we act from a silent center, we reduce the chaos and the noise, rather than add to it.

My Turn from Doing to Being

Each day, as sunlight dims and dusk falls, I stop. For more than fifty years, I've watched the light turn to darkness, then closed my eyes to make the transition from doing to being, from fast to slow, from outward to inward.

For me, dusk, the time when the glare of the day diminishes but the blackness of night has not yet blanketed the sky, is a sacred time. So, I have paid attention to dusk, the time between the world of light and the world of darkness, and I noticed a feeling of loss as another day wanes and a feeling of eagerness as another evening embraces me.

Eager for what? I'm eager to immerse myself in the expansive ocean of silence that is simply there as I close my eyes and enter meditation, breathing in, breathing out, releasing the day's stimulation, emptying the internal noise that goes with it, and sinking into the vastness.

After some years of feeling precious intimacy with my breath, I realized that each meditation is like practicing dying, going deeper within, letting go of it all, and breathing out one last time. Then I realized, while writing this paragraph, that this ritualized practice has helped me to prepare for the greater Dusk—for aging consciously into the twilight of my time here.

Before we cultivate pure awareness, our inner world is splashed with the colors of intense emotions, we believe our fleeting thoughts, and we unconsciously identify with the shadow character that is emerging in the moment. The result is grief, paralysis, shame: "I'm too old or weak for that," rather than "I'm feeling weak today." Or "I am useless," rather than "I'm not feeling like doing much today." We become lost in the shadow character—and have no portal to silence.

After we cultivate pure awareness and learn to witness those characters, we can watch the feelings of the moment and notice our thoughts without believing them. They float like clouds through the sky of our minds. Our deeper identity remains clear, uncolored by the passing phenomena. We might say, "I feel sad with this loss, but I know it will pass." Or "I can't do that anymore, but I know that it doesn't detract from who I am." Or "I can accept that this is how it is, even though I wish it were different."

As we open daily to this state and watch, breath by breath, we begin to realize that we are not those thoughts, those shadow characters that are complaining, judging, or rejecting our circumstances. We are not those feelings that ebb and flow. Rather, we are that simple, silent, observing awareness. And the more we identify with it—rather than with the noise—the quieter the mind grows, the wider the heart opens, and the deeper we sink into the timeless emptiness. And the more we embrace life as it is.

This capacity to break our unconscious identification with the shadow character and return to pure awareness or the silent vastness brings many gifts: It provides the body with deep relaxation and recovery from stress, as our heart rate and blood pressure go down. And meditation alters brain waves in positive ways, as indicated by years of research.

In addition, more recent studies demonstrate that meditation may slow aging at a cellular level. Dr. Elizabeth Blackburn, who won the 2009 Nobel Prize for the discovery of telomeres (the protective caps on chromosomes whose length is a metric for aging), has linked stress to shorter telomeres, meaning shorter lives. If meditation reduces stress, she reasoned, it could increase telomere length. In a series of studies, she found that it did.

Meditation also appears to slow age-related degeneration in our brains. Neurologist Eileen Luders at UCLA looked at the link between age and the volume of the brain's white matter, which typically shrinks with age. She reported that this decrease was less prominent in meditators as compared to non-meditators. On average, the brains of long-term practitioners appeared to be seven and a half years younger at the age of fifty than the brains of non-meditators.

With practice, one day we can sit in silence, watch the flow of thoughts and feelings come and go, and distinguish the voice of a shadow character from the whisper of the soul. In the context of aging, we can identify age—but not identify with it. Rather, the changes that inevitably arise with age become a vehicle for the soul's evolution.

On the other hand, when we hold on and resist change, a wave of grief arises. Everything changes; we don't want it to change. Everything ends; we don't want it to end. We cling for dear life. And we feel terrible grief to the degree that we resist ever-changing change.

Fortunately, in our time, with the democratization of mystical and contemplative methods that used to be kept hidden for a select few, we can now explore many practices and choose one that fits our natural tendencies and/or beliefs. We can cultivate a state of mind—pure awareness or nonduality—that opens an internal space where we can notice how thoughts come and go, how shadow characters come and go, and how bodily sensations come and go. Here, the ego has no agenda and no goal. It's not trying to get anywhere, fix anything, or resist anything. Instead, we let go of the contents of the mind and rest in pure awareness itself.

As George Harrison sang to us, "When you've seen beyond yourself, then you may find, peace of mind is waiting there."

So, from a spiritual perspective, we can't choose the circumstances of our age. But we can choose the quality of awareness we bring to those circumstances. We can open the portal to silent vastness and experience our thoughts and feelings as a quiet witness, freed of the grasp of the shadow.

An Interview with Rabbi Rami Shapiro

I spoke about spiritual practice in late life with Rabbi Rami Shapiro, then sixty-seven years old, whose eclectic practices stem from mystical Judaism, Zen Buddhism, and Ramakrishna's Hindu order. He has worked with Rabbi Zalman Schachter-Shalomi and Father Thomas Keating. Rami's many books and workshops address the deep unifying experience of nonduality, or unity consciousness, in mystical traditions.

"My body reminds me of my age now," Rami told me. "But the awakening to a singular reality feels ageless. We can't describe the indescribable, ineffable, infinite aspect, but it has no birth or death. If we experience that, even for a moment, everything changes. We're no longer afraid of death because we know that we are just a wave returning to the ocean. The form is gone, Rami dies, but the oceanic essence remains the same."

I asked him what he practices now, in his sixties. "Jewish mysticism suggests that we do one practice for each of the five dimensions of life. For the body, I do qigong. For the heart, I do *metta* compassion practice. For the mind, I study sacred texts and write about the links between psychology, religion, and spirituality. For the soul, I practice a mantra connected to the divine mother to become more aware of the interconnection of all things. And for the spirit, I practice self-inquiry from Ramana Maharshi, which involves exploring the many levels of the question *Who am I?*"

This sounded to me like a full-time job. "Whatever we're doing," Rami replied, "our lives are always about exploring *Who am I?* For seekers, it's always a relevant question. Even if they stop meditating for years, the question is there in the shadow. So, just pick it up again."

Even in our later years? "I find that the older I get, the more compelling the question becomes. At sixteen or sixty, ask the question in the same way, and it ripens into the same nondual reality. Beneath the body of X number of years, the timeless essence remains."

I asked him for some examples from his own experience, and he spoke about sitting in a soundproof isolation tank, in zero gravity, when his body/mind disappeared into a nondual state. "This Rami, these labels, these aches and pains, are only the crest on the wave, not our true nature."

Rami described having a similar experience when he sat with an Advaita, or Hindu nonduality, teacher. "I was talking away . . . when he asked, 'Are you?'"

"Everything stopped. Time stopped. Gone. I returned a few minutes later, speechless and free. He had gone behind my mind to just the right question to silence it."

Some of us have at least some basic experience with spiritual practices that gives us a taste of what lies beyond ordinary, daily awareness. Some of us continue and deepen those practices; others let them go. But the tasks of late life require the very traits and skills that meditation cultivates: a capacity not only to slow down but to slow downward, manage the mind, release the ego's striving, be fully present, and attune to the voice of soul.

Today, many of us experience just the opposite state: We are drawn outward to the noise, increasingly agitated, angry, and saddened by the chaotic, violent events of our day. We are compelled to look and listen, and the result is that our bodies and minds are overloaded, feeling the disturbance in the Force. So, in this era, more than ever, we need to find a calm center, a refuge from the noise, a way to clear our minds and open our hearts. Over time, we will see the growing impact of turning our attention within.

There are many spiritual traditions, and each has its own exoteric moral/behavioral practices and esoteric inner/mystical practices, with its own method of turning attention inward. Some of us feel drawn to a particular tradition, say Judaism, Advaita, Sufism, or Christianity. Others sample various traditions and practices through the decades, discovering the gifts and shadow issues of their many teachers and teachings. But the goal of all mystical or contemplative practice is universal: to quiet the mind until it rests in nondual pure awareness.

An Interview with
Kirtan Chant Leader Krishna Das

The Hindu devotional path became renowned when Richard Alpert returned from India in the late 1960s as Ram Dass, telling tales of the spiritual powers of his guru, Neem Karoli Baba, whom he called Maharaj-ji. Alpert metamorphosed from a Harvard psychologist to an advocate of LSD to a lover of God right before our eyes.

Jeffrey Kagel grew up in the 1950s on Long Island and dreamed of becoming a rock star. When a band offered him a job as its lead singer, he happened to meet Ram Dass, who was just back from India, and saw instantly that R.D. had something he wanted. Jeff faced a crucial turning point: to follow his dream of singing rock and roll or to follow Maharaj-ji's devotee back to India and discover the guru for himself.

Jeff turned East—and returned a few years later as Krishna Das. His name means servant of Krishna or Ram.

On the Hindu devotional path, God, guru, and Self are one. The guru is not outside of us; he is our true nature, a mirror to reflect the divine within us. As K.D. put it, "The guru is the presence in which we live—and which lives in us."

So, on this devotional path, the moment-to-moment devotion to, surrender to, and remembrance of the guru is the doorway to the divine or to pure awareness. There is no school of thought or method. There is only this sacred relationship. And this is what Krishna Das learned in the presence of his teacher.

When I interviewed him, he was about to turn seventy-three. "Maharaj-ji taught us to do practice, serve people, feed people, and remember God," K.D. told me. "He didn't teach people to meditate for their own self-gratification. . . . He just loved us from the inside, just as we are. And all the pretense, who you think you are, crumbles when you feel that love in your heart."

K.D. spent nearly three years in India with Maharaj-ji. During his time there, the pandits (singers) who chanted for the guru began to flirt with Western women. So, the guru banished them—and told Krishna Das to chant in their place. "These mantras or divine names are deeper than the mind," K.D. told me.

"They're not about believing anything. We sing them to turn toward ourselves, and the experience changes us."

K.D. wanted to stay in India and become a *sannyasin* (monk), but his guru sent him back to the United States. "He told me that I needed to live through my attachments here. I was heartbroken, depressed for a long time."

Six months after returning to the States, K.D. learned that his guru had died. He made an inner vow: "I will sing for you in the West."

Two decades passed before he became known as the rock star of *kirtan*, or devotional call-and-response chant. Fourteen albums later, he draws sold-out crowds of thousands to sing with him. When I am surrounded by these voices of ecstatic longing, I am reminded of the Hindu legend of Krishna and the *gopis*, the cow-herding girls devoted to him. When Krishna played divine music on his flute, the women left their husbands and followed him into the forest, where they danced around him in joyful devotion. But when the *gopis* became proud and felt special because they were with him, Krishna disappeared, intensifying their spiritual longing. And they wandered, seeking him everywhere.

"In the West, we're raised to be egos," K.D. told me. "Even our spiritual work sometimes polishes ego-centered beliefs. When we do yoga and meditate, our egos grab the results and keep us self-preoccupied." (I wrote about this at length in my book *Meeting the Shadow of Spirituality*.)

He recognized that, as his popularity grew, his ego got involved. So, he returned to India and, at the temple, had a vision: He saw the divine play of people coming and going, coming and going in vast space, like waves in the ocean. They got puffed up, believing they were an important wave, then returned to the ocean. This direct perception freed him to get out of his own way; he returned home and began to sing with 100 percent devotion.

"During that last visit at the temple, Maharaj-ji changed my heart. After that, I knew it was not about me. He was doing it all. I just sing. And I knew that if I didn't sing with people, I wouldn't shed light on the dark places in my heart. So, anything that arises during chanting becomes an object of meditation to let go of. It's not a performance. We're sharing the practice together."

When we watch our parents age, K.D. said, "we see them as more human, too. We see how difficult it is for them to be kind and present. And we have absorbed the same patterns, the same self-hatred or anxiety. So, we need to know that this programming is not us, it's not who we are. We need to plug into what's real."

Everyone longs for the same thing, he told me. "We long to experience our true nature and to relieve suffering. But as we age, it gets harder. Our energies wane, and we have a crisis because we can't project ourselves as important, powerful, charismatic people anymore. We become too weak to follow our lust. We have less concentration and can't take our minds where we want them to go if we haven't prepared. So, the preparation is key.

"We can begin a practice at any time," he said, "not based on faith but based on our own experience. Pay attention to how you feel and see what works. Each time we remember who we are, we return from the dream and plant seeds of awakening."

As a kid, Krishna Das just wanted to sing—and now it's happened, but not exactly as he had imagined. "I'm living my fantasy, but it's a practice, not a career. I sit at the harmonium and do practice. I don't know what else is happening because I do it so completely and so intensely. My knee hurts, my shoulder hurts, but that moves into the background as I chant."

He told me that initially his emotional problems from childhood caused terrible suffering and distracted his mind during chanting practice. As a result, the flow of his attention was diverted outward. But eventually, fifteen to twenty years ago, that flow dried out and turned inward. And that inner stream grew deeper and sweeter with practice.

"As we age, our spiritual practice naturally ripens our life experience. So, how we sit inside ourselves is a ripening experience. For me, it's easier to be here now. I'm less controlled by the obsessive flow of thought. It's not that the thoughts are gone, but they don't grab because the center of gravity has shifted."

Krishna Das explained that his ego is not the one doing it. "I just sing and go with the program."

As we age, K.D. said, instead of sedating ourselves to overcome the fear of death, spiritual teachings can help us. Buddhism teaches that we can die at any moment. In India, he pointed out, Hindus live surrounded by death; it's not hidden like it is here.

But, he added, "without spiritual practice, we have no leverage to let go of the issues that cause us suffering. Letting go is so important because it prepares us to let go of everything in a positive way, not a fearful one. We can live in love, not fear. We can die into love, not fear."

❀ ❀

Mortality Awareness

Portal to Presence

A Baby Boomer dies every 18 seconds. Breathe in. . . .
Our generation will be extinct by 2086. Breathe out. . . .

This is mortality awareness.

Like a thief, death can slip in and steal a life at any age. When we are young and touch death—whether of a family member or friend or even a near-death of our own—we tend to recover and forget, falling back under the spell of youth and the delusion of limitless time.

When we are adults, a close encounter with death penetrates more deeply, acting like a divine messenger and leaving us with an acute awareness of a shortened time horizon. But, after some time, we too tend to fall back to sleep.

Looking at death is a bit like looking at our shadow: We catch a glimpse for a moment, then forget, then remember, then forget again. Most of us just turn away from the breath of death. But this turn has profound consequences for our aliveness. In his classic book *The Denial of Death,* Ernest Becker writes that our "deepest need is to be free of the anxiety of death and annihilation; but it is life itself which awakens it, and so we must shrink from being fully alive."

This denial of death, and hence of life, takes many forms: our heroic striving to be somebody important and to amass a collection of objects, or to lean on what Becker calls "borrowed powers" from a priest class and its magical symbols, all in an effort to fill an inner emptiness. The dizzying rush to construct a false self keeps us from full presence in the moment, full joy and gratitude for the privilege of life. And, at the same time, it reinforces the epidemic refusal to acknowledge *what is,* to acknowledge that we, too, shall pass.

Denial always has its reasons: "I'm special." "I'm a good person." "I'm a good Catholic (or Muslim, or Jew, or other believer)." "I'm part of something important." "I take Lipitor." "I'm vegan." "My mother lived to be 102."

Denial of our own mortality blocks our capacity to see the whole truth. It prevents us from crossing over from role to soul and to being fully present now.

In my interview with Jungian analyst and prolific author James ("Jim") Hollis, then seventy-eight, he kept returning again and again to this theme. "Our awareness of death is part of an examined life. Mortality awareness is not morbid. Mortality, not perpetuity, makes meaning possible. It makes our choices matter.

"We believe that we have a problem because we feel separate from nature," Jim continued. "Death is not a problem for nature or for divinity. But it's a problem for us, for the ego's sovereignty. To really grow up, we need to accept our inevitable death."

Jim linked our capacity for holding mortality awareness to our capacity to live full lives. "People with the most anxiety take the least risk, so they have a big unlived life and tend to have regret when facing death. People with less anxiety live life more fully and don't have that fear at the end. They most fear the loss of others."

The tension between our innate will to live and our ever-present awareness of inevitable death has been a theme of religion, philosophy, and psychology for eons. The existentialists refer to "death anxiety," the psychoanalysts to "fear of annihilation." And both speculate ad infinitum about the consequences.

But there are those few who can feel intensely alive and, at the same time, hold mortality awareness. "I am here now," Father Thomas

Keating told me at the age of ninety-five, as we approached the conclusion of our interview in early 2018. "When you send me the interview to read tomorrow, I may be gone."

I felt a shudder of confusion, not knowing whether to laugh or cry in that awfully vulnerable moment. Then I realized that the ninety minutes he had just given to me were precious. And his capacity to stay connected to me and interested in our conversation, while acutely aware that he could die at any moment, was modeling a high level of presence.

Father Thomas died a few months later. But he was not the only one: As I wrote this book, two other Elders whom I had interviewed passed away—Frances Vaughan and Robert Atchley. I found myself filled with sorrow and gratitude, love and loss, because they had chosen to leave something precious with me near the end of their time. And each of them had been so present to the conversation.

Mortality awareness is a portal to living fully here, now, in presence. Presence is a heightened awareness of our momentary bodily sensations, feelings, and thoughts, which can expand out into a presence for others, attuned to their feelings and thoughts, and then out even further to connect us to all living things. Presence pierces the veil of denial and reveals to us the sacred value of life in every moment, and the sacred value of every circumstance as a teaching, an opening to something larger. It permits us to see through the emptiness of distraction and the meaninglessness of the ego's futile efforts.

As I write this, I can see, in my mind's eye, the clock on the wall in Ram Dass's home: There are no hour numbers. Every hand points to "NOW."

But the ego is so terrified of annihilation that it tries everything to deny mortality, building fortresses in all shapes and colors. The inner obstacle here: the mind's movement to regret about the past or fear about the future. Emotional unfinished business leads us to look back with remorse and wish *"if only . . ."* or to look forward and fear *"what if. . . ."*

Proponents of religious dogma use this existential dread to coerce us to be good children and moral adults and to behave in certain ways so that we can go to heaven or have a positive reincarnation, thereby transcending death.

Secular beliefs can be used in this defensive way, too. As detailed in *The Atlantic* (see J. Greenberg et al., 2012), a group of researchers linked the terror of death to worldviews, which are longer-lasting than we are. We instinctually oppose anyone who violates our worldview by tightening a circle around "us" to keep out "them." This tribal stage of awareness typically includes beliefs about the afterlife and modes of symbolically transcending death. In this way, "we" find a sense of security despite our ever-present mortality.

Even a reminder of death that is not consciously observed can trigger unconscious efforts to bolster the ego's worldview. When the researchers cited above subliminally flashed the word *death* for a few seconds on a screen—too quickly for anyone to notice consciously—their American subjects' reactions to an anti-American author were amplified. In my language, their shadow projection onto the Other intensified when they were reminded of death, even beneath their conscious awareness.

There are some exceptions to cultural denial, such as the Day of the Dead in Mexico and Ash Wednesday, when ashes are placed on the heads of worshippers, who are told, "You are dust." The sixth-century *Rule of Saint Benedict* encourages monks to "keep death daily before their eyes." In Islam, Sufis practice "remembrance of death" by going to graveyards for contemplation, and in Tibetan Buddhism, monks practice *lojong,* awareness of impermanence, the inevitable death of the body and its uncertain timing, which is out of our control.

As the Buddha said, "Of all footprints, that of the elephant is supreme. Similarly, of all mindfulness meditations, that on death is supreme."

When a divine messenger brings us face-to-face with our own mortality, if we are fortunate, we experience a revelation about the whole truth of life, and as a result, our ego may be humbled. If we do not, the ego continues to strive for immortality through heroic deeds, gathering possessions, rank, and even creative endeavors and legacies. Integral philosopher Ken Wilber called this the Atman project—the attempt to find the timeless in time, the striving to find Spirit in substitute gratifications that, in the end, are not That.

With mortality awareness, heat is applied to the psyche, which slowly generates an alchemical shift. In *From Age-ing to Sage-ing*, Rabbi Zalman Schachter-Shalomi explained it this way: "The more we embrace our mortality not as an aberration of God and nature, but as an agent urging us on to life completion, the more our anxiety transforms into feelings of awe, thanksgiving, and appreciation."

Anyone who has a regular meditation practice knows this truth: When the mind wanders, we are not fully present in the moment. With shadow awareness, we open ourselves and deepen our self-knowledge, allowing the fears that are stuffed away into the shadow to enter conscious awareness. With pure awareness, we can learn to witness the noise and sit in the silent vastness. With mortality awareness, we can learn to be present, appreciating the experience of *this moment,* of *what is,* releasing the ego's fears. *Yes, I too shall pass . . . Yes, I too shall pass . . .* Paradoxically, as this happens again and again, the fear decreases, and the energy that was stuffed away with a lifetime of denial returns to us, available for a more vital future.

Mortality awareness may show up in a mundane moment. My eighty-year-old friend went to Costco to buy toilet paper—and found himself wondering whether he would be around long enough to use it up.

It may emerge when we read the obituaries of the rock stars of our youth: Aretha, George Harrison, David Bowie, Prince, Glenn Frey, Leonard Cohen, Jerry Garcia, Barry White, Ray Charles, Gregg Allman, Tom Petty, Mary Travers, Lou Reed, Pete Seeger, Joe Cocker, Leon Russell, Tom Fogerty, Clarence Clemons, Levon Helm, Miles Davis, Freddie Mercury, James Brown, B.B. King. I feel shock as I type this list—this is my generation of artists.

It may sound an urgent alarm, such as with a serious diagnosis. In 2011, two years after Steve Jobs had a liver transplant due to pancreatic cancer, he gave a commencement speech at Stanford University and spoke of a quote by which he had lived his life: "If you live each day as if it was your last, someday you'll most certainly be right." He reported that he had used this awareness to gaze into the mirror every morning and ask himself: "If today were the last day of my life, would I want to do what I am about to do?" If the answer was no for too many days in a row, Jobs said, he knew he needed to change something.

Stewart, a dear friend, at age eighty-four, had been speaking openly to friends and family about his "slow glide to stop." He was deeply enjoying his time with family, his artwork, and cooking. Then a doctor gave him a prognosis: ten to eighteen months.

"It just got real," he told us. "I'm at the top of a roller coaster about to dive. And it's okay. My heart is open. No regret. And deep gratitude for an early mystical experience of seeing deceased loved ones. I know that death is not the end. I don't believe it; I know it."

I felt so grateful to Stewart for modeling not just an awareness but an acceptance of mortality, for all of us. His capacity to be at peace stood in stark contrast to other friends who had struggled with acceptance to the end.

Rob, a client who had watched his father die, allowed that deep loss to become a reflection of his own mortality. He told me that it forced him to reevaluate everything: his ego's agenda in work and marriage, his difficult dynamic with his adult daughter, and his religious orientation. He even saw his shadow's lifelong obsession with sexuality in a broader perspective and wanted to do inner work to let it go.

"My values and priorities for midlife," Rob told me, "don't fit my values and priorities for late life. When I'm dying, I don't want to be regretting that I didn't work harder." He retired soon after to help raise his grandson and to join the board of a conservation group that fights against animal extinction.

Mortality awareness can act as a catalyst, dissolving outworn beliefs and behaviors in every moment and revealing their deeper nature. It is the riddle of late life, an enigma that cannot be figured out but only deeply lived.

During the COVID-19 pandemic, with moment-to-moment reports of increasing deaths around the world, many people were forced to face mortality—the risk of their own, the actuality of their loved ones'. As the fear and grief penetrated people, the world grew silent. Then the denial erupted—in the rebellions of anti-maskers and anti-vaxxers. Of course, their motivations were complex. But, certainly, denial of mortality awareness was at play.

There are some indications that our society is opening to this quality of awareness, with a few bestselling books on the topic and more open discussion of health care directives, hospice care, and assisted suicide. There is even a small movement to form "death cafés" in local communities and online, where strangers gather over cake and tea and openly discuss death, with the intention of bringing this taboo subject out into the open in order to make the most of their lives. They are facing death anxiety and breaking through denial of mortality.

The purpose of aging, then, is not merely to slow down; it is to slow downward. It is to shift our attention and our energies from the outer world to the inner, from role to soul. It is to connect the moment to eternity, the fleeting to the lasting. It is to open the three portals of awareness, each of which opens to a mystery—depth, silent vastness, and presence.

As we cultivate shadow awareness, pure awareness, and mortality awareness, aging initiates us into renewal in late life.

Shadow-Work Practices

🦋 Shadow Awareness

- Which shadow character within you is afraid of looking into the dark?
- Which shadow character works to maintain the walls of denial?
- What feelings and ideas about "old" are stuffed away in the bag you drag behind you?

✿ *Pure Awareness*

- Have you tasted pure awareness?
- Do you have a practice that carries you beyond ego?
- Who within you stops you from doing that practice each day?

✿ *Mortality Awareness*

- When did you first become aware of death?
- Did you forget?
- Did you remember again?
- What are your beliefs about death? Do they trigger fear of death?
- What effect does mortality awareness have on your life now, in this moment?

Spiritual Practices

✿ *Pure Awareness Meditation*

This practice from Ram Dass helps us move our identification from the mind and the senses to identify with pure awareness. We can do it as beginners or as advanced practitioners. First, remove potential distractions and sit comfortably. Take a few deep breaths in and out. As you breathe, practice moving your attention into your belly as it rises and falls. Notice that as you do this your mind grows quieter. Now you can begin:

1. Breathe into your belly and bring your awareness to your eyes, silently saying, "I am not the eyes and what they see. I am loving awareness."
2. Bring your awareness to your ears, silently saying, "I am not the ears and what they hear. I am loving awareness."
3. Bring your awareness to your mouth, silently saying, "I am not this mouth and what it tastes. I am loving awareness."
4. Bring your awareness to your heart center. Pause, breathing in and out of your heart center, resting in pure awareness.
5. If you wish, you can continue downward through the body, including other parts. When you are done, bring your awareness to the totality of your body, silently saying, "I am not this body. I am loving awareness."

As Ram Dass put it, "Only this moment is real, this moment of loving awareness. The past and the future are all just thoughts."

Repeat the above practice, this time substituting each feeling that arises, disidentifying with those feelings and identifying with loving awareness. Practice saying, "I am not this hurt. I am loving awareness. I am not this regret. I am loving awareness. I am not this anger. I am loving awareness."

Repeat again, this time substituting each thought that arises, disidentifying with those thoughts and identifying with loving awareness. Practice saying, "I am not this thought. I am loving awareness. I am not that sound. I am loving awareness. I am not that image in my mind's eye. I am loving awareness."

Bring your attention to loving awareness and identify with it, again, again, again.

If you don't feel drawn to the term *loving awareness,* you can substitute *pure awareness, Spirit, Higher Self, soul,* or whatever term resonates with you. Or simply say, "I am not X. I am that which lives and breathes through everything."

🍂 *Mortality Awareness Practice*

Death can be denied, or death can be a teacher. We practice mortality awareness to make the most of our lives. Please breathe into your belly as you contemplate these questions:

- If you were to die today, what would be your biggest regret?
- What is one change you can make to bring you closer to living the life you want today?

3

Meeting Ageism from the Inside Out and the Outside In

PARABLE

Meeting the Inner Ageist: Beatrice Wood's Story

In The Ageless Spirit, *California potter Beatrice Wood told a story of discovering her own inner ageist at the age of ninety. "I know the absurdity of old age,"* Beatrice said, *"because I've always hated old people, ever since I was young."*

"I remember, for example, that I was ill and had to go to the hospital for three days, mostly to rest. I found myself [in a room] with an old toothless hag who had an accent. I needed sleep, so I went to sleep. And this poor lady chatted and chatted. I was so mad. I tried to avoid her. The next day, after I had a little rest, I said to myself, I'm not nice to this poor woman. She needs someone to talk to. I must be more decent to her. So when afternoon came I got off my high horse and listened to her. She'd had a heart attack, and she was all alone and frightened to death and in a state of crisis. The next day I was leaving. I whipped myself into a kind of decency. . . . I sat on her bed, took her hand, and I looked at her, and to my astonishment this ugly old woman was beautiful. There was no wall between us. It was a wonderful experience.

"You see, we're all really one, and that oneness between us I touched.

When I left I said goodbye, and the next morning I phoned and they said I couldn't reach her. She died during the night. . . . I was sure she died knowing that somebody cared. Now you see the arrogance of the artist who did not want to be disturbed by the old hag. I threw that into the ashcan and met another human being. And that ugly human being became beautiful. This is one of the most important experiences and lessons of my life."

—As told in *The Ageless Spirit,* edited by
Phillip L. Berman and Connie Goldman

In the story above, Beatrice Wood eloquently described an awakening to her "inner ageist," the shadow character within who rejects a compassionate connection with older people and blocks our society from awakening to systemic age discrimination. It is this character in us that projects negative traits onto older people, starting in early childhood and increasingly into adulthood. The irrational insistence that people in late life are "Other" results, eventually, as we ourselves age, in denying that we are becoming "them." In fact, older people form the only group that is discriminated against to which we will all one day belong.

In the moment that Beatrice awoke to her own unconscious bias, she reoriented to her inner world. She recognized her inner ageist— the shadow character that denies age and insists on identifying with youth—and the consequences of obeying it for both herself and another person. As she brought it into awareness, her heart opened, and her behavior changed accordingly. When we do the same, acknowledging, engaging with, and honoring our inner ageist, we open the doors to personal and social change.

While the inner ageist lies in the personal shadow, institutional ageism hides in the collective or cultural shadow. Most of us remain blind to the stereotyping and discrimination that occurs everywhere on the basis of age, even if we have become aware of other forms of discrimination and their harmful consequences. As a result, we organize our attention, values, services, and especially our power without seeing this blind spot: Ageism is a human rights and social justice issue that is critical now, as millions of people cross the threshold into late life. Both inner work and social activism are urgently needed to uproot the insidious forces behind ageism.

Meeting Your Inner Ageist

From the Inside Out

My own story of meeting my inner ageist and building a conscious relationship with it, or romancing it, can serve as a model of shadow awareness opening a portal to depth, or sacred self-knowledge. The experience dramatically reoriented me in late life. And it's an example of how inner work is a service for the common good.

A child of the '60s, I bought into the trope of never trusting anyone over the age of thirty. Then over forty. Then over fifty . . . uh-oh . . . I began to realize as I aged that I was becoming one of *them,* a member of the group that I rejected—those old people.

I was in denial, banishing the "old woman" into my shadow, and thereby rejecting my own future self. But I wasn't aware of this for a long time. In fact, I was continuing to sing to myself the lyrics from Bob Dylan's 1973 lullaby to his young son: "May you stay forever young." The song is an exquisite blessing, and yet, from my vantage point today, I wonder how its ageist overtones shaped its listeners, almost like a prayer.

Then, a few years ago, a divine messenger arrived: A frail, elderly woman sat next to me in a restaurant. I noticed her tattered clothes and dirty hands. She ordered free samples, and I observed that I felt uncomfortable—no, if I'm honest, I felt repulsed. My inner dialogue went like this: "She shouldn't be here at my favorite vegan restaurant. It's so sad—those wrinkles, that frailty, poverty, and neediness. I'll never be like that." The sensation in the pit of my stomach was tight and nauseous. I felt uncomfortable and afraid.

I was meeting in myself an unconscious shadow character that was projecting onto her what I was denying and rejecting in myself—my own loss of youthful vitality, my vulnerability, and my potential dependency, loneliness, and poverty. In fact, I was projecting onto her a dark image of my future self, if I lived long enough to be "old," and deeply disliking what I saw and felt.

I was shocked by this new awareness, especially because I had worked and rallied against the other "isms"—racism, sexism, classism, and homophobia. And I had felt acutely aware of the impact of cultural messaging, media marketing, and biases against identity groups. Yet here, deep in the hidden recesses of my unconscious shadow, ageism, invisible and insidious, persisted into my late life. I was stuck in the primary inner obstacle: identifying with youth and denying age.

After decades of inner work, I was able to catch this one, and I named it my "bag lady" shadow character. That is to say, I became aware of the universal archetype of the inner ageist in myself through this personal image of the "bag lady." She personifies the fear of losing everything, being unable to take care of oneself, and ending up abandoned on the streets.

I followed the same steps to romance my shadow that are outlined in the previous chapter.

First, I heard my inner dialogue: "I'll never be like that." This gave me a cue that I was separating myself, creating an us/them dichotomy.

Then I felt the emotions: disgust and fear. This gave me a cue that I was emotionally overreactive, and a projection was involved.

Then I observed the sensations in my body: nausea in my solar plexus, tightness in my shoulders.

After I recognized the inner voice, feelings, and sensations of the shadow character, it took on dimensionality for me.

Next, I saw the image in my projection onto the woman—the bag lady.

We often meet the shadow in an unconscious projection onto another person, attributing to him or her a rejected part of ourselves. So, if we deny our own aggression, laziness, or sexuality, we may encounter it indirectly in another and feel an exaggerated reaction to that person: He's really a pushy bastard, she's really a lazy couch potato, he's such a sex addict. We shoot the arrow of projection and unconsciously attribute this quality to the other person in an effort to banish it from ourselves, to keep from seeing it within.

With ageism, we project our negative fantasies of "old"—ugly, frail, needy, senile—which leads to condescension and stereotyping: greedy geezer, old bat, over the hill, out to pasture. And when millions of people project what they fear about aging onto elders, the latter try to appear and act as if they are younger. Hence the epidemic of anti-aging marketing, advertising, surgery, and hormone replacement therapy. Further, as our society as a whole—young people, old people, and everyone in between—buys into a stereotype that devalues Elders, as well as our lifetimes of skill and wisdom, a collective inner ageist takes root.

I didn't know it at the time, but the shadow character of the "bag lady" is an epidemic image of the inner ageist within women in our culture. In 2016, a survey by Allianz Life Insurance Company found that almost half of all women respondents said they often or sometimes fear losing their money and becoming homeless, regardless of income level. The fear of becoming a bag lady was highest among single and divorced women. But it also was present among high earners. So, I was not alone in carrying this shadow figure.

Finally, I traced it back to its roots in my personal history, exposing its origins in my childhood, which did not include so much as a single observation of someone aging with dignity, vitality, and creativity. I can recall my mother's discomfort with her own mother, who was a cruel, manipulative woman. I can remember my grandmother's negative gaze at Mom, then at my sister and me, when we visited and felt that we could never please her. In retrospect, I see that my grandmother, who was an uneducated immigrant and stood 4 feet, 10 inches high, used her power trips to protect herself from feeling inferior or weak and used her money to manipulate others to fend off feeling vulnerable or alone. But as a child, I knew only that I didn't want to be like her.

Then I heard in the recesses of my memory a Yiddish phrase uttered by my dad, referring to a neighbor he disliked: "He's an *alte kaker*," which translates as "a washed-up old fart." With that memory, I realized that I had heard critical, dismissive terms for older people many times. How deeply had I internalized my dad's patronizing tone and contemptuous gesture that accompanied that comment?

When we begin to recognize a projection, as I did that day in the restaurant, and create a conscious relationship to an inner shadow character, to material that was previously unconscious, we are romancing the shadow. We are turning within to read the messages encoded in the moments of our daily lives in such a way that we gain depth and self-knowledge.

When we meet the shadow and deny it, turning outward in blame, we live in projection, not reality, and we banish the shadow once more into the dark cavern of the unconscious. When, instead, we meet the shadow and romance the character, it loses power.

During my daily practice of pure awareness, I learned to observe when the bag lady erupted into my awareness and brought up feelings of fear, repulsion, and vulnerability. I witnessed the thoughts and endured the discomfort, opening to it with curiosity because I did not want to succumb to denial.

But I also learned to turn outward, toward the homeless women and men who live in my area in shame, invisibility, and powerlessness. I had felt so ashamed when I realized that I had unknowingly succumbed to the undertow of ageism, and that shame connected me in compassion to the real-life bag ladies crouched in rags on the street corners of my city. As my heart opened to my inner ageist, it opened to them as well.

A colleague called this a "stereo effect"—both inner and outer bag ladies, the symbolic and the real, surround us and enhance our fear of becoming old, poor, and forgotten. The results of unconsciously agreeing with the inner ageist, male or female, are devastating. It warns of a terrible fate beneath the boundary of awareness: the loss of home, love, family, and dignity.

Of course, this is just as true for men as for women. One eighty-year-old male friend told me that when he was forced into retirement, he was terrified of becoming homeless and thought about entering a monastery just to have shelter. (And indeed, he has since outlived his money and is now driving for Uber in order to stay solvent.) A male client, age seventy, told me that his shadow figure is a lazy, ineffective guy who "can't get it done," the opposite of his "go-getter" ego ideal.

When we're young and unknowingly carrying this hidden figure, it drives some of us to make choices to avoid risk, to choose business over the arts, or teaching over music, or one spouse over another to ensure security. As a friend put it, "The bag lady is a slave driver; she haunts and taunts us."

In addition, she leads us to reject whole generations of older people, thereby robbing us of valuable friendship, mentoring, and guidance, as well as robbing them of the opportunity to transmit their love, skills, and wisdom. Furthermore, if we obey the inner ageist, we reject our own future and set ourselves up for a late life filled with shame, fear, and disappointment.

I learned to slowly and gently coax the bag lady out of the darkness, attune to her message for me, respond differently to older people, and deal with the fear and dread of my own aging. When my inner ageist erupts these days, or a homeless woman holds out her hand, my heart cracks open—and my gaze turns toward, rather than away.

So, Beatrice Wood and I both had a disturbing encounter with an inner character that was prejudiced, stereotyping, and unconsciously projecting onto others. As I inched breath by breath toward seventy, I wondered whether the arrow that I had pointed outward, toward the target of older people, had unknowingly been pointed inward, too, toward myself. Unaware of this dynamic, we reject, even hate ourselves and long to be different from how we are.

When we resist *what is,* we block the development of our soul. For me, the discovery of my inner ageist was the first step of my rite of passage to become an Elder. To overcome this obstacle, I needed to let go of this shadow character and its identification with youth. In order to emerge into a new stage of life, as an Elder filled with self-respect and gratitude, I first needed to step into the unknown, asking myself, "Who am I now?"

The Dramatic Consequences of the Inner Ageist

It turns out that *what* we believe about age throughout our lives—consciously and unconsciously—shapes *how* we age. The brain/mind/body connection becomes highly visible here: Living as a target of ageist projection affects our self-image, general health, brain health, and behavior in a dynamic process that takes place across our life span. If we internalize it and develop an inner ageist, we become our own target.

In other words, how we age is not determined solely by physiology. It is a more individual, subjective experience with health outcomes tied as much to beliefs and values as to biology. When we internalize ageist messages and believe that becoming old makes us useless, worthless, unattractive, and inferior to youth, when we believe that it means only decline, dementia, suffering, and death, then we behave accordingly. We cling to denial by striving to remain young, refusing to let go of old habits and roles, even when they are well worn out. We lose a sense of meaning and purpose and may grow depressed and depleted, ignoring our self-care. And we suffer health consequences, losing resilience for the inevitable challenges ahead.

On the other hand, when we reject the negative messaging and build a conscious relationship with our inner ageist shadow, we can shape late life differently: as a vital stage of adult development for continuing our emotional and spiritual growth, cultivating wisdom, and contributing to future generations—that is, as a time to shift from role to soul. Then we can more easily align with the realities of our individual aging, accept ourselves more deeply, and change our lives accordingly. In this way, we become models of aging well for others.

Research by Becca Levy, a psychologist at Yale School of Public Health, has confirmed this link between our beliefs about age and their health consequences. She pioneered research on "implicit ageism," studying how positive and negative beliefs about older people (which she calls age stereotypes) have profound effects on their mental and physical health. In "Mind Matters: Cognitive and Physical Effects of Aging Self-Stereotypes," a review of studies on ageism, Levy reported that age stereotypes are internalized during childhood and young adulthood and embodied as they lead to self-image through the years.

She cited a study that found that children, from preschool to sixth grade, when shown drawings of a man at four stages of life, considered the oldest man to be "helpless, incapable of caring for himself, and generally passive." When these children were asked how they would feel about becoming elderly, 60 percent gave negative responses.

Such childhood stereotypes are reinforced throughout our lives by repeated exposure to ageist messaging, according to Levy. She cited another study showing that college students, when subliminally exposed to the word *old,* made associations of negative traits more quickly than when primed with the word *young.* Levy wrote, "Because the elements of this process seem to be deeply engrained, it is likely that implicit ageism will continue to operate when, for instance, the students are at the 50th reunion of their college class." In other words, eventually, when we reach old age, these age stereotypes become what Levy calls "self-stereotypes," or what I would call the inner ageist.

Levy went on to investigate the effects of these "self-stereotypes" on older subjects.

- *Memory:* Levy developed a technique to subliminally prime subjects by flashing words on a screen at speeds designed to permit perception without awareness. Older subjects exposed to negative stereotypes of age ("senile") performed worse on memory tasks than those exposed to positive ones ("wise"). The results show that even outside of conscious awareness, these stereotypes influence cognitive ability.
- *Will to live:* After exposing subjects to subliminal primes and pos-

iting hypothetical fatal medical situations, she found that older individuals exposed to positive stereotypes of age tended to accept life-extending medical interventions, while those who saw negative primes did not.

- *Cardiac health:* Older subjects exposed to negative primes showed higher heart reactivity, indicating physiological stress, although the participants were unaware of this impact.

- *Survival rates:* In a review of data, Levy found that people who had positive beliefs about growing older, compared against those with less positive beliefs, as measured twenty-three years earlier, gained seven and a half years of life—more than the longevity gained from low blood pressure, low cholesterol, healthy weight, cessation of smoking, and regular exercise!

- *Brain health:* Levy reported, in the *Journal of Personality and Social Psychology* (1996), that activating positive self-stereotypes about age, beneath conscious awareness, improved memory. In 2016, in *Psychological Aging,* she reported that subliminal activation of negative self-stereotypes predicted Alzheimer's disease biomarkers.

Levy's findings are startling and confirm that ageism, operating from the shadow beneath conscious awareness, has ripple effects throughout our bodies and minds as we navigate through a youth-centered, ageist culture. In a different article, "Longevity Increased by Positive Self-Perceptions of Aging," Levy et al. proposed that more positive internal self-images of aging predict better brain/mind/body health over time. To translate into my language: Ageist stereotypes are internalized early as shadow characters and later become self-images. They are then consciously and unconsciously triggered to exert their harmful or beneficial influences on us through several pathways.

Given this complexity, we cannot fight inner ageism merely by replacing negative thoughts or images with positive thinking. That is only a conscious process. The beliefs and images in the shadow, outside of our awareness, are elusive, contagious, and deeply ingrained in our society. Rather, we need to cultivate pure awareness, shadow awareness, and social action in tandem.

Meeting the Collective Shadow of Ageism

From the Outside In

I also traced my inner ageist to its roots in our collective cultural shadow, which worships youth and devalues older people, isolating us from other generations. The cultural shadow is the larger framework in which family and individual shadows develop. It helps determine on a large scale—via the national media, social media, musical lyrics, political dialogue, religious doctrine, education—what is acceptable and what is taboo.

Today we are confronted with the dark side of human nature several times each day, as the world has become a stage for the collective shadow. Racism, sexism, homophobia, ableism, and religious intolerance, and other manifestations of the cultural shadow have erupted across the globe in recent years, sometimes violently. It's as if they were merely dormant in the shadows of many, a primitive beast asleep in the limbic brain, legislated away but not truly overcome, as we had hoped.

As Becca Levy's studies demonstrate, even subliminal priming has great power over our thoughts and behavior, and we are constantly being primed by the culture in which we swim, especially by the media, even unknowingly. I can recall how I felt as a young girl watching Archie Bunker dismiss and patronize Edith, then watching the Golden Girls with their silly, empty-headed banter. I know now that I was being primed to buy into the disrespect of older women. The media was feeding my inner ageist.

In a 2017 report, *Over Sixty, Underestimated,* researchers S. Smith, M. Choueiti, and K. Pieper from the University of Southern California Annenberg School for Communications and Journalism examined the portrayal of older characters in twenty-five films that were nominated for the Best Picture Academy Award in 2014, 2015, and 2016. The findings are revealing:

- Only 11.8 percent of the speaking characters in the films were sixty or older. Of those, 77 percent were men.
- Of the lead actors and ensembles, only one was over sixty—the same one: Michael Keaton in *Birdman* and *Spotlight*.

As the research shows, although 14 percent of film ticket buyers in the United States are over the age of sixty, they are underrepresented on screen. And when they are, those characters are often subjected to ageist put-downs. Some 35 percent of those films with prominent older characters included derogatory, demeaning comments about age.

In a complementary report released that same year, titled *Seniors on the Small Screen,* Smith and her fellow researchers at the USC Annenberg School also looked at two groups of TV series, including the favorite shows of people between the ages of eighteen and forty-nine and the favorite shows of people over sixty-five. The findings: Older people represented less than 10 percent of the speaking characters. Both groups of shows used demeaning language by younger characters and self-deprecating language by older ones, priming all of us with ageism. In 2018, the researchers' follow-up study, *Still Rare, Still Ridiculed,* found that people over sixty in film remain rare and ridiculed.

A year later, in 2019, all nominees for best director and screenwriter were over fifty. And four of the ten actors nominated for their work in leading or supporting roles were sixty or older. We'll see if this is an anomaly or a trend.

A 2013 article about American advertising examined stereotypical portrayals of older adults in TV ads. The researchers found that some 97 percent of ads featuring older adults portrayed them with positive stereotypes, such as "golden agers" or "perfect grandparents," with men portrayed more positively than women. Most of these older adults appeared in ads for health-related products, linking age to poor health. (See E. Lamb and J. Gentry, "Denial of Aging in American Advertising," for details.)

Studies by the AARP show that, along with purpose, health, loss of loved ones, and social connectedness, age discrimination deeply affects older people's satisfaction with life. Women are more likely to feel the negative effects of age discrimination than men, especially concerning appearance. Silver-haired CEOs and silver-haired grand-mas elicit different stereotypes. So, women begin to try to pass as younger than they are.

Ageism at work—denial of hiring, promotion, or training or being harassed or laid off due to age—has been against the law for more than fifty years. But in 2016 alone, 20,857 age-related complaints were filed with the U.S. Equal Employment Opportunity Commission. In our culture, steeped in stereotypes about older people being unproductive, those with hiring power can be reluctant to hire older workers due to their own inner ageists.

A 2017 AARP study, reported by Sarah Kerman and Colette Thayer, showed that 38 percent of older people between the ages of fifty and sixty-four were very likely to apply for new jobs, even though most thought that their age would work against them. Most importantly, the researchers found, job discrimination negatively affects life satisfaction among respondents—interestingly, other expressions of discrimination, such as comments about memory, unrequested offers of assistance, or others' impatience with them, did not.

But it persists. A report by Kenneth Turrell in the November 2017 *AARP Bulletin* cited a study in which researchers sent more than 40,000 resumes for 13,000 job openings posted online. They sent three resumes for each posting, posing as young, middle-aged, and older adults with similar skills. The older applicants received far fewer callbacks.

In a 2017 summit hosted by the Milken Institute Center for the Future of Aging, Patricia Milligan, then a senior partner at Mercer, a human resources consulting firm, proposed that employers need to get over three categories of unconscious bias against workers over fifty: 1) older workers are less productive than younger ones; 2) older workers can't learn; and 3) older workers cost too much. She noted that older workers can be high performing in many ways, reducing turnover and creating stability. (See R. Eisenberg, "Why Isn't Business Preparing More for the Future of Aging?" for details.)

Laura Carstensen, founding director of the Stanford Center on Longevity, concurs. In a 2017 *Economist* special report, "The Economics of Longevity," she asserts that older workers are not less able-bodied, less inventive, or less productive than the young. "This may have been true fifty years ago," she said, but "the point at which workers are physically no longer able to work has shifted much further up the age range."

In the rising tech sector, a youthful tribe like none other, those responsible for hiring typically seek out digital natives who will fit into the workplace culture. Nearly half of all tech workers are millennials. At Facebook the median age is twenty-eight, at Google it's thirty, at Amazon it's thirty-one. Certainly, that doesn't prove ageism; but it's a harsh reality.

Unequal power dynamics have a distinct flavor when age and gender intersect. Like men who lose work and suffer a loss of self-worth, women today risk a loss of identity, influence, and dignity with ageist job discrimination, on top of widespread sexism. "Old" + "female" = dangerous territory.

In the field of education, Jessica Terrell reported in an article, "Make Early Retirement Enticing to Teachers," that experienced teachers, when viewed as "old," commonly face early retirement incentives and denial of promotions and tenures.

In the gay community, research is beginning to reveal "internalized gay ageism," or feeling denigrated or depreciated because one is aging as a gay person. Richard G. Wight and his team at the Fielding School of Public Health, University of California, Los Angeles, studied the intersection of ageism as a social stressor and homophobia as a social stigma and their health consequences in older gay men. They found that, due to experiences of internalized ageism and homophobia, older gay men may be exposed to unique, previously unexamined sources of stress that exacerbate age-related problems and place them at elevated risk for poor mental health, such as depression. Their conclusion: "We hypothesize that the particular overlap between internalized ageism and internalized homophobia among midlife and older gay men generates internalized gay ageism."

Jesus Ramirez-Valles, author of *Queer Aging,* interviewed hundreds of gay baby boomers about the intersection of being gay and old. He found that many felt pride in their accomplishments, guilt about having survived AIDS when others did not, and sadness at the high emphasis on youth in gay culture. He concluded that internalized gay ageism is widespread in the gay community and puts people at risk of depression.

In the field of medicine, ageist misconceptions can affect the diagnosis and treatment of older patients. Some health care providers, engaging in "senior profiling," may dismiss a pathology as an inevitable feature of age or treat a symptom, such as medication side effects, as a disease. In both cases, bias blinds them to treatment options for their patients.

In the United States and Europe, older patients are less likely than younger patients to receive certain life-saving treatments. For example, in 2015 Beth Casteel reported in the *American College of Cardiology Journal* "on a study of older patients who had mild heart attacks but did not receive treatments offered to young patients." "Because people over 80 are underrepresented in clinical trials, they are less likely to receive treatment according to guidelines," cardiologist Nicolai Tegn said. "But more invasive strategies result in better outcomes in these patients."

That type of discrimination may have made sense in 1900, when most people died before the age of fifty. But with the new longevity, and general life expectancy close to eighty, it is no longer valid.

Ironically, even gerontology, the field dedicated to studying the biological, cultural, and psychological aspects of aging, adheres to an ideology that dismisses subjectivity, or the personal, lived experience of people in late life. Harry R. Moody, known informally as Rick, former vice president of AARP, former chair of Elderhostel (now Road Scholar), and a prolific author, told me in a private conversation that at professional conferences on aging (hosted by, for example, the Gerontological Society and the American Society on Aging), he does not see speakers who are themselves very old, talking about their own experiences. "It's as if the NAACP or NOW held events in which all the speakers were White or male," he said. "Even those who advocate aging studies end up reproducing academic discourse, and the subjective experience of age is dismissed. You might say that subjectivity is a shadow in the academic world."

At a recent meeting of the National Academies of Sciences, Engineering, and Medicine's Forum on Aging, Disability, and Independence, Kathy Greenlee, former assistant secretary for aging in the U.S. Department of Health and Human Services, addressed this issue of elders' missing voices. She called for a new wave of advocacy by and for seniors: "We need more older people talking publicly about themselves and their lives. Everybody is battling aging by themselves, reinforcing the notion that how someone ages is that individual's responsibility," rather than a collective responsibility. (See J. Graham, "Learning to Advance the Positives of Aging," for details.)

Meanwhile, the field of geriatrics, which specializes in caring for the complex issues of the elderly, is contracting just as our need for experts is expanding. There are only 7,500 geriatricians in the United States today. On the other hand, the American Academy of Anti-Aging Medicine has tens of thousands of doctor members who promote the idea that aging is a curable disease. Collective ageism is everywhere, even in the field itself.

❦ ❦

An Interview with Ageism Crusader
Ashton Applewhite

Applewhite, author of *This Chair Rocks: A Manifesto against Ageism,* is also a crusader for the cause. Using humor and storytelling in her book and TED Talk, she makes the case for an anti-ageism campaign as an antidiscrimination and health care initiative.

Ashton is working to generate a diverse movement of all kinds of people who are over the age of sixty because she sees our society's different issues—sexism, racism, ableism, ageism, and so on—as all one struggle. She has built a free online clearinghouse, called Old School, which offers a consciousness-raising guide, educational curricula, books, blogs, podcasts, and resources for schools and businesses.

In an interview, Ashton, then sixty-six, told me that she backed into the subject that is now her passion when she wrote a piece about people over the age of eighty who still work. During her research, she realized that everything she thought she knew about late life was wrong. "It's framed as a problem. So, we should buy stuff to fix it. Wrong!" she said. "Aging is hard and complicated, but our fears of it are out of proportion to reality. And we can live longer and healthier if our attitudes are in line with reality."

People used to contact her, she said, about giving lectures to define ageism and its consequences. Now they ask her how to act on it and how to improve their institutional environments. "We've moved from thought to action. That's very exciting," she said.

Medical school students have told her that they are shocked by the ageist curriculum. So, she developed a presentation. Architects have asked how to incorporate elder needs into their building practices. So, she went to Eden Alternative, a group that works to create vibrant, personalized communities in assisted living and nursing homes, and joined forces to create home care programs for elders. Age-friendly universities, such as the Leonard Davis School of Gerontology at the University of Southern California, have requested curricula. All the materials are available free on Old School for others to continue to use.

The aging industrial complex, as Ashton calls it, moves slowly. "Most experts in the field see people at the end of life who are frail and debilitated. It makes aging scary. So, they become invested in aging as decline."

I suggested to her that these experts also each have an inner ageist, who is in denial of their own unconscious ageism. "Yes!" she nearly shouted. She urges us to hack our unconscious beliefs about age. "That's the first step. Once we see our own bias, we are liberated to see it in the culture and become culture warriors. First, we see our own collusion. Then, we see it outside ourselves. And we can't get the genie back in the bottle."

Ashton wants us, as a culture, to tell the whole truth about aging—not only the positive narrative, not only the decline narrative. "People with a realistic attitude, who can see 'old' in all of its individual nuances, will have greater health and opportunities as they age."

🥀 🥀

There are a few signs that an anti-ageism movement is afoot. In 2016, the World Health Organization launched a global campaign, "Take a Stand Against Ageism." In their press release, WHO reported on the results of a survey of more than 83,000 people in fifty-seven countries: 60 percent of respondents said that older people are not respected. The lowest levels of respect were reported in high-income countries.

In a 2016 World Health Organization Bulletin, Alana Officer, a senior health advisor, wrote: "Ageism is highly prevalent; however, unlike other forms of discrimination, including sexism and racism, it is socially accepted and usually unchallenged, because of its largely implicit and subconscious nature. Collective, concerted, and coordinated global action is required to tackle ageism. Given the current demographic transition, with populations around the world ageing rapidly, we need to act now to generate a positive effect on individuals and society. In May 2016, the 194 Member States called on the organization's Director-General to develop, in cooperation with other partners, a global campaign to combat ageism." To date, 196 countries have signed the pledge.

AARP also has a campaign to "disrupt aging" and reimagine what it means to be old. They are attempting to bust myths and stereotypes by telling stories of people who are thriving in unique ways into their eighties and nineties, and even centenarians. They urge us to examine our ageist beliefs and stop letting others define us.

And, in a first of its kind, *Allure* magazine announced in the summer of 2017 that it would no longer use the term *anti-aging* and hired Helen Mirren to be the face of their public relations.

In the corporate world, a few small steps have been taken: IBM built an "Aging in Place" environment in its Austin research lab to study how to use technology to help older people live in their own homes longer; Michelin has rehired retirees to oversee projects and facilitate mentoring; Xerox has instituted an ergonomic training program to reduce musculoskeletal disorders in its aging workforce; and Cisco, Target, and UnitedHealth Group are doing reverse mentorships, where young workers mentor older ones.

Meanwhile, the organization known as Aging2.0, a global innovation network, launched a grand challenge initiative to prioritize innovation in the aging sector. And the nonprofit Radical Age Movement is working to build a grassroots, intergenerational community to challenge ageism in all sectors.

Why don't we protest ageism in the same way we protest other forms of discrimination? Yes, we're distracted today by health and financial issues, by caring for grandkids, by information inundation. But where is our moral outrage against age discrimination? It's systemic, hurtful, and wide-ranging, with personal, family, economic, political, and health care implications. So, why doesn't this issue hit us as hard as, say, racism and sexism do?

I would suggest that, in most of us, the inner ageist is alive and well—and sabotaging our activism. We view ourselves as young or "ageless"; we want to live long but stay young, and we don't want to become the Elders we are meant to be. Our denial of aging puts us in the position of implicitly colluding with ageist policies that fail to support us. If we cannot uncover the inner ageist shadow and accept and align with the unstoppable tides of age, then we will deny its treasures for ourselves and for everyone.

We need to claim our age and reclaim our power, value, status, voice, and beauty. If we can't see it, we can't be it—and we can't change it. Let's romance the shadow of ageism together.

Shadow-Work Practices

🦋 *Meeting Your Inner Ageist*

Look at photos of older peoples' faces and bodies (Google Images is a good place to start). Try to catch your first association to each one. Don't hesitate— just note your first thought or inner dialogue with each one: "She's frail. He's didn't age well. He looks useless. She looks ageless. He's fit for his age. She should dress more appropriately for her age. She must have had a facelift. He looks like a dirty old man."

Notice which feelings arise with those thoughts. Are you attracted? Repelled? Scared? Joyful? Empathetic? Indifferent?

What are the sensations in your body that go with the thoughts and feelings? Tightness of breath? Contracted muscles? Openness? Tension?

Now, please recall a recent incident in your actual life when you encountered an elderly person and the same internal voices and feelings were triggered. Make a note and be with it for a moment.

If you were to imagine these inner voices and feelings as an internal figure with a voice, feelings, and sensations, who is it? You might personify this character by giving it an image.

Please name it and jot it down.

You are meeting a shadow: your inner ageist.

Can you trace your shadow back to an earlier time in your life? Negative messages from an adult? A negative role model in your family?

How old were you? In what period of your life was this shadow character born?

When you listen to this inner figure and agree with its beliefs, how do you feel? What actions do you take or not take?

What does it mean to you to become aware of your inner ageist and to build a conscious relationship with it, rather than allow it to influence you from the unconscious?

Please look in the mirror. How do you feel about being your biological age now that you've uncovered that you may have been discriminating against yourself or others?

Meeting the Collective Shadow of Ageism

- Have you experienced being the target of ageism? How did you respond?
- Should there be a mandatory retirement age to make room for younger workers?
- The world population spends $274 billion per year on anti-aging products. What do you think about this? Would you consider plastic surgery?
- What stops you from political activism against ageism?

Spiritual Practices

Practice meditation to return to pure awareness (see page 66 for an exercise). Allow the shadow character of your inner ageist to arise and learn to make some inner space from it, so that eventually you can witness it.

4

Retirement as a Divine Messenger

Old Man and the Sea: Adapted from Ernest Hemingway

A weather-beaten old man in a torn, sweaty shirt, with rough hands, drags his small boat out to sea, stepping off white sands into turquoise waters. Surrounded by other boats, each with two men chatting, he drifts off alone.

As the sun sets, the others return to shore with their catch. But the old man drifts farther out to sea, mumbling to himself. "Eighty-four days, no fish. I'm a fisherman. I've failed."

Days pass, his lips parch, the last sip of water is gone. He throws the line, again and again, into the depths . . . and waits . . . .

In an instant, there's a tug. Then stillness. Then a big tug—and a huge marlin leaps into the air, dives, leaps again. The fish pulls the boat farther out to sea. The fisherman grips the rope, wraps it around his shoulders, battling the speed and weight of the fish. The man's hands are torn and bleeding, but he can't let go. "I wish I could see what I'm up against. Come out and face me," he pleads.

He speaks to the great fish, as if in prayer. "I'm stronger than you," he says, again and again. "I love and respect you, but I will kill you."

He throws a spear, and the fish goes still. He lashes the fish to the side of the boat. Victorious. He will be respected again. They will call him "the fisherman."

As the boat sails toward home, the man spies fins above the water: Sharks circle his catch. He spears one, and the spear is lost. He ties his knife to a pole and spears another, and the knife is lost. He knows that his victory is past, his prize soon to be gone.

He apologizes to the great fish as it becomes a carcass.

When the old man comes to shore, the people gather, relieved that he's alive and astounded at the size of the carcass. He heaves the mast across his tired shoulders, falls forward, rebalances himself, and carries it, like Jesus carrying the cross.

His young apprentice praises him. And he responds, "A great loss, a great gain."

For some of us, the call to retire is a divine messenger, a force that awakens in us a yearning for something more, a holy longing to transcend a role, an identity, or a purpose and to connect with something larger. It invites us to cross a threshold and change our lives from the inside out.

The end of working for pay may portend new beginnings. It may quicken in us a desire to serve the common good in other ways, to engage for social, political, or moral impact, or to create a greater legacy. It also may stir a desire to turn from doing to being, to slow down and contemplate the lessons learned from the life we have lived—and the life we have not lived, the gifts and dreams that were sacrificed and buried in the shadow. And the end of work may reconnect us to our spiritual ideals, to the dream of aging into awakening.

For others, the time of retirement signifies not a higher vision but simply relief. It is a time to set down the burden of responsibility and enjoy leisure time.

But some of us deny and resist the call to retire. Disoriented, we cannot imagine a life without the structure and purpose of work. Disconnected, we feel empty as we try to imagine what would fill our days. We feel anxious when others interrogate us: What will you *do?*

And that dread stops us from letting go. Another inner obstacle arises: our identification with our doing and our self-image. Unconsciously, our worth is determined by our success and appearance.

The fisherman, in Hemingway's novel, could not put down his rod. His hands were bloodied, his face burned, his spear lost, but he couldn't let go. Is this the essence of masculine strength, courage, and perseverance? Or is it the result of being paralyzed by inner obstacles, which results in a failure of the ego to be humbled in the face of larger forces, and a failure to cross over from role to soul?

What would it mean for this fisherman to stop being a fisherman? What would it mean to put down the spear, appreciate the beauty of the great fish, or simply allow it to reenter the depths and live its life? What would it mean for him to become a grandfather, a mentor to young boys, or a village storyteller?

What stops him from stopping?

Perhaps the loss of his lifelong role is too disorienting to face. Perhaps he fears becoming irrelevant to the village. Perhaps he fears becoming dependent. Certainly, he fears facing his mortality. His inner ageist tells him that if he cannot catch fish, he has no worth. Perhaps it also tells him that if he is no longer a young, triumphant provider, he's not fit to do anything else. And so, like many of us, he just keeps doing the same thing, the only thing he knows how to do.

For each of us, decisions about work in late life—if, when, and how we'll retire, and what we will do afterward—are acutely personal. Each of us has different needs, values, pleasures, and circumstances. For that reason, you won't find here any advocacy for any particular retirement plan, except for this: Late life is a time to turn inward, to make a transition from a heroic focus on *doing* to an Elder's focus on *being*. It's not necessary to stop doing in order to start being. As noted earlier, the evolution from role to soul is not about *what* we do but *how* we do it. It's about the ego's capacity to let go of striving to uphold a self-image. The fisherman couldn't let go. To his ego, that would mean he was a failure. And he could not face defeat; he could not retire from his role.

The question—to retire or not to retire—implies a deeper question: Do we identify with the Doer in heroic mode, or do we act on behalf of something greater as an Elder?

Are we identified with a shadow character who is driving us to achieve? (For example, "I'm not enough." "I don't have enough." "I need to do more." "I need to accomplish great things." "I'm a failure if I stop.") Or are we able to witness the inner voices of a shadow ("I hear that childhood message but don't believe it." "I know my own value beyond doing.") and follow the call of the soul?

Most of us know that retirement requires a baseline of financial planning; we have to make sure that we have the means to support ourselves if we stop working for pay. But emotional and spiritual planning are just as important as finances. Therefore, let's shed light on those shadow characters within us, the "sharks," that are triggered at this transition. They hold us in lifelong patterns that no longer serve us in late life, thereby blocking the soul's evolution.

We must, in effect, explore the conscious and unconscious processes by which we wrestle with one of the big questions of late life: to retire or not to retire? Beneath this inquiry, deeper questions remain. And they hold the clues to our further development at this stage.

To Retire or Not to Retire?

Gerontologist Rick Moody suggested to me that our images of retirement are like a Rorschach test about aging: We project our fears and dreads onto it. And we project our unfulfilled wishes and fantasies onto it, too. Both are carried by unconscious shadow characters.

As we consciously ask ourselves whether or not to retire, perhaps over years of transition, many voices will arise: "I'm a fisherman." "Who am I if not a fisherman?" "If I catch the big one this last time, I will be respected again. If I don't, I'll be no one. Worthless, invisible. Just waiting to die."

In the parable, the fisherman cannot face the first step of this passage: letting go. He cannot let go of more than the obvious fishing rod; that is to say, his ego is identified with his role and his past achievements. He cannot let go of the fight, the hero's eternal battle with the adversary. The fisherman has not made the shift from the midlife heroic values of action and victory at any cost to the more reflective late-life values of inner work, self-care, service, and compassion.

I like to imagine that the fisherman knows, in his heart, that his pride ruined both the great fish and his own soul; that his reach exceeded his grasp, and his gain became a loss.

In an essay on *Old Man and the Sea,* Jungian analyst Michael Conforti points out that Hemingway's novel speaks to everyone's struggles with aging, letting go, facing limitations, and sacrifice: "The call to be Santiago [the fisherman] is present at every corner and experienced as we desperately cling to outdated behaviors and attitudes. As sanctity and spirituality are eclipsed by the promise of temporal gains, we share in Santiago's long and fruitless journey home."

So, if we approach the threshold of retirement in denial, like the fisherman, we too will hold on to past identities, worn-out patterns, and empty meanings. We too will allow our fears of change to keep us from leaving the battlefield and entering the field of the unknown—that is, liminal space. And we too will collude with a culture that values human doing over human being.

On the other hand, we may, even from a young age, eagerly imagine that the end of work makes all our wishes come true: having enough money to feel carefree, travel the world, and learn new things. This, too, is a projection onto retirement that doesn't account for late-life realities of financial limits, health crises, family needs, and emotional loss.

However, if we can turn within, quiet our minds, and witness our thoughts, other whispers can be heard: "I will have more time to follow my own flow, rather than live on the clock." "I can return to the creative dreams that I put aside to support the family." "I will be able to take care of the grandkids." "I can become more engaged in that charity that I love." "I will finally be able to meditate for as long as I want."

"Perhaps something will arise in the open space—a surprise."

In this way, using self-observation, we can engage in retirement as spiritual practice. We can start to orient toward our inner lives and to notice the shadow characters that are either refusing the call to retire or romanticizing the call. We can witness these obstacles, rather than obey them. And, perhaps, we can heed the call of the soul as it urges us to a new stage of life—new beginnings or aging from the inside out.

Shadow-work is a bit like fishing: We dip into the depths and wait, watching. We feel a tug, then it disappears. We feel another tug, a stronger pull. Then our whole boat is pulled off course, the line breaks, and we are adrift, floating in liminal space between work and retirement or between retirement and a new purpose.

"I wish I could see what's pulling me off course," we say to ourselves, just as the fisherman did. "I wish I could see what's upsetting me, making me feel off-balance, leaving me unsettled." But the source of the pull is hidden in the depths.

"I wish I knew what I'm up against." But our adversary, an inner obstacle, is invisible, outside of conscious awareness in the shadow. "I'm afraid of the unstructured time," we say. "I'm afraid of giving up the income. I'm afraid of losing all my colleagues, of feeling irrelevant and purposeless."

If we listen even more closely, we may hear, "I'm afraid that retirement means the end, that it means death is right around the corner." This is dreaded mortality awareness, which often arises with thoughts of retirement.

Perhaps you can allow this awareness to lead you to a deeper question: "If I don't stop working, will I die with regret?"

My client George, at the age of seventy-three, continued to manage daily operations of his insurance firm. Although he was bone-tired and missing time with his grandkids, he didn't want to slow down or retire. When asked why, he told me that both his grandfather and his father became useless in retirement.

"Grandpa watched TV all day and basically bossed around

Grandma. Then, when Dad quit his job, he did nothing but play bridge and eat, until he became obese in his seventies. They both seemed sad and useless after they stopped working, so I dread retiring. I don't think I ever will."

As we explored further, George came to see that the men in his family were negative role models for retirement. He had embodied an unconscious image of his grandfather sitting in a rocker, watching TV, that he carried throughout his life. Now, he was unable to switch gears himself and move toward letting go because he believed, unconsciously, that people in retirement were "useless" to others and to society.

"When men are no longer providers, who are we?" he asked.

I shared with him the following: In a seven-year study, researchers compared two groups of people, all between the ages of seventy and seventy-nine. People in the first group felt useful to friends and family; people in the second group did not. Over the course of seven years, those who felt useless were more likely to become disabled, losing mobility or capacities to care for themselves, or to die. So, the researchers surmised, the subjective feeling of usefulness shapes health in older adults. (See T. Gruenewald et al., "Feelings of Usefulness to Others, Disability, and Mortality in Older Adults.")

Thinking about all this, George came to understand his inner obstacle: A shadow character was defending him against feeling useless by continuing to push him at work. But, by unknowingly relying on this strategy, he was failing to let go and enter liminal space. He was failing to enjoy a new rhythm, explore the dreams he had left behind in his shadow, and shift from role to soul.

Gradually, George became ready to romance his shadow character of the "useless retiree" and to make some time to help his grandchildren learn to read, which opened a new avenue of usefulness. In one session with me, he recalled a boyhood trip he'd taken with his grandmother to a museum, where he saw masterpiece paintings for the first time. He recalled the wonder he felt while looking at those canvases. On a whim, he now enrolled in a watercolor class and, to his surprise, became captivated. The decision to work part-time followed, and then he shifted to a consultancy for his company. When it became clear that the vice president could replace him, he retired. And the "useless retiree" shadow receded.

"I feel a sense of freedom that I didn't know was possible," he told me. "When I'm painting, it's as if I'm doing something that I've always wanted to do. And I didn't even know it until I recovered that memory." He had found the gold in the dark side.

George had a gradual experience of letting go, releasing his role slowly. He managed his liminal time, rather than allowing himself to feel lost. But he emerged with a newfound passion for creativity and a surprising joy as a painter.

Retirement can serve as a divine messenger that carries us across a threshold—or it can be denied. It can be a call that ends the midlife journey and launches a new stage of life—or it can go unheeded. When I discovered that the root meaning of the word *retire* is "to draw back," I was struck by the similarity with the root meaning of *yoga*—"to draw back to the source." Perhaps retirement can be viewed as a time to return to the source, pure awareness.

Retirement from the Outside In

In an article in *Forbes* magazine, Joseph Coughlin, director of MIT AgeLab, noted that there are roughly 8,000 days between birth and college graduation, 8,000 days between college graduation and a midlife crisis, and 8,000 days between a midlife crisis and retirement. And, if we've planned well, there are another 8,000 days after retirement.

Like aging, retirement happens in a larger context: The nature and timing of life after full-time paid work differs by economic class, race, gender, and marital status. In this way, retirement is socially constructed. And that means it can be reimagined.

As baby boomers began to reach retirement age over the past decade, the demographic expectation was that ten thousand of them would exit the workplace every day. But that expectation has come up against two new realities: Many potential retirees simply don't want to stop working; they find that work gives them meaning, purpose, and structure. Others don't have the option of retiring; they can't afford it. The financial stats (as compiled by T. Campbell in *Motley Fool,* March 2016) tell a disturbing story:

- 59 percent of baby boomers rely heavily on Social Security, which is not a safe foundation due to the size of our generation.
- 45 percent of boomers have no retirement savings. At the same time, health care costs continue to rise.
- 30 percent postponed their retirement plans, and many don't expect to retire until age seventy or later.
- 44 percent carry heavy debt.

For those in such dire financial circumstances, to retire or not to retire may not be the right question.

How we retire, and how we imagine retirement, may be more important than when we retire. Negative beliefs and images, hidden in the shadow, influence health as we age. Yale psychologist Becca Levy, whose work we looked at in the preceding chapter, has demonstrated that age stereotypes and prejudice can be internalized in the brain, mind, and body, leading to self-images, such as the inner ageist. She tested this idea for the transition to retirement. In a study of more than a thousand older adults over a twenty-three-year period, she found that those who embodied positive images about physical health during retirement lived 4.5 years longer than others. Those who embodied positive images of mental health during retirement lived 2.5 years longer.

Rabbi Laura Geller, of Temple Emanuel in Beverly Hills, California, is a pioneer in creating Jewish ritual for girls and women, extending the Torah of tradition, as she put it, into the Torah of our own lives. Today she is extending that work into late life for older people in the Los Angeles area, where she organized several hundred members of local congregations into Wisdom Circles to explore their feelings about late life, ageism, and retirement.

When I interviewed her, Geller pointed out that religious congregations do a great job of serving families. But many people in this late, unnamed stage of life—post-family and post-career—are not well served and are, therefore, leaving their churches and synagogues. Religious communities could help make this time of life more meaningful, she said, by creating rituals to honor their transitions.

"Let's start by noticing what is happening, to make it conscious," she said. "What are the moments of transition now? Empty nest, downsizing, becoming a grandparent, losing a family member, job, or driver's license."

I suggested retirement. Geller quickly responded, "First, we begin to imagine a ritual that would mark and honor that transition. What values do we want to communicate? Do we want a private ritual or a public event? What are the symbols we might use? And is there an analogue in your religious tradition, a story or myth that could help frame the transition?"

Geller told me that, for her, a transition is an invitation to experience the divine, to open to the sacred. But if we don't stop, give it attention, and create a ceremony that gives us both a conscious ending and a new beginning, we miss the spiritual potential of the invitation.

In the language of the inner work of age, we need shadow-work to address our own ageism and anxiety about aging, including how it relates to retirement. A ritual might involve a circle of retirees who help a friend bless and close an office, removing the props of a career. Then they might support their friend in stepping into the unknown through a talking circle, expressing fears that arise. Finally, they would welcome him or her across a symbolic threshold, celebrating their friend's entry into the new stage of life.

Even before the outer transition of retirement begins, shadow-work helps us prepare emotionally. For instance, as we approach late life, having now worked for the majority of our years, we may feel conflicted, resentful, burdened, or resigned about our work, whether or not we are planning to retire soon. If we learn to uncover the shadow characters behind these feelings, we may be able to bring them into the light of awareness and work with them. Through meditation, we can learn to witness these shadows, so that they lose their charge. We may even be able to break our ego's identification with the Doer and experience a different sense of doing at work, a flow state that is not the ego's heroic pushing.

Many of us, whether by choice or necessity, will continue working well beyond sixty-five. But as we've discussed, the capacity to age consciously is not about what we do but how we do it. If we learn to be more present with *what is,* rather than resisting or resenting what we cannot change, we may be able to discover the hidden gifts of continuing work: a community that prevents isolation, a meaning besides money, a contribution that connects us to something larger. By connecting outer work to inner work, we may have a surprisingly new experience: the beginning of the internal shift from role to soul, which is not dependent on outer circumstances.

For people with assets, the end of work may be anticipated and welcomed, imagined as a time for leisure, family, travel, or service. For people without assets, the task is more complex. A 2013 report from the National Institute on Retirement Security by Nari Rhee stated that people of color are less likely to have an employer-sponsored plan. In fact, three out of four Black households and four out of five Latino households have less than $10,000 in retirement savings. The same institute explored gender differences. According to a 2016 report by Diane Oakley, women are 80 percent more likely to face poverty in retirement than men. Women's reliance on Social Security, pension, and savings is inadequate because we are more likely to have earned 75–80 percent less than men, worked part-time, done more caregiving—and live longer. Financial insecurity may make inner work seem like a luxury; but the first does not have to preclude the latter. The practices here can offer respite and rejuvenation to face the most difficult challenges on the journey.

Finally, the nature and timing of life after full-time work depends on our constitutional types or innate inclinations. In my interviews, I found that people who were more extroverted tended to want a more active social life and more service-oriented activity. They gain vitality through exchange with others. And those who were more introverted tended to want to design a more contemplative period for solitude, meditation, reading, and inner work. Therefore, it would be useful to know this about ourselves as we face this rite of passage and begin to design our inner and outer work accordingly.

Retirement as Reinvention

Encore Careers

For many people, retirement ushers in a new life stage, one following career and family-building and preceding the frailties that may come with older age. For many, it's a time of reinvention without a blueprint, a shift to flextime, part-time, volunteering, service, lifelong learning, or caregiving.

Some large companies are catching on, becoming aware of the reservoir of talent, knowledge, communication skills, and resiliency of older workers. CVS Health's Talent Is Ageless initiative builds public and private partnerships to recruit older workers. The Hartford, an insurance giant, even goes to senior centers to find older employees. And AT&T reports that they intend to keep older employees at work for as long as possible.

However, all this emphasis on working and doing has a shadow side: it stresses that purpose comes through productivity and doesn't appear to include more service-oriented doing or more contemplative, spiritual development. Therefore, I was encouraged to find the results of a study by Anne Colby and William Damon at the Stanford Graduate School of Education, in collaboration with Encore.org: Large numbers of older people rank "purpose beyond the self" very high on their lists of priorities and are taking steps to realize it. In fact, this desire was expressed by a majority of respondents across differences in income, education, race, gender, and health status. (The study was reported by Katie Remington and Matt Bendick in the Stanford University Publication *Cardinal at Work*.)

In addition, for those surveyed, finding purpose doesn't require the sacrifice of personal growth. When asked whether their views of late life are reflected in the statement "It's a time for personal growth," 67 percent responded that this descriptor is accurate.

This finding helps explain an ongoing trend among older workers, which can be seen as an expression of personal change from the outside in. Nearly half of older workers have changed jobs since turning fifty, altering a century-long cultural pattern in which people tended to work at the same job or profession until they retired. And many more want to, we have to assume, but are reluctant. Some may need "bridge income" on their way to their destination, to take courses or get certified, or to pay bills while they search for the right position or vision of how to take an idea into action. Others may need to uncover the inner obstacles in their shadows—fears of age discrimination, failure, health problems, technology, or loss of time for other activities.

But many older people today are taking the reins and launching their own start-ups. In New York, for example, the growing number of entrepreneurs over age fifty defies the stereotype of the young twenty-something in blue jeans. The number of those over fifty who became entrepreneurs in 2016 rose 63 percent from the number in 2000. In comparison, as reported by Winnie Hu in the *New York Times,* the total number of residents at that age rose only 28 percent over the same period of time.

According to Encore.org, an international community that creates intergenerational solutions to pressing problems, more than twelve million older people are "encore entrepreneurs" who want to put their experience to work for the greater good. Many plan small, local ventures to meet needs in their communities. Intel, the giant tech company, partnered with Encore.org to offer Encore Fellowships to its retirement-eligible employees. They receive a $25,000 stipend and placement with a high-performing nonprofit as a stepping-stone to redeploying their skills in a new career.

Research suggests that age may be an advantage for entrepreneurs: One study found that there were twice as many successful founders over fifty as under twenty-five, and twice as many over sixty as under twenty. Ray Kroc was in his fifties when he launched McDonald's; Colonel Sanders was in his sixties when he started Kentucky Fried Chicken; Steve Jobs was as creative in his second stint at Apple as in his first. (For details, see the 2012 blog post "Enterprising Oldies," for *The Economist*.)

Heather, a colleague, had several positions in education: high school English teacher, assistant principal, and principal. Then she moved to Alaska and worked for a college education program where she taught teachers. She also ran conferences to train caregivers for older people. Her role as an educator took many different forms until her mother became seriously ill and moved in with Heather and her husband. Then Heather became the caregiver and switched over to part-time work.

Heather found purpose as a caregiver, as a mother to her mother, as she put it. She identified more and more deeply with the role. "For me, every day is Mother's Day," she told me.

Then, at the age of 101, her mom died. And Heather's purpose died as well. She took a family leave from her job and, while grieving, drove up and down the West Coast doing mobile coaching on her phone. Soon after that, she quit her job, aware that she was looking for the next stage.

"I took off all the hats that gave me power—principal, teacher, even caregiver. It's been really humbling," she told me. It seemed that she had released her identification with those roles and moved into a liminal, formless space.

After drifting for a while, she went to a ten-day meditation retreat and realized that she was in a late-life identity crisis. She was no longer a mom or an educator. She had no professional label and no defined role.

She read books on aging, did volunteer peer counseling, practiced yoga, and waited. It took three years in liminal space—the time between one identity and another—before she knew that she wanted to work with people undergoing this very transition from career to post-career, from hero to Elder.

Heather began to organize Elder groups around Julia Cameron's book *It's Never Too Late to Begin Again*. As she sat with her fellow Elders and explored together, she was no longer the educator. She retired the Expert. "There was no rank and much more equality," she told me. "It's humbling not to be an expert, to do the inner work right along with the others." When an eighty-one-year-old woman told her that the group changed her life, Heather felt deeply grateful.

"Those old hats gave me cover," she said. "Now I'm finding self-confidence based on my essence, not my job. And that's what we do together in the groups."

Another story comes from Harvard Business School (as reported by Kanter et al.). In 2008, at the age of fifty-six, Doug Rauch, then the president of Trader Joe's, felt restless and decided to leave the company. After floundering for a year, he discovered the Advanced Leadership Initiative at Harvard, which offers fellowships to business leaders who want to transfer their skills to the social sector. He became a fellow and began to explore an issue he felt passionate about: More than 35 million Americans suffer from hunger or food insecurity (per the USDA's 2019 report). But because they can't access or afford more healthful food, many working-class people get an excess of empty calories from fast food, and as a result, many are obese.

Rauch had a vision: a nonprofit chain of stores in low-income areas that would sell groceries and prepared foods at a low price. To keep prices down, he would recover excess food that might be wasted and surplus goods that were close to their sell-by dates, also reducing food waste. Daily Table, his nonprofit, opened its first store in Massachusetts in 2015. In 2021, it opened its third store.

Rauch was able to transform his knowledge of the food industry, his management skills, and his heart's desire into a service that met the needs of a community. It became his soul's mission.

New options for reemployment and self-employment are everywhere. Some roles also include opportunities to explore new parts of ourselves, to live out those unlived qualities and fantasies that were buried in the shadow. An introverted mom joins the Women's March, runs for state office, and wins, discovering her voice to protect women's health issues. A retired small-town doctor joins Doctors Without Borders and lives in Asia, caring for underserved communities and fulfilling his dream of life in another culture. An architect, who always imagined rebuilding communities after natural disasters, takes his family to Ecuador after an earthquake to live simply while following his mission.

But beware: With reinvention from the outside in, new roles may be more of the same in disguise, merely holding a past persona in place and requiring the same emotional and creative sacrifices. When this is the case, new roles simply rob us of the developmental tasks of late life. And they rob us of connecting to soul.

Shadow-Work for Retirement

From the Inside Out

A recent survey of people who are seventy-five or older, which intended to explore the issue of identity after retirement, found that only 9 percent felt that their identity remained wrapped up in their former career or parenting. Instead, post-retirement, they identified with their current activities and interests (reported by Dan Kadlec in *Time*). Even high achievers, like doctors, lawyers, and executives, reported that success quickly faded into the background as they redesigned their lives.

After retirement, most people make a shift in identity away from work and toward encore careers, service, hobbies, creativity, or leisure. A 2016 study by Age Wave, titled *Leisure in Retirement,* found that 90 percent of retirees felt they have greater flexibility to do what they want, with two-thirds preferring to spend time trying new challenges.

Nine out of ten retirees reported that they enjoy having a less structured life and that they often feel happy. The poll also found that seniors will spend $4.6 trillion on global travel, so the call to adventure as a retirement fantasy is being lived out by many.

So, if most people who let go of career identities really enjoy the years after retirement, why are we so afraid of retiring? Our own inner obstacles—our identification with youth, success, and doing—are the guardians at the threshold of retirement that keep us from crossing over. Shadow-work, which reorients us to our inner depths, can help us release these past identities and attune to soul.

My friend Steve Wolf likes to point out that shadow characters begin as protectors and end up as saboteurs. Let's examine this idea. The inner ageist, the part of us that denies aging, protects our identification with the youthful, carefree spirit in us who revels in possibilities. Our inner ageist also may protect us from mortality awareness until we are ready to deal with it.

When we are mature and need to adapt to aging, but we continue to unconsciously identify with the inner ageist, then we are locked into denial—and it sabotages us. In late life, this keeps us from self-acceptance, self-care, and self-actualization. It keeps us in *puer aeternus,* the eternal youth, who lives in dreams and possibilities, but not in reality.

My client Gina grew up in a family in which her father was a successful lawyer and her mother and disabled sister were severely depressed, spending most of their lives at home. Gina became the family savior, the only one capable of following in her father's footsteps. She earned a Ph.D. from UC Berkeley, then immediately started law school and pushed herself into burnout through long hours, perfectionism, and lack of self-care. She couldn't imagine doing anything but study and work. She'd never had an intimate relationship, was disconnected from her feelings, and was so exhausted that she feared becoming ill.

After a decade of work, she gained partnership at her firm and her career was established. Another decade went by on autopilot. She found that she was not thriving in the world of law. And, although she had thought it was all she wanted, she began to question her choices and daydream about a new direction. I met her at this juncture, when she realized that she needed some support and guidance.

As we began to do shadow-work, Gina uncovered an internal shadow character that had protected her from being like her mother and sister. "I'm smart and capable—not like them," this character insisted. This shadow figure gave her confidence and a sense of identity that was distinct from her mom, whom she did not respect. So, she had continued to work relentlessly to prove herself different from her mom and to avoid the feelings of emptiness that she might feel if she stopped—and, of course, to avoid the dreaded depression of her mother.

As our therapy proceeded, Gina identified this shadow character and named it the Driver. Slowly, she began to see how it was sabotaging her. She could not slow down, or the Driver would criticize her intensely. She could not rest, or the Driver would whip her into a frenzy. She couldn't even eat well; the Driver felt it was a waste of time. At fifty, she *was* the Driver; it was the only identity she had ever known. And the Driver would never tolerate letting go.

At my urging, she began to do yoga. When she experienced moments of slowing down, breathing deeply, quieting her mind, and connecting with her body, she sobbed. Again and again, she allowed the feelings of isolation, grief, and fear that had been stuffed away for a lifetime to begin to surface. And she began to open, like a flower.

As we meditated together, Gina learned to observe her thoughts and identify the Driver and the consequences of listening to it and obeying it: She would work instead of eat. She would work instead of sleep. She would work instead of experience her feelings.

And then a man entered her life, and a tender romance began. She learned how to open her heart, express her needs, and even slow down enough to be present with him. She wanted time with him; she wanted to love and be loved. And the Driver began to recede.

This is not a romantic solution to an emotional problem. This is simply what happens with an internal shift of a shadow character: There is an opening, and something new appears.

As her relationship deepened, she began to connect to the femininity that she had rejected along with her mother. At last, she could reclaim her connection to her body, sensuality, intuition, and feelings. For the first time, she began to feel compassion for her mother and to grieve about how her mother's life had passed her by.

The question surfaced: to retire or not to retire? In the end, for Gina, the answer was not about leaving work; it was about retiring the Driver. She shifted to a different area of law where she could serve a community in need and take care of herself at the same time. She worked at a different internal speed limit, honored herself and her relationship, and found a larger purpose in service to others.

The Driver shadow character is epidemic in our workaholic culture. In fact, in many work settings, it's encouraged or even required. And it is this habitual internal drive, which assured our survival in childhood, that goes on unconsciously for decades in many of us—and that keeps us from stopping. We are not even aware that it's stopping us from stopping. Even when we do stop, it lingers in the shadow, an unconscious identification with role that is an obstacle to shifting our identity toward soul.

For people who are connected to their dreams, this shadow character can appear while we are sleeping. Rick Moody shared with me a retirement dream that he had, which he called "Meeting the Stranger," from his unpublished manuscript "Dreams for the Second Half of Life."

> I dreamed I was back at AARP [Rick's former employer] in a huge skyscraper. People told me that the boss was out and that I would have to chair the staff meeting. I protested that I didn't work there anymore but soon found myself among colleagues, rushing to the meeting. As I moved through the building, I was pushing an empty shopping cart. Suddenly, I saw a guy standing in line at the cafeteria. The other man recognized me and greeted me, but I was

embarrassed that I didn't know him and moved on. We met again, but I still didn't recognize him. So, I made an excuse, asking the Stranger to help attach my watch to my wrist, so that he would have to bend over, and I could read his name tag. When I looked closely, I realized that the Stranger's name tag was on backward—and I saw my own name written on the back of his name tag.

Upon waking up, Rick realized that, although his full-time work for pay had ended, and he believed he had given up the "big-shot" role, his internal identification with it in the shadow had not ended. Internally, he was still back there, feeling important, wanted, and needed. His encounter with the Stranger is a classic meeting with the shadow: He tries to avoid the encounter but cannot. He tries to see the man's name—but instead sees his own.

"He is me, but he is not me," Rick said. "He is a Stranger." And that is the dilemma of the late-life identity crisis.

Each archetype is expressed in diverse images in different times and places. We saw how the archetype of the inner ageist may be expressed as the bag lady. The archetype of the workaholic may appear as the Driver. Another client called her overworked shadow character Chicken Little—because it believed that the sky would fall if she stopped.

In his book *Soulcraft,* Bill Plotkin gives this archetype another name: Loyal Soldier. He tells the story of hundreds of Japanese soldiers who survived shipwrecks and plane crashes during World War II and became stranded on islands in the Pacific under extreme conditions. When they were found many decades later, they expressed fanatical loyalty to their mission and were ready to return to the war, unaware that it had ended. They were not human beings who had acted as loyal soldiers; they *were* Loyal Soldiers.

Back in Japan, civic leaders recognized that these men were not ready to reenter society and become citizens. So, a communal ritual was designed: The whole community thanked them and praised them again and again. An elder stood and announced, "The war is over. The community needs you to let go of the battle now and return as men—to retire the Loyal Soldier." This collective ritual enabled the soldiers to let go of their warrior identities. Some naturally fell into a liminal space, disoriented for a while. And some crossed the threshold, letting go of a past identity and emerging into a new one.

Those of us who lived through the wars in Vietnam, Iraq, and Afghanistan are aware that our own veterans receive no such ritual of gratitude and welcome. Many struggle mightily to let go of the inner Loyal Soldier and return as healthy, vulnerable human beings. But without a rite of passage reentry can be traumatic and difficult.

As an analogy: For some, the workplace is like a battlefield. The exit from work is like returning from war after decades of obeying orders, engaging in power struggles, working tirelessly, and sacrificing dreams in an effort to feel secure, powerful, important, needed, and safe. The Loyal Soldier is the part of us that needs to retire. In late life, it no longer protects us; instead, it sabotages our ability to turn within and cross over from role to soul.

If we don't retire the Driver or Loyal Soldier—that is, if we don't learn how to romance it as a shadow character and break our identification with it—then we will continue to live in survivor mode, becoming more rigid, stubborn, and arrogant as we age. And the shadow figure will plod on, defending against a slowing pace or a dropping of defenses, effectively refusing to acknowledge that the war is over. Tragically, it will continue to defend against a range of hidden feelings, such as vulnerability, sorrow, anger, and disappointment, so that emotional unfinished business cannot be completed.

On this path, we will fail the developmental tasks of late life: the further cultivation of emotional, cognitive, and spiritual gifts, the softening and opening of the heart, the call to service, and the cultivation of pure awareness.

In addition, those traits and talents that were banished to the shadow because they do not suit the Driver or Loyal Soldier—our critical thinking, vulnerability, creativity, playful spontaneity—need to be reclaimed. This is the key lying in the darkness of our fear of retirement; this is the gold in the dark side.

Retirement from Clinical Practice

My Story as a Helping Professional

In each week of my career as a therapist, I shared intense intimacy with my clients and guided them where others fear to tread—into the shadow. I felt privileged to mentor them and watch them alter deeply ingrained patterns and lead more fulfilling lives.

I deeply loved my clients. My heart was filled by their openness, vulnerability, and honesty. It was filled with compassion for their suffering, too. I enjoyed the stories of their lives, their eagerness to learn shadow-work and plumb the depths of the unconscious, the seeker in their souls who longed for more awareness. My days were filled with depth and intimacy, and I felt gratitude.

But during my sixty-eighth year of life experience, I noticed a restlessness, a stirring that I had felt several times before at the end of a cycle and the beginning of another—when I had stopped teaching meditation full-time but had no vision of a new career and felt like I stepped off a cliff; when I had stopped working in journalism but didn't hear a new call and stepped into the dark unknown; when I had left book publishing and decided to go to grad school to become a therapist, but without financial or emotional support. Each time, my soul had whispered to me, and I had agreed to leave behind my former self and enter liminal space, not knowing what lay ahead. Each time, a path appeared, with allies and guides and, eventually, a fulfilling destination.

Now, I was aware that I was approaching a threshold again, although no one else in my friendship circle was using the "R" word. After many years of attuning to myself, I listened to the conflicting inner voices:

"I wonder what else I could do with the time I have left?" Then "I wonder what I need to stop doing."

"I think I should do more." Then "I think I should do less."

"I don't want to travel." Then I book more trips.

"I want to slow down." Then my calendar fills up.

As I reflected on these internal contradictions, I became aware that it no longer bothered me when clients disappeared without a formal closure. Previously, I felt that I was left holding the relationship when a client stopped communicating. Now, I could let it go. Previously, I looked forward to traveling from the Santa Monica mountains into my office in town. Now, I didn't want to do the drive. Previously, I enjoyed traveling into others' inner worlds. Now, I wanted more time to explore my own.

It wasn't that I cared any less about my clients; it was that my attention was moving away from the work, and my heart was opening in other ways. What was it moving toward? I was hearing the call of a divine messenger for a new orientation to time—less structure, more flow. A new orientation to responsibility—less obligation, more choice. A new orientation to service—from one-on-one therapy to teaching large groups. A new orientation to purpose—from role to soul.

Then, the most essential question arose: Who am I, if I'm not Dr. Connie, a therapist, the shadow expert? What would it mean to let go of my role and my brand? What have I sacrificed to maintain that role? Who am I if I am no longer the Doer? How do I overcome resistance to letting go in this transition?

First, I stopped accepting new clients. When they emailed, I took a breath, wished them well, and referred them out.

Next, I began discussing my own departure with clients. We explored the range of their feelings and moved slowly, each in a unique way, toward completion.

A few months later, the opportunity came to give up my city office. I went for it—and let go into the unknown.

I suspected that, with the gain of freedom, there also would be loss. I would feel less needed and less important for a while. I would feel less secure and more uncertain for a time. I would feel less independent with the loss of income from therapy. It would change my partnership with my husband, who was still working, and the way we cared for one another. And I might feel less purposeful and a bit disoriented, with the path ahead still hidden.

Perhaps hardest of all, I would lose the precious vehicle, the clinical relationship, in which to transmit all that I've learned from my own inner work, intellectual development, and spiritual growth to others. It has been a sacred container to radiate my level of development to others, who willingly received it.

Of course, I cherish my clients for who they are, but also for who they are for me. Aside from my husband and grandkids, who would I love with such fierceness? Who would receive my consistently positive gaze and devotion? That would be a terrible loss—and a potential gain, if I turned my loving gaze back to my family, friends, and self.

My clients love me back in a certain way, of course, in the projection of a good parent. For some, I'm the only good mother they've ever had; for others, the only kind sister or wise grandmother or spiritual mentor. As I've carried that positive projection over the years, I've become accustomed to wearing it like a gown and standing in the archetype for them, rather than disclosing my personal story. It will be a loss to give up the power and status of that projection—and a gain to cultivate more equal and reciprocal relationships. It will be a loss to give up the "brand" of shadow expert—and a gain to extend it into this whole new territory of late life.

Finally, I had to acknowledge the grief I'd been feeling about the direction the field of psychotherapy has taken. Some hundred years ago, the discovery and exploration of the unconscious was at the center of therapy. Freud, Jung, and their colleagues were like the first humans on the moon, traveling through entirely unknown worlds. As depth psychology evolved to include and transcend their findings, the unconscious remained the therapist's territory of choice. It came to be called the psyche, which is Greek for soul. I was fortunate to find a graduate school in the 1990s that still taught depth psychology, training us to orient to the unconscious and to honor the life of the soul.

Enter the American Psychological Association's school accreditation system, which has forced transpersonal and depth-oriented grad schools to either accommodate to their medical model or close. Enter the pharmaceutical companies. Today, psychology is a science, not an art. It's about the brain—transcranial magnetic stimulation, neural feedback, EMDR, and meds, meds, and more meds. Enter the ranking of psychiatrists as M.D.s at the top of the field, who only prescribe medications and no longer practice therapy. And it's about behavior—brief, cognitive-behavioral therapy, which posits that human beings have no soul, that we need only change our thinking to relieve symptoms, and that the relationship with the therapist is not relevant to healing. In the end, therapy has become no longer a spiritual journey guided by the precept "Know thyself."

As I approached the threshold, during many conversations with my husband, Neil, I began to see how offering therapy had become a spiritual path for me. Yes, my meditation, shadow-work, and primary relationship were the key psychological and spiritual practices for my development. But now, with a 360-degree view, Neil and I could see how the practice of psychotherapy had cracked open my heart, helped me eliminate judgment, resolved some of my personal shadow issues, and pulled me into presence, hour by hour. It taught me to orient to the unconscious and attune to the hidden fears and unspoken dreams of others. It taught me to guide each of them as a soul on a journey.

In the first stage, I viewed the therapist/client relationship as subject/object. I was the expert who assessed, diagnosed, and treated the client. This created a superior/inferior dynamic in which the parent-child relationship could be relived. This is how therapists are trained to work, and it reinforces their ego needs to feel smart, admired, and special. This is a shadow side of all "helping" professions; it risks keeping those being helped in an inferior position. It risks splitting opposites into self/other and blocks a more unified experience.

In the second stage, I viewed the client and myself as part of a larger system, a mutual process of intersubjective experience, shared caring, love, and respect. I discovered that I learned from my clients, too, that there was something larger holding us both in the field of the unconscious. Poet Robert Bly referred to this energy as a "Third Body" that can emerge between two people, as if another energetic presence were in the room, joining us but larger than us at the same time. This more reciprocal dynamic transcends and includes the earlier stage; that is, I'm aware of the parental projection but I'm not operating from it. I feel less separate but not yet spiritually joined.

In the third stage, I discovered that therapy opens to something larger still—what's inside the room is connected to what's outside the room. The Third Body, holding our conscious and unconscious minds, is a reflection of the collective unconscious in the world at large. In other words, I am not only working on a client as the client works on me; the whole culture is in the room within us and between us, shaping and influencing us as we change, and as we shape and influence it. Our inner work, the evolution of soul, is affecting change in all living things. The work is happening in the room and outside the room at the same time—because everything is connected in a unified flow. This is the end of separation and the emergence of unity.

When I came to this stage, I was not operating from my mind; my speech became a manifestation of spontaneous, direct intuition. My client brought what I needed, as part of a collective process. I brought what the client needed. Sometimes every client came through the door with the same issue, and synchronicity appeared again and again. This collective stage transcends and includes the earlier stages; that is, I was diagnosing, while holding the projection and the unity all at once. We were working on the story of humanity not as two isolated people with egos and shadows, but as integral parts of humanity's evolution as a species alongside other species.

So, retirement from clinical practice is not simply stepping away from the office. It means retiring a spiritual path to my own deepening and widening awareness. It means retiring the need to help; it means retiring the need for answers; it means retiring the need to be appreciated. It means retiring from a life that's known and facing an unknown, liminal time. And it means retiring a practice of love that has connected me to the depths of the human soul and to the journey of the human species. It has been a privilege.

My Retirement Ritual: A Late-Life Rite

One night I gathered a circle of friends and colleagues to ritualize my retirement from clinical practice. I had never created a rite of passage before, but I had been seeing one in my mind's eye.

I lit candles and lowered the lights. I read for a few minutes from the opening to this chapter so that my observers would share my framework. Then I lifted each of four white cards, one at a time, that had my careers written on them: meditation teacher, journalist, book editor, therapist. And I lifted the five books that have been my gifts to the world.

I spoke for a bit about who might have been influenced by my work, including the known influences, such as my meditation students and therapy clients, and the unknown influences, such as readers of the books I wrote or the hundred books I edited, whom I would never meet. And I acknowledged myself for these contributions and deeply felt the value of those years spent working.

I held up these symbols of my work, roles, and responsibilities and offered them to the world: "I bless and release you to find your way now." And, letting go in my heart, I set them down.

Then I asked each member of the group to offer a blessing. I stood for a moment, then crossed a threshold of silver tape on the floor, empty-handed, into open space.

When I wake up now, I breathe deeply and look around in wonder. I'm retiring the past. I'm retiring the future. I'm practicing presence. Just here. Aging breath by breath. Intending to live as a soul.

Retirement as Spiritual Practice

From Role to Soul

As I've said, life transitions demand that we change more than our roles or outer activities. They demand that we change from the inside out. When we cross a passage to become an adult, change careers, marry or divorce, have children, or suffer a serious illness, we also change archetypes—we step into a new life pattern. For most people, this is not a conscious process because our society doesn't offer adult rites of passage.

But with retirement, this shift in archetypes from role to soul may become more conscious when the obvious roles and responsibilities fall away, the structure of our day dissolves, and the people who formed our teams and work families go on without us. At a deeper level, the ego's lifelong identity of Doer may be shattered, and a primary source of meaning and purpose is gone. A late-life identity crisis may be triggered, and it takes time to hear inner guidance for the next stage.

Some of us will rush to fill the time and the inner emptiness with other activities, as we discussed. We want to construct new roles and continue to feel useful, valuable, and relevant. Some will want a sabbatical year to sit fallow in liminal time. Others will be more oriented to inner work. Among the people I interviewed, some had begun a contemplative practice when they were young but stopped it during midlife childrearing and career building. When they picked it up again in late life, they found the inner stillness to be like coming home.

I'm not suggesting that this turn within is easy after a lifetime of doing, building, creating, and achieving—and of identifying with doing as who we are. But our ability to internally retire the Doer—or the Driver, the Dominator, the Competitor, the Provider, or whatever you want to call it—is greatly enhanced when we experience pure awareness daily and romance these shadow characters. A quiet mind helps us retire fixed ideas, a need for others' respect, and a need to control, all traits that no longer serve us.

In this way, we cultivate spiritual work for retirement and cross the threshold from role to soul. And in this way, we uncover new sources of meaning and purpose from our inner lives.

When I interviewed Carol Orsborn, then age seventy, a prolific author of thirty books about aging, she said that when she retired her to-do list, she also retired her solid "I," her successful identity as a marketer and author. "The roles were not sustaining me anymore," she told me. "I had to squash too many parts of myself to be useful or successful. Now I've gotten old enough to have the experience and the trust to take off the lid of performance and see myself naked. I'm painfully alive and joyfully alive."

She also retired the concepts of success and failure. She explained how she had used her success to cover her vulnerability and authenticity, to push them into the shadow. "I'll sell the next book, then I'll be okay for a year," she used to say to herself. Now she is letting go of those defenses, allowing herself to shed layers and, slowly, become something else.

"In the past, I would wake up and write or market all day. I was always trying to make things happen. Now I walk a mile along the lake to the senior center for exercise. And the world opens, full of surprise. I've even grown a braid. And I've let go of friends who don't understand. I'd rather be alone than go back to that ego place."

Like many of us, Carol believes she is an introvert who was trained to live as an extrovert. She's no longer fed by public speaking or by conversations in which she can't be a "courageous truth teller." Rather, she has returned to a meditation practice that she learned decades ago and has added yoga and tai chi to her routine.

Unfortunately, we live in a culture that hypes only achievement and consumption and dismisses contemplative practice and spiritual development, even in late life. But these inner values have been woven into the social fabric of other cultures, such as the Christian monastic traditions, Buddhism, and Hinduism.

In the Hindu tradition, the stages of life are known as *ashramas*, and the human journey aims to fulfill the developmental tasks of each stage. The first stage is student, which is focused on education and discipline, preparing a person for the second stage of householder, which is focused on marriage, family, and work. If the tasks of these stages aren't completed, one remains immature, missing key qualities that develop with the roles and responsibilities of those years.

The third stage is grandparent and retirement, which emphasizes letting go of work, household responsibilities, and past roles and identities and shifting from material values to spiritual values. It also includes letting go of old thought patterns and feelings that create stress and no longer fit the stage of late life. For most people, it also includes grandparenting, mentoring, and teaching younger colleagues or children. In that culture, retirement is recognized as a vital physical, emotional, and spiritual transition that is universal.

The final *ashrama* is renunciation, whose focus is letting go of worldly life and the ego's concerns and turning attention to spiritual practice in preparation for death.

I learned about the *ashramas* from my first meditation teacher when I was in my twenties, and it struck me that, at that time, just like today, so many people were studying meditation and turning inward for spiritual practice at a young age. In practicing spirituality first, not last, we were turning the traditional progression of stages upside down. We were cultivating spiritual values before we built the foundations of our material lives.

I began to realize that, in the West, these are not sequential stages; they are archetypes that live in potential within us during our whole life span. Traditionally, they were actualized in a specific sequence. But we can become a student at any age, a householder or retiree at any age, and a seeker or spiritual practitioner at any age.

In addition, as we become Elders, we can gain access to all these energies simultaneously: We can continue learning with openness and curiosity. We can reimagine love and family in new or old marriages. We can enter the "forest" of solitary introspection on regular retreats. And we can focus on spiritual practice and letting go from the inside out when the final quest for meaning and transcendence beckons.

Retirement is not generally included in the traditional Buddhist teaching of divine messengers. But today, in our world, it certainly is one. With our extended longevity, the call to retire is a call to turn within, whether we remain outwardly active or not. It's a call to ask again the key spiritual question: Who am I?

Shadow-Work Practices

- Who is the shadow character within that stops you from stopping? Who is your Doer, Driver, or Loyal Soldier?
- How is your inner ageist involved?
- Who is the shadow character that feels "not enough" when you are not the Doer?
- How is your fear of death involved?
- How did the Doer protect you in the past? How does the Doer sabotage you now in the present?
- Can you create a ritual that would allow you to retire the Doer?
- If you cannot afford to stop working, how can you change your internal experience of work? Can you bring a different awareness, a quality of presence, and a renewed meaning to your work? Can you see that your individual contribution is connected to a larger contribution to life as a whole?

Spiritual Practices

These contemplative practices continue to turn your attention from role to soul. When you find yourself in the grip of a shadow character, practice addressing it out loud ("I see you now, Doer, trying to get me to rev up again." "I feel you, Loyal Soldier, and your intention to get me to stay with the company and not let go."). Then practice internalizing the deeper identity, thinking it, feeling it, embodying it. Write about this experience in your journal and explore what arises as you shift your attention.

Fill in your own role: "I am a CEO. I am a provider. I am a salesperson. I am a lawyer. I am a writer. I am a teacher. I am a caregiver." Who are you if you are not that role?

Please practice saying to yourself, "I am not the Doer. I am pure awareness." Or, if you prefer, "I am not the Doer. I am that which lives and breathes through everything."

5

Life-Changing Illness as a Divine Messenger

PARABLE

The Story of Tiresias: A Greek Myth

In Greek mythology, a mortal named Tiresias was walking through the woods when he unintentionally saw the goddess Athena bathing in the nude. Enraged, Athena blinded him.

The other gods and goddesses asked Athena to reverse the curse because he was a good man.

Athena did not restore Tiresias's outer sight; however, she gave him inner vision, the ability to see the future in smoke and fire, the capacity to understand the language of the birds, and the gift of communicating with the dead. These gifts increased as he aged, and he became known as a wise seer.

In this way, his loss became a gain, and he lived in the liminal space between humans and the gods.

Illness, affliction of body and soul, can be life-altering. It has the potential to reveal the most fundamental conflict of the human condition: the tension between our infinite, glorious dreams and desires and our limited, vulnerable, decaying physicality. In the shadow, no number of trophies can quiet this internal contradiction. No amount of anti-aging products can resolve this existential paradox. No amount of positive thinking can crack this koan. It is given to us as part of the whole truth.

The tale of Tiresias is easy to dismiss, but it's a teaching story about loss and gain, about endings and beginnings in late life. It's about a man whose terrible wound became a sacred wound, opening him to the inner worlds and elevating him to the stature of Elder. It reminds me of the great impressionist Claude Monet, nearly blinded by cataracts in his eighties, who nevertheless was able to alter his painting style enough to create his masterpiece series on water lilies. It also reminds me of the renowned painter Henri Matisse, in a wheelchair at eighty-three, whose hands were crippled by arthritis, so he used a scissors to cut paper and invented a new art form.

Illness also can be a divine messenger: It can lead us to shadow awareness, pure awareness, and mortality awareness. It can open the portals to depth, transcendence, and presence. It can even lead us across a threshold from our identification with the body to our identification with soul.

I have heard a man say, "Cancer changed everything. It set me on a different path."

And a woman told me, "I had cancer. They took it out, and nothing changed."

In the first instance, with diminished vitality to keep doing what he always did, Tom became deeply disoriented and ultimately was forced to slow down and turn within. He deepened his contemplative practice to rest in the silence and create some spaciousness from his anxiety. He also began a shadow-work practice to uncover the emotional issues that may have contributed to his form of cancer. As a result, he severed his codependent overpleasing behavior, letting go of deep patterns. And he learned how to express his own needs, while accepting what he was given.

Tom explored the lifestyle issues that may have contributed to his illness and began to make very different choices about his nutrition, letting go of a lifelong sugar addiction. He committed to dying without regrets, which meant doing the emotional repair work that was required to mend his family relationships. Facing the whole truth about his current condition, Tom woke up to mortality awareness and radically changed his priorities.

As Tom did this profound self-examination, his illness became a rite of passage: He died to his heroic past self, spent an uncomfortable liminal period in treatment, not knowing the outcome, and emerged slowly in remission to a more conscious stage of life.

"I went through a door," Tom told me, "with no way back. No do-over. Cancer became my path, and it opened out into a larger view of life than I ever could have imagined."

In the second instance, Shelly did not heed the call. She underwent surgery, but her mind, heart, and soul remained unchanged. She returned to the same high-stress job, the same high-stress emotional relationships, and the same self-destructive coping strategies, using caffeine and sugar to stay awake and alcohol to slow down at night. She just kept doing what she had always done because she was caught in a common inner obstacle: denial of illness and a resulting lack of attention to self-care and self-awareness. She failed the rite of passage.

When the Buddha left the palace of his father, he observed illness, old age, and death—and he woke up. When we suffer an illness, especially a life-threatening one, we are faced with many choices at once. Perhaps, most invisibly, we are faced with the choice of whether to allow this crisis to serve the soul and wake us up.

From Terrible Wound to Sacred Wound

The more mythic version of this ordeal, as it appears worldwide, is characterized as a death and rebirth motif: The hero/ego must die to be reborn. She must suffer and sacrifice her old life before resurrection can happen. If she overcomes the ordeal, she attains another stage of awareness, with new powers and insights and a reorientation to life.

This is the hidden power of life-changing illness, the alchemical transformation of the terrible wound into a sacred wound, as told by the myths of Jesus's crucifixion, Job's boils, Persephone's rape, Inanna's torture, Orpheus's dismemberment, and the Fisher King, who holds the secret to the Grail but whose wound will not heal. For each, the wound cracked open a larger spiritual reality, which is always blocked by the ego's habitual patterns and habitual awareness. The wound was the catalyst for the ego's reduction and the encounter with the divine.

This same tale is told in our time by those who have had near-death experiences, left the body yet maintained their awareness, and returned to the world as survivors with a new story about the nature of death and life after death. And it is told in our time by those who have been violated by rape, incest, abuse, war, and torture and returned to the world as survivors with a new story about meeting the dark side of human nature and how it broke them open to compassion and service to other survivors. Today, this is how the wound becomes a sacred wound.

As Leonard Cohen sang to us, "There is a crack in everything. That's how the light gets in."

This crack, this wound, is the reason for choosing the time of illness, when we are weak and afflicted, to examine our souls. Poet and novelist Deena Metzger wrote in her essay, "Cancer Is the Answer," "At the very instant when our life is slipping out of our hands, when we recognize how little of it is remaining to us, we are called to scrutinize our lives, to sacrifice comfort for truthfulness, to re-value everything. In this deciding moment, we come to see that our life has value only as it is lived authentically, that it is measured not in years but in understanding."

We might add that the value of our lives is measured not in years but in self-awareness, forgiveness, and gratitude. It is measured not in cure but in letting go into the unknown, crossing each threshold as it appears, and emerging anew. It is measured in our capacity to experience illness from the inside out.

This may sound like a high ideal, a romanticized image of the awful and terrible suffering that accompanies a shocking diagnosis, severe pain, or physical degeneration leading to disability. It's not my intention here to set up "successful" health vs. "failed" illness. That is much like preconceived notions of "successful" aging, which create an ego ideal and resulting feelings of self-blame and shame for not living up to society's standards. Rather, we aim to place illness in the context of the soul's journey, with all its complexity and mystery. And, as with aging, I wish to explore its dark side and its light side, its descent into pain and its potential ascent to new meaning and another level of awareness. In this realm, when we talk about victory and defeat, we speak of the soul's evolution.

As one client told me, "I have a 50 percent chance of living for five years with this disease. This awareness of my mortality is always there. It's as if I've dialed in the binoculars until I can see perfectly clearly. Without cancer, I was not willing to look at my life."

Closing the Mind/Body Split

In the Judeo-Christian tradition, the human body and its animal impulses, sexual passions, and inevitable decay were banished to the shadow and characterized as taboo by a priesthood that valued only the "higher" realms of spirit, mind, and rational thought. Like a riverbed, the split runs deep in our collective terrain, creating false opposites: flesh/spirit, sinful/innocent, animal/divine.

With the advent of the scientific age, the body was confirmed to be a mere sack of chemicals, a machine with no soul. And the mind/body split became so embedded in a cultural blind spot that we can no longer see it.

The ego sees the mind/body split as a given; the soul does not. From its point of view, the brain, mind, and body are interconnected organs of the soul.

Today it's increasingly clear that our shadows—our denied, unlived, bound-up material—are not isolated in some corner of the head. Because we know that the brain/mind/body is a web of interrelationships, mediated by peptides and hormones, our shadows inevitably take on substance in our bodies, as well as our minds, and may appear as symptoms of disease.

These symptoms, of course, can be denied and banished. Faced with recurring headaches, shortness of breath, changing blood pressure or blood sugar, back stiffness, bladder infection, and other issues, we turn away. In denial, we ignore these premonitions.

Trudy, at the age of sixty-two, told me, "I had a heart attack. I considered myself to be healthy, strong, and young. I was newly married, learning ballroom dance and snorkeling. Sure, my blood pressure was high. And, yes, I smoked cigarettes occasionally. And my job was sedentary, but I exercised once a week. It was not that I was unhealthy; it was that I was in denial about aging. Even during cardiac rehab, I was telling myself, 'This is a fluke. It won't happen again.'"

That had been two years ago. "I can see now," Trudy said, "that I had refused to enter the gateway to this most important part of my life. I had continued to live as if I could drag this aging body and this aging psyche around without consequence. But, deep in my unconscious, my heart was breaking."

A cardiologist, Jeff, then at the age of seventy, worked long hours at the hospital and deeply identified with his role as the expert. When he took a bad fall, he was filled with shame and refused to use a cane, fearing to be seen as disabled. Then he fell again and needed a walker. He continued to resist: He refused to clear space in his home to make room for the walker. He refused to permit the help of a home health aide.

Jeff was struggling with a dependent shadow character, an unconscious part of him that refused and denied the loss of independence and the need for help. "I'm a doctor," he told me. "I help others. They don't help me." His identification with his role continued to sabotage him, preventing him from accepting a new reality, and preventing his family from supporting his needs.

Nevertheless, loss of mobility and chronic illness are widespread, particularly in older populations. The U.S. Centers for Disease Control and Prevention (CDC) reported in 2018 that two out of five Americans over age sixty-five have a mobility disability, one in five has diabetes, 40 percent are obese, and more than half take medication for hypertension. Among men, 70 percent will suffer an enlarged prostate by age seventy. Among women, one in eight will develop invasive breast cancer during her lifetime. In addition, because women tend to live longer, they are more likely to experience life-threatening illness later in life, when it's harder to recover and sometimes also harder to pay for health care.

Social isolation among older people is epidemic, too—and it's bad for their health. Researcher Angie Leroy and colleagues surveyed more than two hundred healthy people to see how lonely they felt. Then the team gave them the virus for the common cold, kept them in separate hotel rooms, and asked them to record how they felt while sick. "Lonely people feel worse when they are sick than less lonely people," she reported in the journal *Health Psychology*.

In a prime example of the mind/body connection, chronic loneliness has bodily consequences: It triggers the stress response, raising blood pressure and leading to insomnia and indigestion. And it lowers the immune response, creating chronic inflammation, which has been shown to contribute to heart disease, cancer, and brain disorders. (While researchers are still exploring the genetics of loneliness, they suggest that to combat the effects of loneliness, we should eat anti-inflammatory diets and find a shared mission with others.)

Clearly, cutting-edge medicine and psychology are moving toward closing the split between body and mind. But this two-thousand-year-old habit of thinking is embedded in the increasing specialization of every arena of science.

Illness of the Body

Cancer as an Answer

We are told to think positively about health, and the idealist in us wants to comply. Yet, particularly in late life, we are surrounded by reminders of illness in both ourselves and others. How do we hold these opposites: a positive vision alongside mortality awareness?

For some, in the face of a diagnosis, a tension arises between that inner idealist and the bodily reality of *what is,* a fine line between optimism and denial. A friend of mine struggled to come to terms with her cancer diagnosis because she insisted on "a miracle." I understood: Her sister had survived the same kind of cancer, and her mother had lived to be a hundred. So, she refused to acknowledge her progressive decline, complete her unfinished business, and make plans for the end of life. She died angry and heartbroken.

Contemporary notions of health sometimes promise an unending state of well-being if only we practice self-care, eat the right foods, and do the right exercise. But that is not nature's plan. Rather, for all of us, no matter how well we care for our bodies, health and illness, birth and death, are inextricably linked in the natural, organic cycle of life.

One of our constant reminders is the epidemic of cancer. No one remains untouched. Each year, 12.7 million people are diagnosed with cancer, and 7.6 million die. So, if we hear the words, "You have cancer," the shock and disorientation are understandable.

Like aging in general, cancer occurs in contexts: male or female, affluent or poor, well served or underserved by health care. It's not experienced collectively—that is, all cancer patients don't share the same suffering, don't have access to the same resources, and don't have the same outcome. Cancer is experienced as individually and idiosyncratically as aging itself.

But the metaphor used for cancer is collective: We are told we are fighting a "war on cancer," mobilizing against an enemy invader, with a commander (our doctor), a fighter (the patient), and chemical, biological, and nuclear weapons. This imagery of power and aggression may work for some physicians and their patients, who are motivated by it. But it's paternalistic and violent and may disempower others. It implies a win/lose outcome, with the patient as a "winner" who keeps fighting at all costs, or a "loser" who didn't fight hard enough.

In addition, this metaphor pushes other qualities of the cancer experience into the patient's shadow: It ignores the emotional, social, existential, and spiritual dimensions of a person's life, while turning the body into a battlefield. So, for some patients, the conventional language of cancer can add to the suffering because they come to believe they must be "courageous," which may mean denying their feelings of fear, vulnerability, anxiety, grief, and helplessness. They must be "proactive," which may mean denying their need for support and dependency, even their need for rest. They must be "compliant," which may mean denying their need to question authority and find their own path.

This creates a "cancer persona," a false self whose intent is to preserve the ego's ideal as a "Fighter." One cancer patient told me that her Fighter character would never stop trying new treatments, regardless of their awful side effects. The Fighter would always fight for life, regardless of her suffering.

"Why?" I asked.

"The people who love me would be so disappointed if I were a quitter," she replied.

As we explored her illness from the inside out, she realized that, despite her lack of further medical options, she could not accept letting go and moving into the final stage of her life. She could not retire the Fighter because the Quitter was a loser, bringing shame on her and devastation to others, and forcing her to face mortality.

Whatever the illness, the treatment, and the predicted outcome, the inner work of illness remains constant, calling on us to ask: Who am I if I am not well? Who am I if I get better? Or don't get better? Will I continue treatment even though it causes me to suffer? Why? What feelings and fears am I avoiding here and banishing into the shadow? What stops me from making certain choices?

The cancer Fighter persona can prop up the ego and form an obstacle to deeper change, keeping us from slowing, even for a moment, to reflect on all of our options.

There's another risk, here, too: A patient turns the Fighter into a new role and deeply identifies with it. My patient Sheila, at the age of seventy, went through a painful ordeal with breast cancer before finally going into remission. Entering a liminal space, she lost her orientation and no longer knew who she was. Her work role was gone, her purpose lost. When the cancer returned six months later, she confessed that she felt relief. "Now I have a purpose again. And people will show up with love."

She hesitated, then asked, "Do I want to be sick?" She sat with this question.

Then she continued: "Living with cancer is familiar now. And the uncertainty of the last six months was disorienting and scary. It's as if I know who I am and what I need to do when I'm a cancer patient."

The term "war on cancer" also can lead to an identity crisis for anyone who depends primarily on alternative medicine. "I'm an environmentalist, a vegetarian, and a meditator," a friend with lung cancer told me. "Now I need radiation! That's not who I am. That doesn't align with my values. What do I do?" She gazed at me with alarm and helplessness.

The other common metaphor for cancer likens it to a journey, which implies a movement from one place to another with others on the same path. It may be easier for people who see themselves on a journey to include a spiritual practice, a gentle regime of self-care, and the loving support of a community, all of which can contribute to a healing environment. And, most of all, it may be easier to transit the stages of a rite of passage with this positive metaphor, leaving behind past identities and habits, moving into the unknown, and reemerging a different person.

In her essay "Cancer Is the Answer," Deena Metzger pointed out that cancer is growth out of control. Its devouring nature seeks to spread and dominate everything it touches, giving nothing in return. She drew parallels between cancer's imperialistic behavior and humanity's predominant political modes: As the military war machine invades and occupies territories, slaughtering inhabitants and devouring resources until people are starved and forced to become refugees, cancer cells also invade and occupy territory, creating a toxic, uninhabitable environment.

"These diseases are mirrors of the prevailing political moods and activities," she told me. "They are microcosms enacted on the human body of larger events enacted on the social and political body."

When Deena herself had cancer, she said, she examined her internal defense department: "What weapons do I create against what enemy? What voices do I silence? Which inner selves have I imprisoned because they objected to the system that makes me ill?" These are, indeed, the questions of shadow-work, on behalf of herself and the world.

Since her illness decades ago, Deena turned her terrible wound into a sacred wound by accompanying many people on their healing journeys. Almost without exception, she wrote in the essay, she found that the moments of wrestling with illness and dying were identified by them as the most profound moments of their lives. They told her that, short of making these discoveries by other means, they would not change their circumstances. The process of healing and of dying was a process of waking up that they valued above all else. In each case, they woke up to something beyond ego, and their ego became relativized, smaller and less important in relation to soul.

Cancer might be an *answer,* as Deena called it, in the sense that it often serves as a divine messenger: It breaks us down until we question our totalitarian habits of mind, our ego's efforts to dominate and control ourselves, others, and the natural world, all to the point of near death. Only a death sentence—to an individual or to a planet—may force us to change course, to wake up to the greed, gluttony, self-righteousness, aggression, and total disconnection that hides in our behaviors. We live in a global culture that denies our interconnectedness and so is separated from the life force. It denies the compassion that is owed to every human being, animal, tree, and life form. Only with this deep reflection on individual and collective shadows will we survive.

I have heard many clients tell stories that are similar to the one told by Deena. Karen told me that cancer cured her specialness. If she could get cancer, Karen said, then she was just like everyone else, despite her meditation practice and organic diet. It leveled her ego so that she felt more deeply connected to every human being than she ever had.

Stephanie was forced to give up her driver's license due to the effects of chemotherapy on her cognitive function, and her loss of independence triggered a late-life identity crisis. As she reached out for help, uncomfortable feelings of dependence arose, but her circle of care widened. The loss was traumatic, but gradually, it led to a sense of being loved and cared for that she had never experienced before.

My friend Andy reported that only cancer could have brought him to his knees. Through the course of his experience with the disease, he finally found that he could release his lifelong effort to fix everything, to make himself and his loved ones perfect. "I can't fix it," he cried, throwing his arms into the air. "I'm powerless in the face of something larger. And I have to stop now, turn in a different direction, live in a different way." His powerlessness forced him to seek something greater than his ego for the first time in his life, and his spiritual search began.

A colleague, Christine, rejected chemo treatment, telling me that she wanted to "let her body heal itself." She threw herself into research and learned about GMOs in foods and carcinogens in her shampoo and cosmetic products. And she found healers who became mentors, guiding her through herbal, dietary, and emotional treatments. Christine went into a temporary remission and became a "wounded healer." As she transmitted her wisdom, turning her wound into a sacred wound, her intuition shined, and she found herself becoming an Elder.

Not every loss that comes with illness has a commensurate gain. But none of these people went "back to normal." They moved through letting go and liminality, continuing to do their emotional and spiritual work, and allowing themselves to be transformed by cancer. Some were able to release their identification with the body and move their attention to soul.

In a piece titled "In the Valley of the Shadow of Death," Jungian analyst Steven J. Frank wrote about his ordeal with multiple myeloma, a cancer of the plasma cells in bone marrow. Following chemotherapy, with its horrific side effects, and stem cell transplants, he went into remission and began to recall those sources of inner support that had gotten him through the ordeal: his experiences of a power greater than his ego.

Surfing, he wrote, confronted him with the power of the ocean and taught him to know when to flow with its force, when to push against it, and when to let go and be carried by something larger.

While doing transcendental meditation and sitting in pure awareness, Steven felt the boundaries of his body and head disappear, opening and connecting to everything around him, as if he had no limits. "Through the experience of meditating, I not only felt the smallness of the ego and the sense of something greater, but I also learned the skills of concentration, relaxation, and the ability to focus my attention. These skills proved extremely valuable in my efforts to tune into myself during this time and to not attach to some of the effects of the treatment."

Finally, Steven credited Jungian analysis, working with his dreams and shadow issues, with his capacity to watch thoughts and feelings arise as he went through the ordeal.

Of course, he was not perfect at all of this. He worried about his death and how it would affect his family. He ruminated, "Why did this happen to me?" He questioned God: "Am I done serving you?"

One night he reflected on the disease metaphorically, like a dream image. "What does it want from me?"

The answer: "It gets me in the marrow, in the core of me. What is at my basic core? God/the Self. What more do you [God] want?"

"I want greater service, devotion, much greater attention."

He fell into self-blame. How perfect did he have to be to prevent getting ill?

Steven pointed out that it's common, with serious illness, to discover that we have neglected something in ourselves. But that doesn't mean that if we hadn't, we wouldn't have become ill. The point is that illness causes us to look inward. Any self-blame is the ego imagining that if we do everything perfectly, we won't get sick. "We can no more control all aspects of the nature of our health than we can control nature itself."

Of course, this stems from a shadow character, a Critic, that compares *what is* to an imaginary standard, whether about body image, our choice of romantic partner, career success, or our health.

Steven developed a visualization practice to focus on light/presence filling and surrounding him. As he did this, his anxiety decreased. "Eventually the meditation shifted from taking in the light to seeing it move back out from me to its source. I realized that to love with all my heart, all my soul, and all my might meant that I could not just take; I had to give back too. To feel the light come into me on the in-breath and then go out from me on the out-breath was opening and peaceful. It wasn't just about me and my disease anymore. I felt a greater connection to something larger."

Eventually, Steven found that he did not need to identify with his body's cancer and could release its centrality from his inner world. By practicing shadow awareness and pure awareness—"I am not this cancer . . . or heart problem . . . or arthritic knee. . . . Rather, I am pure awareness"—we might come to the same experience.

To be clear: Steven didn't deny the illness; he relativized it in his inner world and opened to something greater—to shadow awareness and to pure awareness. In this way, the illness guided him to shift his attention away from ego concerns and toward higher meanings, or from role to soul.

Hence, cancer was an answer.

Today, some diseases that used to kill us can become chronic, and death can be delayed even several times with transplants, bypass surgery, and medications. But what does life look like after we meet the shadow of death? Do we maintain the same values, routines, and priorities? What do we need to be doing? What do we need to stop doing?

In late life, an encounter with life-threatening illness can lead us to speak what has been left unsaid, to complete what has been left unfinished. It can be a portal to presence, to designing a legacy, and to becoming an Elder. It can open us to profound spiritual experience.

But there is no institutional or social support for medical crisis as a rite of passage. Most doctors, family, and friends would urge us to return to life as we knew it and to move on. Our shadow characters may take control and unconsciously collude with this advice, preventing us from hearing the divine messenger's call to radically change our life.

The Driver, who won't let us stop doing, may push us to get back to work and continue to do what we've always done. The Loyal Soldier will obey the orders of an authority, like a doctor. The Dutiful Daughter views the doctor as a parent and hasn't individuated enough to question him or her or get other opinions. The Addict may resist any change in consumption or lifestyle. Even an Inner Child, who is overwhelmed and panicked, may grip a patient's attention, causing emotional regression and helplessness, so that the patient loses agency and becomes passive and childlike.

So, it's important to identify these shadow characters that are obstacles to this rite. And it's essential to practice pure awareness so that we learn to witness them and thereby respond consciously and authentically to our illness, our caretakers, our doctors, and our loved ones.

Shadow-Work for Illness
From the Inside Out

Illness of body/brain/mind demands a reorientation to the inner world. It triggers the shadow in myriad ways, and with each of these, a shadow character emerges to grip us. The uncertainty of our fate provokes anxiety that can re-create childhood fears. We feel deeply unsafe. We don't know who to trust. We are too frightened to make decisions. We need to be loved but can't receive it in the way that it's being offered. We feel isolated among others, who cannot understand. We feel worthless without vitality, unable to work. We feel helpless, unable to change things, unable to accept *what is*. We fear being seen merely as a "patient," who carries the stigma of death. We want to fight for life; we want to just rest and give up. And we are terrified of dying.

A client, Mary, at the age of seventy-three, was rushed to the ER with severe abdominal pain. She awoke the next morning to a doctor announcing, without any preparation, that she had stage 4 cancer and must be rushed into surgery. Soon after, chemo began—and life as she knew it ended.

"I don't want things to be what they are," she told me. "I'm alone. No husband, kids, grandkids. Who can I rely on? I've been totally independent, never depended on anyone."

"Who would you be if you depended on someone?" I asked.

"Needy . . . ugh!" she said.

Her repulsion told me instantly that this was a shadow character, a denied and rejected part of herself. "What do you say to yourself when you need help now that you're so sick?" I asked her.

"Oh, no! I'm hungry and can't cook. Oh, no! I'm too tired to drive. I need someone. I'm so ashamed." Mary hung her head.

"What are the feelings that go along with those thoughts?"

"I feel trapped and silenced. I can't ask for what I need. I feel disgusted with myself. I'm old and sick. I want to hide, to just disappear."

We agreed to call this shadow character Needy. "What's your earliest memory of Needy in childhood?" I asked.

"I couldn't have needs. I had to be what my mother needed. It was all about her. I was unwanted for who I was. I was just an extension of her so that she could feel good about herself."

So Mary learned not to have needs and not to rely on anyone. And in this way, Needy protected her in childhood. But now, as a single woman in late life, Needy was sabotaging her, keeping her from depending on others who wished to be her caregivers.

Decades before, Mary had been instructed in meditation by a swami and had continued to meditate and chant for years. She had let her practices lapse since the diagnosis. When I reminded her that it would be helpful to begin to witness Needy as it arose in her awareness, so that she could get enough inner spaciousness to do shadow-work, she began to meditate again.

A circle of friends spontaneously formed around her, the result of lifelong connections that she had nurtured over decades. One, who lived nearby, brought groceries whenever she asked. Another came to cut her hair as it fell out and helped her find hats that she liked. Others drove her to medical appointments. Others brought gifts of a robe, movies, books. One woman cared for her garden so that Mary could sit outdoors among the flowers.

Although Mary had been unable to trust one significant other, she had formed deep bonds with many. But she was so anxious that she wanted her loved ones to be perfect. Of course, they made mistakes that challenged her: too distant, too intrusive, too Pollyanna, too dark, saying too much, saying too little.

As she learned to witness and romance Needy and spent more time in meditation, she began to explore ways in which she could bring herself to consciously depend on others: If she controlled the schedule and managed her time with them, and if she delegated her chores and made clear communication boundaries, then she could begin to rely on them. She could begin to feel loved, meeting her deepest need. And the shadow character began to recede.

Then Needy got triggered with Nina, one of Mary's closest friends— and Mary cut her off. It took her several weeks of journaling and speaking with me to understand what had happened. Unconsciously, within Mary, Nina had seemed to share traits with her mother: needing her to be affectionate, needing her to eat certain foods, needing her to follow certain treatments, and, most of all, worrying about her. Projecting her mother onto Nina, Mary felt repelled and unable to tolerate the feelings.

She knew that Nina was hurt, that she must have felt unwanted and unseen. But Mary could not reach out because she didn't have the physical and emotional energy to deal with the feelings aroused by Needy. Since her illness, she had been learning a mature dependency on others. But when her negative mother shadow was triggered, she regressed to young Needy, could not speak up, and just wanted to get away from her dear friend.

A month later, the two women met to explore what had happened.

Mary explained that she had unconsciously projected her needy mother onto Nina. She felt very young when this happened, but she also felt the anger and resentment that she hadn't been able to risk feeling as a child and, therefore, pushed Nina away. Mary told Nina that she had uncovered her shadow projection and deeply apologized for hurting her. But she also wanted their interactions to change. So, she expressed her adult needs as well.

Nina took the opportunity to explore the nature of her emotional attachment to Mary and its underlying, unconscious needs. She saw through her worry about her friend as her ego's effort to control life, rooted in her own fear of losing Mary. And she felt grateful for this insight and vowed to herself that, as an Elder, she would set an intention to retire her worry.

Later, Nina asked, "How can I love you now? Show me how to be with you at this difficult time." And she learned how to better attune to Mary, listen without judgment, give advice only when it was invited, and stay inside her own boundaries. She was delighted when her giving could be received.

Mary told me that uncovering the unconscious shadow character through her work on this relationship had healed her fear of being dependent. "Needy isn't a dirty word anymore," she told me. This experience taught her about Elder friendship, a kind and conscious exchange of love and wisdom. "Like two wise elders sitting by the riverbank, she and I have lived so much life, we have done our inner work, we have practiced for this moment. We are here now. Together. Alone."

There are also occasions to find gold in the dark side of illness, such as a passion that may have been dormant for decades but emerges with mortality awareness. In his wonderful book *The Creative Age,* gerontologist Gene Cohen tells a personal story about meeting the shadow of illness. His left calf muscle was cramping and appeared larger than the right. As a physician, he became alarmed and went for tests. Two months later, he was told he had ALS, Lou Gehrig's disease, meaning that he would lose control of his body and die within three to five years.

A profound darkness descended upon him. Dread invaded his world. His mind raced: "What should I do now? How could I tell my family? Should I resign from work? Go on a long trip?"

Then the denial emerged: "Maybe they're wrong."

Then the anger: "Why me, why now?"

Then the bargaining: "Maybe, if I do such and such, I will be an anomaly and survive this thing."

One beautiful morning, he asked a different question: "Are there things I always wanted to do but didn't?" In other words, he was asking, "What is the unlived dream in the shadow that I could live out now?"

This question launched him into a life review. Cohen had always wanted to design an intergenerational learning game but had pushed the idea aside during his medical career. When he reconnected with this dream, he felt excitement and vitality coursing through his body. So, he began to envision a game in all its complexity.

Then synchronicity happened: He ran into an old acquaintance who had the skills that he needed to execute the game. They worked diligently, entered a judged contest for games as works of art, and won the competition. Cohen wrote, "I realize that it was my first significant personal experience of aging that adds as it takes away. It was my most vivid experience of creativity transcending loss—the loss of my health and hope for the future."

Unable to change his health, he focused instead on something he *could* do, reclaiming a lifelong desire from his shadow and living it out fully.

As life would have it, the diagnosis of ALS was incorrect. With this news, Cohen's dark mood began to lift. As painful as this ordeal was, he wrote, "it elevated me to a new vantage point in life in understanding myself and my capabilities. I was able not only to cope with the dreadful forecast but to emotionally transcend it through a creative process. I felt I would be able to help others with grave conditions because I had gone through it."

Cohen went on to establish the interdisciplinary Center for Aging,

Health, and Humanities at George Washington University and his own game company, GENCO, with a mission to develop new ways to expand intergenerational creativity.

Caregiving from the Inside Out

Becoming a caregiver, or requiring a caregiver, is another transition that may come gradually or suddenly. But when it happens, we're instantly uprooted and transplanted into foreign territory. Our former aptitudes and strengths may no longer matter; our former vulnerabilities, once hidden, may roar to the surface. But given the new longevity of our population, at some time we will either give or receive care. As Ram Dass put it, we all transition from asking, "How can I help?" to "How can you help me?"

This major life shift triggers many shadow issues: for caregivers, resentment of the lack of freedom, impatience with the other's demanding needs, betrayal about the loss of a dream. As one woman put it, "When my husband got sick, we lost our future." As a client said, "When my brother was diagnosed, my life became about nothing but him. I can't cope." As a friend said, "Did I stay healthy just to take care of him?" And a husband told me, "I adore her, but I'm not built for this kind of patience."

Our default shadow characters, and their coping strategies, may take over: The Savior will try to cure the loved one. The Victim will feel helpless, overwhelmed, confused, and alone. The Researcher will obsess with googling possibilities. The Denier will turn away, unable to see *what is.*

For those receiving care, this shift may trigger a dark night in the liminal zone, a loss of identity, purpose, and meaning—and an uncertain end. As a cancer patient told me, "Don't ask how I'm feeling. I am not a cancer patient. That's not who I am."

In addition, it may bring up denial, or the Fighter, or the Rebel, or the Obedient Patient. Beneath the roles, the shame of dependency, the loss of agency, and the fear of death linger. As one man told me, "I was so competent. Now I can't even drive." A wife told me, "I never had to depend on him for anything. Now I feel trapped and ashamed."

For both caregivers and receivers of care, shadow-work can help us move toward conscious caregiving, crossing the threshold from an outer orientation of role—the helper and the patient—to an inner orientation of two souls on a healing journey.

Caregiving can become a portal to self-knowledge through shadow awareness. It can become a portal to silence through practicing pure awareness and dropping our identification with the body. In this way, we can more openly bear witness to suffering. And it can become a messenger of mortality awareness.

For example, my colleague Anna told me that, for a full year, she attended to a friend with cancer, taking her to doctors, buying food, and listening to her struggles. When that woman went into remission, Anna was exhausted and resentful. "She never really appreciated all that I did. She didn't thank me in any meaningful way."

Anna's early childhood injury, feeling unseen and unacknowledged by her parents, had been triggered during her long year of caregiving. In her shadow, she was striving mightily to be seen and appreciated by her friend in a way that she had not been by her family. And she had been unknowingly over-giving, neglecting her own self-care, and, most importantly, expecting something in return—to be acknowledged and valued.

When Anna reflected on her own responsibility for her reactions, she saw that her ego had a secret agenda: She admitted that a part of her—her inner Savior—wanted credit for her friend's remission. When her friend complied with Anna's recommendations, they got along. But when her friend made different choices, Anna's ego was offended.

As she examined the hidden motives in her shadow, she could feel more accountable for her reactions, and her heart opened again to her friend. She learned how to serve differently, to move in and out of the caregiving more fluidly, without identifying with it. And she learned to see her friend as a soul undergoing an ordeal, rather than another person she could fix.

When a person is caring for a spouse, it's likely that the shadow will erupt at some point. When my client Paula was caring for her husband Jim, and it became clear that his undiagnosed illness was becoming chronic, she began to feel trapped. "Three months is enough," she said. "It's looking more like three years of cooking, cleaning, chores, and driving to doctor's offices. What about me?" she asked.

Paula needed to talk about her accumulating feelings as the situation worsened, or they would be stuffed into the shadow. She felt that she couldn't burden Jim with them, so she brought them to me. I explained how important it is for caregivers to have a safe place for their own self-care, sometimes just to vent, sometimes to explore shadow-work. Once she could reorient and focus on herself, Paula expressed difficult feelings.

"Who am I, now that my freedom is gone, now that my future is gone? Jim was my rock, my refuge. Now, as he deteriorates, and I rush around to care for him, I'm lost and disoriented."

Paula felt growing resentment and concern that, if this was her life from now on, she would become bitter and depressed.

"The other day I felt so frustrated that he couldn't help with anything that I lost it. I yelled and stormed out. Now, I'm so ashamed. He doesn't deserve that."

We explored how she could identify the anger and resentment before it boiled up to the surface: Her skin felt hot and her throat closed. Her body felt like it would explode. She named this shadow Resentment and learned how to romance it by slowing down this reaction with deep breaths and telling Jim that she needed a break before the anger erupted. Then she would go for a walk and release the energy from her body.

Paula also felt helpless and useless. As we traced these feelings back to her childhood, she recalled how helpless she felt in the face of her father's alcoholism. This had shaped the "Helper" role that she took in the family, which was now reemerging and triggering intense early-childhood feelings.

"I had to be there for my mother's needs with Dad. But who was there for mine? Gosh, here I am again, helping others and feeling invisible and unappreciated."

For most of us, the re-creation of early dynamics in our adult circumstances can add emotional charge to our current responsibilities. Paula came to realize that the Helper part of her was not what her husband needed. She was not trying to fix him or to earn love. Paula saw that the Helper emerged when she couldn't tolerate her own feelings or Jim's feelings, so she tried heroically to fix things. She wanted to be a successful Doer, as she had been in her midlife years.

But Jim mostly needed her loving presence, not her heroic doing. He didn't need advice or solutions. He didn't need to be cheered up. And she mostly needed to give love. So, their deeper needs, beneath the roles, actually fit.

Paula decided to hire a professional for two days a week to fill the role of caregiver. In this way, she could set limits on her own doing, focus on her own creative projects, and begin to orient from role to soul in her marriage. Someone in different circumstances might join a caregiver support group, find a friend or relative who can provide relief care, or seek help from a local social services agency.

This self-care allowed Paula's higher emotions to emerge in her caregiving: compassion, empathy, generosity, patience, and nonjudgmental awareness. Rather than contracting into her narrow new role, she began to expand out of liminal space and find space in her new reality. She found patience with Jim's slower pace and eventually understood that patience was now her spiritual practice. She opened to it, breath by breath.

Eventually Paula saw that caregiving contains many pairs of opposites that, at times, feel like they are pulling her apart: doing/being, obligation/choice, resisting/accepting, dependent/independent, and especially self/other. Eventually, she learned to recognize when she moved into one side and fell into identification with it. Slowly, she expanded to hold the tension of these opposites and to witness them from a broader vantage point.

This kind of caregiving from the inside out can become part of our sacred service or *karma yoga,* a path to greater unity. It can lift us out of habitual roles and labels, such as husband, wife, patient, helper, father, mother, son, or daughter, which can limit our capacities for giving due to shadow issues. And it can move us into the realm of soul. When we encounter one another behind these masks, in moments of profound joining, our feelings of separateness dissolve. Now, as our ego barriers fall away, we often can intuit the other person's needs.

Here is an anonymous story about this shift from the book *How Can I Help?* by Ram Dass and Paul Gorman:

In the early stages of my father's cancer, I found it difficult to know how best to help. . . . Toward the end, I was called to come suddenly. . . . When I entered the hospital room, I saw that I'd made a mistake. There was a very, very old man there, pale and hairless, thin, and breathing with great gasps, fast asleep. So, I turned to find my Dad's room. Then I froze. 'My God, that's him.' I hadn't recognized my own father! It was the single most shocking moment of my life.

All I could do was sit next to him and try to get past this image before he woke up. I had to look through him and find something besides his astonishing appearance. By the time he awoke, I'd gotten part of the way. But we were still uncomfortable with one another.

Later, I came into his room and found him asleep again. So, I sat and looked some more. Suddenly I heard the words of Mother Teresa, describing lepers she cared for as 'Christ in all his distressing disguises.' . . . What came through to me was a feeling for my father's identity as . . . a child of God. That was who he really was, behind the 'distressing disguise.' And it was my real identity too. I felt a great bond with him, which wasn't anything like I'd felt as father and daughter. . . .

For the remaining months, we were totally at peace and comfortable together. No more self-consciousness. No unfinished business. I usually seemed to know just what was needed. I could feed him, shave him, bathe him, hold him up to fix the pillows, those very intimate things that had been hard for me earlier.

In a way, this was my father's final gift to me: the chance to see him as something more than my father. The chance to see the common identity of spirit we shared. The chance to see how much that makes possible in the way of love and comfort. And I feel I can call on it now with anyone else.

As this story shows us, the shift in awareness from role to soul can actually be a legacy of caregiving from the inside out.

Illness of the Mind

Depression or Disillusionment

A 2012 report from the National Academy of Medicine, edited by Jill Eden, et al., stated that 5.6 to 8 million older adults—one in five—have one or more mental health and substance use conditions. These can be serious enough to affect their functioning and may lead to increased disability, poor quality of life, and a higher death rate. For example, older adults with depression, the most common disorder, have higher rates of mortality following hip fractures, heart attacks, and strokes.

In addition, although the rate of suicide for women typically declines in older age, it increases with age among men. There are many known risk factors: chronic illness and pain, certain medications, emotional losses, economic insecurity, social isolation, and the fear of being a burden. A growing mortality awareness may influence depression, as well as our will to live, which changes as we age.

The diagnosis of depression in older people is complicated by the side effects of multiple prescription drugs, alcohol abuse, emotional unfinished business (such as unresolved trauma and personality disorders), grief, and neurological conditions (such as tumors, strokes, and memory loss). Today, psychologists are trained to view depression through the medical model as a disease of the brain, rather than as an emotional and potentially symbolic journey. (In my book *Romancing the Shadow*, I explored midlife depression as a symbolic journey at length.)

However, in late life, with the loss of capacities and the loss of loved ones, forbidden feelings of rage and helplessness may emerge from the shadow. With the loss of dreams and ideals, secret fears and fantasies may emerge unexpectedly. And, with an altered sense of time, unanswered questions of meaning and purpose sneak up and pester us. The shadow forces us to face the unlived life and the limits of the choices we made. For some, this encounter is emotionally and spiritually destabilizing.

Rick Moody has pointed out that depression is distinct from disillusionment, and some degree of disillusionment is inevitable with age. Our high expectations for ourselves, others, and institutions will no doubt go at least partially unmet—and this can be heart-wrenching. Writing in "Baby Boomers: From Great Expectations to a Crisis of Meaning," Moody distinguishes disillusionment from garden-variety disappointment or regret: "It is a deeper existential loss of confidence in institutions and in those values, principles, and practices upon which we have based our lives." That is, it can stem from the loss of a dream, both personal and collective. And most of us have big dreams for both ourselves and the world.

Disillusionment also can stem from a meeting with the shadow in ourselves or our loved ones, politicians, mentors, mentors, clergy and spiritual teachers. This loss of faith in others, in whom we placed our trust, can be shattering.

Moody cites the 2016 election of Donald Trump by 53 percent of older voters as a sign of profound disillusionment and loss of hope. Many voters surveyed said that the world had become dangerous; they feared immigration, crime, terrorism, and globalization, and they expected things to get worse.

"The current epidemic of disillusionment is global and reflects a profound misalignment between rising longevity and population aging, on the one hand, and structural elements that promote greater risk for individuals over the life course," Moody asserts. In other words, the world's population is living longer, but the world's institutions are shifting under our feet. And some of this uncertainty is creating a crisis of meaning among us, which, if misunderstood, may be diagnosed as depression.

Let me be clear: Depression can be seen in the brain as an alteration of neurotransmitters, and that is why medications like SSRIs (selective serotonin reuptake inhibitors) may help. Each mental event, whether sorrow or ecstasy, has chemical correlates. But are those neurochemical changes causes or effects? Are they rooted in untreated early family trauma, family biology, or late life circumstances? Certainly, as we age, there are valid reasons for sorrow, grief, and disillusionment. But also, like retirement and illness, depression may be a divine messenger—a call to a symbolic path and a rite of passage.

Why can some people face decline, grieve losses, and cross a threshold into a new stage, while others cannot? The latter remain stuck in past identities and roles, fixed ideas, and resentments; they are unable to let go of one trapeze bar and withstand the emptiness—the liminal space—for a moment before catching the next.

A Japanese American client, after being diagnosed with a serious cancer at the age of eighty, grew depressed and hopeless. But she kept on doing what she had always done, what was expected in her culture; she could not let go of her roles to cook, clean, and care for her husband and grandkids, no matter what. And her family maintained those traditional expectations of her, despite her changing circumstances. So, she faced both a cultural and a familial role expectation that was difficult to release.

But slowly, with support, she began to understand that this was a time for herself, a time to slow down, attune to her own needs, rest when she needed, and even say no to her loved ones. As she began to say no for the first time in her life, setting limits on her service to others, the depression lifted. She stopped pushing herself and began to feel a flow to her day, even in the face of acute mortality awareness.

There are few supports for undergoing depression as a conscious journey, a descent to the soul. But the unlived life is waiting there to be recognized and invited out into the light of awareness. Depression or disillusionment in late life may be a call—if we heed it and honor it.

Illness of the Brain

Memory Loss as Epidemic

The quality of our brain's hundred billion neurons—how they fire, form pathways, make connections, and age—shapes the quality of our momentary experience—how we love, learn, innovate, organize, feel joy, make meaning, feel pain, and self-reflect. The mysterious intersection of the brain/mind/body and consciousness has evoked questions for materialists and mystics alike for eons.

But now there's an urgency to this issue: In the United States in 2019, according to the CDC, an estimated 5.6 million people aged sixty-five and older had Alzheimer's disease and related forms of dementia. With longevity, the risk of dementia grows. Globally, according to the World Health Organization, 50 million people already suffer from dementia, and that number is projected to rise to 152 million by 2050.

Mythologist Michael Meade calls this "the great forgetting" among our Elders. What is this epidemic of memory loss among those who are meant to remember what is most important, those who are meant to be the carriers of family and cultural story and the guardians of wisdom?

The great forgetting is like a myth in which countless people lose their way, finding themselves alone and wandering in a fog before the end of their stories. It feels like the Greek goddess of memory, Mnemosyne, has abandoned us, and in her absence, millions of stories are erased.

I am reminded of a terrifying film, *Invasion of the Body Snatchers,* which was released when I was very young. In the movie, people were alarmed to find that their loved ones seem to have been replaced by emotionless impostors. Today, who or what are the memory snatchers of our loved ones? Environmental toxins? Unresolved emotional trauma? High-carb, low-nutrition diets? Sedentary lifestyles? Why is this happening to millions of us?

Like aging and illness, memory loss happens in social contexts. According to a press release from the 2017 Alzheimer's Association International Conference, African Americans are 50 percent more likely to develop Alzheimer's than their White, Asian, or Hispanic peers. Researchers speculated that those living in disadvantaged neighborhoods—with food scarcity, few exercise options, air pollution, poverty, and violence, and hence higher stress—are at greater risk of cognitive decline. Several studies confirmed this finding. In addition, the American Psychological Association has noted that the stressor of racism takes a toll on the brain.

Yale psychologist Becca Levy, whose research on negative stereotypes about age was cited earlier, also examined how they influence changes in our brains. In an article called "A Culture-Brain Link," Levy and her team reported that participants holding more negative age stereotypes earlier in life had greater hippocampal-volume loss and accumulation of neurofibrillary tangles and amyloid plaques in their brains—the biomarkers for Alzheimer's—in later life. These findings suggest that our unconscious thoughts and images about aging (our inner ageist), which are lived out through our life spans, have a biological impact on how our brains age and potentially lose memory.

There is widespread debate today about how to care for those living with memory loss. When I interviewed professional caregiver Elizabeth, she was working for 102-year-old Flora, who had dementia and was in hospice care because her doctors believed she was near death. Flora was combative, agitated, and depressed. But Elizabeth learned how to calm her patient and treat her with respect. She was able to look past her immediate state and see a charming, funny, and intelligent woman. "I saw through to her beauty and wit," Elizabeth told me.

She also learned not to try to get Flora to be rational. She aligned with her, rather than arguing with the dementia, by simply agreeing with Flora's statements. "Elders want to be heard," she said. "When I listened to her, she felt valued."

"Also, they are dismissed as givers, as if only we are giving and they are receiving," Elizabeth said. "Flora gave me so much; she healed my lack of mother love."

Flora bonded with Elizabeth. When she was released from hospice care after a few months, Flora told her, "It's official. We've adopted you into the family."

For two more years, they cared for each other, body and soul.

Elizabeth's experience as a caregiver echoes my own. When my father was diagnosed with Alzheimer's, I wrote the following piece:

Who is this man before me, taciturn, where once he was gregarious, vacant and empty as a Buddha, where once he was full of opinions? Who, only moments ago, gobbled chicken pizza with relish and now cannot recall what he ate? Who, only months ago, drove to lunch with his best friend of sixty years to debate the events of the day? Who, only a year ago, lost his home and his possessions, only two years after losing his wife of sixty-five years, and now remembers none of it?

I sit in a red upholstered seat, across from him, and take his hand. It's mottled, knotted fingers with the big gold band are so familiar to me. But nothing else is familiar.

I recall myself, small and helpless, and this man, a raging bull, throwing words at me like weapons; this man, slamming his fist on the table, insisting the Vietnam War was right—the communists had to go. And this man, taking my hands in his to the sounds of 1960s swing, twirling me around the floor.

Who, then, is my father?

I seek out his hazel eyes, and he pulls his glance away. Not toward something else, but simply out of focus. Gone. Where does he go? Until recently, he went into memory . . . Where do memories go when the ego/mind is gone? Or he went into jokes . . . Where does humor go when the ego/mind is gone? Or he went into love . . . Where does love go when the ego/mind is gone?

Who is he? A simple set of traits—bossy, smart, doting, loyal, liberal, foodie, impatient, critical, generous, provider—that simply vanishes one day?

Or do those traits mask who he really is? Do we mistake them for the man, for the real person? And is that man naturally revealed when they are gone? Or do we have to *do* something, uncover something, to detect the real thing—the soul of a man?

The disappearance of ego/mind into oblivion in Alzheimer's raises the question: What was there to disappear? Like a photon vanishing before the physicist's observing eye, did the ego ever have any life of its own? Did it have any substantiality that arrived for a while, then vanished?

When my father's mind dissolved in slow motion, he appeared to sink into his heart. It opened like a vast canyon, and the depth of his feeling, previously hidden in the shadow, became evident. Not the loud political passion and moral indignation about social injustice that I had heard all my life, but the quiet, tender sentiments of gratitude for my presence, empathy for others, and even tears during romantic moments in film—those feelings that had been covered over during eighty years of the ego's reign. His own vulnerability opened him to the vulnerability of others in a deeply heartfelt way, even though his intellect was gone, his short-term and then long-term memory was gone, his wife and friends were gone, the life he had always known was gone.

My dad's journey with Alzheimer's, and my sister's and my own as his caregivers, sheds light on the kind of experience that is available to some people during different stages of the great forgetting. Yes, he had outbursts that clearly stemmed from the remains of unresolved emotional injuries. But as some of his faculties declined, I observed that others emerged. As he lost the capacity for new cognitive learning, I found myself grieving. Then I discovered that music evoked great emotion in him. We sang show tunes and listened to the bossa nova from his early life, and he lit up with joy.

As he settled into a wheelchair, he needed to look up at us, rather than down. This physical repositioning altered a lifelong power dynamic between us. As I tried to join his reality in the moment, day after day, rather than impose my own, his mood lifted. And we met in a new psychic space, a zone of presence that we had never previously found between us when we were trapped in rigid father-daughter roles.

In a moment of insight, as he saw through the ego's drama of the past, my dad looked at me quizzically, shaking his head, and asked, "What *was* all that about?"

I knew, then, that he had a direct perception of the fleeting, dream-like nature of his life. He could see the self-importance, the striving, the urgency from a new vantage point. His forgetfulness was a portal through which he could see his life beyond the constructs and the drama to its essence.

My dad did not survive into the final stages of Alzheimer's, when he may have lost language or failed to recognize us, for which I am grateful. But his journey reinforced for me the fleeting reality of everything, and the substantiality of something else: a self-reflective consciousness or soul that exists behind and beyond the ego/mind.

Many decades ago, my first meditation teacher used to say that before we meditate, our experience is etched into memory like a line in concrete. As we continue to meditate, it's etched like a line in sand, then a line in water. Eventually, it's like a line in air.

So, I had imagined, at the innocent age of twenty, this spiritual goal: One day the traces of my experience would make no imprint on my brain/consciousness. Some fifty years later, I understand that losing our mind is not the same as transcending our mind.

Today, I can hold this paradox: the aim is to retain the traces of my experience but to be less emotionally attached to them. That is, I seek to witness them, rather than lose them. I seek to see through the essentially constructed nature of my mind. Of all mind. And to remember that it is not who I am.

In our society, most people are deeply identified with their rational minds and personal memories. Some believe they are their beliefs or their histories. Many tell me that they will live on in the memories of others. From that point of view, this epidemic of memory loss is deeply disturbing.

In generations past, books carried the collective recollections of history, science, philosophy, and literature. And now bookstores are gone. It's difficult for us to imagine the past before the printing press, when knowledge had to be memorized and genius was attributed to people with superior memory, such as Aquinas or Talmudic scholars. But now we need to imagine a future where nothing needs to be memorized.

Today we are replacing individual memory with an immense supertechnology that contains it all for us. This boundless external hard drive has taken humanity from the need to remember everything to the need to remember nothing. As the Cloud becomes the vast carrier of individual and collective memory, what becomes of imagination? Will our grandchildren and great-grandchildren learn how to read, write, and tell stories with the Cloud at their fingertips? Who will they be as Elders?

Delaying Memory Loss and Enhancing Plasticity

The brain's plasticity—its ability to adapt its neural pathways in response to change, loss, and risk—is an ongoing source of surprise and innovation. New findings indicate that cognitive impairment can be prevented or delayed with only changes in lifestyle and behavior. They suggest that the Mediterranean diet (fish, vegetables, fruit, olive oil), aerobic and strength training, cognitive training (especially speed of processing), and management of cholesterol, blood pressure, and blood sugar all protect against the onset of memory loss.

Mila Kivipetto and Krista Hakansson reported on a Finnish study in *Scientific American* in which researchers found that overall cognitive performance improved 25 percent more in people who followed this program than in the control group. Even those with the ApoE4 gene, which has been linked to a higher risk of Alzheimer's, received benefit from the program and showed a slower rate of cellular aging.

Dale Bredesen's research on reversing memory loss through lifestyle changes has shown exciting results. The author of *The End of Alzheimer's* and his team personalized treatment approaches for patients with varying degrees of memory loss, based on extensive testing to determine what might be affecting signaling in each patient's brain. In his book, Bredesen describes the protocols.

For one patient in a high-stress job who was having trouble finding her way home, for example, the program included:

- eliminating all simple carbohydrates, leading to a weight loss of twenty pounds
- eliminating gluten and processed food, with increased vegetables, fruits, and non-farmed fish
- reducing stress with yoga
- meditating for twenty minutes twice per day
- taking melatonin nightly
- increasing sleep to seven to eight hours per night
- taking vitamins B_{12} and D_3, fish oil, and CoQ10 daily
- optimizing oral hygiene using an electric flosser and electric toothbrush to avoid bacterial infections that travel to the brain
- reinstating hormone replacement therapy, following discussion with the patient's primary care provider
- fasting for a minimum of twelve hours between dinner and breakfast, and for a minimum of three hours between dinner and bedtime
- exercising for a minimum of thirty minutes, four to six days per week.

The results for nine of the ten patients suggest that memory loss may be reversed and sustained with this therapeutic program. Since that pilot study, the protocol has proven successful for hundreds of people with memory loss. And several hundred medical practitioners have been trained in the Bredesen protocol around the country.

(I will add here that I put myself on a similar regimen following my father's diagnosis, with the guidance of Bredesen's book. With the exception of hormone replacement therapy, I followed the protocol but added more supplements and nootropics for the brain. So, my case cannot confirm Bredesen's results. However, my experience has been astounding.)

The brain's plasticity also may be enhanced by silence. A 2013 study by Imke Kirste, a biologist at Duke University, exposed mice to various types of noise to monitor the effects on their brains. The researchers used silence as a control. But they made an unexpected discovery, as reported by Daniel Gross in the article "This Is Your Brain on Silence": When the mice were exposed to two hours of silence per day, they developed new cells in the hippocampus, a brain region associated with memory and learning. Silence may be an especially important factor given today's noisy, chaotic world.

Noise also activates the amygdala, a part of the brain associated with memory formation, and elevates stress hormones, which increase our blood sugar and heart rates. It also reduces cognitive performance in reading, memory, and problem solving.

Silence seems to have the opposite effect: It releases tension in the brain and body, reducing blood pressure even more than listening to music, and reducing the stress hormone cortisol. Meditation can do the same.

A study reported by Sue McGreevey in the *Harvard Gazette* described the results of research at Massachusetts General Hospital in which participants in an eight-week mindfulness meditation program showed increased gray matter in several areas of the brain, including the site of memory, in contrast to non-practitioners, who showed no brain changes.

Another study, by Harris A. Eyre and his team at University of California at Los Angeles, showed that a practice called kundalini yoga resulted in short- and long-term improvements in subjects with mild cognitive impairment, as compared with controls.

According to the theory of "attention restoration," sleep is not enough to rejuvenate the brain. To recover from the fatigue of information overload and distracted attention, we need time in quiet, pristine, natural environments, where we can breathe in the stillness and perfection of an old-growth forest, an ancient mountain, or a shimmering lake.

There is also a link between cognitive health and a felt sense of purpose. In a study published in 2012, Patricia Boyle and her team at Rush University Alzheimer's Disease Center found that people who feel a high degree of purpose, who derive meaning from their experience, were 2.4 times more likely to remain free of mild cognitive disorder and Alzheimer's. In other words, finding and maintaining purpose in late life has all kinds of ripple effects.

Some people doing genetic testing make a disturbing discovery: They have one or two copies of the ApoE4 gene that is linked to Alzheimer's. As scientists work to develop blood tests for early detection, these people may be living with undetectable pre-Alzheimer's conditions. But they are finding purpose by becoming patient-advocates and creating an online community, ApoE4.info, where they gather, collaborate with scientists, and share the results of research findings and lifestyle changes. In this way, by refusing to be stigmatized or live alone with this risk, they are turning this wound into a sacred wound, feeling informed and empowered.

An Interview with
Buddhist Psychologist Rick Hanson

Rick Hanson learned to meditate in 1974 during the human potential movement, which opened doors for many of us. After a time of exploration and experimentation, he went to grad school and became a psychologist. Twenty years ago, when neuroscientists began to map brain states, Rick's worlds came together: clinical psychology, neuroscience, and Buddhism. And he found his soul's mission: to write and teach about well-being, growth, and contemplative practices. Rick wrote *Buddha's Brain* and *Neurodharma*.

I interviewed Rick, who was then sixty-seven, and asked him about ways to prevent cognitive decline and enhance brain plasticity in late life. "The growth of new neurons in the brain's memory center takes place in two steps," Rick told me. "First, stem cells are converted into neurons, then they wire up with other neurons. During this process, they need to be protected. And we now know what achieves that: stimulation with complexity, such as walking while talking or walking while listening to a podcast."

"Does this happen automatically?" I asked.

"No, we need deliberate effort to turn our transitory experiences into lasting change," he responded. "That's what I call a superpower: being an active agent of lasting change by acquiring self-knowledge and using our capacities through deliberate efforts."

What interrupts that process?

"Stress reduces the insulation along nerve fibers, and it generates cortisol, which degrades certain areas of the brain. So, we need mental training, such as meditation, to reduce stress in our nervous systems."

Rick called meditation "marinating in who we want to be and how we want to be."

I asked him about his current practices. "Each morning I reestablish the fundamental intention of my activities," he said. "I take refuge in what's personally meaningful to me, my sense of the divine. This is especially important as our social structures feel less and less supportive."

He continued, "I inhabit the Third Noble Truth of not craving by resting in a feeling that my needs are met. The Buddha taught that craving arises from lack, from something missing. So, I build the resources to meet my own needs and internalize the feeling that they are met. Then, I can rest in peace, contentment, and love for a few minutes."

I asked if this is what he means by *neurodharma*. "It means steady mind, warm heart, rest in fullness, come into whole mind, receive the Now, open to All, and find timelessness," he told me.

These terms resonated for me with resting in pure awareness and practicing presence.

Finally, I wondered whether mortality awareness was having an impact on Rick. "I've had a fortunate life along with my own share of sorrow and mistreatment," he said. "But I'm acutely aware of the miracle of evolution from a one-celled organism to the human body/mind. Think of it: Our bodies are made of stardust, the atoms in them are billions of years old. That leaves me in awe and gratitude every day."

Illness as Spiritual Practice

From Role to Soul

Some stages of life-threatening illness pull us into a liminal space: We feel as if we are between worlds, between identities, no longer this, not yet that. For example, the waiting between diagnosis and treatment can seem interminable, full of uncertainty about who we were and who we will become. During chemotherapy, when the ego's props fall away, hair falls in clumps, food tastes metallic, and muscles waste, the old life passes away and a new life is not yet born. When we are in remission or recovery, we can swing between hope and fear, between birth and death, living in a kind of bardo between worlds. Each of these is a transit space, a holding station, much like the chrysalis for the butterfly.

With some illnesses, a liminal period between identities can last a long time as roles fall away and a physical or psychological renewal fails to appear. My dear friend Corey, a beloved professor, psychologist, and author, was forced into retirement at age sixty-eight by chronic fatigue syndrome. Previously, he had longed to give up the urban commute, the noise, and the stress of his position and locale. But he felt too planted there, until the illness forced his hand. He unplugged from his life, quit his job, sold his home, and moved with his wife to a small island where he knew no one.

"I've gone from being somebody to being nobody," Corey told me. "I live in a twilight, although it's spring outside. My old self feels like a zombie that could be reanimated, but I don't want that. The Dr. Corey show is over. I let it go."

For a few years, he would say to me, "When I recover . . . when I have energy . . . when I'm productive again . . ." He imagined a future after this holding pattern. Then Corey realized that he was imagining action driven by ego in his heroic mode, and it didn't fit anymore. He no longer needed to be seen as smart and to impress people with his intellectual fireworks. He no longer needed to make money to accumulate stuff. Everything he had dedicated his life to, everything that had seemed so real and important, was gone now.

Corey didn't even need to live in linear time. "I've been forced into a slower wave frequency," he told me. "I'm moving at the pace of nature, not the pace of culture."

As he stopped resisting and let go into the new life, no longer living in his mind, no longer seeking outer affirmation, but instead enjoying presence, the beauty of the sea outside his window, the eagles soaring above, making his breakfast, and resting when he needed to rest, something began to shift.

Corey had never focused on self-care and self-love before. And he had never been loved without heroic doing, without providing for others. Yet his wife loved him as much as ever, without his titles, without the status of his roles, without his earnings. He discovered sources of renewable energy in small things—the taste of cherry pie, the sea air, a song he loved. And his sense of humor began bubbling up, along with moments of vitality. He had outgrown adulthood and was on his way to donning the mantle of an Elder.

Then the fragments of a story, which had been gestating deep within him for many years, became the beginnings of a novel.

"The hand of fate washed me up on a desert island," he told me. "If not for chronic fatigue, I would still be driving that commute and working myself to the bone."

Ram Dass wrote and spoke of his life before and after a paralyzing stroke in his book *Still Here*. Always a scout for our generation, just ahead on the path, he continued into his eighties to teach about illness as a vehicle for spiritual knowledge and experience.

After the stroke: "I can no longer drive my car. Now, my attendant drives the car, and I sit in the passenger seat. So, each time I get into the car to go somewhere, I can either be an ex-driver, who can no longer drive, which will bring up suffering for me on that trip. Or I can say, 'Far out. I'm being chauffeured.' One brings up suffering, and the other brings up joy. It's a projection of my mind on the phenomenon of a trip to the post office."

Illness calls in new gods—new archetypes and identities—and ushers out the old. And it can shift our focus from fixing what's broken to connecting with the unbroken soul.

Shadow-Work Practices

Which shadow character in you is a patient or victim of an illness? What are the inner words, feelings, and sensations of this shadow character? Can you witness this character and return to pure awareness?

Which shadow character is dependent? Please practice this visualization: Sit with your eyes closed and become present, breathing slowly. See and feel your illness or limitation and the dependency it creates. Expand your vision outward to encompass your home's dependency on the surrounding resources, your garden's dependency on the larger natural world, your community's dependency on its surroundings. Sit in the whole truth of the interdependence of all living things, each one as precious as the other. And imagine, just for a moment, that your dependency is not shameful or unnatural. It's just a part of the whole truth.

Spiritual Practices

Continue breaking your identification with changing, limited phenomena and moving it to soul:

- If you are struggling with changes to your face, practice breathing in, move your attention to your face, and repeat: "I am not this face. I am pure awareness."
- If you are ill or losing physical capacity, practice breathing in, move your attention to your body, and repeat: "I am not this body. I am pure awareness."
- If you are struggling with feelings of fear, grief, and despair, practice breathing in, move your attention to your heart, and repeat: "I am not this feeling. I am pure awareness."
- If you are struggling with memory loss, practice breathing in, move

your attention to your head, and repeat: "I am not this mind. I am pure awareness."

I have written repeatedly about coming face-to-face with the question, "Who am I?" You can adapt this inquiry to illness by contemplating the following questions:

- Who was I before this illness?
- Who am I now, during this illness?
- Who will I be after this illness?

If you are a caregiver and feel trapped, isolated, and powerless, try to detect the source of these feelings in your early life. Who is the shadow character? What is its message? As you recognize it, remember that, instead, this is the spiritual truth: You are free, interconnected, and powerful. Imagine an internal message or mantra from this truth: "I am not trapped. I am choosing to love this person, one breath at a time. This is what I've been given. Caregiving is a noble task. And I can offer it, as I also care for myself."

When you look at the person you are caring for, who do you see? A suffering body? A suffering mind? What are you missing when you look at, listen to, or touch that person? How can you move closer to seeing a soul?

PART 2

Life Review and Life Repair

Part 2 explores two tools for the inner work of age—life review and life repair—that may be familiar to you, especially if you've done a lot of therapy. Life review is a focused reflection or emotional inventory of the key events of our lives and how we experience them in retrospect. Following your life review, you will be able to identify more clearly where you need to give attention to life repair. Life repair is rooted in the desire to find reconciliation or even forgiveness with those who betrayed, disappointed, and hurt us. It's also an effort to forgive ourselves for those words and actions that brought us shame or regret.

Throughout this section, we'll deepen our exploration of two aspects of the inner work of age: shadow-work to uncover the unconscious aspects of our heroic journeys and their wounds; and spiritual work to help us let go of past self-images and identities, such as victim or victimizer, live more fully in the present moment, and begin the passage from role to soul.

6

A Review of Your Lived and Unlived Life

Fatima the Tentmaker:
A Sufi Tale

Hoping to find a handsome, affluent husband, Fatima, a spinner by trade, joined her father on a trip to several islands in the Middle Sea. On the way to Crete, a violent storm destroyed her father's ship, killing everyone except her. Poor and alone, she befriended a family of weavers in Alexandria, and they taught her their craft.

Years later, in the marketplace, Fatima was captured by slave traders and sold to a man who made masts for ships, her world collapsed for a second time. But she adjusted to life with the mast builder.

When her life was disrupted once again, she cried out, "Whenever I try to do something, it comes to grief! Why? Why should so many unfortunate things happen to me?"

Yet she refused to lose hope. She traveled to China and learned that the emperor was looking for a female stranger who, according to legend, would be able to make him a tent. By this time, Fatima had worked as a spinner, a weaver, and a mast builder. But she was unaware that each career, each

164

disruption in her life, each grief, had prepared her for her final roles—as the emperor's tent maker and eventually his wife.

—Paraphrased from a story told by Idries Shah in
Fatima: The Spinner and the Tent

Like Fatima in the parable, most of us live our lives in reaction to changing circumstances, in the details of the moment that require our energy and attention to meet our survival needs, our emotional needs, and the needs of those we love. We are lost in those moments as if they are disconnected from what came before and what comes after, as if they are single, separate entities, like the many-colored threads of a tapestry before we turn it over and stand back to view the finished pattern.

As the great existential philosopher Søren Kierkegaard said, "Life can only be understood backward, but it must be lived forward."

The effort to understand a life, repair it, and find meaning in it is a natural developmental task of late life. With the loss of the ego's agenda, we can suffer disorientation, and a life review can help us reorient to the soul's mission and give us a deeper purpose for late life.

But no one teaches us how to do this in a thoughtful, organized way. No one teaches us how to digest the life we've lived, distill the lessons from it, and turn them into wisdom. So, we watch older people trying urgently to tell their stories or reminiscing in a way that makes them appear to be lost in the past.

Fifty years ago, experts in the field of aging believed that this reminiscence was a sign of senility, which reinforced ageist stereotypes. But in the 1960s, renowned gerontologist Robert Butler discovered that many older people seem to be experiencing a profound internal effort to come to terms with everything that happened to them in the past. He coined this phenomenon "life review" and concluded that it is a normal, necessary task of late life, not a pathological one.

Butler suggested that the purpose of life review, whether spoken or written, is to recall unresolved conflicts and reconcile with them through seeing a larger picture or reframing the events. This may lead to reconciliation with estranged loved ones, making amends and forgiving them, or forgiving ourselves. In the best case, it leads us to give up denial or blame and become accountable for the life we've lived.

The call to review our lives may come as a gentle nudge to see it from the long view, not through the eyes of youth or of middle age. We want to recognize what we have made with the life we were given, or what it could have been if it had unfolded differently. We want to detect the patterns in our choices, the results of our actions, the coincidences in seemingly chance encounters, and the residue of unfulfilled desires—the full weave of the tapestry and the images revealed there.

Sometimes, the shock of mortality awareness triggers the desire to review our life, evaluate our achievements, and possibly design a new direction. Or the reality of retirement may catalyze a process of self-reflection about the past and inquiry about the future. Sometimes the event of becoming a grandparent stirs a need to tell our stories, to record them in the memories of our family members or in an actual written or video document to create a legacy for future generations. In other cases, a nagging feeling of guilt or shame brings up a need for emotional repair, which requires us to look back and examine when we were harmed or harmed others.

In a less intentional way, people in late life may repeatedly tell the same stories from their past, in a dreamlike, nostalgic reverie, as if to digest something that's stuck somewhere or to complete something that's unfinished. They may fantasize about the life they did not live, which they could be living if only this had happened or not happened. Their minds may wander between reality and fantasy, between *what is* and what's out of reach, between choices made and not made, opportunities lived and missed, loves gained and lost. And they are haunted by internal shadow characters that grieve lost potential, regret abandoned gifts, long for ideal lovers, and mourn unfulfilled dreams.

In late life, these shadow characters inhabit us and inhibit us from redesigning our lives now. They form an inner obstacle: remaining stuck in denial about the past or stuck in fear about the future. The result: We live in a narrow band of time, unable to make the shift from role to soul.

Instead, with a life review, we can gain the opportunity to see the full arc of a lifetime from a higher, broader vantage point. We can see how the key moments in our lives were interconnected and became sacred passages with a hidden purpose: the evolution of the soul.

My client, Alan, had been harboring resentment toward a woman who had rejected his marriage proposal decades earlier. He just got stuck there. But when he looked at his full life span in the way that we will explore here—backward and forward, above and beneath—he realized that the painful rejection by one person was not isolated from the rest of his life. That pain carried with it a pattern of feelings from his early childhood. This insight led him to seek therapy and to learn how to have a much more rewarding relationship. At last, Alan could reframe that apparent failure as a turning point that took him in a new direction, an ending that became a beginning, a loss that became a gain in awareness and maturity.

Seeing from this deep and wide vantage point, we can release the past and live more fully in the present moment, opening to love of family, creative impulses, and the beauty of the natural world. A life review can be a portal to presence. And it can help prepare us for death by lessening feelings of fear, guilt, anger, and regret as we move toward life completion.

On learning that he had terminal cancer, the late neurologist and prolific author Oliver Sacks wrote, six months before his death, "Over the last few days, I have been able to see my life as from a great altitude, as a sort of landscape, and with a deepening sense of the connection of all its parts. . . . I cannot pretend I am without fear. But my predominant feeling is one of gratitude. After all, I have been a sentient being, a thinking animal, on this beautiful planet, and that in itself has been an enormous privilege and adventure" ("My Own Life," *New York Times,* February 19, 2015).

As a scientist, Sacks viewed life through a material lens. Others, with a more philosophical or spiritual lens, seek to address questions of existential or spiritual meaning in late life: Could we have made different choices, or was our life fated to unfold in this way? What is the meaning of coincidence or synchronicity? Of karma or fate? What is the larger tapestry that is hidden behind our own small story? And who is the weaver?

To see the shape of a life, we need to stand back from it and reflect, as if the tapestry is hanging on the wall. We need to soften our gaze, step out of the immediate moment, and let go of the apparent randomness of events to see the order and beauty of our one-of-a-kind story.

We may be asking: Can we accept ourselves more deeply now? Can we accept our losses and our limits? Should we let go of relationships that continue to disappoint us, or should we use the time remaining to try to repair them? Can we accept our unmet goals and unlived dreams? Or should we use this time to reclaim those dreams, such as write a memoir, learn to play guitar or paint, or travel to exotic lands, even as we move toward life completion?

Some of you will read this and feel immediate resistance: "I don't care about the past." "It's too painful to look back." "I can't do anything about that now." "I don't have enough time or energy for that."

This denial or resistance to inner work may be the voice of a shadow character that does not want to face our many disappointments and disillusionments. Perhaps our memories of a trauma or betrayal are too painful, and they have been stuffed away in the shadow for too long. Perhaps a Critic shadow judges us for "sinful" behavior, such as lying or cheating, and we don't want to face that rejected aspect of ourselves. Or the Critic compares us to an invisible standard of success that we did not attain, creating self-doubt and regret.

It's also possible that our "inner ageist" is part of the resistance to life review, whispering, "Oh, nostalgia and reminiscence, that's just for very old people. That's not me."

But our denial of this opportunity also denies us the chance to repair the past, forgive ourselves, and pass on what we've learned to future generations. And this denial puts us at risk for depression about the past or unhealthy obsession with it. A lack of self-reflection leaves us with a lack of insight, which is needed to become an Elder. It's as if we've gathered a lifetime of bounty and just don't bother to harvest it.

When I was in my sixties, it never occurred to me to do a life review. For most of my life, I was future-oriented, never interested in looking back. But something began to call me to contemplate my life patterns and digest all that I had learned. For me, this call came through the music of the 1960s and '70s, listening to Dylan, the Dead, the Band, the Stones . . . and discovering that my brain lit up with joy and my body rose up to move. The rock sounds of my youth connected me to those times. The lyrics arose from my memory like buried sacred texts. And I became ready to look back.

If we do not consciously choose to undertake a life review, it may take place spontaneously, as has been reported by people who've had near-death experiences when their lives "flashed" before them. And it may take place unconsciously while we sleep. Jungian analyst James Hollis told me that his older clients, over the age of sixty-five, often dream about unassimilated material from the past, which they need to digest now. "It's not merely nostalgic," he said. "It's how the psyche is making meaning of the life story."

For instance, Hollis had several physicians as clients who were burning out from work and looking at their futures with dread. Their dreams led them to understand that they had become doctors for the wrong reasons—for their parents' dreams or cultural expectations. "They were in pain from doing the right thing, which turned into the wrong thing. But they didn't know it. If they didn't pay attention to their dreams, they wouldn't know what was really going on behind the ego's story."

Hollis suggested that this kind of connection with the unconscious, or shadow, equips us to deal with the many losses and diminishments of age, including mortality awareness. Through our dreams, we have a felt sense of an ongoing dialogue with something larger than the ego, something deeply meaningful.

In a conversation, Rick Moody reminded me that life review can occur spontaneously in dreams and that this was famously illustrated by Charles Dickens in *A Christmas Carol*. The novel's protagonist, Ebenezer Scrooge, now an older man who has been miserly and unkind all his life, hates Christmas and refuses to give donations to people in need of food. In three dream episodes, Scrooge sees the ghost of Christmas past, when he was an innocent, lonely child; the ghost of Christmas present, where some families celebrate in generosity and joy, while other children starve; and the ghost of Christmas future, which reveals Scrooge's own funeral that no one attends.

This dark review of his life and his mortality prompts a painful question: "Is it too late for me?" Scrooge wakes up a changed man. He spends time with a family, gives his worker a raise, and sends a turkey to a needy family, finding generosity and renewal in his own heart.

Like Scrooge, many of us meet a shadow part of ourselves in late life and vow to take a different direction. It may not be such an extreme turning as Dickens's character. But with a life review, we can turn away from harmful or limiting habits and turn toward a larger embrace of life.

Physician Rachel Naomi Remen on Seeing Her Life with New Eyes

Rachel Naomi Remen is cofounder of Commonweal Cancer Help Program and author of the bestsellers *Kitchen Table Wisdom* and *My Grandfather's Blessings*. In an article for the Institute of Noetic Sciences *Review,* titled "Seeing with New Eyes," Rachel wrote about the turning points in her life that led her to "see with new eyes." She called these moments "initiations" because they resulted in a new stage of awareness.

Rachel was born into a family of doctors, and her life goal was to be the first woman to head a department of pediatrics. Then the human potential movement and the field of holistic health emerged, and she was invited to join a research team at Esalen Institute in Big Sur,

California. She agreed. Her discoveries about the mind/body connection and the field of complementary medicine took her by surprise and forced her to question her lifelong ambitions. "If I had known what I was going to have to surrender, I wouldn't have gone."

Months later, confused and disoriented about her purpose as a doctor, Rachel suffered a series of panic attacks and wanted to leave Esalen to return to the safe, familiar world of science. A colleague encouraged her to do an imagery exercise that slowly revealed a mystery: an image of a marshmallow squashed under pressure, flattened out of its natural shape. "The shape most familiar to the marshmallow was not its true shape," she wrote. "But something in it remembered its own shape and was puffing up and reclaiming it now."

Rachel cried as she realized that this was her life story. Her family of scientists worshipped logic and facts and scorned other styles of learning. Her colleagues reinforced this view. She had been under a lifelong pressure to flatten herself and conform. But by nature, she was an intuitive, even a mystic. And at Esalen she had, for the first time, found like-minded souls.

"Before that, I felt like I was dying," she said. "But I was going toward a way of being I had never been able to live, a way that would fit me perfectly when I got there. I was going home."

Having left Esalen and taken a teaching position at Stanford University, she received a faculty promotion and achieved her conventional career goal. But instead of celebrating, she felt trapped and suffocated. Then a synchronicity triggered a memory: "I stepped through a doorway into another reality in which all the odd parts and pieces of myself turned toward each other, and for the first time they fit together seamlessly. I who had always felt an outsider, always felt like the wrong person, I remembered—and knew I belonged."

She quit her job and, as she put it, went from being a person who was always fixing a broken world to a person who felt privileged to serve a holy world.

"But this hadn't happened as a single event," Rachel said. "It happened slowly over time through a series of events. And I could see it only by looking back."

Rachel pointed out that these moments of initiation happen as a natural part of living, a return to what is most genuine and unique in each of us. "They seem to be moments when the personality recognizes what the soul has always known," she said. "At such times something familiar is lost, but something of great value is found. Our true life is offered to us—a life more transparent to our deeper values."

In the trajectory of a lifetime, this turning toward soul happens not once but many times. "With each initiation we come closer, we turn more easily," she said, "until that final initiation, death, when we turn away from the personality and become the soul."

Rachel had the intelligence and discipline to become a doctor, but to do so, her intuitive, mystical nature had to be buried in the shadow. Like many people in family professions, she could have pushed herself to become a gifted physician. But she realized, in the early years of the holistic health movement, that the sacrifice of her innate, constitutional design (or typology or calling) had too great a cost.

It was only later that she could see the ebbs and flows of her life with new eyes, the eyes of a sage.

The Ego's Life Review

What Was Expressed

To find the threads of the tapestry of your lived life, I suggest you prepare by sitting still, taking a few deep breaths, and sinking into presence. With your mind quiet and alert, write down a horizontal time line from birth to one hundred years old across a long, horizontal sheet of paper. Then divide the time line vertically into decades. For each decade, recall the key events and key people of those years. Write them down above the horizontal line, that is, in the realm of conscious awareness. It may help to note the numbered years, beginning with your birth year, to jog your memory.

For instance, for your first decade, from birth to age ten, what do you know of the key events, transitions, gains, and losses? Who were the central people in your story, families, romances, and mentors? How did they influence you?

Taking your time, continue through each decade, remembering as much as you can about the forces that shaped you. What were your major transitions in each decade? What insights did you gain coming out of the transitions? How did you grow, open your heart, and develop new awareness?

A key event may be a beginning or end, a gain or loss, a success or failure, a birth or death, a rite of passage, a gift or trauma, or a meeting with a remarkable person. Given the rich and unique life that my husband has lived, I was surprised to hear him say that his key event was immigration—leaving his country of origin, family, friends, and financial support to come to the United States. He believes that the trauma of immigration shaped his traits of resilience and determination, as well as his capacity for letting go, leaving behind the road not taken, and embracing change to build a solid foundation for his children.

There are many possible dimensions to a traditional life review. For example, you can go through each decade from the point of view of your body, which has its own life story—its seasons of youthful vitality and beauty, midlife potency and responses to stress, and late-life slowing, resilience, limitations, and perhaps illness.

Sara, a client, told me about the difficulties of her own birth, as told to her by her mother, and an early childhood illness that affected her gait. Although she grew stronger and healthier, she carried a self-consciousness about her body into adolescence, which affected her early romances. She described the pain of her first menstruation, the awkwardness of her first sexual experience, her failed efforts to dance well, and a surgery that left scarring on the neck, which she wore as a badge of courage. At sixty-five, Sara survived breast cancer, which triggered her desire to do a life review. She told me that her body's story left her in awe of its beauty and strength, even though it's now scarred and sagging.

"I never felt such appreciation and gratitude for my body before looking back over its journey," she said.

Or you can go through each decade from the point of view of your heart, which has its own narrative—its seasons of hope and disappointment, of widening compassion and heartbreak, of empathy and generosity.

When she was in elementary school, my friend Jeanne watched her aunt enter a convent to follow the religious life. Jeanne followed at the age of nineteen; she opened her heart to God with all the love and longing of a young woman and took her vows. She left eleven years later with no knowledge of how to live in the world. Eventually she married, and she worked for Bank of America for twenty-seven years.

During that time, Jeanne discovered the Myers-Briggs Type Indicator, a personality test that is built upon Jung's work with personality typology. To her shock, she discovered that she was an intuitive feeler, but she had been raised at home and in the convent to be a sensate thinker. That is, her feelings had been banished into the shadow long ago, and she had been living a false self.

During one brief period, Jeanne's husband left the marriage, her parents moved to assisted living, and her job disappeared. "Then the real shadow-work began," she told me. Her perfectionism, reinforced in the convent, hid secret feelings of fear and anxiety. Her "good girl" persona hid secret longings for freedom and self-expression.

A former priest told her that the only difference between her and Jesus was that Jesus realized that he was God. In that moment, Jeanne woke up to the myths that she had been living, read widely in mysticism, and completed her master's degree in transpersonal psychology. She also rekindled an intimate relationship, which led to a conscious partnership for the first time. "Now, when I react, I know it's me, and that changes everything."

Her partner also had stuffed his feelings into the shadow. "So now we're learning feelings together," she said. In other words, Jeanne was reclaiming long-lost feelings from the shadow in late life.

The ego/mind has a narrative, too—its seasons of fluid curiosity and love of learning, then attachment to beliefs in black-and-white thinking, then receptivity, and then close-mindedness.

Bob, a colleague and former minister, was unconsciously identified with his religious beliefs, holding himself and others to a moralistic, right/wrong way of life. One day, his spiritual director pointed out that God is not the same as the dogma of the church. Shocked, Bob began slowly to see through the thoughts and beliefs that he had internalized and taken for granted and to explore what he really believed, gradually recovering his independent thinking and discovering a more direct connection to his God.

"I became disillusioned for a while," he told me. "Although I was no longer a true believer, I became more interested in other traditions and open to interfaith dialogue." Eventually, he became a spiritual director to nurture people's religious curiosity, rather than their dogmatic beliefs. In other words, Bob broke his identification with unconscious thinking patterns that created egoic arrogance and self-righteousness, reclaimed his critical thinking, and opened his mind to other paths. At the same time, his moral development advanced as he let go of rigid rules and came to follow his inner, intuitive guidance.

Your work life has a narrative. So does your creative life. How have they intersected in your story? How has one disrupted the other or supported the other?

You also might review your life through the lens of romantic relationships. What do the patterns tell you? How have your partners resembled your parents? How have they been reactions to your parents? Have you chosen the same partner over and over, or have you chosen very different people?

While undergoing a divorce, Sue, a client, reviewed her relationships. She had married her first husband, John, at a young age and had several children, who now had children of their own. John had been an addict and, eventually, they divorced. Judging herself through a conventional lens, she felt regret that she had not stayed with John and tried to tolerate his addictions. But after the divorce she met and married another man, who brought emotional and financial stability to her family.

Over the ensuing years, Sue felt stifled at home and returned to school, where she was shocked to be drawn to another man and pulled into an affair of the heart. Wracked by guilt, she cut off the connection. But her romantic yearning awakened her holy longing and carried her onto a spiritual path. Eventually, when her second husband wanted to end the marriage, she agreed. Several years later, she met a man who also was a seeker, a practitioner of centering prayer, and they formed a more conscious bond than she had ever experienced.

"I feel some regret for the divorces and the emotional affair," she told me. "From the life review, I can see who I was then and feel compassion for my younger self. But now I'm living real love. And any earlier choices that had been different would have had different results. My ego feels guilty, but my soul knows that something bigger happened."

Another client, who had never married or had children, told me that it was only after she reached her sixties that she could see this truth: Her father had tied her to him for his own needs. It was only then, years after his death, that she could see how he had prevented her from bonding with other men.

"He put me in a trance. I believed only he could be relied upon. No other men. Only he would provide for me always. Only he really knew me and loved me." Now, she was free at last to choose whether to begin seeking out a relationship or come to terms with the reality of her life and the life that will never be.

All our personal stories are parts of the larger story of us, invisibly woven together as the tale of our lives. You might look at how the key events of your life story intersect with the key events of your generation—wars, scientific breakthroughs, political clashes, legal victories, environmental crises, heroic leaders, even musical hits. These and other cultural highlights are the context in which your personal key events took place in that decade.

A National Life Review

Many voices now are calling for a collective life review, a social and political accounting of the history of the United States. We can explore our ancestral histories and all the many ways in which we came to be here, together, on this land. We can explore our cultural histories and our family roles in the blessings and the sins that shaped this nation. We can explore our national collective shadows, speaking the truth about genocide, slavery, internment, torture, and immigrant policies that have been committed in our name. Without this kind of rite of passage, profound shame and grief lie buried in our collective shadow. Without it, we cannot understand the underlying roots of privilege and injustice.

If we looked back together with honesty, perhaps in time the grieving would ripen us. And we could witness the evolution of the soul of our nation. In that way, we could decide how to move forward together. Some politicians are calling for reparations to the descendants of African slaves. Some White people are exploring the impact of privilege on their lives. One woman I know, whose early ancestors stole land from Native Americans, is meeting with tribes today to grieve the past and make amends. She told me that she bought land in the Southwest and is leaving it as her legacy to the local tribe.

On a different level, when we stand back to look at our stories and reflect, we may be able to uncover a mythic tale: the archetypal hero's journey. This narrative was popularized by mythologist Joseph Campbell, who found it to be a universal tale in which we as heroes venture forth from the ordinary world into an unknown, wondrous, perhaps frightening territory. We meet mentors, allies, and enemies; we undergo ordeals, victories, and defeats. And we return from the great adventure, as if reborn, with gifts to offer our fellow human beings. Many screenplays and novels are based on this tale; perhaps your life story is too.

Take some time to examine your life review in this framework:

- The hero hears the call to adventure;
- first refuses the call,
- then heeds the call and leaves the ordinary world,
- meets a mentor,
- crosses a threshold,
- undergoes a test (such as meeting the shadow),
- finds allies and enemies,
- stops to face inner doubts and fears (shadow characters),
- undergoes an ordeal (physical death or symbolic/ego death),
- receives a reward (object, secret, insight),
- follows the road back,
- has a final resurrection (following an encounter with death),
- and returns with a boon (a solution, a new awareness, a new beginning).

Here's an example from my own life review: A childhood infatuation with a blue-eyed boy stirred my holy longing and led me to yearn for the divine. A seemingly chance comment by my father about UC Berkeley led me to choose that school and wake up to my own racism, and I lost my suburban, White naivete in the heat of the Black Power movement, and Eldridge Cleaver became my hero. I became radicalized, rejected my father's money for college, and volunteered in West Oakland schools.

A year later, a seemingly chance meeting with a pony-tailed hippie, who told me that he wouldn't date me unless I began practicing transcendental meditation, led me on a spiritual journey. Books by Ram Dass and Paramahansa Yogananda opened wide the windows onto the spiritual realm. And my priorities shifted from activism to inner work. After meeting Maharishi Mahesh Yogi and listening to his vast integration of science and consciousness, spiritual awakening became the purpose of my life.

A decade later, after practicing and teaching transcendental meditation, I faced a painful encounter with spiritual shadow and left the community, disillusioned and alone. But I read *The Aquarian Conspiracy*, the first comprehensive vision of the "new age," and made a seemingly chance phone call to the author, Marilyn Ferguson. She told me that the editor of her newsletter had just quit and it must be synchronicity—I should come in. I had never called an author; I had not been seeking a job. But when we met, we felt a deep recognition. And Marilyn offered me the position of writing *Brain/Mind Bulletin*. She became a life-changing mentor and writing teacher, opening yet another door.

The first call I received on that job was from Steve Wolf, who was seeking publicity for a project. Fifteen years of friendship later, we became coauthors of *Romancing the Shadow* and remain close friends today, forty years later.

During those heady years with Marilyn, I was privileged to meet many of the leaders of the human potential movement and the pioneers of consciousness exploration—neuroscientists, psychologists, shamans, psychedelic researchers. But this cycle of my life would end in heartbreak when Marilyn fell into a spiral of addiction, which became an ordeal for all who loved her.

During that time, I met her publisher, Jeremy Tarcher, whose publishing house was the first, in the 1980s, to popularize books about alternative health and conscious business practices. We became friends, and eventually he became my mentor in the publishing world, where I spent a decade as an editor developing a hundred books, including my first two anthologies.

I had begun to study Jung seriously and to work with an analyst, who introduced me to my shadow in dreams. With my analyst as my guide to the underworld, I decided to return to graduate school in depth psychology and learn to teach others to work with their shadows.

I also had been grieving a broken marriage engagement for several years. On a seemingly chance evening, I received a dinner invitation from an acquaintance. A dark-haired man entered the room in a white

T-shirt, and my life turned again—upside down. Five years later, I married Neil, becoming a stepmother and, now, a grandmother. This rite truly initiated me into a new life of conscious relationship. If I had gone through with the earlier marriage, I never would have been emotionally prepared for this journey with Neil.

As Neil and I studied Hindu, Buddhist, and Sufi mystical practices, guides have continued to appear in person, in dreams, and through books. In each case, we met remarkable, highly evolved people. In each case, their shadows appeared. One man, in an extremely high stage of awareness, acted out a money shadow. Another Indian swami had unique attainment but was sexist and narrow-minded.

More recently, as I approached seventy, I wondered about the possibility of an initiation to become an Elder. I wondered what might need to be learned and what might need to be sacrificed to cross this threshold. I certainly no longer wanted a teacher or spiritual guide. I was becoming the Elder I had been seeking.

Today, after completing my life review, I can see that my life's initiatory moments happened through a series of meetings with remarkable men and women (or their books). I feel incredibly blessed for the appearances of my guides along the way, for their loving support and their generous transmissions to me. But in each case, I had to heed the call, undergo the tests, and earn the gifts. And I had to return the boon to the larger world.

I feel grateful for those people whom Rabbi Zalman Schachter-Shalomi called the "severe teachers," those who betray our trust by acting out their shadows, creating terrible suffering. I can see now how these "negative" experiences were "teaching experiences" that initiated me into the shadow, ending the innocence of childhood, humbling my ego, and moving me toward maturity. During this period of facing spiritual shadow, I had the following dream: *I dreamed of a man on a mountain who throws a boomerang out to the sky—and watches as it always come back to him.* I can see that each betrayal or disappointment boomeranged back to me, to my own responsibility for giving away some power or some gift. Each time I painfully reclaimed a projection, I regained a part of myself, again and again, in an alchemical process. Each loss, in this way, became a gain. Each failure, a victory. Without the severe teachers, I would not have become a gifted therapist. I would not have become an expert in shadow-work.

With my life review, I now understand the difference between the ego's purpose and the soul's purpose in my own life. When I look back on my four distinct careers—meditation teacher, journalist, editor/author, and therapist—there are no obvious external commonalities. But, at the level of soul, they share the same mission: to transmit information about consciousness. It's been deeply satisfying to uncover this motif in the warp and woof of my life.

I had been living this mission like a vow, which oriented me to something larger than myself, to the whole of humanity. And today, with this book, my legacy is extended into transmitting information about consciousness in late life.

Stepping back, I also see that my life was not a string of unrelated events, a series of random changes or unnecessary sufferings that left me empty-handed. Rather, something larger was at work in me and beyond me—this thread, purpose, mission, dharma, Tao, whatever we call it—and I was following it, unknowingly, all along. If I listened and obeyed, it held me and carried me across threshold after threshold.

To put it differently, as Mick Jagger crooned, "You can't always get what you want. But if you try sometimes, well, you just might find you get what you need."

The Shadow's Life Review

What Was Repressed

The ego's story, the hero's journey, is the conscious tale we tell ourselves. But as we know from Freud and Jung, as the ego develops, a lot of material gets buried in the shadow. In fact, what is not expressed gets repressed. So, as we live out our life, another story is running beneath the threshold of awareness, which Jung called the unlived life. And because the task of late life is not to reinforce the ego with our accomplishments but to connect with something larger, our life review needs to uncover those unlived shadow figures that have been secretly writing our stories and blocking the transition of role to soul.

A broader, deeper life review links the story of our conscious life with the story that's been running beneath conscious awareness—our unexpressed feelings, unexplored gifts, and unlived shadow figures, including their archetypal forms. It adds a whole new dimension to the traditional life review: We look not only backward and forward but above and beneath the boundary of ego awareness, creating a panoramic 360-degree view of our lives.

This 360-degree view may uncover those places where we got stuck, where our development stalled, and a rite of passage failed. It may reveal unconscious identifications that kept us stuck in past, limiting roles. And it may show us those sacrifices in which we lost essential parts of ourselves to the shadow. This kind of life review can be a portal to depth and presence.

Then, if we choose to, we can reclaim from the shadow specific material that we want to express now—new identities, mythic patterns, creative gifts—to enrich this stage. Or we can work to make peace with ourselves and with *what is*.

So, I ask you to return to your horizontal sheet of paper with your decade-by-decade time line. Begin with the first decade, looking at an event you've listed above the line—the level of conscious awareness. Ask yourself: For that to be expressed, what had to be repressed? Then write down that repressed trait, feeling, or action below the line—in the shadow. And pose this question with each key event.

Here's a simplification: The ego and shadow typically develop opposite qualities, so if one trait or tendency is cultivated, such as academic performance and identification with being smart, the opposite will be banished into the shadow, such as fear of not knowing and looking stupid. If independence is praised in the family, dependency may be forbidden. If kindness or politeness is demanded, anger may be punished and vanquished into the dark. If happiness is praised, sadness becomes taboo. If artistic talent is accepted but athletic talent is not, then it goes into the shadow.

I'll continue with an example from my life. During my twenties, when I primarily practiced and taught meditation, two major kinds of development went into the shadow. First, I didn't focus on building a career, so I wasn't building skills to find a place in the world. And I was banishing money into the shadow. The desires and abilities that go with career building—the desire for power, status, money, impact—were not expressed, so they were repressed.

Second, I wasn't focused on building relationship skills. Without a relational focus, I wasn't engaging emotional development, learning how to explore my feelings or share them with a partner. Of course, I had friendships. But I wasn't learning the tools needed to build a safe, trusting, intimate, lasting relationship—how to express needs, how to listen deeply, how to be vulnerable, how to be emotionally accountable. Those abilities were repressed.

Anyone who, like me, did spirituality first, then career and family later, may have similar shadow issues. Ken Wilber called this a "spiritual bypass": We skipped stages of growth, believing we could get beyond them by "transcending" them. But in that way, we derailed our development.

Now, focusing on one decade, see if you can link your ego's story in that decade to your shadow's story during that time. What was expressed? What was repressed?

If you identify that connection, can you see it as a shadow character, with a name and image? For example, I lived out the spiritual Seeker with such singular-minded commitment that I rejected the archetype of the feminine, and the Girlfriend/Wife/Mother was banished into my shadow. I lived the myth of enlightenment; I longed for spiritual awakening only.

Today, as a wife, stepmother, and grandmother, I can open the invitation to what was unlived and reclaim and redesign those roles and qualities for myself.

If you had a family early, how did that determine what was expressed and what was repressed? If you had a high-powered career, how did that determine what was expressed and what was repressed? Can you now say yes to something that you said no to before and, in that way, alter your late life from the inside out?

If you resonate with archetypes, see if you can detect the mythic level of the story that's playing out. Because of my early years, I didn't identify with my apparently powerless mother but became a father's daughter and eventually lived out the story of the Greek goddess Athena—a fierce, independent warrior born from her father's head.

If you're not familiar with the Greek archetypes, use other terms that speak to you, such as Hero, Caregiver, Victim, Lover, Mother, Tyrant, Inner Child. If you spent decades as the Caregiver, what was repressed? If you lived the myth of the Victim, what was repressed?

Take the time to slowly and gently recall each decade. Then look to see how each contributes to your whole life story, lived and unlived. It's as if you're standing in the twilight, gathering the fruit of your life.

When you've had time to fully review your lived and unlived lives, see if you can detect an overall thread—your soul's mission in this life, your higher purpose or *dharma*. This can help you reorient from the ego's midlife agenda to a deeper purpose in late life. It can help you witness your story from on high, rather than get lost in identification with it.

When the threads of the story are connected and the tapestry revealed, we can see our lives with a 360-degree view—backward and forward, above and beneath. Some people feel a certain sense of inevitability about how their journey unfolded, a sense that it couldn't have happened any other way. If we completed the developmental tasks, our key transitions became sacred passages, key people left their gifts with us and we digested them, and our heartbreaking encounters with the shadow became initiations into soul, then we became who we were meant to be.

Ultimately, at the level of soul, we are not our stories. The narrative self, which constantly tells these stories and unconsciously identifies with them, is not the spiritual essence of who we are. When we meditate and listen to our mental chatter—stories about the past or the future, stories about who we are or who we are not—we can begin to detect shadow characters and their agendas. We can learn to listen from a more spacious silence, from pure awareness.

When we witness the noise for long enough, we can begin to break our identification with the stories of the narrative self or shadow characters that have lived the hero's myth, the romantic myth, the victim myth, or the caregiver myth. And we can begin to identify with pure awareness, moving beyond ego to a more spiritual identity. In this way, a life review can help us complete the ego's story and go beyond it. To include and transcend it. A life review can be a portal to soul.

An Interview with Father Thomas Keating, Founder of Centering Prayer

When I interviewed the late Father Thomas Keating at the age of ninety-five, from St. Benedict's monastery in Snowmass, Colorado, he looked back on his life in the context of his changing relationship with the divine and "a growing consciousness of relationship with the mystery," as he put it. The conversation was a spiritual life review, although we didn't call it that, because for him that was the primary thread in the tapestry.

At the age of five, Thomas had had a life-threatening illness and heard the doctor say that he might die. So, he made a bargain with God: "Let me live to twenty-one, and I'll become a priest."

As he recovered, he would sneak out of the house in the early mornings, before his parents awoke, to go to mass. He loved these secret visits and joyfully watched the monks "talking to God." Gradually, he disconnected from worldly concerns and knew that he, too, wanted to be a monk. He wanted to keep his promise to God.

His parents were dismayed, hoping he would become a lawyer and create financial security for a family. This created a rift for many years, as Thomas felt unsupported in his vocation.

As a young man at Yale, he read Tolstoy's controversial views of the Catholic Church and became disillusioned, realizing that it was not teaching the real Gospels. He delved into the mystics, St. Teresa, St. John of the Cross, and the Desert Fathers, and he discovered ancient Christian contemplative practices, which seemed to have been lost since the Reformation. This discovery would open a way for him.

In his first spontaneous spiritual experience, Thomas felt "surrounded and penetrated by a powerful love." He saw that on his land the hay, the trees, the heat were emerging out of this reality. And it was all that mattered. The perception of That was all that mattered. Everything else lost meaning for him.

Thomas learned transcendental meditation and discovered pure awareness, a taste of silence. "Silence is God's first language," he told me. "Just keep quiet and find this out."

Slowly, he became more austere and eventually chose to become a Trappist, giving up contact with his parents and the outside world. Thomas felt their anguish, he told me, but needed to follow his calling.

At St. Joseph's Abbey, where he served as abbot, Thomas found that many people failed to mature emotionally and intellectually because they had missed developmental steps and couldn't integrate the spiritual energies that arose. He explained to me, "We can have a mystical experience at any stage of development. But if we have no guidance and no practice to heal our early emotional wounds, that energy is not digested. If you have high graces and mystical unions, but other lines of development are incomplete, then the shadow will appear even as you move forward spiritually."

Thomas told me, "God calls us to interiority through the purification of unconscious traumatic wounds." From my point of view, he was affirming that our emotional suffering can lead us to therapy and self-reflection, as well as to spiritual practice.

For him, this understanding meant that he needed to reconcile with his father. Eventually his father came to accept his son's life choice and offered financial support for the monastery. "I saw new parts of him then. And I saw my own failure to forgive him, even feel concern for him. I had wanted him to change the script. But through this reconciliation with my father, I realized why forgiveness is at the center of Christianity."

When I asked Thomas about the purpose of long life, he said, "It gives us the opportunity to see ourselves with deeper honesty and transparency, to see through the false self. It's different from St. Benedict's time in the sixth century, when the elders were forty. With ninety years, we can do purification and uncover unitive states. We can use old age for contemplative prayer, to surrender the ego, and abandon ourselves to God's will.

"Spirit works in us when we let go of the obstacles to It," he continued. "It's not about earning God's love. It's about looking inwardly for divine presence and allowing God's love to flow into us. It's always present, just hidden under debris. It's not an image or a concept. It's being free of thought, becoming everything. It's the reverse of a hero's success story."

In this context, the things we give up or the things we might do are unimportant, I thought. Our personal history is unimportant. He continued: "The experience of God absorbs your faculties. Awareness without content is home. And the construction of a separate self is the radical problem of humanity."

In 1984, drawing on ancient Christian practices with two other Trappist monks, Father Thomas founded Contemplative Outreach, an interdenominational community of people practicing centering prayer, in which a person chooses a word or symbol "to turn our will toward God and rest in the presence of that which is."

Thomas urges us to move beyond method to a relationship with the divine. "It begins in prayer and meditation, it weaves itself into activity, and eventually we see it in everything. Then we feel awake in aliveness, as if we're embraced and held by God."

He also "transcended the bounds of the Church" by entering world religious dialogue. "I wanted to use Catholic doctrine to speak universally. I saw Nature as the Book of Revelation—infinitesimal and immense. The spiritual journey does not require going anywhere because God is already with us and in us."

Years later, no longer abbot, Thomas was free to meditate, write, and teach, becoming a Spiritual Elder and modeling an inclusive, nondogmatic, mystical Christian way. "The gift of living long enough is to pass through the phases of human development to higher levels of unitive consciousness. This gift has been given to us," he told me. "It just is. We can bring ourselves into relationship with this reality. The only condition is consent—say yes."

Father Thomas lived his vow: to move into intimate relationship with the reality of the divine. He passed away while I was writing this piece. Many teachers and practitioners now carry on his work of teaching centering prayer.

We have moved far beyond the traditional life review. We have moved from telling our conscious tales to reframing them with new eyes. We have moved from detecting our unconscious tales to reclaiming them in late life. And we have moved from identification with past stories and their wounds, past roles and their limits, toward identifying with soul.

At the deepest level, we are not our stories. We are not what we do—or what is done to us. But the shift in identity from story to soul is a radical one. Letting go of our stories runs against the cultural grain. Elders everywhere today are writing memoirs and recording videos. And when they say "I'll live on in people's memories," they mean their stories will live on.

So, this shift may be aspirational. But in the next chapter, we'll explore how we might make it manifest.

Of course, in pursuing a life review, some of us may not find the thread hiding beneath the stories of victory and defeat, gain and loss, suffering and well-being, meaning and meaninglessness. We may continue to feel sorrow or regret about how our lives turned out. We may grieve that we have not fully lived.

So, let's continue with life repair to reclaim what was banished into the shadow, take responsibility for our choices, speak our truths, forgive ourselves and others, realign our values, and make meaning for this time of life, here and now.

Shadow-Work Practices

🍁 Ego's Life Review

- What is an early formative experience that shaped your later life?
- What is a less obvious, more hidden event that led inevitably to your unique journey?
- How did your body's story unfold?
- How did your mind develop and change over the years?
- How did your heart open and close over the years?
- How has suffering become your teacher?

🍁 Shadow's Life Review

- Which shadow character in you wants to avoid examining the past? What is it telling you?
- Which shadow character ruminates about the past without distilling wisdom?
- Who is the critical voice that creates regret or "If only . . ." statements about the past?
- What essential part of you had to be repressed for your personality to develop in the way that it did?
- What do you want to reclaim from the shadow to rewrite your story now?

Spiritual Practices

🍁 Spiritual Life Review

- What is the myth that you have lived?
- What were your key spiritual experiences over the years?
- What is your soul's mission or the vow that you have lived?
- Following your life review, can you see the evolution of your soul through new eyes?

7

Emotional and Creative Repair to Release the Past and Live in the Present

The Cracked Water Pot: An Indian Tale

A water bearer in India had two large pots, each hanging on one end of a pole, which he carried across his neck. One pot was perfect and delivered a full portion of water after the long walk from the stream to the master's house. The other pot had a crack in it and leaked, so that it always arrived half full.

For two years the bearer delivered only one and a half pots of water to the master. Of course, the perfect pot was proud of its accomplishments. The cracked pot was ashamed of its imperfection and miserable that it was able to accomplish only half of what it had been made to do.

It spoke to the water bearer one day by the stream: "I want to apologize to you."

"Why?" the man said.

"I am only able to deliver half of my load because this crack in my side causes a leak. Because of my flaw, you do all this work and don't get the value of your effort."

The water bearer responded, "As we return to the master's house, notice the beautiful flowers along the road. Do you see that there are flowers only on your side of the path? Because I knew your flaw, I took advantage of it and planted seeds on your side of the path. You've watered them every day. And I've been able to pick them to decorate the master's table. Without you being just as you are, he would not have this beauty to grace his house."

—Adapted from a folktale cited by Judith Helburn
in her "Making Peace with Death and Dying" course

Like the cracked water pot in the story, we each have a flaw, a crack, a shadow. We are vessels with imperfections, wounds, and regrets.

Our injuries and wounds can leave us feeling disoriented, lost, and without meaning. But they also initiate our longing and bring us into therapy or self-reflection. It is our suffering and imperfections that turn us toward something greater than ourselves and bring us to spiritual practice. So, the wound sets us on the path of awareness.

Our wounds are openings that make us vulnerable to others. Our wounds also give us empathy, allowing us to walk beside others. Our wounds can bring shadow awareness, revealing a deeper self-knowledge and a portal to the soul.

Following a life review and gaining a 360-degree perspective, we can slowly see how our "severe teachers," those people who betrayed us and broke our hearts, and those events that disappointed us and left us without hope, shaped a story that we have told ourselves over and over again. Whether the person who hurt us was a parent, spouse, child, friend, or mentor, that hurt formed within us a shadow character that gripped the wound perhaps for many years—and may still keep us locked into the past.

"I was a victim of my father's anger." "I was abandoned when my mother went to work." "My brother bullied me." "After I married Will, he changed." "My best friend betrayed me." "When I got sick, God abandoned me." "My son broke my heart." "My minister lied to all of us." "My guru was a hypocrite."

For many of us, these wounds remain open, even raw. Years later, we are still identifying with the story of a wound and continue to burn with resentment against those who failed us. We continue to rage in fury against those who abused us. We continue to judge and blame others. Our vitality is sapped as these feelings remain unresolved and get pushed, again and again, into the shadow. Our relationships are fractured. Our creative impulses are blocked. And our open, broken hearts do not mend.

On the other hand, we may carry in our shadows guilt and regret about how we failed others, or how we treated our parents, spouses, or children, or how we did not live up to our own internal standards and failed ourselves.

But no one teaches us how to reconcile these feelings and forgive ourselves and others so that we can move toward closure. No one teaches us how to look back on our lives to reframe the story, break our identification with the Victim shadow character, break the projection onto the Victimizer, and reorient toward reconciliation.

Now, in late life, mortality awareness urges us toward life repair. We fear becoming dependent on people who feel hurt by, resentful toward, or angry at us. We fear dying without fully expressing our feelings and attempting to be understood. We fear dying without attempting to give and receive forgiveness with loved ones. We fear dying with that ache in our heart.

Research confirms that this desire for emotional repair in late life is widespread. Laura Carstensen of the Stanford Center on Longevity studies the links between our perceptions of future time and our motivations to achieve goals. When time is seen as open-ended, she found, we want to experience learning and novelty. When time is seen as limited, we prioritize deepening and reconciling emotional relationships (see her 2006 *Science* article).

Emotional repair follows naturally from a life review, which enables us to see where we suffered disappointment, hurt, shame, and anger, which may lie dormant in our shadows and keep us locked in the past. With life repair, we can begin to heal the wounds that fester and find forgiveness, even a sense of resolution, whether with a family member, friend, clergy, or teacher. When we let go of the past, we are free to be present to our lives now in a richer, more authentic way. We are free to become Elders.

Of course, for some people in the face of this challenge, denial rears its head: "I could never speak to him about that." Or "It happened so long ago, who cares?" Or "She's dead now, so it doesn't matter." This is another inner obstacle: We identify with regret or feel like a victim of the past, thereby losing the opportunity to free ourselves by giving and receiving forgiveness.

We can move past this denial to see the possibility that we can, to some degree, create compassionate closure for ourselves and others. We can reframe "negative" events when we examine them from a 360-degree view. We can begin to see how a loss led us in a different direction, how a rejection or disappointment opened another door, or even how a betrayal initiated us into another stage of awareness.

If we are fortunate, we can even begin to see the gifts of our wounds and the beauty of our cracks—and even the beauty in the cracks of others. We begin to see how our wounds gave us our uniqueness—how the light shines in through them.

We may feel an urgency to break the pattern of wounding for future generations. For example, if as children we were not seen, and we recognize that wound, now we can strive to see deeply into our own children and grandchildren, to see them as we wish we would have been seen. If as children we were abandoned, and we recognize that wound, now we can attempt to hold commitments sacred, to remind our loved ones that we are available to them. If as teens our boundaries were violated, and we recognize that wound, now we can respect the boundaries of others with reverence. If as spouses we were not heard, and we recognize that wound, now we can listen deeply to the next generation, and tell them that we hear them, thereby breaking the family pattern. For some of us, after decades of inner work, our wounds can be made sacred.

We may not be able to perfectly resolve everything with everybody.

But we may be able to move toward acknowledging both the possibilities and the limits of life repair. And that alone can bring us acceptance.

These developmental tasks of life repair move us toward the threshold of becoming an Elder. They lighten the long bag of shadow material that we carry into late life, freeing us to be more fully here now. And they hold the promise of breaking our identification with the wound, the Victim shadow, and turning us toward soul.

Emotional Repair

Reinventing Relationships from Role to Soul

Many years ago, before I had deeply explored shadow-work, I read an essay by archetypal psychologist James Hillman that was brilliant and shocking. The essay, "Betrayal" (published in *Senex and Puer*), was so memorable that it has stayed with me all these years later. In it, Hillman tells the story of a father who was teaching his son courage by having him jump down from progressively higher stairs, promising to catch him each time. The boy jumped, the father caught him. The boy jumped, the father caught him again. Then the boy jumped from a very high step—but the father moved back, and the boy fell on his face. As the young one picked himself up, bleeding and crying, the father said, "That will teach you never to trust . . . even if it's your own father."

To explore emotional wounding, Hillman poses these questions: Why must a boy be taught not to trust? And not to trust his own father? What does it mean to be betrayed by one's father or by someone else close to us? On the other hand, what does it mean for a person to betray someone who trusts him or her?

As he was known to do, Hillman takes our conventional assumptions and turns them upside down. Before betrayal, he writes, we live in unconscious primal trust: The ground is safe, the sky won't fall, the sun will rise. Like the image of God, the image of father to a child is stable, reliable, and safe. This innocent stage of our development, for Hillman, is eternal youth, or *puer aeternus,* like the archetype of Peter Pan.

But, he writes, "we are betrayed in the very same close relationships where primal trust is possible. We can be truly betrayed only where we truly trust—by brothers, lovers, wives, husbands, not by enemies, not by strangers. The greater the love, the greater the betrayal. Trust has in it the seed of betrayal."

After betrayal—when the promise is broken, when the violence erupts, when the secret is told, when the Betrayer is revealed—we are initiated into the shadow. "The father willingly shifts from the ego's commitment to stand by his word . . . to deliberately allowing the dark side to manifest itself in and through him." So, the boy is thrown out of the Garden, his innocence lost, his trust betrayed. The naive youth dies, and the young man with shadow awareness is born.

Hillman cautions us that after betrayal, we may retreat into denial, attempting to forget abusive moments; or we may seek revenge, the Victim blaming and pursuing the Victimizer; or we may take refuge in cynicism, losing all ideals and hope for loving bonds. We may even fall into paranoia, attempting to control others so that their flaws will be contained, such as by becoming strict moralists or demanding loyalty oaths.

Conversely, we may be taken over by our own inner Betrayer, acting in the same cruel ways and thereby betraying ourselves. In other words, instead of identifying with the powerlessness of the Victim, we identify with the power of the Perpetrator and treat others abusively, continuing the pattern.

Human development from primal trust through betrayal to forgiveness, Hillman suggests, involves a movement of consciousness. We grow from unconscious innocence into our suffering to the death of the eternal youth and the integration of shadow in maturity.

For many of us, these moments of betrayal lie locked away in a vault outside of awareness for decades. When we do life review and life repair in late life, we can shine the light of awareness on them, set them in the context of our life span, and possibly see them with a 360-degree view. This is the next step on the path toward life completion.

So, let's begin, as always, by taking a few breaths and sitting down inside yourself in presence. When your mind is quiet and alert, choose an adult wound that you suffered at the hands of a "severe teacher" or a Victimizer—a parent, spouse, friend, child, mentor, spiritual teacher— and write down that story in the way that you've always told it: as the Victim.

The Victim's point of view of the event is clear: You were innocent, and someone hurt you, disappointed you, harmed you in some way. You didn't deserve it. And you were powerless to prevent it. So, you blame him or her, you hold a grudge, you feel self-righteous. The shadow character of the Victim tells the same story again and again without being able to mend it.

Next, return to your life review and set this painful moment in the context of what followed: How did your life direction change from this event? Which doors opened, and which closed? Which people appeared, and which disappeared? What did you learn about yourself or others? How did it change you?

My client, Suzanne, at the age of sixty, married Dan, who was sixty-two, after dating for six months. They had never had any major conflicts, and they shared a love of sailing and of their grandchildren. She had already been through a rocky divorce earlier in her life, but she felt safe and familiar with Dan and told me that their values were aligned.

Then, one night, she came home an hour later than he had expected her. When she entered the room, Dan screamed, "You don't care about anyone but yourself. You don't care about my dinner. You always have to do things your way. I don't know if I can be married to you."

Suzanne went into shock. She felt betrayed; this was not the way Dan had presented himself during dating. Frightened, she felt like a Victim.

After several days, he calmed down and revealed to her that his rage had destroyed his last relationship. Suzanne felt betrayed again because he had kept this a secret from her. She insisted that they go to therapy.

Dan was not aware that he was emotionally triggered by an abandonment wound. He just knew that, at times, he raged in a childlike tantrum in an effort to be heard and seen by his partner. Because Dan had never learned to communicate his needs from his adult self, he just criticized and blamed Suzanne for his intense feelings. Beneath the rage, shame remained hidden.

In response, Suzanne froze, growing cold and shut down, because she was being retraumatized, experiencing her own childhood injury from her father's rage. She was thrown back into a Victim shadow, unconsciously ashamed that she felt so small and powerless.

Her response was the opposite of Dan's hopes for an empathic understanding of his frustration and feeling of unimportance. So, he felt like a Victim, too. Both felt betrayed—and shocked to see the Betrayer in the other, whom they thought was safe.

They decided that they would stay together for at least another six months to do couples therapy and learn some tools for communicating. Eventually, they committed to another six months, then another. Slowly, over several years, Dan learned to use inner child work and meditation to soothe his wounded Abandoned Child, rather than project onto his wife the Good Mother, who was obligated to nurture him in the way that his own mother did not. This led him onto a path of slowly developing his own autonomy, passions, and friendships apart from the relationship. And, as he moved into emotional adulthood, his shame lessened. In addition, he learned to speak about his emotional needs to Suzanne as an adult, with "I" statements, thereby ending the blame game.

Suzanne discovered the depth and complexity of human nature, sacrificing her dream of an ideal husband, who would never be angry and always be kind and generous, to live a more nuanced, adult understanding of Dan and herself, of both their wounds and their gifts. After she understood that she had been traumatized because his rage reenacted her own childhood with her father, she felt less like a Victim in present time. And after she felt the pain of her husband's early abandonment, she was able to open her heart in compassion toward him. She was so moved by their journey of emotional repair that she left her job and entered graduate school in psychology to learn to support other couples.

This betrayal, in which the shadow acted out early childhood wounds in each of them, could have broken the vessel of their marriage, as it does for many couples. But, instead, it led them on a path of late-life individuation, a path of growing up. Eventually, they could see the Victim and Victimizer in each of them, so the shadow projection was broken. They learned to take responsibility for their own shadow characters and to communicate in their adult voices. In this way, the relationship became a vehicle for their evolution—and reoriented each of them from role to Victim to soul.

After two years, they were able to perform a shadow marriage, vowing to honor and cherish all parts of one another and of themselves. But without that first initiation into shadow, they may have lived a superficial, role-based marriage for a long time. And their attempts to forgive one another would not have arisen from this depth of compassion.

A similar dynamic is evident in many couples: One repeatedly criticizes, and the other cheats. Or one overworks, and the other drinks. Which shadow characters are cause, and which are effect? Each wound has the potential to initiate the partners into their own and the other's shadow. Each wound has the potential to lift them out of fixed roles and into a fluid soul dynamic whose intention is ever-growing awareness. With a conscious relationship, the cracks in the pot are watering new growth.

An opportunity to complete unfinished emotional business may arise while caregiving a parent. Rene, at the age of fifty-two, was at the peak of her career. Then her parents, in their eighties, began to have serious health issues. While her mother was depressed and resistant to advice or assistance, Rene was surprised to find her father receptive to her suggestions. An internist, he had always radiated a remote superiority. In addition, he had had a long-term secret affair that had devastated the family.

Rene learned to practice presence with her father, to move more at his pace and to reflect slowly on their decisions. She let go of trying to fix things, especially her mother's depression. As she drove him to appointments and helped to write the family's living trust, she told me, her father was more real and more authentic with her than he had ever been. And, for the first time, they were able to discuss the way in which her father had lied to the family and betrayed them. He suffered from terrible guilt, a profound burden near the end of his life. As he imagined his death, he asked her for forgiveness.

In conversation with me, Rene acknowledged that her ego couldn't forgive him because his behavior had been so immoral and had affected so many people's lives. But as her intimacy grew with him in his vulnerability, so did her compassion. And she felt less like a Victim of his behavior with their growing openness and his imminent mortality.

In the end, Rene came to understand that her father's marriage to her mother must have been lonely and unfulfilling. She could see him, then, not as her heroic, idealized father but as a suffering human being. She could see his own inner Victim, as well as the family Victimizer. Rene and her father continued their open, authentic conversation until his death.

An Interview with
Jungian Analyst James Hollis

When I interviewed psychiatrist and Jungian analyst James Hollis, who was then seventy-eight, he described a daily life of morning meditation, seeing patients, teaching, and writing. He had just published his fifteenth book, *Living an Examined Life*, in which he explores how to complete our unfinished business. He refers to this accountability for our own wounds as "growing up," taking responsibility for the choices we make and the ways that they shape our lives. He summarized his principles for me, which are guidelines for emotional repair in late life.

"It's *now* time to pay attention. How much of your behavior is in service to old defenses that bind you to a disempowering past? It's *now* time to recover personal authority: What's true for you really? And to find the courage to live that truth.

"It's *now* time to make amends. Ask others where you have injured them, and vow to change those behaviors.

"Reflect on where you're stuck, identify the task you need to address, and choose the path of enlargement, not the path that diminishes you.

"Free your children from your unlived life, from your expectations that they ratify your values. And release them as you wished to be released from the dreams of your parents.

"Construct a mature spirituality. What is your connection to what is larger than you? And seize permission to be who you really are."

Finally, Jim commented on the urgency to break through our denial of mortality. "I'm continuing to live fully in the presence of mortality. This is not morbid," he said. "It only seems that way because we are separate from nature. Mortality makes meaning possible, not perpetuity. It makes our choices matter."

In other words, mortality awareness is a central task of life repair on the way to life completion.

❦ ❦

There are many circumstances in which we cannot do emotional repair with another person. Perhaps he or she is unwilling, or unable to communicate, or has died. When Patty's husband, Greg, died suddenly of a heart attack at age seventy-two, she came to my office with an excruciating mix of emotions: shock, grief, fear, disorientation—and relief. It had been an unhappy marriage for twenty years, in which she accommodated and placated him, giving up her independent thinking and personal agency in exchange for financial security and the familiar role of Accommodator, which began in her early life.

Patty insisted to me that they had loved one another but, sadly, didn't have the emotional stability or the tools to work through their painful issues. As a result, Greg demanded what he wanted: Give up your desire to travel because I can't. Give up your friends because I don't like them. Give up your holidays with family and stay with me. And the Accommodator shadow character in her just said yes. When she tried to say no, Greg was so critical and rejecting that she felt hurt and gave up.

Now, at sixty-four, Patty felt devastated by the loss of her husband and the familiarity of their marriage. Yes, she lost someone to nurture. Yes, she lost her home, too. And it would take some time of grieving for the shock to recede. It would take some time to overcome the guilt about her complicated feelings. And it would take some time for his critical voice, ringing within her, to recede.

But for the first time in her life, she had also gained the opportunity to break this insidious pattern and grow up. When she told me that she planned to drive across the country to see her son, I suggested that she do it as a pilgrimage to her soul, following her own impulses from moment to moment, making her own choices, discovering her own flow. It was such a foreign idea to her that she said, "It's hard to imagine doing this without someone to follow, without someone to please."

When she returned from the long, solitary drive, Patty told me, "I faced my fears. It wasn't easy, but I can be alone now. I can hear my inner voice, even when Greg's voice criticizes me inside my mind. I'm not buying it now. I'm terribly sad, but I'm reclaiming the power and independence that I lost in my marriage. I'm not the Accommodator anymore."

Initiation into Shadow

My hope is that now you can see your betrayals as initiations into shadow. In that framework, you still suffered a painful loss, which shouldn't be minimized. But now you may be able to see the gain. You still suffered a humbling defeat, but now you may be able to detect a victory. You still suffered an ending, but now, in retrospect, you may see that a beginning emerged there, too.

You are no longer the Victim in this story. You can let go of your identification with this unconscious shadow character, who keeps you in a powerless, childlike position. You can step into a more accountable adult self. That means, for example, that you see clearly that you could have left, but you chose to stay. You could have gotten help, but you chose to go it alone. You could have created better boundaries, but you chose self-sacrifice.

In each case, you made a fundamental choice, whether you were aware of it or not at the time. In each case, you probably forgot about your own choice and slipped into blame and resentment, the roots of the Victim.

Now you may be able to see your portion of the responsibility, the way in which your shadow character colluded with the other person's shadow, creating this painful situation. And that means, from this vantage point, that the Betrayer is no longer the Victimizer. Rather than clinging to this terrible image of opposites—Victim and Victimizer—you can end blame by reclaiming the shadow you've projected onto him or her.

You may be able, at some time in the future, to see the hurt child in this other person who hurt you. You may be able to trace back generations of hurt, an ancestral line of those who carried the same flaw—the same Abandoner, Liar, Cheater, Addict, Critic. And you may able to become so aware of the flaws in you and in the Other that you can vow to break the chain here and now, for future generations.

Eventually, you can reframe the hurtful event and see that the one who betrayed you is the one who initiated you out of naivete and into shadow, into the complexity of human nature, and into the profound alliance of opposites.

Just as the seeds of betrayal lie in primal trust, as Hillman pointed out, the seeds of the Victim are in the Victimizer. And the seeds of the Victimizer are in the Victim. None of us is without shadow. And this insight breaks the projection. We are no longer innocent, while the Other is guilty; we are no longer good, while the Other is bad. This new stage of awareness, in late life, is a developmental leap.

This profound shift brings with it another insight: The past is structured in consciousness. We view events in time through subjective filters that are colored by our level of awareness. The past is not a frozen object somewhere behind us. Our view of it and our relationship to it are fluid, depending on the quality of our awareness. This insight can free us of guilt, regret, and resentment about past events if we reframe them with shadow-work.

It offers a picture of "post-traumatic growth," the possibility of finding a positive outcome—enhanced resilience, deepened empathy, the end of blame, a full view of the Other's humanity—from a negative emotional crisis. One outcome might be a widened lens through which we see that our perception of reality is a projection of our own mind. Many of us have had that insight in a meditative breakthrough or through the use of psychedelics.

Finally, we attempt to see a personally painful event from a 360-degree view, from the vantage point of the soul's journey. From the ego's point of view, the drama is real. But from the soul's point of view, the drama is grist for the mill to work out our issues. The soul is not here to be right or even to be rid of suffering. The soul is here only to learn—that is, to gain awareness.

A caveat is needed here: These concepts are not meant to rationalize or excuse physical or emotional abuse; they are not intended to say that hurtful behavior was not wrong or that any cruel or criminal behavior can be reframed. And it certainly doesn't apply to childhood physical or sexual abuse, in which children are truly innocent, not just naive.

I'm aware of my own fortunate life, the privilege I have enjoyed as a White woman in the West. I have suffered my own share of trauma and grief, but it pales when compared to so many around the world who have experienced such profound harm and deprivation.

But if you are reading this book, you have the inclination and the capacity to repair your past. And you have the capacity to see that betrayal, as initiation, has the potential to open a portal to shadow awareness and to soul. It can open our heart wider than the ego could ever imagine—both to others and to ourselves.

Now, only now, we are ready to cross the threshold to forgiveness. We have stepped out of our identification with the Victim shadow character, who is locked in blame. We have stepped out of the ego's point of view, which is locked in being right.

Forgiveness does not arise from the shadow or ego. It arises from the soul.

And a lack of forgiveness in our hearts—holding on to a grudge, resentment, or feeling of anger—hurts us as much as it hurts our betrayer. Rabbi Zalman was fond of saying that the refusal to forgive someone is like stabbing yourself in the stomach to hurt the person standing behind you. This is a startling image, but it makes clear that Victim and Victimizer are joined, in perpetuity, by the absence of forgiveness.

Forgiveness is not forgetting an event; it's not condoning; it's not a passive assent. It's an active letting go, sometimes over years, as we bear the pain and grief and allow our soul to turn gently toward peace. Forgiveness is an eventual acceptance of another's shadow parts, or our own, as part of that soul's journey.

Viewing betrayal as initiation and forgiveness as a movement in the soul allows us to see the hand of fate at work in our lives. Whether or not we forgive a person who abused or betrayed us, we can be reconciled with an event as an initiatory process. For a rare few, this allows us, in late life, to look with a 360-degree view and embrace our fate—without false hope or childlike illusions and without hopelessness or despair. It allows us to align with larger, invisible forces that carry us, like the wind, through this human lifetime.

Reimagining Kübler-Ross's Stages of Grief

With aging, a key part of emotional repair is learning how to live with our grief. As the losses keep coming, whether from divorce, illness, the passing of our beloveds, the loss of a home, a career, a role, we begin to inhabit grief. Or does it inhabit us?

If grieving does not happen consciously, if we don't turn to face our lost loved ones, unmade choices, and unopened invitations, then our sorrows remain hidden in the shadow. Their meanings remain secret. And we are blind to the full range of human life, unable to ripen into adulthood.

Like aging in general, grief is an individual, subjective journey. It's not a tidy, linear road with a beginning and end, with a right and wrong way to do it. It happens in contexts: alone, with families, with support groups. It happens whether or not we hold religious or spiritual beliefs, and without regard for our economic, social, familial, or cultural circumstances.

Thankfully, Elisabeth Kübler-Ross, in her work on death and dying and, subsequently, on grief, drew a map for us. It's not a set of steps but a pattern of stages that can help us identify and understand our feelings through the process of grieving:

1. Denial
2. Anger
3. Bargaining
4. Depression
5. Acceptance

As I sat with my own grief one afternoon—climate grief, democracy grief, and personal, aching sorrow—I realized that I needed to add another dimension to her framework. I'm not redrawing the map but incorporating the portals of shadow awareness, pure awareness, and mortality awareness to expand and deepen the landscape. It's as if the map was drawn before we did the inner work of age and had a 360-degree view of our lives.

1. Denial

Denial has been a central theme throughout this book. It's buried within every inner obstacle to the shift from role to soul. But the psychological defense of denial also has a value: It gives us time to adjust to shocking news, a diagnosis, a loss. Just as we titrate a medication to the right dose so that our bodies adjust, we titrate our awareness with denial. We avoid the full truth for a while; we distract ourselves with less weighty things. And it helps us acclimate by allowing in only so much information and only so much emotion.

When we can begin to attune to our feelings and inner voices, from the shadow we hear, "No, it can't be true. Maybe the doctors are wrong and it's something else." "No, he can't be leaving me now. Who am I without him?" And we detect denial.

In many cases, hidden within our experiences of grief and loss lies denial of mortality awareness. Loss reminds us of our own short time horizons; grief echoes with our own deaths. "It's not my time." "I don't have limits." "My mother lived to a hundred."

2. Anger

When anger wells up, the shadow looks for a target to blame: "It's her fault." "It's that surgeon. He messed up." "It's my boss. He's ageist." "I hate God. He's so unfair."

But beneath this secondary emotion lie deeper, more vulnerable feelings of fear, abandonment, frustration, and betrayal. In our helplessness, our inability to control a situation that seems out of control, anger gives us a momentary sense of power. It energizes the Fighter in us and can motivate us to act on our own or another's behalf.

Anger also blinds us to mortality awareness. As adrenaline sweeps through the body, we don't feel the vulnerability and deeper truth of limitations and death.

3. Bargaining

At this stage, we are telling the story of our loss in an effort to find meaning in it. We are negotiating with doctors, loved ones, or higher powers to change the outcome that we've been given. The shadow says,

"If only . . . then I will . . . " When you detect this quiet, prayerful voice, you are in a moment of bargaining.

For some people, beneath the negotiation, self-blame lies dormant. If we are carrying unconscious guilt and secretly blame ourselves, we are bargaining to atone for a sin. The shadow, in this case, is targeting the bargainer. And it's essential to tune in to this unconscious process and decide, more consciously, if we are accountable in some way for this situation or if this is an ancient pattern of self-blame in the shadow.

4. *Depression*

Now the Fighter concedes. The Bargainer rests. And we sink into an empty, meaningless moment of despair. The shadow speaks: "Without that job, I'm nothing." "Without her, I'm no one." "There's no future for me now. I'm hopeless."

For some, depression is an appropriate response to a crisis or loss. Overwhelmed with feeling and bereft of meaning, we sink with the heavy weight of the new reality. But it's vital to move through it without getting stuck and allow it, slowly, to alter us. (In *Romancing the Shadow* I wrote extensively about depression as descent to soul—if the descent is done consciously.)

5. *Acceptance*

This is what I call being present with *what is*. We are no longer trying to change it or fix it. At the same time, this is not a passive, impotent response to a situation. Rather, it's an active quality of adjusting to a new reality, along with a deep trust that there is some invisible purpose, some evolutionary direction, hidden in our suffering.

I came to see that the stages of grief describe the steps of a rite of passage: letting go, the struggle to release precious attachments to loved ones, loved objects, and loved belief systems. It requires release of a past reality and its meaning to us.

First we deny, then we feel angry. The anger subsides and we bargain. We plead. Eventually our pleas subside, and we pass into a liminal time in which we float for a while, unmoored from our past reality. This period, between the past and the future, in which our identity and meaning are lost, can be frightening and disorienting. We may feel depressed.

Eventually, we emerge into another reality: The loss is real. We are ill, separated, widowed, retired, caregiving . . . The word *acceptance* doesn't quite imply the full outcome of this rite of passage. *Renewal,* rather, suggests that we have undergone a transformative transition and accepted that we are, now, a different person in a different reality. We are shifting from role to soul.

For grief to initiate us in this way, we need to experience pure awareness. Each loss carries us beyond the ego's control. Each loss carries us toward a sacrifice. With a practice that offers the experience of pure awareness, we can more easily witness our sorrow and disorientation, more easily return to center and remember who we are.

Let's be clear that shadow awareness, pure awareness, and mortality awareness are not "cures" for grief. Rather, they can deepen our journey through grief so that it becomes, like age itself, a rite of passage enabling the evolution of soul.

As author and teacher Jeff Foster put it, "Loss has already transfigured your life into an altar."

An Interview with Psychiatrist Roger Walsh

When I spoke with transpersonal/integral psychiatrist Roger Walsh about his own spiritual practices, he told me that he moved through a sequence of Buddhist practices from Vipassana (mindfulness) to Zen to Vajrayana (Tibetan) to Dzogchen (also Tibetan). "The sequence was essential for me," he said. "It took twenty years of spiritual boot camp before I could practice Dzogchen."

But Roger reminded me that he was always using each moment of life as an opportunity to awaken, including his relationship, work, friendships, and writing. "Anyone who is deeply committed to contemplative practice and to cultivating the qualities it enhances—empathy, compassion, clarity, insight—will want to practice as continuously as possible. This means finding a way to use our daily activities and work as part of our practice. The Hindus call this karma yoga, which aims to turn the act of living into an uninterrupted yoga practice."

He continued, "What really educates us is not more theory or becoming a better doer. It's the internal practice of awakening to ourselves, to our minds, to the nature of reality."

When his wife, Frances Vaughan, passed away in 2019, Roger's grief was disorienting. Aside from losing his beloved, he lost his forty-year practice of intimate relationship. He told me that his meditation was a godsend for dealing with grief. "For many people who are not seasoned meditators, more active practices might be best," he said. "But I was used to sitting, which rubs your nose in mortality. And Frances was older than I am, so when it happened, I was not surprised. But I was shocked—shocked to be alone, to be single again, to be making decisions alone. For a while, it was like walking in a cloud bank."

Five months after Frances died, Roger entered a meditation retreat. He sat with a central pain in his chest, entered into it, and watched his mind spin off into a shadow character: "Poor me. I'm alone now." He recognized that this voice caused a secondary pain due to associative thoughts, and that it was more painful than the primary one.

With meditation, he worked to let this pain be, without his thoughts telling a story about it. Rather than deny it, resist it, or defend against it, he acknowledged the pain and let it be.

Roger also had a spiritual community of friends for support. He told me that his spiritual worldview continued to give him meaning and purpose. And he began a deliberate practice of gratitude, at the beginning and end of each day, "for all of the gifts that remained in my life."

Lost Creativity Found
The Gold in the Dark Side

As we discover from our life review, while our conscious personality develops, we express certain traits, feelings, and talents and don't express others. Those that remain unexpressed get stuffed away into the shadow, creating the "unlived life." But that material is not merely "negative"; our forbidden and unexpressed gifts and talents and our unfulfilled dreams and desires also lie dormant there.

For instance, in some families, athletic gifts are praised and encouraged; in others, they are devalued as trivial or meaningless. In some families, artistic or musical talent is praised and encouraged; in others, it's seen as a waste of time. In some families, academic performance is praised and valued; in others, it's seen as a way of avoiding "real" work. So, if we grow up in a family in which our unique gift is not valued or supported, it gets banished into the dark closet of our minds.

In addition, as adults, our financial and emotional needs may limit our creative expression. Marriage, family, and work may inhibit our creativity by keeping us in narrow roles with few outlets for imagination.

The result: Spontaneous creativity cannot arise naturally from the soul, which always seeks to express itself in innovative ways. But in moments of transition, the barriers to connecting with the creative soul grow thinner and the call to create grows stronger. At midlife, we may stop and reflect on our journey, eventually reclaiming lost creative impulses and exploring new forms of expressions. Facing illness or accident, many people reevaluate their lives in a shortened time horizon and seek to fulfill an unmet dream, such as painting, photography, dance, or writing a novel.

My friend Phil told me that he felt fortunate that he was able to earn a living as an author. However, after writing twenty-five nonfiction books to pay the bills, his long-lost dream, a novel, was calling to him. He had continued to fantasize that it would be a labor of love in his seventies—and it would be the one thing left undone that would lead to regret on his deathbed.

With retirement, too, the soul's longing for self-expression can be unleashed. For the first time, many people feel freedom to heed the call, follow their intuition, pay attention to their daydreams and night dreams, and explore their unlived creative lives. As I was writing this section, a woman, age seventy, emailed me and described her late life: "I'm a writer, sculptor, and member of two choirs. And I'm playing in a recorder quartet, after not playing the instrument for many decades. I didn't know that I was an artist until now!"

Howard, a psychologist colleague, and his partner bought a condo on the Big Island, in Hawaii, anticipating that they might retire there. He went back and forth for a decade, seeing patients in L.A., then returning to the island. I spoke with him during the week that he completed the transition to live there.

"I'm nervous because I'm a busy beaver," he told me. "And I've never lived without accomplishment. So, I was worried about what I would say when people asked, 'What do you *do?*'"

But the cultural rhythm in Hawaii is slower and easier, he told me. "So, the setting supports where I'm at. I'm choosing to change life now, and for me, that means focusing on creativity—sculpting and writing."

Howard described how, when he's working with clay, he's fully present and lost in the moment, in a creative flow state. "The reason for doing it is the sheer joy of the process, not the outcome." He's letting go of his ego's goals of earning money or helping people and learning how to practice presence while sculpting, writing, eating, walking, or tying his shoes. He's letting go of busyness and changing his pace by attuning to his body, conserving his vitality, and connecting to his inspiration.

In this way, creativity becomes more than a hobby; it becomes a practice. Responding to the clay in his hands, Howard is not the Doer. The creative muse is doing the work.

The link between creativity and aging is complex and profound. It urges us to ask: What is possible in late life? Not what is impossible due to the inevitable limits. Not what is possible despite aging. But what is possible because of it?

What can we create because of our extended life experience, because of our resilience, because of our 360-degree view? What can we create because of our personal history of wrestling with shadows, inner critics, or creative blocks? What can we create because of our ripeness, our capacity to get out of the ego's way and open to soul time?

Stories of late-life creative renaissance abound. Marjorie Forbes retired as a social worker in New York City at sixty-eight and began to study the oboe. At eighty-one, she had joined chamber ensembles at the 92nd Street YMCA and at a community arts school. She told a reporter, Abby Ellin, "I've reinvented myself to do something I've always wanted to do." Her colleague, Ari L. Goldman, plays with the New York Late-Starters String Orchestra and wrote a book about learning an instrument later in life. (Ellin, *New York Times*, March 20, 2015.)

Research indicates that the range of creative potential across a life span has been underestimated. Ageism has robbed us of the vision of late-life creativity, leading in part to the disorientation many of us experience today. Our own inner ageist, in collaboration with this cultural blind spot, stops us from engaging in innovative pursuits and engaging with them from the inside out.

In a way, the call to be creative is a portal to shadow awareness. We may hear "I can't learn that now." "It's too late." "I can't remember or concentrate." "I don't know how." "I'm doing it wrong." "I'm too slow."

If our inner ageist blocks our soul's yearning to create, we must simply take a breath, observe it, and remember that it's not who we are. Then we can look at the consequences of obeying it—stopping ourselves again—and make a different choice.

Ageist conventional wisdom tells us that creativity peaks in young adulthood or at midlife, so if we haven't made a breakthrough discovery, written our novel, or painted a masterpiece by then, it's over. But the whole truth is this: Late-life wisdom, nostalgia, longing, and mortality awareness are sweet ingredients for poets, novelists, composers, painters, sculptors, and more.

These people defy the peak-and-decline narrative: Verdi and Strauss wrote some of their greatest operas in their eighties and nineties. Georgia O'Keeffe, nearly blind, enlisted assistants to help her paint from memory into her nineties. Grandma Moses didn't even begin painting until she was seventy-eight! Boris Pasternak wrote *Doctor Zhivago* at sixty-six.

I. M. Pei designed the pyramid for the Louvre at sixty-six. Frank Lloyd Wright designed the Guggenheim Museum in New York at seventy-three. Margaret Atwood published the sequel to *The Handmaid's Tale* at age eighty-one. Leonard Cohen released his last album just before his death at eighty-two. And Bob Dylan, approaching eighty, continues the never-ending tour.

These exemplars may be called geniuses, but they are not exceptions as late-life bloomers. Karl Pillemer, a gerontologist at Weill Cornell Medical College, and his team asked more than 1,500 people who were seventy or older a single question: *What are the most important lessons you've learned over the course of your life?* Many reported that they had achieved a creative life dream or embarked on a new and meaningful endeavor after reaching the age of sixty-five. They finally felt that they were "getting it right," he wrote in *30 Lessons for Living*. They were discovering the secret as Elders to creatively change their lives. Karl Pillemer's work continues as The Legacy Project: Lessons for Living from the Wisest Americans.

In his seminal book *The Creative Age,* psychiatrist and gerontologist Gene Cohen explores the unique combination of creativity plus life experience, including creative stimulation as medicine for our brains, immune systems, and moods. He examines three obstacles to inventiveness that we face as we age: fixed psychological patterns, fixed ideas, and unresolved family relationships. In other words, he is calling for emotional, cognitive, and relational life repair to liberate repressed creative forces from the shadow. Free of anger, resentment, and disappointment, we may heed the call to explore brand new forms of self-expression.

There is yet another level that is rarely talked about: creativity as spiritual practice. Many decades ago, as a new meditator, I believed that sitting practice alone was a spiritual act; meditation alone constituted a spiritual life. I drew a clear line between sacred and profane activities.

But my heartbreaking experience of spiritual disillusionment led to my surprising discovery of writing as a spiritual practice. In 1981, after leaving my spiritual community, I met Marilyn Ferguson, author of *The Aquarian Conspiracy,* who hired me to write her publications, which explored innovations in consciousness research. I vividly recall my first day on the job: I sat with a blank mind facing a blank screen— paralyzed. As I began to take assignments, become engaged with cutting-edge research, and articulate fresh ideas, I found that journalism fit my temperament. I loved gathering information, synthesizing it, and transmitting it to others.

Then I submitted it to Marilyn. She took a red pencil (in those days!) and deleted or altered every word. The text came back unrecognizable. My heart sank. She demanded a dense, telegraphed style without a trace of me; in the objective voice, the subject disappears.

I wrote and rewrote . . . and rewrote . . . and rewrote. Finally, an article was accepted. And I began again.

One evening, staring at the screen, tears running down my cheeks, I threw up my hands. "I will never become a journalist. I will never please this woman."

And yet I felt such joy in finding the right word to make a sentence fly. In that moment, I recalled a story from the Tibetan Buddhist tradition: A solitary monk named Milarepa lived in the woods, practicing meditation day and night and eating only nettle soup. For years, he tried to attain realization, but his fasting and prayers were not enough. One day, another man, Marpa, emerged from the woods. Their eyes met, and Milarepa recognized Marpa as his teacher.

Marpa told him to build a small stone house in a certain corner of the woods, "over there," then disappeared among the trees. For the next year, Milarepa gathered stones, one by one, lifted them slowly, and carried them to the site. Then, with painstaking attention, he fit them together until they formed a sturdy structure.

Marpa emerged from the woods, glanced at the stone hut, and pointed in another direction: "Oh, no, over there!" Then he vanished.

Milarepa's heart sank, but he set about his task as if he had no choice. He took apart the hut stone by stone, carried each one to the new spot, and fit it into place. A year later, the task was complete.

Marpa reappeared, shook his head, and proclaimed, waving in yet another direction, "Oh, no, over there!"

Again, Milarepa submitted. He took it apart and rebuilt it. Again, Marpa appeared and said, "No, over there."

This time, as Milarepa placed the last stone, the story goes, he became enlightened.

I stared at the screen, tears dried, smiling. I had believed that only my sitting practice was spiritual practice. But the work of writing and rewriting, submitting and letting go, concentration and surrender, was a kind of yoga. It also could teach me about self-observation, unattachment, and impermanence, breath by breath.

I began to write as if setting words in a sentence were setting stones in a house. I wrote as if my awareness of the writing process were more important than the content. I saw fewer red marks!

Then another discovery emerged: I would do intensive research, then sit to meditate for an hour, emptying my mind, relaxing my body, letting go of all words and images. When I returned to the screen, words flowed through me in an easy river. No Doer. No struggle. No time. Writing practice, sitting practice, writing practice, sitting practice, became the rhythm of my life.

Slowly, I learned to trust this process: exploring ideas, sitting in pure awareness, filling the mind, emptying the mind, getting ego out of the way. And the red marks disappeared.

The cycle of mentoring was over. During the next few decades, the Muse came to me, through me, in quiet moments as my ego receded. And I opened to Her. The Muse has given me six books—literary children that gestated in my body/mind, entered my cells, married my soul, and moved through me out into the world. Like a mother, I have released them to live their own lives, to find their own way to those who seek them. My gratitude to Her is boundless.

Ultimately, as I have been saying, we are not our stories or our wounds. And we are not our creative endeavors. Our ego may be tempted, as we age, to deeply identify with them, to build castles in the air in order to fend off the transitoriness of our own body and the impermanence of the world around us. We may be tempted to believe that our creative projects can trump our mortality.

When I began to gestate this book, I asked myself: Is this book my ego's last stand? One more attempt to hold on to my name, my brand, my role in perpetuity? To compensate for the loss of charms and powers that comes with age? Or is it a call of the soul, something I must write or risk betraying myself?

As I sat with this inquiry for two years, a response eventually emerged. I would heed the call of my soul to write—and I would let go. I would sit at the screen and sit at the cushion. I would fill my mind and empty my mind. The work would be a practice in opening to the voice of my soul. It would be a gift that only I could give.

But I also would monitor my energy, my self-care, and my relationship needs. And I would not lose balance, as I had as a young, single person. I would not identify with the Doer and allow that internal character to pressure me or drive me from within toward a heroic achievement. Rather, I would open to flow and to my soul's mission: transmitting information about consciousness.

With a closure of unfinished business to release the past, with emotional and creative repair, we can feel profound gratitude for how our lives unfolded. We can forgive, bless, and release people and feelings so that we can begin the shift from role to soul.

Shadow-Work Practices

Please take time to slow down, turn within, and breathe deeply as you contemplate these questions. Have your journal nearby.

🍁 Emotional Repair

- Do you have unfinished business with parents? Siblings? Children? Partners or ex-partners? Friends?

- What goes unspoken or undone that will lead to regret?
- Which shadow character stops you from forgiving others? What does it gain from holding on?
- Which shadow character stops you from forgiving yourself?

◄ *Loving Your Shadow Characters*

Take a few breaths and move into presence. Put attention on one of those parts of yourself that is still young or small or hurting, living in shame or rejection. Attune to that part as you would to a small child. Locate it in your body. Sense it and listen to it, becoming very quiet, present. Then pour your love into that small child or angry teen or disappointed young adult. Love him or her deeply, fiercely, until you feel a shift.

Creative Repair

- How did your family encourage or limit your creative expression? Which talents or dreams were buried in the shadow?
- How do your adult relationships encourage or limit your creative expression?
- How does your work encourage or limit your creative expression?
- Which unfulfilled creative impulses do you want to reclaim from the shadow now?
- How can you incorporate creativity as a spiritual practice?
- What is your creative legacy, which only you can leave behind?

8

Spiritual Repair to Reimagine Our Beliefs and Reclaim Our Practices

PARABLE

The Soul's Yearning for the Divine:
Carl Jung's Case Study

Carl Jung told the story of a patient who projected Spirit, or the Light, onto him as her analyst. Rather than analyze her fantasies to be rid of them, he urged her to elaborate on them. As she did so, they became more and more fantastic, endowing him with superhuman qualities and her with a daughter-like dependence. She dreamed that she was a tiny child in the arms of her father, who was a giant. The giant stood in a wheat field. As the wind swept over the field, the giant swayed back and forth, rocking the child.

In response, Jung asked himself whether the patient's unconscious was "trying to create a god out of the person of the doctor. . . . Could a longing for a god be a passion welling up from our darkest, instinctual nature, a passion unswayed by any outside influences, deeper and stronger perhaps than the love for a human person?"

—From Jung, "The Personal and the Collective Unconscious"

While Freud's insight into patients' projections of a parent onto an analyst was groundbreaking, Jung took the next step: archetypal projection. This unconscious mechanism establishes a link between the two in which a patient imagines that the god-like figure of the therapist can renew or even save the patient. The exact same process takes place between a believer and a religious or spiritual teacher.

Archetypal projection has hidden within it a divine image, a symbol of God or Self, which gives meaning to life. When a living teacher or analyst becomes the object of this unconscious ideal through projection, the link is made: the student/believer longs for union with the teacher/beloved, who is unavailable, thus creating an agonizing separation, which fuels the longing.

In a classical spiritual apprenticeship, the student is encouraged to meditate on the teacher as an image of God, merge with him or her, and give over spiritual authority and control. This process can relieve our existential uncertainty because we are in the presence of someone who knows the truth.

But this dynamic leads to a questionable assumption: A human being can have divine authority and so must be infallible, immune to the corruptions of the shadow. Therefore, whether the teacher is a priest, rabbi, or guru, his or her words and actions cannot be questioned. If and when a therapist or teacher acts out in emotional, physical, or financial abuse, the result is devastating: The patient/believer feels betrayed, disillusioned, and lost.

Whether or not we have experienced such spiritual disillusionment during our lives, whether or not we have met darkness on our paths, spiritual repair is an arena for rich exploration in late life.

Shadow-Work for Spiritual Disillusionment

Recently, I lost one of my best friends to cancer. Cindy's death left me sitting in a well of grief—but not for the reason you might think.

Cindy was a student of Swami Muktananda, who brought Siddha Yoga to the West. Cindy was heartbroken when it was revealed that he had seduced female students, and the scandal was covered up. Later, she was a follower of Swami Vishwananda, with whom she also met sexual shadow. While studying with him, she attained a high stage of witness awareness and inner bliss. So, when Swami Vishwananda's sexual acting out and lies came to light, she was devastated again and conflicted about whether to stay or leave. Cindy's projection of the light onto a mortal person led her, again and again, to meet spiritual shadow. Her resulting heartbreak brought with it a dark night of the soul.

When she was diagnosed with cancer, after a lifetime of spiritual practice, she was able to maintain her witness awareness during the first cycle of chemotherapy. But during the second cycle, with her body full of toxins and her brain increasingly foggy, she lost that awareness and reverted to an earlier stage of development, in which fixated emotional issues surfaced. Eventually, near death, she no longer knew what she believed or whether her practices meant anything at all. She faced death with feelings of anger and betrayal at God.

I was able to help her complete legal and medical unfinished business. I was even able to help her complete some emotional unfinished business. But I was unable to help her complete her ongoing spiritual unfinished business by accepting the human fallibility of her teachers, along with the gifts that accompanied their stages of awareness. I was unable to help her reclaim the spiritual projections she had given away and bring the light back into her own circle. And that is the source of my sorrow: Cindy did not die in peace.

The soul's yearning for transcendence carried many of us, in youth, toward spiritual community and contemplative practice. We explored and experimented, and some of us found a practice that opened a portal to pure awareness.

But many, like Cindy, also suffered betrayal by religious or spiritual teachers and institutions, which led to spiritual disillusionment and a shattering of our belief systems. Uprooted from our teachers and communities, we may have lost our way, feeling no connection to the divine or to something beyond ego.

Today, as Elders, it's vital to contemplate what we believe about the divine, what we most cherish and most highly value. It's vital to reflect on our past beliefs and to revise those beliefs if they no longer serve our development. In this way, it becomes possible to create a late-life philosophy that's unique to our own journey and the lessons we've learned. And that reorients us to life now.

Are we connected to something larger than ourselves? Is it knowable or unknowable? Are we actively seeking to connect with it now?

As the mystic poet Kabir put it, "Who have we spent our entire life loving?"

Is there a deeper purpose to our life that we can see now? Are we connected to it?

What is the role of the mind? The heart? The body? Are we caring for them in a balanced way?

What is our connection to service? Do we feel responsible for alleviating the suffering of others?

Is death a final end, or is it the beginning of a new cycle?

What is the end of a human life? Toward what end do we move? The word *end* has a double meaning. The end of our endeavors is both an aim, or intention, and a conclusion, a termination in time. And we may want to reconsider, rethink, and re-feel into both meanings.

If we deny this task, we miss out on a key step in the shift from role to soul. Our religious or spiritual beliefs will remain stagnant, hidden in the shadow, rather than developing along with other parts of us. If we unconsciously identify with past beliefs and they remain outside of our conscious awareness, they will hinder our ability to shift our lives from the inside out today.

This is yet another inner obstacle: We continue to unconsciously identify with past religious beliefs and fail to repair our relationship to the divine.

For example, a friend of mine, who was raised Methodist, was taught to "get up and do good works." Several years after retirement, she no longer wanted to wake up and do. She longed to sit by the lake and watch the birds. But guilt gnawed at her. So, she needed to become aware of her early childhood religious teachings and choose consciously whether to obey them now.

A client, who was a Christian Scientist, watched as her parents, in their eighties, became gravely ill and were forced to choose between using medicine, which is forbidden by church doctrine, or facing imminent death. They both went to a doctor for the first time in their lives. As a result, their church shunned them.

"It was awful to watch them being abandoned by the church they had supported," my client said. "With the community's judgment and rejection of my parents, all of my own doubts came crashing in, and I left."

As I write this, Elder statesman and former president Jimmy Carter, at the age of ninety-four, resigned from the Southern Baptist Convention after sixty years. He publicly said that he could no longer tolerate its institutional sexism and use of scripture to justify the subordination of women. He was aligning his beliefs with his values in late life.

Many of us have spent decades thinking and reading about these existential questions of meaning and purpose. We may have found a religious dogma, or an anti-religious dogma, and deeply identified with it—mysticism, mindfulness, Gaia, Buddhism, yoga, Judaism, Advaita, Christianity, Sufism, existentialism, science.

In some cases, we unconsciously identified so deeply with our beliefs that we thought that's who we were: I am Evangelical, I am Muslim, I am Tibetan Buddhist, I am a meditator. In the same way that we identified with our work roles—"I am a fisherman"—our ego identified with our spiritual roles and philosophical ideas. We became fundamentalist thinkers, grasping our beliefs with a death grip, without realizing it.

"Veganism will cure you." "This is the only path to enlightenment." "My church can save you." "I only trust what I can see." "Life's a bitch, then you die."

This identification with dogma is evident on the world stage today as Democrats and Republicans inhabit separate spheres of belief and project their shadows so intensely that they cannot speak to one another, let alone collaborate. It's evident as globalists and populists fight for control of governments, as jihadis and capitalists fight for control of minds. People are not free to think independently and come up with solutions; they are enslaved by dogma.

In late life, we need to ask ourselves whether we have in any way been fundamentalist in our thinking—that is, whether we have believed in something so fervently that we failed to see other points of view, became blinded by self-righteousness, and sacrificed into the shadow certain parts of ourselves that were essential to our well-being.

For some of us, that is precisely what happened in our spiritual communities. And then, in some cases, we watched our teachers, clergy, guides, or institutional dogmas express shadows, violating agreements or morals by displaying hypocrisy or committing overt abuse. With their actions, our faith and beliefs were shattered.

Faced with these betrayals, we told ourselves: "He cannot be enlightened, or he wouldn't want my money." "She has secrets and is not who I thought she was." "Those priests were child molesters." As a result, many of us lost faith, no longer believing in the precepts or practices that had been precious to us."

As James Hillman pointed out, the very place where we put our trust is the place where we are most open to betrayal. When our faith has been shaken, spiritual repair becomes necessary. And in order to recover from these wounds and clarify our values now, we'll want to understand how this happened.

Just as we unconsciously project the dark shadow onto others, so we unconsciously project spiritual light—and unknowingly ask others to carry it for us. We might say, "Jesus talks to him, and I want that." "She has the light that I'm seeking. I can get it if I obey her." "He is liberated, and I'm not."

In this way, we direct our spiritual yearning toward a person who may or may not have a higher stage of awareness, but who definitely has human flaws, limits, blind spots, and shadows. We look to this person to mediate divine energy for us. When that effort fails—when we witness the shadow in the very people whom we have entrusted with our most sacred bond of faith—we feel betrayed by God, the ultimate loss. And as a result, our longing for the light evokes its opposite: a shattering encounter with spiritual darkness and an emptying out of hope and meaning and previous images of god. (I explored this theme at length in *Meeting the Shadow of Spirituality.*)

Consider the reports of pervasive, horrific scandals of sexual abuse among Catholic priests, who acted out their shadows in the most destructive ways, leaving innocent believers traumatized and lost. Many people left the church in heartbreak, telling themselves, "These are not men of God. How did the Church ignore this? Does God, as I believed in Him, even exist?"

Before spiritual betrayal, we are innocent, trusting believers. We are the chosen; we will be saved; we can be enlightened; God is on our side.

After spiritual betrayal, we enter the night sea journey, the *via negativa* or way of darkness. The longing for ascent turns abruptly and becomes a great descent. In the Christian mythos, this is the time of the cross. "My God, why have you forsaken me?"

At first, we may try to deny what we see. "If I believed such stories, I would disbelieve my whole life." "The more I meditated by day, the more I drank by night. And my teacher colluded with the problem." "I don't want to know what my minister did—I don't want to see." In this effort, we deny the reality that human beings are imperfect. We deny the reality that their institutions are imperfect.

Internally, our denial pushes our thoughts and feelings into our own shadow—a gnawing doubt, a buried question, an inexplicable discomfort. But few of us can live indefinitely cut off from our own intuitive knowing or emotional and bodily cues. Few can live indefinitely in a passive, dependent state. Few can live indefinitely with our connection to the divine projected onto a limited, mortal human being. With so much denial, the evolution of soul is derailed.

Then, one day, when we can no longer tolerate it, our inner know-ing erupts into awareness. We admit that, despite our faith in a church's teachings or in a guru's promises, despite our diligent worship, service, meditation, or yoga practice, we still struggle with darkness—our teach-er's and our own.

If we strive for spiritual perfection, our teachers and our practices inevitably fail us. The ego's quest for perfection traps us in isolation and in a longing that can't be fulfilled. For many people, the ideal spiritual practice and community is a forgotten dream, a melody lost in the noise of busy life. No one taught us how to recover from the betrayal and rekindle the flame of longing in our heart. So, we just turned away and tried to forget, banishing any dreams of communion or transcendence into the shadow.

Some of us continued to study or practice and found different teachers and methods. And for still others, the dream was diverted into a watered-down form of mindfulness in everyday life.

However, a fortunate few of us eventually found the narrow path through the darkness and experienced betrayal as an initiation into shadow: We traveled from spiritual innocence through the dark descent, into a liminal world, across the threshold, and toward a new stage of awareness—spiritual maturity. We evolved from Victim and Victimizer, from childlike dependency on a spiritual parent, through meeting the shadow and accepting it as part of the path, the *via negativa,* toward spiritual maturity.

On this winding road, our projections collapsed: wise/innocent, right/wrong, enlightened/ignorant, saint/sinner. We learned to meet the darkness in ourselves and in our beloved clergy and teachers, gradu-ally coming to accept it as a part of being human. We saw through the veil of our projections to the humanity in the Other—his shadow and wisdom, her humanity and divinity. Slowly we came to see that our beloved teachers and clergy are not responsible for carrying the divine for us. And, slowly, we came to recognize that what they carried for us was inside of us all along—the light, pure awareness, our basic spiritual nature.

As with emotional repair, when we took responsibility for our projection and for giving away our spiritual power, we broke our identification with the Victim/Victimizer dynamic. The opposites within were no longer split. We carried them consciously. As a result, we no longer held on to certainty; we let go into mystery.

Having been emptied of fixed spiritual ideas and images, having been left fallow for a dark season, we became fertile soil for new life— open but not naive, eager but not impatient, ripe for blossoming. As we began to carry our own wounds *and* our own greatness, we began to need others in a different way—neither to parent us nor to connect us to the divine, but, rather, to join us in the dance between love and freedom, between union and autonomy. That is the promise of spiritual shadow-work.

For those of us in late life who have suffered religious betrayal or spiritual abuse and have not yet repaired these wounds, for those of us who long for a direct connection to something greater before we die, we need, first, to retrieve those qualities that we banished into our shadows by projecting them onto a teacher or clergy person. We can use our practices for their original intent—to open a portal to silent vastness or pure awareness—and we can carry our own light.

Reclaiming the Light

Perhaps our spiritual light, our innate divine essence, frightens us more than our shadow's darkness. Perhaps our natural radiance is diminished as a need to feel safety, or belonging, or approval takes over. And perhaps that's why, when we find a priest, teacher, or guide whose words and stature we respect, we so easily give away our light and permit another to carry it. We come to believe that this person alone, or this institution alone, can mediate the divine for us. Then we are no longer burdened with a direct relationship to our own light, our own radiance, our own spiritual authority.

As a result, we come to identify with a narrow role in our spiritual lives: student, seeker, believer, follower, parishioner. But when we take an obedient position, we repress many of our own best qualities—our inquisitiveness, ambition, insightfulness, openness, creativity. Our spiritual development is derailed by virtue of being limited to another's fallible interpretation of the divine. Our light dims.

To reclaim our light, we need our own direct experience of pure awareness or the silent vastness within. A belief about it is not enough. We need to put our belief into practice and experience it daily, allowing ourselves to dip into the inner silence and expand into the vastness.

We may avoid or resist this contemplative time. Even with retirement, most of us are living hectic, distracted lives filled with activities, families, self-care, and social media. So, it's challenging to stop and sit and breathe.

But deep inside, many of us feel a restless stirring, the soul's longing for something more. This is the teaching of every mystical tradition: We yearn for something beyond ego, a transcendental awareness that connects us to the divine. There are many paths, but they all lead to this direct inner experience. As our personal connection to pure awareness stabilizes and our awareness rests in it more and more, we begin to reclaim our light—and would not imagine giving it away.

This does not mean that we stop learning from wise people; it means only that we stop giving them our spiritual authority. We can respect and even revere others without projecting our light onto them. In this way, we reinvent spirituality from the inside out.

Reclaiming Our Beliefs

We all need guidance and mentoring, at times, for spiritual instruction or direction. But, most importantly, we need to cultivate a connection to our own inner wisdom through growing awareness of our thoughts, feelings, intuitions, images, and actions. If, in the past, in a church or spiritual community, we shut down our intuitive or bodily cues that something was wrong, if we silenced our doubts to gain approval and belonging, then we may have struggled with a tension between our own inner knowing and outer authority.

If we gave the power of definition over our lives to others, and if they circumscribed how we spent time, energy, and money and what we believe, then our questions become taboo. If they defined right and wrong thinking, who is on God's side and who is not, who is going to heaven or becoming enlightened and who is not, then we didn't think for ourselves for a while. We were unknowingly identified with dogma that was given by others.

In our unconscious, the shadow character of Doubter may have carried our questions for us. Or a Rebel wanted to break the rules of religious or spiritual life. At some point, these inner characters erupt out of the shadow.

"I've lived all my life as a good Catholic. What if it's all a lie?" "Why am I even doing these Buddhist practices at all? What do these practices have to do with me?" "Is this Sufi belief system true or just a crutch to keep me from having to think about things on my own?" "Is this swami/priest/rabbi/yoga teacher really more spiritually evolved than anyone else?"

When I was younger, I belonged to a meditation community that, in the Eastern tradition, described emotional attachment as a trap. And I conformed; I believed that the only path to liberation was to remain free of all attachment, whether to love, comfort, money, beauty, or another person.

But then one day my inner Rebel spoke up: Emotional attachment must have some value! And that rebellious thought opened a tightly shut door. I could see that my attachment to nonattachment had deeply personal roots. It supported my fears of intimacy, failure, and death. Gradually, I came to believe that I needed to face those fears by going through them, rather than avoiding them. I needed to take a psychological journey through my fears (Growing Up) before I reached a stage of awareness in which nonattachment, or the witness, emerged spontaneously (Waking Up).

This led me to sort out other teachings that I had absorbed without discrimination. For instance, when I came to believe that meditation alone reached the source of problems—consciousness—I stopped my political and social activism. Today I see that a practice that is purely introverted and without social engagement risks self-absorption. And it risks colluding with unjust political and economic systems, furthering the suffering of others.

I came to conclude that, while meditation holds immense value for spiritual development, as I have said many times in this book, some of the teachings around it, in any tradition, may be outdated, rooted in monastic cultures, or even destructive to emotional, cognitive, and moral development. This distinction enabled me to reclaim my independent thinking while continuing my practice. As I learned, it's the direct experience of pure awareness, not our beliefs or theories about it, that brings rewards.

I began to hold both the positive and the negative sides of my spiritual experience, healing the internal opposites that accompany black-and-white thinking: believer versus infidel, sacred versus secular, immanent versus transcendent. And I could see the beauty in paradoxical opposites, such as a wise human being who has a shadow. As my past spiritual persona died, I crossed a threshold into a new stage of spiritual maturity. I could view my Victimizer as my Liberator. My life was much lonelier without community and more challenging without the certainty of a given belief system. But it was also more of an adventure and a mystery, as I learned to attune to the voice of my soul and become my own guide.

Reclaiming Our Images of Divinity

Just as we may be unaware of the inner voice of a shadow character and how it sabotages us, we may be unaware of inner images that have guided us and now sabotage us in the same way. Our spiritual yearning often has a hidden object of desire—an image of God, guru, paradise, the beloved, or Higher Self. And our souls long for it and follow it like a fragrance.

At times, we catch a glimpse of the sacred image—a Madonna inspires purity, a judge inspires moral fitness, a Kuan Yin inspires compassion, a king inspires nobility, a goddess inspires connection to the earth, a Buddha inspires stillness, a holy book inspires learning.

Carl Jung wrote extensively about the god image as he uncovered it in his patients' transference onto him—that is, their projection of the light onto him. He believed that the god image, which develops in humanity over eons, does not refer to anything in the outside world but is alive in the psyche. He proposed that we gain consciousness through a growing awareness of these evolving images, which free us from traditional religious imagery.

In the psychology of religion, researchers have found that a sacred god image can develop through an individual's life span, transforming from an unconditional mother to a protector father to a Creator to a more symbolic savior/protector. We learn to pray to it in both conscious and unconscious ways, and it changes in response to our life experience.

But most of the time our god images lie dormant and neglected, casting a spell over us from the shadow, outside of awareness. No one teaches us how to unearth them and reimagine them. Therefore, they may remain unchanged for decades. If they remain static while we grow into adulthood, and we remain in bondage to childhood representations of God, then our minds are in idolatry and the soul's longing is misdirected.

This is a little-known developmental task for late life: We need to reclaim and reimagine our images of the divine. If they don't fit us— our stage of life, gender, ethnicity, experience—they may no longer serve as divine guides but, instead, act as shadow figures by sabotaging our conscious spiritual intentions.

When I interviewed Jungian analyst Lionel Corbett, who has written extensively about depth psychology and religion, he affirmed this idea: "Aging has a function. It's to renew our inner image of God. And that's a kind of spirituality that's more authentic than the collective, given traditions offered to us."

My client Steve, at the age of sixty-five, identified himself as a Buddhist and practiced mindfulness. But, in his shadow, a wrathful Pope-like figure was sending him to hell for his sexual fantasies, no matter how much he tried to purify his mind.

Such long-neglected images lie at the source of much spiritual suffering at the end of life if we, even unconsciously, imagine a deity that is shaped by an early experience with a spiritual authority, such as an angry father figure, a punitive nun, or a yoga master whose enlightened standard of perfection cannot be met. I knew many meditators who, for decades, struggled with a shadow character that carried the shame of not being enlightened enough, the shame of failing to match their idealized inner image.

Jung pointed out that we don't experience a god or archetype directly; rather, we experience an image of it, which is filtered through our subjectivity. Once we see through our filters, the personal and social influences on our images, we can no longer identify with a single image of god. Instead, we come to see it as a living reality in our own souls.

As Bob Dylan put it, "You're gonna have to serve somebody." If, unconsciously, we are obeying divine images that do not encourage the evolution of our soul, then we need to replace them.

But these images, including archetypal god images, are not pure awareness, or consciousness without an object. They are not nondual. Therefore, as far as I understand, despite all of his genius, Jung did not delineate this stage of awareness beyond the archetypal. Ultimately, the goal of awakening is nondual awareness—that is, the disappearance of all images in the unity of pure awareness.

Spiritual Work

Reclaiming Our Practices

Every mystical or perennial tradition teaches that it's only through our direct experience of pure awareness (or emptiness, or the divine, or whatever name we use) that we can move beyond ego, truly crossing the threshold from role to soul. They also teach that now, in late life, is the time to turn our attention within. We no longer need to go, go, go, carrying the burden of big responsibilities. Instead, we can slow, sit, breathe, and allow our minds to settle down into an open, spacious, contentment, without struggle or resistance. We can discover how our minds work and who we really are.

If you have reviewed your life and faced your severe spiritual teachers, releasing the betrayals, losses, and disillusionment of the past; if you have reclaimed the light from your projections onto teachers; if you have reclaimed your beliefs and reimagined your sacred images of the divine, then turn within and listen for the whisper of your soul's holy longing.

By now you have become aware of the Seeker within you, who has carried a lifelong yearning for something more. And this spiritual restlessness continues today, even if it whispers more quietly: "There's more . . . I want something more before it's too late. I yearn to connect with Spirit, to allow it to guide me. I long to be free of the mind's noise. I long to be free of the ego's grasping. I long to open my heart more . . . to be silent, fully present, fully connected to *what is*. I long to fulfill the purpose of my soul."

Make a commitment, in this moment, to find a spiritual practice that fits who you are now, in this stage of life, and what you seek now. Look for a practice that is resonant with your soul and appropriate to your circumstances, emotionally, culturally, physically, and in all other ways.

When I spoke with Mirabai Bush, founder of the Center for Contemplative Mind in Society, about how to choose a practice, she said, "Different practices work at different times in our lives. I used Vipassana [mindfulness] for fifty years, but I needed other practices, too. When I had an emotionally hard time, I learned aikido, a Japanese martial art. It was wonderful for body/mind centering in the moment. My attention was fixed and never wandered. When I'm with friends, I practice chanting, or *kirtan*. And as

I age, I find *hatha yoga* more important to maintain flexibility."

It's fine to change practices, Mirabai told me. "But be patient so that they can deepen, rather than constantly shopping around."

How to Choose a Spiritual Practice for Late Life

You may find your spiritual practice through reading and an intuitive recognition of a fit with a lineage. You may find it through people who share your values or demonstrate some quality that you want to cultivate. You may find it by opening to synchronicity and allowing its connections to lead you. You may find it by recording your dreams and heeding their timeless messages. You may find it by hearing a friend say something that points the way. You may find it by traveling to another culture and feeling deeply at home. You may find it in a sacred place in nature or in a church or temple. And you may find it by returning to a practice from your youth with your rich life experience in tow. If you trust your inner guidance and know how to attune to your intuition or Inner Elder (see chapter 9), then you may find it by asking and looking within.

But listen for the voices of shadow characters that may try to stop you: "I can't concentrate." "It's too late for this." "I can't cross my legs." "It didn't help before, so it won't help now."

Allow yourself to witness the shadow characters without obeying them. Instead, listen to the quiet whisper from the soul: "I feel drawn to try that." "I wonder what that would be like." "This one feels familiar to me." And trust this guidance.

Whatever practice you choose, look for the *fit,* the felt sense of resonance or familiarity to a lineage or to a teaching. But use your discrimination, too—beware of shadow issues, projection, dogma, group think, and subtle allusions to hierarchy, shame, or requirements that you sacrifice essential parts of yourself.

You can take a breath, then begin to contemplate these questions:

- What were you seeking during the heyday of your hero's journey?
- Did you want a wise, compassionate teacher, guru, or guide who provided beliefs, practices, and rules to live by?
- Did you want a community of like-minded others?
- Did you seek a religious/spiritual solution to emotional problems (or what Ken Wilber calls a "spiritual bypass")?
- Did you seek an otherworldly paradise?
- Did you long for a level of awareness beyond suffering?

What are you seeking now in late life? Do your former spiritual desires still pertain? If so, how can you explore them now with new eyes and greater awareness?

By the time you reach late life, you may have been deeply disillusioned by a life's worth of heroic spiritual efforts. So, how can you heed the call today, while maintaining an acute awareness of the pitfalls and shadow issues of spiritual life? How can you stop being a heroic seeker and become an Elder seeker, thereby aging into awakening?

If your former spiritual desires no longer pertain to you, what is the object of your longing now? Pick up a pen and quickly write the first ten spiritual desires that come to mind. Choose three of them that stand out. Use these intentions as guides for your late-life spiritual path.

Spiritual practice has the potential for great impact on the aging body and mind. As we struggle with, among other things, potential depression, anxiety, negative thoughts, emotional unfinished business, illness, chronic pain, and emotional loss or memory loss, extensive research indicates that meditation can help. Today there are many YouTube videos and apps, such as Sattva and Headspace, that teach practices from all traditions.

To move past denial of aging and death, you might begin with the book *The Blooming of a Lotus* by Thich Nhat Hanh. Its mindfulness practices will center your attention on the universal truths of the divine messengers: aging, illness, and death.

If you are drawn to ceremony and ritual, after you complete the inner work of age, you can design a rite of passage for yourself to become an Elder. Imagine symbolically letting go of past roles and identities and crossing a threshold into your new awareness of yourself as soul and your offering to the common good.

All contemplative practices aim to open a portal to pure awareness and pull us into presence, away from the past or future, into the timeless now. Mirabai Bush suggests that a basic sitting practice with an anchor, such as breath or a mantra, can ease negative thoughts and emotions and teach us beginner's mind. Later, it can deepen into silence and then open out into pure awareness and more advanced spiritual states.

Ken Wilber told me that contemplative practice is so important in late life because now we need to let go and detach from limited identities and self-images to continue to evolve. "We continue to have experiences but learn to witness this and let go, witness that and let go. Our longevity gives us more time to rest in pure awareness, to include and transcend past roles and identities, allowing higher stages of development, with greater freedom and happiness, to unfold."

For beginners, you can try mindfulness, guided visualization, transcendental meditation, centering prayer, or a mantra practice from any tradition, such as the Jewish Shema. These practices reduce negative thoughts and enhance concentration and a sense of self-control.

Calming practices include *japa* (counting sacred beads), *dhikr* (Sufi chanting), rosary, transcendental meditation, guided visualization to a safe space, and breath awareness. Or you can contemplate Bible passages, yoga *sutras,* or other scripture.

To increase concentration, you can use Zazen (Zen meditation), walking meditation, breath awareness, chanting psalms or *kirtan,* or focused gazing on a candle or a *yantra* (a visual image that aims to induce mystical states).

To maintain bodily flexibility and cultivate inner calm, you can use *hatha yoga* and adapt the postures to your body's abilities. It can reduce pain and increase vitality.

To open the heart and enhance devotion to God, you can try *kirtan* chanting to increase feelings of love and joy or Christian devotional prayer to the deity.

To increase self-love and empathy for others, you can use loving-kindness (*metta*) practice, the Dalai Lama's "just like me" compassion practice, or the Tibetan Buddhist practice of *tonglen*.

To increase a sense of connection, you can try sacred service or *karma yoga* to offer your gift to humanity and enhance a felt interdependence with a wider world.

To increase happiness, use smiling Buddha meditation with *mantras* and *mudras* (hand positions) or Thich Nhat Hanh's smiling meditation practice. Also use Brother David Steindl-Rast's gratitude practices to focus on *what is,* rather than what is not.

All these practices can open a way, leading you to pure awareness and experiences of higher stages of awakening.

If you don't quickly discover your path, I suggest that you continually listen to the whispers of your soul and ask Life or Spirit for your spiritual practice with great sincerity and seek to find the current of life, as a surfer does, which takes you out to sea.

Seeing through Our Beliefs

Remember: We are not our beliefs. Although we unconsciously identify with the mind and its positions about right and wrong, it is not the essence of who we are. When we stop and listen to ourselves, it can be shocking—a choir of dissenting opinions, unquestioned assumptions, and self-righteous positions. But when we learn to listen from a more spacious silence and witness the noise for long enough, we can begin to see through our beliefs; we can see that they are constructs of the mind, and we can break our identification with them. We can begin to identify instead with pure awareness, gradually moving beyond ego/mind to a more spiritual identity. In this way, we can use the mind to transcend the mind. We can discover that we are pure awareness, not the contents of awareness.

About a decade ago, I was sitting with my *satsang,* members of a meditation group who speak about their internal experiences in meditation and give one another reflection and mirroring. Each time I would speak, someone retorted, "That's a concept." I would speak up again, and I would hear, "That's a concept." I would try to say something else, and I would hear, "That's a concept."

This went on for some time until, in an instant, my mind stopped and emptied out onto the floor. The contents of consciousness were unloaded—and I sat, open-eyed, with a hollow head, grinning.

I had experienced this state many, many times in meditation, but never in the waking state with others. This was pure transcendental awareness plus waking awareness, known by many names—*satori, kensho.* It was expansive, free, and liberating.

Hours later, the first thought arose: I am not my mind.

As time passed and more thoughts returned, I could see through them, as if they were thin veils, not the concrete realities they had appeared to be. I could see through my ego's constructed separate self-sense, and how hard I had worked to build it, defend it, and use it to my advantage. And I came to understand that we all use these constructions of mind to cover our wounds and our existential fears of what lies beneath.

Since that awakening experience, I no longer live in or through my mind. I enjoy it fully, even as I write this sentence. But it's no longer the central mediator of my experience or primary source of my identity.

With the completion of spiritual repair, we deepen, accept, and open to the life of the soul, while being stewarded toward the next threshold. This process leads naturally to becoming an Elder.

Spiritual Practices

Please take time to slow down, turn within, and breathe deeply as you contemplate these questions. Have your journal nearby.

- Do you feel the yearning of your soul to connect with something greater? How can you heed this messenger? Which shadow character seduces you into denial or distraction?
- Do you have unfinished business with a clergy person, mentor, guru, or God? How can you use the tools in this book to address this?

🍂 Reclaiming the Light

- Have you given away your spiritual light to another?
- What do you need in order to let go of a longing for an ideal parent or teacher?
- How can you reclaim your projections and take back your own light?

🍂 Reclaiming Your Beliefs

- Have you projected certainty and banished doubt, accepting others' definitions of God or of moral behavior? Do those definitions still work for you today?
- If not, what do you believe now about the divine and your own connection to it? Is it *transcendent,* outside of us, or *immanent,* within us? Is it an all-nurturing Mother; a personal savior, such as Jesus; or an impersonal interconnectedness, such as pure consciousness or Gaia?
- How do your current beliefs about the divine shape how you live your life now?

🍂 Reclaiming Your Image of the Divine

- What do you see when you close your eyes and say "God" or "Spirit"?
- Does this image fit your current understanding of spirituality, shaped as it has been by your unique life experience? If not, what do you need to reimagine your image of the divine today?

🍂 Reclaiming Your Practices

- What kind of spiritual practice fits who you are now? What stops you from learning it or doing it regularly? What are the consequences of not doing your practice?

• Where is your attention while you are driving, walking, cooking, typing, eating, reading, speaking? How can you extend your spiritual practice into these everyday activities?

⌒⌒⌒

Please practice repeating:

"I am not a Victim of my spiritual story."

"I am not my spiritual beliefs."

"I am not my god image."

"I am a soul [or whatever you call your spiritual essence]."

PART 3

From Hero to Elder

Part 3 explores how to make the late-life transition from the heroic doing of midlife to the inner tasks of later years. Our unconscious identification with outer roles and achievement can block a new myth from emerging: How do we become Elders and reorient to the inner world? How do we live as Elders? What is Elder wisdom? How do we transmit wisdom to future generations? How do we reorient to spirituality? Do we hear the call to serve something larger than ourselves?

9

Elder with a Thousand Faces

Master and Butler: A Sufi Tale

According to an ancient Sufi tale, the master of a large household needed to go abroad for a long period. He decided to leave his trusted, capable butler in charge of his affairs. When the master returned after many years, he discovered that the butler no longer recognized him; the butler believed that he himself was master of the house.

"I'm in charge," the butler said when he first took over. "I have my own priorities. I have power over people. But the people don't know who I really am, so I have to hide." And the butler hid so well that he forgot how he got the job in the first place. He identified with his new role, and his power was aimed at maintaining his position and proving that he was worthy of love and respect.

In fact, the butler became so immersed in his role that he was unwilling to give up control of the household when the master returned. So, the master needed to send in his henchmen. They appeared to the butler as obstacles to maintaining his power: depression, anxiety, envy, competition, projections onto others. As a result, the butler felt afraid that he would be found to be a fraud, afraid that he wouldn't have enough, afraid that he would be left alone. He dreamed about being attacked or killed by unseen enemies.

Eventually, having faced the henchmen and his own pain and struggle, the

butler was humbled and forced to surrender to the master's authentic power,
and the master returned to his place as head of the home.

—Paraphrased from a story told
by Idries Shah in *Tales of the Dervishes*

Now we have become ripe for a profound rite of passage. We have faced the divine messengers and heeded their calls. We have opened the three portals to shadow awareness, pure awareness, and mortality awareness. We have met the inner ageist and explored retirement and illness from the inside out. We have viewed our life stories with new eyes and repaired our life wounds with new tools. We can see the evolution of the soul in this inner work of age. And it has prepared us for the next leap: becoming Elders and reimagining the nobility and sacred power of age.

As each of us chooses not to merely grow old but to grow whole, to intentionally step across the threshold and become an Elder, we discover that aging can be a spiritual path. The foundation for our late-life development has been described in every spiritual tradition as ego transcendence, a shift in identity from butler to master, from a separate sense of self to a transcendent, universal sense of self.

Ego transcendence is often referred to as a symbolic death because our bounded, limited identity "dies" into an expanded identity. As Jesus put it, "Not my will, but Thy will be done." In Sufism, students are advised to "die before you die." Jewish Kabbalists speak of "the kiss of death." In Zen Buddhism, satori or ego death is called "the great death." Carl Jung articulated this point (in *Mysterium Coniunctionis*) when he said, "The experience of the self is always a defeat for the ego."

The conscious aging movement sometimes refers to this internal leap as "gero-transcendence," a term coined by Swedish gerontologist Lars Tornstam. He described an intrinsic shift in older people from a materialistic, rational view of the world to a more cosmic, transcendent view. This evolutionary step includes an increased feeling of affinity with past generations, a diminished interest in superficial social interaction and material things, and a greater need for solitary, contemplative time.

In early life, our connection to pure awareness or a transcendent self-sense goes dormant, and the ego takes control of our conscious lives. It runs the house like an efficient servant and eventually forgets that the master even exists. Here, again, the ego creates an unconscious inner obstacle to the evolution of the soul: We deny and resist the inner work of age because the butler/ego cannot let go of control.

The ego is not inherently bad; it's not our aim to be rid of it. In fact, our ego serves us to develop our talents, adjust to society, build our careers, create our families, and follow the hero's journey of life. From my perspective, we develop ego to work out *karma,* or the issues of soul.

Years ago, some young students told mythologist Joseph Campbell that, thanks to their guru, they could move from youth to sage without having to pass through the suffering of adulthood. Campbell responded, "Yes, and the only thing you lose is your life."

So, the ego is not the enemy. But in late life, we seek a changing of the guard from hero to Elder, or from ego/role to soul. When we want to transfer our center of gravity from small self-interest to larger communal and planetary well-being, and from self-aggrandizement to self-actualization, the ego can no longer reign supreme. The call of the soul must be heard. We must allow the ego to recede to permit a more spiritual identity to emerge, reconnecting us with pure awareness.

For the ego/butler to move aside, an Elder needs to travel through the three portals—shadow awareness, pure awareness, and mortality awareness—and connect with the source. That means centering in deep silence and letting go of our identification with the noisy mind. It means witnessing those thoughts that appear as shadow characters and block this transition.

For example, we can overcome our own inner ageist by letting go of our unconscious identification with youth. It's our inner ageist who associates being an Elder with being elderly and resists the transition that is needed now for us and for the world.

Through our inner work, we can overcome the ego's identification with image and success and its desire for control. We can let go of our denial of mortality and allowing it to penetrate so deeply that it humbles our ego. My "Connie-ness" is not permanent; it will not endure. No matter how I live or what I write, my name will be forgotten.

We can welcome the grieving and gratitude that follow a life review, which opens a 360-degree view of our lives. The self-exploration and self-acceptance that follow life repair allow us to take on a higher purpose for the sake of others, for the sake of our soul, and for sake of the soul of the world. Just as we left a fleeting childhood behind, now we move beyond the fevered ambitions of adulthood and follow the ambitions of the soul.

As storyteller Michael Meade told me in our interview, "Elders are made, not born."

In other words, this is not an automatic transition. The Elder is not another role to be put on like a change of wardrobe. We don't become Elders simply because we move more slowly or even more wisely. Rather, it is a deep interior shift from role to soul and from soul to higher stages of awareness.

What Is an Elder?

Joseph Campbell's renowned telling of the hero's journey ends with the hero, reborn, returning to the ordinary world with a boon. I like to think of this boon as the deeper, wider awareness of the Elder, which is then transmitted to the next generation.

In myths and tales, we see the Elder, teacher, or mentor aiding or training the hero, like the fairy godmother with Cinderella or Merlin with King Arthur. This figure is inspired by divine wisdom and a connection to the spiritual realm. And his or her aid or advice brings power with conscience. Consider how Q, as mentor to James Bond, teaches him to use new technology. Or how Mr. Miyagi trains Daniel in martials arts in *The Karate Kid*. Or how Obi-Wan Kenobi gives Luke his father's lightsaber.

I spoke about this motif with Jungian psychiatrist Allan Chinen, whose books *Beyond the Hero* and *In the Ever After* explore Elder fairy tales. "In fairy tales all over the world, elders are a bridge between the young and the spirit world," he told me. "Elders move out of egocentricity and become more authentically themselves. If they reclaim the inner child, they act more playfully, sometimes outrageously, in a newfound freedom. If they break out of conventional rationality, they act more spontaneously. If they release their identification with 'I am what I do,' they transcend roles. If they release their identification with 'I am this body,' they move toward identification with soul. If they accept their death as part of a larger story, they may find peace."

Allan distinguished these positive developmental steps from the risks of potential backward steps: "If Elders don't release conventional beliefs, they can regress to rigidity and bitterness. If they don't release past social roles, they can regress to grief and depression. If they don't release identification with the body, they can regress to hypochondria. Finally, if they don't confront their shadow and connect with soul, they can regress to childishness, rather than becoming childlike."

Just as heroism dominates tales of youth in every culture, ego transcendence illuminates tales of Elders around the world. But our own stories also are full of guidance, warnings, and reconciliations, if we know how to read them. In late life, as we look back, most of us can see mentors and elders who appeared to aid us in crisis, train us in worldly skills, pass on their knowledge to us, and connect us to another, more magical reality.

After our dramatic heroic journeys from youth through midlife, we can now reenter the story as those wise men and women who mentored us on the path—and give our hard-won knowledge and boons to the next generation. To do this, we need to take the empty seat that awaits us. We need to welcome a new generation of seekers and change agents, pass the lightsaber and transmit values to them, and support them on their own journeys. For the world needs the wisdom and gifts of older adults. It's nourishment for a world starved of meaning.

Some of us will hear the call to be Earth Elders, fierce guardians of our habitat at this crucial moment of history. Others will hear the call to become socially or politically empowered Activist Elders, joining the youth in the streets who are fighting for the end of income inequality, hunger, homelessness, gun violence, money in politics, mass incarceration, and rampant sexual assault. Activist Elders may look like Gloria Steinem, Bernie Sanders, Al Gore, Bill McKibben, Deena Metzger, Nelson Mandela, Joanna Macy, Kofi Annan, Roshi Bernie Glassman, U.S. Rep. John Lewis, Rabbi Arthur Waskow, Nancy Pelosi, John Sorenson, and Michael Meade. Activist Elders may look like you . . .

Some of us will hear the call to become Spiritual Elders, teaching contemplative practices to those who are lost in digital distraction. If we are grounded in pure awareness, we can hold space for the highest human possibilities for those who are coming; we can anchor presence for the next generations. Spiritual Elders may look like the Dalai Lama, Thich Nhat Hanh, Ram Dass, Rabbi Zalman Schachter-Shalomi, Desmond Tutu, Roshi Joan Halifax, Ken Wilber, Pema Chodron, Mirabai Bush, Sharon Salzberg, Hameed Ali, Richard Rohr, Joan Chittister, Thomas Berry, Brother David Stendl-Rast, Jack Kornfield, Roshi Wendy Egyoku Nakao, Matthew Fox, Luisah Teish, Father Thomas Keating, Jon Kabat-Zinn, Jean Houston, Eckhart Tolle, and B. K. S. Iyengar. Spiritual Elders may look like you . . .

Some of us will hear the call to become Creative Elders, allowing visual or performing art to move through us and offer inspiration. They may look like Bob Dylan, David Hockney, Ai Weiwei, Leonard Cohen, Maya Angelou, Jeff Bridges, Meryl Streep, Paul McCartney, Mick Jagger, Judi Dench, Mel Brooks, Mary Oliver, M. C. Richards, Clint Eastwood, Willie Nelson, Jackson Browne, Norman Lear, Neil Young, Helen Mirren, Samuel L. Jackson, and Yo-Yo Ma. Shirley MacLaine recently said that she was making three new films so that people could see what a woman in her eighties can do. Creative Elders may look like you . . .

Of course, these Activist, Spiritual, and Creative Elders are not without their own personal shadows, emotional issues, cognitive limitations, or even moral lapses. But, because they are publicly recognized, we can be aware together of their attainments and take inspiration from them. We can be aware that they are exemplars who call us to our own depths and our contributions.

So, let's remember: The Elder may wear the face of a shaman, factory worker, healer, political leader, singer, storyteller, ecologist, inventor, CEO, scientist, author, therapist, craftsperson, educator, gardener, grandmother, artist, warrior, or friend. He or she may wear your face.

Joseph Campbell pointed out in the title of his famous book *Hero with a Thousand Faces* that the hero archetype has a thousand faces—that is, it appears in countless images. In the same way, the Elder archetype appears in countless images. There are as many faces of the Elder as there are Elders.

Today, as those who have reached the late stages of life, we ourselves are the Elders we have long been seeking. Our search for others to serve as mentors, gurus, and guides is over. We are the ones to pass the torch. We are the ones who are blessed and who will bless others.

In his book *From Age-ing to Sage-ing,* Rabbi Zalman Schachter-Shalomi put it this way: "Elders are the jewels of humanity that have been mined from the Earth, cut in the rough, then buffed and polished by the stonecutter's art into precious gems that we recognize for their enduring value and beauty. Shaped with patience and love over decades of refinement, each facet of the jewel reflects light that awakens our soul to intimations of its own splendor."

Elder is a verb more than a noun, a dynamic process that reveals the ever-present but invisible urge toward more awareness or self-actualization in the human soul. *Eldering* is the same as *evolving,* a holy longing of the soul that, once recognized and directed, is purposeful and joyful. Eldering is an internal demand to honor the voice of the soul.

My friend Jason described his shift this way: "I look back on the busyness and see it so differently now. I went from being somebody to being nobody. It all seemed so dramatically important at the time—

rushing around to earn money, approval, respect. Now, I'm just being, meditating a lot. I'm mentoring young men locally and writing that book that was gestating in me for decades. But the way that I do these things now is entirely different: I follow my body, feel immersed in the moment, and meet the needs that appear. The only respect that matters now is self-respect."

Renowned painter David Hockney, slowed and hard of hearing in his late seventies, wanted to continue to follow his creative passion. So, he redesigned his circumstances by asking his subjects to come to him and pose for three days. He painted eighty portraits of people in the same chair, each one a distinct glimpse of an individual's essence. In this way, he followed his soul's mission to the end.

My friend Sally described to me the internal shift she experienced when she completed the training with Sage-ing International to become a Sage. "I used to build million-dollar businesses. I would see the goal and make it happen. Now, I see the goal and live in each moment with intention, connection, self-care, and loving awareness—and the goal unfolds. Elders create success by being who we want to be, rather than by railroading it through our egos."

This move from productivity to creativity, from strategizing to intuition, from pushing to flow, reflects the larger transition from role to soul. Whether we call the new direction a greater authenticity, a growing wisdom, or a newfound freedom, it reprioritizes our values, energies, and actions as aging erodes our masks.

Elders know what we don't know. Elders know how to listen because we know how to quiet our minds and be present. We know how to ask the right question for the right moment. And we know how to be—not to be a hero, a mother, a CEO. Just be.

Elders know the end is near.

Given our 360-degree view, we have a sense now of the privilege of age. We have a sense now of how small we were back then, how overcome we were by small things, how used we were by small purposes.

And we have a sense that the heroic ego's mission is over. That the culture's teachings about endless work, endless striving, and endless growth no longer pertain.

With this perspective, the ego cracks. The light floods in. The butler recedes; the master returns. We are not that smallness; there is something larger in us. We are That. And age nudges us to go beyond ego and connect with That.

In each of my interviews, people mentioned that they had tried to plan and organize their lives, but they can see now, in retrospect, that their life events had a rhyme and rhythm of their own. They were not under their ego's control. Of course, things don't always turn out as we had expected, but from the long view that's neither good nor bad, neither right nor wrong. Those dualistic concepts arise from heroic thinking, not Elder thinking. They reflect fixed ideas and the ego's need to control outcomes.

For some, as the ego recedes, the mind's chatter about the future and the past grows dim. The narrative self, the voice of the inner storyteller, grows quieter.

The restricted emotions that accompany ego may loosen their grip and the "higher emotions" may emerge. As we become less self-centered, it may lead to greater empathy and compassion. As we feel less "hurry sickness," it may lead to greater patience. As we feel less regret, it may lead to greater gratitude. As we feel less obsessed with money, it may lead to a previously unknown generosity. As we connect with our inner child, we may feel more awe and wonder. As we experience an appreciation for the interconnectedness of all life, it may lead us to feel a greater reverence for every living thing and for the infinite.

In his book *Portraits from Memory and Other Essays,* British philosopher Bertrand Russell said it this way: "Make your interests grow gradually wider and more impersonal, until bit by bit the walls of the ego recede, and your life becomes increasingly merged in the universal life. An individual human existence should be like a river—small at first, narrowly contained within its banks, and rushing passionately past rocks and over waterfalls. Gradually the river grows wider, the banks recede, the waters flow more quietly, and in the end, without any visible break, they become merged in the sea, and painlessly lose their individual being."

The Elder stage of life also introduces an altered experience of dualities. We hold opposites more consciously in the body/mind: young and old, doing and being, resilience and vulnerability, holding on and letting go, victory and defeat. We feel perfect as we are—and also in need of improvement. We feel connected to life in the face of imminent death. We experience more directly the losses within gains and the gains within losses, and even the beginnings in endings and the endings in beginnings.

In a 2017 essay, "Wondrous and Wild," Carol Orsborn called it a time full of irony: "We find ourselves brimming with unexpected passion, but frequently lack the energy to see things through. We experience ourselves to be at the peak of our knowledge and abilities, only to realize that we are masters of a world that no longer exists. We who are old discover untapped reservoirs of compassion for humanity, while having less patience for individuals than ever before. We crave to be included while yearning to be left alone. We worry we won't have enough for the demands of a cavernous future while fearing that tomorrow may be our last."

In addition, we notice an altered sense of time: Following our life review, our 360-degree vantage point can reorient us by placing our personal story in a larger history, a multigenerational family history or a centuries-old national history. But the span of time can extend even more to include human history and our place in the evolution of our species. This long view can help us feel less hostage to fleeting events and fleeting feelings.

We also observe that time seems to pass more quickly as we age. A month feels like a day, a year like a month, in contrast to childhood, when a summer holiday seems to last forever. It's a mysterious shift in awareness. James M. Broadway and Brittiney Sandoval, at the University of California at Santa Barbara, reported in *Scientific American* on a study that confirmed this subjective experience: Older people tended to perceive time moving faster than young people. They explained it this way: When faced with novel situations, our brains record more richly detailed memories. The older we get, the more familiar we become with our surroundings. We don't notice the detailed environments of our homes and workplaces. But for children, the world is an unfamiliar place filled with new experiences, so their brains are actively making memories. The theory suggests that this difference in brain activity makes time run more slowly for children than for adults stuck in a routine. Perhaps we can slow our sense of time passing by keeping our brains active with novel experience and living more fully in presence, allowing emotions to arise and move through us.

Mortality awareness also affects our sense of time. It shortens the horizon, yes, but it also opens our awareness more easily into a flow state. One woman told me that mortality awareness acts on her like a catalyst, awakening her to those inner shadow characters that say, "Put it off until tomorrow." Or "I remember when . . . " Or "I should take care of that." When she returns to mortality awareness, it pulls her back into presence and the call of this moment. This enables her to sense the flow in the river of life, rather than trying to control it with "what ifs" or "shoulds."

In addition, if we practice meditation and regularly experience silent pure awareness, we immerse ourselves in "no time." The clock stops, the calendar disappears. We dissolve into the timeless mystery behind it all. We experience this truth: Time and the timeless coexist.

Because the term "wise Elder" is such a common cliché, we assume that we know what it means and to whom it refers. But because the Elder has a thousand faces, we must take care not to define Elder too tightly. That puts us at risk of creating another static stereotype, or ego ideal, with a whole set of shoulds. Instead, we can circumscribe its limits by describing what it is not.

An Elder does not reject the face in the mirror, denying aging or mortality awareness by trying to look young, and suffering under the negative gaze of the inner ageist.

An Elder does not avoid facing fear, suffering, and loss by numbing out with substances or digital distraction, losing a connection to shadow awareness.

An Elder does not resist change or impermanence.

An Elder does not live paralyzed between a wistful past or an anxious future, denying the portal of presence.

An Elder does not need to be right.

An Elder is not shame-based.

An Elder does not succumb to cynicism, bitterness, or resignation.

An Elder does not unconsciously serve a shadow character that no longer inspires inner development—a workaholic hero, burned-out caregiver, inner critic, perfectionist, victim, know-it-all, or inner ageist who is "forever young"—and therefore denies a connection to soul.

An Elder does not project a shadow character onto others, believing that he or she is a victim and others are to blame for his or her suffering.

An Elder does not project his or her wisdom or spiritual authority onto others, denying it in him- or herself.

An Elder does not refuse to give his or her gifts to future generations, denying the transmission of a legacy.

Several years ago, I met a not-Elder. I went with therapist friends to see a renowned psychoanalyst whose writings had affected all of us deeply. We looked forward to sitting in his compassionate presence. However, we found a man, at seventy, whose ego was arrogant, competitive, and self-referring. He put down other therapists and bragged about his impact on the field of psychology. He clearly needed recognition and strived to find it through the "superiority" of his ideas.

I was deeply saddened to observe his lopsided development: His cognitive abilities shone, but his emotional and spiritual development were derailed. He was like a philosopher king spouting decrees, who had no access to pure awareness beyond his ego/mind. And he clearly had no access to shadow awareness, for he was blind to his own flaws.

In a more devastating intimate experience with an Elder, I spent several years in close friendship with a man who was a hidden spiritual adept. His spiritual development was so advanced that, as I listened to him describe his inner world in detail from moment to moment, I was transported into his heightened stage of awareness. I felt that I was sitting with a rishi on the Ganges or with a Jewish zaddik in the temple or with the Buddha himself under the bodhi tree. It was the most precious offering, an answer to my prayers for a spiritually awakened guide who was not a guru.

However, when a shadow issue arose between us, and he lied about it, I was heartbroken. I have no doubt about the authenticity of his spiritual experience. But his emotional and moral development did not match his attainment. He was a Spiritual Elder—but not fully an Elder human being.

There also are many tales of fallen Elders who, like Darth Vader, align with the dark side, descend to the shadow, and become lost there. In these stories, they can lead heroes, like Luke Skywalker, into danger. When I watched the film *Wild, Wild Country* about Bhagwan Shree Rajneesh (Osho) and observed the slow moral degeneration of his character and the widespread denial among his followers, I was reminded of this ever-present possibility. I also was deeply disturbed upon hearing about the violent, tragic death of Jungian analyst and author Robert Moore (whose seminal work on masculine archetypes advocated for Kings/Elders to mentor younger men), which reinforces this point. Clearly, both Osho and Moore were teachers with extraordinary talents, and both got possessed by unconscious demons.

Thank you, Ken Wilber, for this understanding of distinct lines of development. That is, there is no global development. We develop in different ways and at different speeds along cognitive, moral, kinesthetic, emotional, interpersonal, aesthetic, and spiritual pathways. In *Integral Spirituality*, Wilber writes, "Evidence shows that a person, *in the same act and absolutely simultaneously*, can be at one level of cognition, another level of self-sense, and yet another level of morals."

In other words, no human being is fully conscious along every line of development. Wilber's work on Integral Life Practice attempts to address this need by designing inner work for every line of development.

Becoming an Elder

A Rite of Passage

The shift of archetypes from Hero to Elder is not automatic, and, unlike our qualification for Medicare, it's not linked to a particular age. The Elder is a stage, not an age. It's a qualitative transition, like liquid to gas. That means that a fifty-five-year-old who serves her soul's mission with authenticity and gravitas may be an Elder, while an eighty-five-year-old who believes he is a victim and deserves revenge may not.

This shift requires a rite of passage. As we discussed earlier, every rite of passage requires three steps, through which the soul evolves to another stage of awareness. In addition to this classical model of transitions, shadow characters can block our movement through any stage, so they are added here.

1. Letting Go of the Ego's Agenda

When we disidentify from the roles and values of midlife, the rushing and struggling, the duties and yearning, we can release the preoccupations of adulthood. When we do an ego life review and a shadow life review, we can see who we have become, our strengths and weaknesses, our contributions and wounds. If we are fortunate, we can see the larger arc of our soul's mission. When we do life repair, we can allow ourselves to feel those dark emotions that hide in the shadow and begin to symbolically let go of grief, resentment, disappointment, and anger. In this way, we sever ourselves from the past of our youthful and adult stages, preparing to enter another period.

At this stage, a shadow figure may deny the call to Elderhood and cling to life as it was. Too fearful to tolerate change and loss, this part of us is unable to let go of the past.

2. Moving into Liminality or the Neutral Zone

When we let go of the familiar identities and strategizing for personal gain, we may feel undefined, lost, disoriented, purposeless, as if we're waiting . . . But for what? During this phase, we feel alone, facing our fears and limits and the symbolic death of the ego.

This stage is completed via shadow-work. The shadow characters— the henchmen, in the parable at the opening of this chapter—provide the means by which the ego is humbled. We begin to observe that we can't control the increasing limitations in our body, brain, and mind. We can't control the losses of our loved ones. We can no longer strive for accomplishment without limits; we can no longer believe our ego's fantasies of omnipotence. If we are fortunate, the ego bows, even reluctantly, to the guidance of greater wisdom. And the door opens for the master's return.

At this stage, a shadow figure may grow complacent with the formless uncertainty of the neutral zone, perhaps during an illness, early retirement, or lull in a spiritual practice. It grows lazy, perhaps, and denies an emerging intuition, fantasy, or vision of the future, keeping us lost in the forest, waiting.

3. New Beginnings

On the other side of the threshold now, our center of gravity has moved from ego to soul. We have pinpointed our unique offerings and committed to give them in service to others, thereby seeding the next generation. To complete this rite, it helps to be witnessed by other "initiated Elders."

At this stage, a shadow figure cannot incorporate the tender new shoots of growth due to self-doubt or distrust of change and clings instead to a frantic adulthood, missing the opportunity for deeper change.

If the shadow character or internal obstacle successfully sabotages any step, the rite can fail and the evolution of the soul stalls.

An Interview with Ron Pevny,
Founder of the Center for Conscious Eldering

I knew that I needed to speak about this topic with Ron Pevny, then sixty-nine, author of *Conscious Living, Conscious Aging* and founder of the Center for Conscious Eldering, which offers wilderness rites of passage for seniors to become Elders. These retreats empower participants to let go of the security of past self-concepts, beliefs, and behaviors, move into the liminal, amorphous passage of late life, and emerge with the skills, resources, and spiritual connection necessary to become an Elder.

"Although modern culture doesn't acknowledge the Elder," Ron told me, "as we age the inner call to elderhood is still there. It's an archetypal dynamic built into each of us that seeks expression as we begin to move from the stage of midlife adulthood to our next chapter."

There is a danger in our failure to recognize the call, he said. "If we stay overactive because we're pretending to be fifty, the Inner Elder cannot emerge."

Ron learned this through a personal ordeal. Until 2007, he had been living a divided life: working to uphold his financial responsibilities to his family and trying to uphold his soul's responsibility to his calling, which was to assist people in becoming Elders. He prayed for an experience that would confirm his calling and credibility to guide others, but no signs appeared. He was paralyzed and could not let go of the past.

"The stress was immense as I tried to honor both realities. In retrospect, it makes sense that it would take its toll."

Ron began to suffer from atrial fibrillation: His heart was beating to two different rhythms. (What a symptom as metaphor!) X-rays revealed a tumor on his lung, which the doctors believed was causing the arrhythmia. The fear that his life was about to end triggered the inner work that Ron needed: facing the awesome vulnerability, the recognition of unfinished business, the need to communicate his legacy, the deep gratitude for his blessings, and the valuing of all that he had taken for granted.

"It showed me in the most compelling way that my calling had to be honored as my highest priority," Ron said.

With this new perspective, Ron could take a leap and release the past. The health crisis led him from living a conflicted life to the decision to devote all of himself to his soul's mission. But the ordeal was not over. He let go of a past role, but a deeper sacrifice was required.

Following lung surgery, his heart's arrhythmias continued, despite the doctor's beliefs that they would cease. "As I tried to fall asleep amid the frightening heartbeats, I entered a state of consciousness where I saw and felt a black shadow that felt like death itself about to smother me. I cried out to God, saying that I had done all I could do and only God could help me now. If there was still work for me to contribute to the world, I needed God to save my life."

For Ron, this was a release of his ego's control and a giving up to something greater. "It was a moment of complete surrender to a wisdom greater than me. In that moment I felt the darkness explode out of me. I awoke knowing that something profound had happened. That release marked the end of the heart arrhythmias and the beginning of a new chapter in my inner and outer life."

Only then, having severed the past and endured disorientation and uncertainty in the neutral zone, could he emerge to redefine himself from the inside out as a conscious Elder, who guides others to become Elders.

A couple of years later, in a wilderness setting with friends and a mentor, Ron realized that his rite was missing something crucial—acknowledgment and support from others in his community. He asked his mentor to create a baptism ceremony in a river to mark his passage into a new life chapter. As others observed the rite, he felt like he was finally embodying this stage of life.

If millions of people made this sacred passage into late life, our rapidly aging world culture would shift from a "sibling society" (Robert Bly's apt term for a culture of adults without Elder supervision) to an "elder society." Elders would aid heroes, who would then become Elders and aid more heroes, who would become Elders.

This cycle is like old trees dropping their seedlings, and young trees gaining height and strength in their shade. Then the young trees grow tall, drop their seeds, and initiate fresh growth.

Letting Go

Inner Work for Resistant Heroes

Let's apply the stages of this rite of passage so that we can see more clearly the evolution of soul in the transition from hero to Elder. Most of us think about letting go of material things as we age, giving away our career wardrobes, selling the family home to downsize. Others think about letting go of physical and mental capacities, learning to live with less independence, less physical beauty, less sexual potency, less short-term memory. Others think about letting go of resentments, judgments, broken promises, and blame that bind us to past relationship habits. And, of course, others think about letting go of deceased loved ones, whose absence becomes a presence within us. Each of these is a kind of sacrifice, leading to a liminal time and a whisper of new beginnings.

But there are volumes written about the losses and diminishments of age, about this kind of letting go from the outside in. Rather, we're concerned here with letting go from the inside out, downsizing our heroic egos and sacrificing the inner idols they have created—the drive for speed, fame, wealth, physical perfection, or salvation, or the need to be special, smart, or right. As we have unconsciously identified with these idols over decades, they have become embedded in who we think we are. So, when we begin to clear the altar of our heroic idols, we may feel the vast emptiness they have covered up—and the vast openness of liminal space.

In that formless space, our shadow characters arise, attempting to block our path from becoming an Elder and connecting with soul. "I'm scared of being an Elder because that's old and close to death." "Who am I to become an Elder? I'm not special or wise." "I need to keep going, I haven't finished building my empire." "I have so much regret." "I can't seem to control anything anymore." "Everyone talks about being over doing. But how is just being different from being a slug?"

Sometimes the obstacle has the voice of recurring resistance or denial. Sometimes it's the inner ageist. Sometimes it's an unmet childhood need or an incomplete heroic task. Sometimes it's a fear of the unknown.

Each of these shadow characters sabotages our development by denying the call of the Inner Elder. We become resistant heroes by gripping on to past roles, listening to the noise in our minds and defending rigid, metallic ego structures. We continue to do what we've always done, running in place, clinging to control, ambition, conformity, blame, and self-interest.

As a result, we are not aligned with *what is.* The more we hold on, the more we resist *what is,* the more our unconscious fear builds charge in the shadow. The more unconscious the fear, the tighter we grasp, whether to our self-image, beliefs, roles, or stuff.

As a result, the three portals remain tightly closed. No contact with pure awareness means no experience beyond ego. No contact with shadow awareness means no self-knowledge, life repair, or preparation for life completion. No contact with mortality awareness means the heights of denial and the depths of lost opportunity to live fully now and to consciously prepare for death.

On the other hand, with shadow-work, we begin to sort through our internal clutter. We seek out those parts of ourselves that resist a closing or an opening, a longing for more or a need for completion. When we release the obstacle, we can pick up whatever connects us to a larger life.

I remember, in this moment, a paradoxical Zen saying: "Grab hold lightly, let go tightly."

So, stop and ask yourself: Who or what, within you, stops you from crossing this threshold from hero to Elder? What needs to be sacrificed for you to become an Elder? This is letting go as a season of the soul.

In her autobiography, *Such Stuff as Dreams are Made On,* Jungian analyst Helen Luke described a dream she had about this theme at age eighty-eight:

> I dreamed of a house in which I was living, with other people living
> in other rooms of it. There was a fire in the adjacent property and

the firemen were at work, but it began to look as though our house was threatened. I was talking to a fireman and he asked whose house it was. I realized that it was not a place I had rented temporarily but my own house. I said so clearly, yet at the same time felt a kind of clarity and release, as though, if it burned down, no one but myself would be the loser, and it didn't matter to me much.

In dreams, a house is a symbol of the dreamer's unconscious sense of self or identity. A house on fire tells us that this identity is burning up, undergoing a great change into something else. Helen Luke, by then long familiar with her shadow, recognized that the destruction and loss of what she had taken to be her identity was not a danger. She expressed no resistance or fear of letting go because she accepted *what is.*

Most of us, on the other hand, resist the sacrifice. We say to ourselves, "God, why me?"

With shadow-work, we can identify the shadow character that resists the shift from hero to Elder, from grandiosity to simplicity, from persona to authenticity. We can witness the repeating voice, the repeating feelings, and the accompanying body sensations in order to personify a shadow character. We know that it's activated when it's loud, repetitive, and uncomfortable.

My client Joe, at the age of sixty-three, worked brutally long hours and suffered from insomnia and migraines. He told me that his age was not a factor. "I'm still young, and besides, I haven't met my financial goal yet." He was in the grip of denial, unable to listen to his body because his chronological age didn't match his picture of "old" and because his fear of not having enough money was deeply rooted in childhood poverty.

When I asked him how much money he had saved, as a reality check on his fear, I was shocked at his answer. It was a lot of money.

When I asked what else he would lose if he slowed down, he responded, "I would be useless. My kids and grandkids would see a useless old guy, not the hardworking provider that I've always been."

What else? "I would lose my productivity, my status, my power." He sighed, appearing to be puzzled. "I wouldn't know who I am."

So, we had an image of a shadow character, an unconscious figure projected into his future that resulted, like the inner Bag Lady, in his feeling such terror that he could not get off the treadmill. He gave the shadow character a name: the Wimp.

"What is the Wimp, this useless, lazy, powerless guy, saying to you now?"

"You can't stop, Joe. You'll lose everything. You'll be a nobody. No one will respect you. No one will love you." I thought I detected a tear in the corner of his eye.

"When did you first hear those words, Joe?"

"As a kid, my dad told me, 'Men work. Be a man and you'll get respect. Be lazy and you'll get nothing.'"

Joe's identity, value, power, and self-respect were bound to the working warrior. His self-importance was tied to his rank. So, letting go of this identity would not be easy or quick. It would be a complex, slow process that included honoring his past, grieving it, and releasing the energy that was bound to it. He would need the courage to let go deeply, enter the neutral zone, face his fear of the Wimp, and trust life until another source of identity and self-respect emerged.

During his time in the neutral zone, many feelings emerged that Joe had banished to the shadow—his vulnerability, grief, and anger. At first they felt intolerable, and he tried to push them back down into the darkness. But slowly, gradually, he allowed himself to feel all those forbidden feelings, and his stoic persona began to soften. He spent many therapy sessions in tears, acknowledging what he had sacrificed by following the working warrior and stuffing the Wimp into the dark. As he reclaimed lost feelings and deepened his self-knowledge, Joe understood that his heroic work ethic had served his ego well in midlife—but now it sabotaged his soul in late life.

He gently put down his sword, making the shift from success to significance, from money to meaning. He began to ask himself, "What is the real meaning of this time of my life? How do I complete unfinished business? How do I contribute to the common good?"

Joe's ego was humbled as he faced himself with honesty. As his fear receded, gratitude arose within him.

"This letting go into the unknown is a bit like lying on your back in water," I told him. "You're terrified, then you float."

Another common shadow character that stops us from making this shift arises from an epidemic psychological issue: Late life is a setup to retrigger narcissistic injury, the early childhood feeling of being excluded, unseen, unimportant, or dismissed by parents who did not see our soul's essential value but, instead, made us perform for love and approval. The invisibility that goes with age is widespread in our age-ist society. So, to become an Elder, we need to recognize that this is an early injury resurfacing in a new circumstance.

My client, Diane, at the age of seventy, was struggling with a lack of contact and appreciation from her family members. A shadow character kept saying, "I'm invisible. I'm irrelevant. I'm unimportant to them. I'll never get my needs met."

Diane named her shadow character the Invisible Woman. I suggested that she could communicate her need to family members by saying, "I'm feeling vulnerable and would really appreciate more communication. Can you check in with me once a week?" She responded that she had never expressed her needs and couldn't do that now.

Alternatively, she could stop trying to get her needs met by the family and seek to receive validation and care from others, such as friends or professionals.

Or she could meet the need herself with inner work. By being present in the moment, validating her own life, and remembering who she is, she could complete the essential tasks of becoming an Elder. And she also could use her Inner Elder as a resource to transmit the love and acceptance that she hadn't received from her parents. In other words, this injury of invisibility can stop us from crossing this threshold—or it can open the door.

Another client, Rowan, age sixty-five, reminded me of a different trait of resistant heroes: "I don't know enough to be an Elder. I have nothing to teach."

A lifelong pattern of self-doubt left him feeling unqualified and therefore reluctant to make this transition. He had an idealized image of an Elder, as he had had an idealized image of being a father. In each case, the Critic shadow character told him that he didn't match up to the standard, and that he wasn't good enough.

As Rowan completed his life review, he began to see a potential contribution that he hadn't made conscious before: He was a foodie and, as a result, had learned a lot about cooking, nutrition, and food as medicine. He did have something to teach, and he began to focus his passion around volunteer organizations that linked food education with hunger in poor communities. When I last saw him, he carried himself with more confidence and lit up when he spoke about his soul's mission. Rowan was an emerging Elder who found the intersection between his offering and a great need in the world. He had moved from self-centeredness to a felt sense of interconnection with a larger system in which he gives and receives.

My client Craig, sixty-five, also felt like he was living between worlds, not young but not old, no longer conquering but not yet stopping, no longer a hero but not yet an Elder. When he awoke one day and realized that he was older than his father had been when he died, Craig felt strange and disoriented.

"I was following his footsteps through life, but now those footprints are gone," he said. "I have no map."

As a hero, Craig built a big career in screenwriting, chased women and peak experiences, and always wanted more of everything. Now, that inclination to chase It, the elusive something that would bring him peace, had begun to subside. He started to see that he didn't need more experience; he needed more depth and more inner orientation.

Craig had entered the liminal zone, where past roles lose their meaning, and his world felt empty. Because he had not consciously chosen this path, he could get stuck there, wallowing in the formlessness, feeling hopeless and powerless. Or he could add more hobbies to his to-do list, trying to change from the outside in. Or he could enter a kind of hibernation and do the inner work of age to cross a threshold into Elderhood. I presented the dilemma to him.

At first, he tried to find his way as he had done everything else: pushing, striving, reading, and intellectualizing his task. He went to a workshop, read three books about Elders, and returned, saying, "Okay, I get it. I'm fixed now. Next?"

Then his mother died, then his sister. And, in my office, he sobbed uncontrollably. "It could happen to me," he whispered.

"It will," I replied. "One day."

He looked up at me, clear-eyed. He had taken in mortality awareness. He was recognizing that he was not in charge. He was allowing age to initiate him.

I sent Craig home to do a life review of his lived and his unlived life. Through the next few months, we explored the events, people, and transitions that he had lived out. We also discovered those parts of him that were sacrificed and remained in the dark. He slowly began to realize that he had been unconsciously resisting entry to this stage of life—"Old, ugh!"—because he had been so identified with an internal Rebel character, who had been telling him, like Peter Pan, "I won't grow up!" Without having deeply accepted adulthood, how could he accept Elderhood?

Because Craig had softened and opened in the face of mortality, he continued to romance this shadow character, which had kept him youthful but unable to accept the full responsibilities and limits of adulthood. I watched as he became more grounded in his body and took up the guitar, a long-lost dream.

When I noticed that his spoken language and body language had changed around aging, I gave him the exercise below to help him meet his Inner Elder.

Meeting the Inner Elder

An Initiation

For decades, in psychology, the Inner Child has been a widely known internal figure who carries, in the unconscious, our woundedness and our wisdom, our early trauma and our sweet innocence. It became popular in the 1970s recovery movement as a subpersonality or shadow figure that held the keys to healing from abuse, trauma, and addiction. Many decades earlier, Jung had written of the Divine Child within us, focusing on the light side of the archetype, with its wisdom and innocence.

In the same way, we all have an Inner Elder, a hidden figure that is banished from conscious awareness but carries our intuitive wisdom, ethical guidance, and spiritual connection. Jung wrote of this archetype as the "Wise Old Man" (or Woman), the "speaking fountainhead" of the soul, who appears in our dreams and myths. The shift from hero to Elder requires the cultivation of a conscious relationship with the Inner Elder, or this Wise Old Woman or Man who knows, who guides, who initiates, who is connected to the source.

The Inner Elder can be seen as an individual image of the universal archetype that connects us to a transcendent or spiritual source. To become a true Elder, we need to attune to our own Inner Elder and begin a dialogue with him or her as part of this rite of passage.

While a living Elder may not have intentionally practiced meditation and cultivated pure awareness, his or her Inner Elder has access to it. While a living Elder may not have consciously practiced shadow-work, his or her Inner Elder has a connection to soul. While a living Elder may not have consciously practiced mortality awareness, his or her Inner Elder always knows and has always known death as a possibility in any moment. This archetype lives out of time and carries the awareness of an individual's end of time.

As you see in the opening parable, this inner guide is master of the house. When the ego or butler bows to the Inner Elder or spiritual source, the internal dynamic changes. We then have intuitive inner guidance, more witness or spaciousness from the voices of our shadow characters, and a link to something beyond ego.

For a rare few who have positive, loving experiences of Elders and some awareness of the inner world, the connection to the Inner Elder may begin early. A woman who was reading my blogs wrote me a lengthy email about herself. As a child, she wrote, she was surrounded by five generations of family who had survived pogroms, the 1918 pandemic, the Great Depression, tuberculosis, Hitler, McCarthy . . . She was awed by them.

They offered her their family stories, their cherished artifacts, and their precious songs. And she wanted to be like them. So, she imagined herself recounting these tales decades into the future to her children and grandchildren. "In the voices of my grandmother's grandmother and my grandfather's grandfather was my destiny. I knew what I wanted to be when I grew up: very old."

From a young age, she had a picture in her mind's eye: a woman with long white hair, wise and solitary, older than God and younger than springtime. She lived in a cabin on a stream in a forest. Wild creatures sought her out: Birds came at her whistle; raccoons brought their babies onto the deck. She was an ancient gypsy who played guitar and sang songs in a foreign tongue, read the Tarot for travelers, and spun a Russian dance with wild abandon.

When she wrote to me, she was seventy years old. She told me that she is manifesting that ambitious internal image, becoming "one really spectacular old lady."

She wrote: "More than any of the grand successes, and there have been some grand successes, I realize that during every meaningful challenge, this Me that I have become appeared to that girl who was becoming—I showed myself, I showed *this* to that defensive, turbulent girl, and said, 'Look at who you'll get to be!'"

Unlike most of us, this woman's lifelong relationship with Elders and with her Inner Elder countered the rampant ageism of our society.

She grew up without an inner ageist and eagerly looked forward to her future self, to being old, colorful, eccentric, and wise.

She reminded me of a Joni Mitchell song: "Songs to aging children come. Aging children, I am one."

Here is the Inner Elder visualization exercise that I recommended to my client Craig. It is paraphrased from the book *From Age-ing to Sage-ing* by Rabbi Zalman Schachter-Shalomi and Ronald S. Miller.

Please read this through, then put down the book and try it.

Sit quietly, close your eyes, and follow the inflow and outflow of your breath as you become calm and centered. When you are ready, visualize in your mind's eye walking up a set of stairs leading to the door of your Inner Elder. When you knock on the door, your realized Self, the embodiment of boundless compassion and wisdom, greets you with a warm embrace. As you gaze into the Inner Elder's eyes, you feel unconditionally loved and reassured about your progress so far.

As a pilgrim confronting the highest, most all-embracing source of wisdom, ask the Inner Elder for guidance about an issue that puzzles you. It can range from practical concerns to metaphysical inquiries. After posing your question, remain in a state of receptivity, allowing an answer to imprint itself in your consciousness as a sign, symbol, or inner sense of knowing.

When you receive an answer, rest in silence for a while. Then, as you look again into the eyes of your higher Self, you receive these parting words of encouragement: "Journey on with confidence and with blessings as you proceed on your path. Visit me again whenever you need further guidance."

With deep gratitude, take leave of your Inner Elder and walk down the stairs to depart. Sit quietly for a few moments, slowly open your eyes, and return to waking state. Record your impressions and intuitions in your journal.

When my client Craig returned to my office after doing this visualization, he was clearly shaken. "I didn't really believe you until this happened. I saw him, an old Native American man with a long braid and deep wrinkles. He was wrapped in a blanket. His eyes pierced me with kindness. No one ever looked at me like that before."

"I asked him what to do with my life, now that I'm not young and not old," he continued. "I asked him about my mission for the time remaining. He said, 'The war is over. Put down your weapons, your strategies, your shields. Grieve your losses. And learn to trust that something larger than you is carrying you forward. The rest will take care of itself.'"

Craig sat there, hands in his lap, eyes wide open. We were silent for a while. Then he asked, "Is that man me? Did I know that?"

The Inner Elder is a latent blueprint that dwells within us, waiting to greet us, waiting to guide us. For so many years, we have been unknowingly obeying the voices of shadow characters, listening to the noise rather than the signal. We've been taking in the inner critic, following the compulsions, and acting out the self-sabotage. It's time now, as Elders, to attune to the voice of the Inner Elder, to make a conscious relationship with it and allow it to guide us across the threshold.

As we embrace the invisible Elder within, breath by breath, we will more readily embrace the invisible Elders without, the many marginalized older people around us. And we will discover the gold hidden within them.

New Beginnings

Reimagining the Elder from the Inside Out

If you, fellow traveler in late life, are reading this book, you would naturally reimagine the meaning of Elder as you age. And, as all of us face the opportunities and constraints of late life, we would naturally embody it in our own ways.

When I entered my year-long training at Sage-ing International to become an Elder (or Sage, as it's called there), I felt a bit anxious and disoriented about late life. I was letting go of past roles but was very uncertain about my future and the meaning of this stage of life. I was facing losses but not yet aware of potential gains; I was facing endings but not yet aware of new beginnings. I was floundering in liminal space.

I knew that, to reorient, I needed to uncover a new archetype and a new myth for this cycle of life.

To prepare for the training, I completed the inner work described in the book *From Age-ing to Sage-ing,* while adding the dimension of shadow-work. I set an intention to let go of my heroic striving and my need to be right and to be certain. I wanted to attune to the Mystery that was emerging and follow the Mystery, rather than my ego/mind.

The training was inspiring and profound. After the final rite and recognition by other Elders, I felt exhilarated and purposeful. I wanted to share this orientation to late life with other people as a natural extension of my lifelong mission to transmit information about consciousness.

Many members of my cohort in the training, ages sixty to eighty, had similar experiences. When asked about their visions of becoming an Elder, one woman said, "My vision is being grounded in essence, engaged in love, fully alive to all that is."

Another said, "My intention is to see me in you and you in me. I'm invited to see this oneness everywhere."

A man said, "My vision of being an emerging Elder is a radiant non-judgmental awareness, speaking truth to power, and being less attached to outcomes."

Another said, "I'm moving from accomplishment to contribution."

And a woman said, "I intend to make life sacred by ritual, befriend my shadow, and choose the path of the Sage from moment to moment."

In other words, a vision was calling them, rather than a "should" pushing them. In this stage of awareness, many of us feel a silent deepening for the sake of service, and we can act as wisdom holders, advocates, mentors, guides, caregivers, volunteers, grandparents, and guardians of the Earth.

Another Sage told me, "I'm slowly coming to see the rightness of aging, of the body's decline, the loss of my roles and identities. I can't quite explain it, but I'm in a transition to another, deeper identity." When I suggested that she was moving from role to soul, she lit up. She hadn't had the language to describe her inner experience, but it fit.

An Interview with Mythologist and Storyteller Michael Meade

When I interviewed renowned author, storyteller, and mythologist Michael Meade, he told me that, at his sixty-fifth birthday, surrounded by his kids, spouses, and old friends, he declared himself now outside the law. He had traveled through the zodiac five times and was free of categories. "So, now I will be an outlaw, instead of an in-law," he told them. "No more expectations because I see and serve a higher law now."

Michael explained to me that Elders have a foot in each world, this world and the other world. "And there are no normal, conventional Elders. We have lived with our shadows, spent time there, fallen and recovered, found self-knowledge and empathy. As a result, Elders are off the map, living outside the dynamic of the village."

In addition, Elders have made a sacrifice, which means "making sacred." They are less heroic, less egoic, and more connected to beauty and to nature, he said.

As a child, Michael felt unmentored. When an older man told him, "You've got something," this led him to question his purpose and to ask, "What am I here for?" rather than "How do I fit in?" He set out to explore this question.

He spent time with traditional indigenous Elders and absorbed their presence, which activated something in him. In traditional cultures, Michael told me, trees and animals act as Elders, too. People draw blessings from nature. "I suggest that Elders show youth how to engage nature as a force of initiation," he told me.

Thirty years ago, Michael found his soul's mission to bring initiation to at-risk youth and Elders. For three decades, he held retreats for endangered youth and older men who blessed and mentored them. "The missing ingredient for young men has been Elder initiation. These youth long for Elders who can inspire them and earn their respect."

One day on the street, a young man, whom he hadn't seen for years, approached him. He told Michael that, thanks to the mentoring he had received from Michael, he now mentors others. "I still keep your books next to my bed. You are my Elder," he told Michael.

"When someone sees you that way, you become an Elder," Michael told me.

This gift can be reversed: Youth can mentor Elders, too, such as in technology. I told him that I had hired a local high-school girl to teach me about social media and had come through my "click" fears and judgments about Facebook and Twitter to a joyful experience of connecting online.

Michael suggested that there is an Inner Youth in every Elder—and an Inner Elder in every youth. Our Inner Youth carries our vitality, hope, and vision of the future. I can reconnect with this part of myself when I'm playing, carefree, with my grandkids.

Our Inner Elder carries our wisdom, timelessness, and fate. I can sense this figure in younger people who stand up for the social causes of our time and shift the sands of fate in their direction.

"Those who continue to grow as they grow older," Michael wrote in an essay, "Where Have All the Wise Men Gone?" for *Huffington Post,* "are able to develop long-term vision where most become blinded by near-term needs and common neediness. Growing older happens to everyone. But growing wiser happens to those who awaken to a greater sense of meaning and purpose in life." (And to those who connect with their Inner Elder, I would add.)

Without this added dimension, Michael pointed out, society produces "olders," who blindly hold on to life at any cost, rather than seasoned Elders, who help others find meaningful ways to live.

Seventy-four at the time of our interview, Michael had transitioned from traveling for conferences to publishing books and podcasts from a studio near his home. With his nonprofit Mosaic Multicultural Foundation, he has built an intergenerational business to continue to get his voice out to the collective as he is physically slowing down. Through technology, he has set up his living legacy, while attending to his own self-care.

"Whereas the '60s were characterized by change brought on by a youth revolution," he wrote, "the current morass may only be changed by an Elder awakening. The revolution waiting to happen in this country may involve an awakening to the necessity of the role that Elders can play in the great crises facing both culture and nature. Issues like poverty and joblessness, climate change and sustainability require long-term visions combined with self-sacrifice and genuine courage. Elders are not elected, so the short-term thinking characteristic of ideological politics and winning elections can be superseded. Since the Elder part of us accepts the inevitability of death, decisions that truly serve the future become more possible."

As Native Americans teach us, Michael told me, "All Elders have medicine—physical, emotional, musical, story. Let's give our unique medicine to the world."

An Interview with Poet, Novelist, Activist Deena Metzger

To find a living Elder, I knew that I needed only to walk up the hill to a neighbor's house. Deena, eighty-two at the time of our interview, lives in a small home on a large piece of land overlooking the mountains, where for more than three decades she has seen clients for counseling and held large community councils for healing rituals.

Deena's passion is the healing power of story, and her recent focus has been on ReVisioning Medicine, uniting Western medical practices with indigenous medicine traditions. She is the author of many books that explore the links between the human and natural worlds, and most recently a novel about climate change.

When I entered her tree-lined patio and crossed into her cozy living room, I felt a wave of familiarity. I had attended Deena's writing group many years before. She had been a mentor to me, as to many others.

Aware of the subject of my book, Deena began our conversation with a story.

"In the 1980s, I went to the Omega Institute to teach. It was the site of my childhood summer camp—same building, same dining room. Back then, my parents went upstairs to eat, and we kids entered downstairs. As I walked upstairs, I was aware of time passing and who I became during those years.

"A young woman suddenly walked up to me and said, 'Thank you for being an Elder for us.'

"I thought, 'When did I volunteer for this?' I was only in my fifties then.

"But I heard the call in my heart. Like it or not, I needed to find out what an Elder might be. I knew something of indigenous Elders among Native Americans and Africans. But nothing of Elders here, now, in my world. And that led me on a path."

Deena became a well-known teacher through her books, workshops, activism, and community building. She trained people to do no harm and to give up their self-centered material values and live in greater harmony with the Earth. She taught them to open to the creative flow in writing, heed their dreams, honor the ancestors, and speak truth to power.

In the 1970s, Deena was diagnosed with breast cancer and rejected conventional treatment. She had a mastectomy and tattooed a tree onto the scar, having decided to convert her wound to a sacred wound. She eventually published a book about her experiences with healing, *Tree,* and a photograph of her bare-breasted and open-armed became a popular poster.

As she told me, "I could never have choreographed this life. If I hadn't had cancer, I would not have thought about healing, written that book, or traveled the country teaching about it."

Cancer speaks in a language that we don't understand, she said. "A symptom talks in particularities to tell us to take a certain path. It orients us to connect with Spirit because, with illness, Spirit enters the field of your life."

Her essential insight: Heal the life and life will heal you. Disease and illness can be messengers guiding us to change our lives, she said. This idea developed over the years into her practice of "Healing Stories," the therapeutic use of "the story that the affliction is telling," as Deena put it, to address diseases, spiritual and emotional crises, and community, political, and environmental disintegration.

Through the decades, her passions and her boons were being woven together by life, as she followed the clues that appeared in synchronicities, dreams, and encounters with people and allowed them to guide her.

"Years after that young woman thanked me for being an Elder, I had a dream: I won a contest that I had never applied for three times. The prize was to go to New York for training to become an indigenous Elder. Questions haunted me: Can I incorporate that consciousness? What might a noncolonized indigenous Elder do?"

She followed this question for years, eventually writing *A Rain of Night Birds* in response. "This Elder is within us as a cellular presence. It's self-aware and ethically rigorous, holds a broad view, and responds only on behalf of the best interests of the whole Earth community. It has no concern for the small stuff."

When I asked her about the current turbulent social and political climate, she stated, "I need to communicate sufficiently about how dire the times are and how responsible we must be. I never thought I would say this: I'm past tolerance. The NRA has no right to an opinion. Climate deniers have no right to an opinion. Those who wish to undo democracy have no right to an opinion. We must meet the times as they are and bear witness, not looking away but still having hope."

Deena walks her talk. At eight-one, she went to Standing Rock and told the youth who were fighting against the installation of an oil pipeline on Sioux land, "I've got your back as an Elder."

Her legacy? "*A Rain of Night Birds* is my legacy. Readers can step out of the Western mind, the willful, ego-driven, power-hungry view and see remnants of wise cultures from within. They can learn to sense the presence of Earth and live in relation to its intelligence."

When I asked about her spiritual practices, she told me, "My practice is an ongoing conversation with Spirit—no inner chatter, just prayers, offerings, praise, and gratitude."

An Interview with
Jungian Analyst Lionel Corbett

Lionel Corbett was a professor at the Pacifica Graduate Institute in California, where his work focused on linking Jungian psychology and spirituality, when I was a student there. At an earlier stage of life, he trained in England as a geriatric psychiatrist. He is the author of *The Religious Function of the Psyche* and *Psyche and the Sacred* and is a co-editor of the anthology *Jung and Aging*.

"Aging has psychological and spiritual significance," Lionel told me. "I teach to contribute to the next generation and enjoy my role as a grandparent. But my vocation, my calling, has become clearer with age. It's given, not a choice of my ego. It's to write about Jung and spirituality."

In comparing Jung's encyclopedic work with renowned Indian Vedanta philosophy, Lionel pointed out that Jung focused on the movement of images or thoughts in the psyche, while Vedanta focuses on the emptiness of pure awareness that underlies these phenomena. "Jung focused on becoming, while Vedanta focuses on being," he said.

However, Lionel found nondual strands in Jung's thinking: He defined the Self as the totality of the psyche and wrote extensively about *unus mundus,* one world or unified reality. Jung believed that the dynamic between ego and Self changed with development (individuation), but he ultimately emphasized that ego is indispensable. "There was no possibility of ego transcendence for Jung," Lionel said.

Lionel speculated that Jung "was not in the habit of meditating in a way that stills the mind, removing the contents that obscure pure awareness. So, he may not have directly experienced pure awareness. Therefore, his work aims to transform the contents of consciousness, whereas in nondual philosophy these very contents and the way we relate to them must be understood and seen through."

He described to me how many Elders who have an experience of something transpersonal can develop from a material, pragmatic approach to life to a more introspective, less self-centered approach. For others, he said, who don't have a connection to the sacred, losses may result in bitterness and withdrawal.

"We need to let go of the baggage of ego and allow it to move into the service of something larger," he told me. "If we look at the mythic themes of our own lives, we can gain a larger perspective. We can come to see that everything was necessary for the larger unfolding. We can align ourselves with the deeper flow of events and recognize our place in them.

"When I look back, I can see how people arrived in my world, and there's a meaningful sequence to things. It wasn't in my control. But now, seeing this, I practice radical acceptance of the inevitable. I don't protest much anymore."

Lionel suggested that late life is also the time for creativity. "Creativity and spirituality both stem from the transpersonal dimension. Creativity liberates our voice, provides meaning, and relativizes the ego. When we follow the inner creative impulse, we participate in a larger reality."

When I asked him about mortality awareness, he said, "Death is a part of life, not a separate meaningless event. When the ship is leaving, there's no point in holding on to the dock."

Honoring One of My Elders

Jungian Analyst Marion Woodman

The last time I sat with the late Jungian analyst Marion Woodman, mentor and friend, the space in the room opened out to a larger field. As we spoke, I could feel our hearts and minds joining and the room expanding to hold us in a larger container. We had moved beyond ego, behind our roles and labels, to experience a soul connection.

Marion was still vibrant and lucid then. Although she would later succumb to dementia and pass away in 2018, on that spring day in Santa Barbara, in that precious moment, she spoke to me about "the crown of age." And I confess that, at sixty, I did not know what she meant.

I had no awareness yet of my inner ageist and no experience of the inner work of late life. I listened deeply but didn't get it.

Today, I am aware that I wear a kind of crown, an inner symbol of the culmination of my inner and outer development. It reminds me of the glorious moment in the life of Queen Elizabeth, portrayed by Claire Foy in the Netflix series *The Crown,* when the crown is set upon her head for the first time—and we watch as she shifts from an individual to an archetype, from a personality with small concerns to a regal presence with cosmic concerns.

This is not to say that we Elders should reign as kings and queens in the profane realm. This is to say that Elders, who may not be perfectly healed, stand in a new archetype in the realm of the sacred. Elders, who may wear the battle scars of our histories, stand in our resilience. Elders, whose hearts have been broken, stand in compassion for all living things.

I feel gratitude to Marion Woodman for the many teachings in her books and in private conversations with me. I feel especially grateful for this image: the crown of age.

Shadow-Work Practices

Becoming an Elder

- Who were your Elders and mentors on your hero's journey?
- What boons and legacies did they give you?
- What shadow qualities of an Elder did they act out? Were they controlling, dogmatic, arrogant, judgmental, or something else?
- What is your vision for becoming an emerging Elder?
- What kind of ritual do you envision to carry you across the threshold? Who are your observers?
- What is your special gift, knowledge, talent, or insight that the world needs now?

Letting Go

- Which identity or story remains gripped by your ego and stops you from crossing the threshold to Elder?
- Which shadow figure from the past keeps you obeying it or rebel-

ling against it, holding you captive in the past and unable to achieve life completion?

- What stops you from releasing self-importance and giving up center stage?
- Which shadow character is addicted to the drama of busyness and refuses to tune in to stillness?
- What stops you from asking for respect or help or care?

🍂 *A Ritual for Letting Go*

This ritual is offered by Ron Pevny in his 2017 online course, "Navigating Life's Transitions," for Spirituality & Practice. (It is used here with permission.)

1. Reflect on what's most important for you to let go of while becoming an Elder and choose one. Imagine how liberated you will feel after you let it go.
2. Imagine the price you will pay if you don't let it go.
3. Assess your readiness: Do you need to do further emotional repair work to prepare for this?
4. Find a physical object, such as photos, mementos, or letters, that symbolizes the old skin to be shed. Place it in a special place and invest it with your energy.
5. When you are ready, build a ceremonial fire or a small grave in the earth.
6. Invoke the presence of the sacred and affirm your intention to honor and release this object and its meanings.
7. Re-affirm how you will feel after you let it go.
8. Burn or bury your sacred object and honor the feelings that arise.

🍂 *Liminal Time: Living between Worlds*

- Have you sensed that you are in a cocoon, not old, not young, but waiting to reemerge?
- What are your fears?
- What are the voices of shadow characters telling you?
- Do you want to push your way out or remain enclosed? Or can you simply be here now?

❦ *Meeting the Inner Elder*

1. Go over your life review from the point of view of your Inner Elder. Ask him or her to bless your life history. Ask him or her to validate you now and to affirm your vision for your life now.

2. Ask your Inner Elder to bless your parents' life histories and to affirm the gifts they left to you.

3. Write a letter from your Inner Elder to a younger self—an inner child, teen, young adult, or midlife adult. What would you have needed to know or to feel as this younger person that was not provided to you? Your Inner Elder can provide that now. He or she can heal your wound of feeling unseen and unvalued. He or she can be a divine presence for you, as you, now.

Spiritual Practice

❦ *Reinventing the Elder*

- Who are you free to be now?
- How do you travel through the three portals of awareness as an Elder?
- How do you attune to your spiritual purpose? How do you embody it as an Elder?

10

Elder Wisdom and the Call to Age into Awakening

The Rainmaker: A Chinese Tale

There was a great drought. For months there had not been a drop of rain, and the situation became catastrophic. The Catholics made processions, the Protestants made prayers, and the Chinese burned joss sticks and shot off guns to frighten away the demons of the drought, but with no result. Finally, the Chinese said, "We will fetch the rainmaker."

From another province a dried-up old man appeared. The only thing he asked for was a quiet little house somewhere, and he locked himself in for three days. On the fourth day the clouds gathered, and there was a great snowstorm. The town was so full of rumors about the wonderful rainmaker that a visitor went to ask the man how he had done it.

"They call you the rainmaker. Will you tell me how you made the snow?"

The man responded, "I did not make the snow. I am not responsible."

"But what have you done these three days?"

"Oh, I can explain that. I come from another country where things are in order. Here they are out of order. They are not as they should be by the

ordinance of heaven. Therefore, the whole country is not in Tao, and I also am not in the natural order of things because I am in a disordered country. So, I had to wait three days until I was back in Tao, and then naturally the rain came."

—Paraphrased from Carl Jung, in *Mysterium Coniunctionis*,
retelling a story told to him by Richard Wilhelm

This tale of a world without water, and a wise man who brings rain, is not a tale of heroic feats. He is not running around seeking solutions in the world, trying to fix the problem on the same level as the problem. He's not trying to change people's beliefs. He's not doing magical ritual to wrestle with demons. The rainmaker knows that no amount of action, physical or magical, will create a connection to the waters of life.

Rather, this is a tale of a wise Elder as a tuning fork, a man aligning with something greater, here called the Tao, so that the world can come back into harmony. This story offers us a vision of a Spiritual Elder who looks within and recognizes when he is out of the Tao and knows how to return to the Tao. The rainmaker feels the disturbance in the Force inside himself. He feels it in the world that he is visiting. And he knows that he is not separate from this dried, broken world.

The rainmaker becomes aligned with source, nature responds, and the whole community is realigned. So, his inner work is not separate from his outer work for the community. Rather, as he heals his own soul, he heals the soul of the world.

In ancient Chinese Taoism, this is the principle of *wu wei,* or non-doing. It can only be performed in a state of mind or stage of awareness in which we are attuned to the inner and outer conditions so that action arises spontaneously, out of the needs of the moment. It is not action that arises from a sense of willfulness, separateness, anger, or self-righteousness. It is not action to "help," or "fix," or "control."

Of course, the rainmaker's ego does not take credit; he credits the Tao. He is an initiated Elder, a bridge between dualities: being and doing, inner and outer, human and nature, spirit and matter. He is aligned with pure awareness, fulfilling his fate. To say it differently, he achieves his task through who he is, through his stage of awareness, rather than what he does.

Many of us, on the other hand, will deny and resist this possibility. Perhaps, even now, you say to yourself, "This is just a legend. No one is really like the rainmaker." But this denial is yet another inner obstacle: If we continue to identify with a narrow, separate sense of self, we lose the opportunity to reorient ourselves by connecting to something larger—whether we call it Spirit, Being, intuition, or God—and moving into higher stages of awareness, as is described by the mystical traditions in every culture. We lose the opportunity to shift from Elder to Spiritual Elder.

Rather, as you read this chapter, allow the Spiritual Elder to become an aspirational image for you, an archetype that stirs in you, even now.

The Final Divine Messenger

The Monk's Call to Awaken

With this image of the rainmaker, we return to the opening story about Siddhartha, the Buddha, having his first encounter with the divine messengers. After he sees illness, old age, and death, the Buddha spies a monk, who embodies the potential for spiritual awakening. Disoriented by his many shocks, Siddhartha now reorients to Spirit.

Most of the perennial spiritual traditions refer to late life as the time to focus on this transition and fulfill the promise of spiritual evolution. In traditional India, after people completed their duties of student, householder, and grandparent, they were free to leave their possessions and responsibilities behind and turn inward. The image of an Indian monk or *sannyasin* wandering the streets in orange robes, with a begging bowl in hand, may seem extreme to us living life in comfort. So does the image of a Christian monk in brown robes, or a cloistered nun in black, who does not step outside of the monastery walls. But these images communicate the potential of letting go of past identities, roles, and meanings, stepping into the unknown while trusting something larger than ourselves, and emerging as a Spiritual Elder.

In our culture, as Spiritual Elder, we can use aging as a "natural monastery" by allowing our sensory diminishments and physical limits to lead us to turn within, away from outer distractions. We can allow our natural slowing to open out into an altered sense of time. We can allow our emotional losses to lead us to deeper compassion for the suffering of others, away from a sense of separation. We can allow our body/mind's decline to lead us to let go of our personal story, its feelings and beliefs, and practice nonattachment as the final part of the soul's journey to connect to something eternal. This is not merely disengagement from the outside. Rather, it is disengagement from the ego, finding freedom from the inside out by surrendering the ego's control and releasing its belief that it has power over age. Breath by breath.

Finally, as aging alters our awareness and our experience of the world, we awaken to our deeper identity: We are not our bodies. We are not our minds. We are not our stories. We see through our thoughts and slowly drop into the soul's point of view. Eventually, the world is no longer separate from us. As Hindu scriptures say, "I am That. Thou art That. All this is That." The duality of opposites dissolves, and we are home.

Of course, there are as many versions of potential Spiritual Elder as there are people. In a 2017 course on Spiritual Elder activism ("Spirituality & Practice"), Robert Atchley, whom I interview later in this chapter, described the qualities that led him to identify someone as a sage or Spiritual Elder:

- deep familiarity with spiritual depth (pure awareness)
- equanimity in the face of challenges
- openness, rather than judgment and premature closure
- the ability to focus attention here and now, rather than in the mind (presence)
- clarity unclouded by desire or fear

- compassion for the suffering of others
- contemplative, big-picture knowledge, a product of deep reflection (shadow awareness)
- humility beyond ego

Although the many familiar losses of old age are all around us, these gains also are part of the full truth. Aging is both descent and ascent.

Ram Dass described his inner experience following a disabling stroke at age sixty-six to Katy Koontz of *Unity Magazine*. "After the stroke I became a new person. Before the stroke, I played my cello, played golf, flew my plane, and drove my fancy car. I was all a good bachelor could be. The stroke left my right side pretty much useless, and it cut those things out of my life . . . I stopped looking outside myself for happiness. I started looking inside and started to feel joy, joy, joy! This was grace. From that point on, I felt my soul . . . the perception that everything was lovable and the whole universe was giving me love."

He continued: "You can bring your attention and your identification with those thoughts down to your heart by using a mantra, such as 'I am loving awareness . . . I am loving awareness . . . I am loving awareness.' That brings you to the heart, which is a doorway to the soul or *soul land*, as I call it—another plane of consciousness."

Awakening into Higher Stages of Awareness

There are many maps of advanced stages of human development from the mystical paths within yoga and Advaita Vedanta, Buddhism, Sufism, Christianity, Judaism, and other esoteric schools, as well as within humanistic psychology, transpersonal psychology, and integral theory. Whether your favorite map is India's chakra system, Buddhist stages of awakening, Maharishi's levels of consciousness, or Ken Wilber's stages of awareness, it's valuable, when you do a spiritual practice, to hold a vision of advanced human development and to know the landmarks along the way. Although language and specifics may differ, each one describes the internal steps of letting go, liminality, and rebirth. And all of them describe one goal of contemplative practice: the realization of ego or small self as Self, the nondual experience of unity or one reality.

In their book *Altered Traits,* Dan Goleman and Richard J. Davidson present the latest brain research on advanced, long-term Buddhist meditators who have attained a higher stage of awareness that brings them to or near this goal. If you are hearing a shadow character expressing skepticism ("This is great in theory, but no one ever attains it," or "I've been meditating and don't feel any different"), you may be curious about their findings: Through a series of brain scans, the researchers found that advanced meditators' brains were aging more slowly. In addition, meditation became an ongoing feature of awareness during every activity, which included open senses, empty clarity, and effortless concentration. In response to stress, they showed less reactivity or spacious equanimity. These practitioners had achieved the goal of transforming transient higher states into stable higher stages of awareness.

Andrew Newberg, a neuroscientist who studies neurotheology, or the relationship between the brain and religious experience, scanned the brain of a rabbi while he was praying the Shema and then again while he was singing a nonreligious song. He compared the results to scans of his own brain while doing those activities. Newberg found that the rabbi's brain showed more intense focus and a sense of letting go or being taken over by the prayer process, while his did not. I wonder if the rabbi, over years, had developed an "altered trait." (Newberg published his results in his book, *The Rabbi's Brain,* coauthored with David Halpern.)

Ken Wilber, whom Jean Houston called "the Einstein of consciousness," has spent decades mapping the stabilization of altered traits into higher stages of awareness. He tracked them from prepersonal to personal to transpersonal, or from Growing Up to Waking Up, as he put it. He suggests that as we evolve in awareness, we integrate and include each stage of growth as we move beyond it.

In other words, we let go, move into uncertainty, and emerge into a new stage with our past identities and meanings still within us. But they no longer rule our values or sense of self. The new stage governs how we interpret our internal and external experience of life. And each stage has both its gifts and its shadows, or blind spots.

In *Integral Spirituality,* Wilber describes his map of stages of awareness. The first level of *egocentric* awareness appears in infants or mentally ill people as instinctual survival needs. The ego is not yet differentiated from the Other, so there is no personal self-awareness.

Then we become childlike, with impulsive, amoral action, taking what we want. In a step toward self-control, we begin to feel separate and vulnerable and react for self-protection by the fight-or-flight response.

Moving into the *ethnocentric* stage, we create identity, stability, and purpose through conformity with group norms, such as duty, patriotism, self-sacrifice, and black-and-white rules. We can observe this stage in American Puritanism and fundamentalists of all religions. Group or tribal identity is reinforced by shadow projection of Us vs. Them. Wilber points out that people are held captive at this stage by traditional organized religions, which arrest their evolution by emphasizing dogma over individual direct experience.

Moving into *worldcentric* stages, first we act rationally and honor progress, strategy, and winning, as seen in corporate businesspeople and politicians (perhaps until recently). Next, we seek peace and harmony with others, sensitivity to the environment, equal opportunity, and pluralism, as frequently seen in those in the helping professions or in Vatican II's pronouncement that salvation is available in other religions. At this stage, because we see ourselves in relation to a larger system, we are open to other points of view and allow our own needs to be relativized. This stage points to what it means to be an Elder.

Wilber points out that, during the 1960s, 10 percent of the population made the shift from rational to pluralistic, evoking the postmodern era. He suggests that, in 2015, 10 percent of the population had moved into *kosmocentric* or integral stages, living the truth of interconnected systems. Gradually, we move into a deeper experience of this wholeness in mind and spirit, until we see through the ego and reframe life as the interplay of awareness, thought, and action. And finally, with ego transcendence, we let go of identifying with the Doer and live as a being in interdependent systems, with the capacity to flow with life, while remaining connected to Spirit and the unity of all. In this stage, letting go becomes spiritualized as nonattachment.

At integral stages, we understand that every previous stage has its value as part of the evolutionary scheme and that each unique perspective need to be included. These stages point to what it means to be a Spiritual Elder.

Wilber proposes that, carried by the evolutionary impulse or holy longing, those of us in these higher stages will continue to expand our awareness and saturate the culture with values of inclusion, holism, harmony, interconnection, and nonliteral spirituality.

You can reflect on these stages and try to see yourself on the map. Of course, we are typically blind to the stage in which we live, unaware that it is shaping our perceptions, beliefs, values, and actions, even about age. We are unaware that knowledge is different in different stages of awareness. But if we can detect the stage of other people, whether we know them personally or not, we may feel a greater compassion for those whose values and behavior seem incomprehensible to us.

Let's take climate change as an example, using Wilber's frame: If older people in an egocentric stage live with food or housing insecurity, lack of safety, and unmet emotional needs, the overwhelming reality of climate change may be too much to acknowledge. Instead, they feel separate, isolated, and unable to care about others in danger or to hold a bigger picture than their own survival.

If their survival needs are met, they become able to move to an ethnocentric stage, in which they join a group and take on a tribal awareness, a set of beliefs that prescribe a behavior about the environment. If they join a church that advocates the end of days so that believers will be raptured up to heaven, they will see climate change in one way. If they identify with this dogma for a long time, they may fail to transcend this stage and their growth may be stopped.

On the other hand, if they join a church that views creation as God's gift and humanity as its steward, they will see climate change in another way and may have the opportunity, with time, to evolve into a more rational autonomy, and then into more relational, compassionate, and tolerant people in a worldcentric stage. Perhaps they begin to hear about the growing extinction of species and discover the idea of the interdependence of all living things.

Finally, with a spiritual breakthrough, our hypothetical seekers will move through this rite of passage and emerge as Spiritual Elders in Wilber's kosmocentric stages, which means not merely knowing about the interdependence of living things but actually living within those systems. Now they see climate through a new lens: Humanity's blindness to nondual reality has led us to the heights of hubris and the brink of destruction.

In this example, we see the evolution of soul through the stages of awareness. We see our subjects' identities shift from unconscious instinct to ego/mind, with its beliefs and stories, to soul and its deeper evolutionary purpose and then to unity with all things. This map shows us the territory to be traversed, from one stage to the next, until we join those at the leading edge of humanity.

We also see that our culture wars about climate change are a symptom of humanity's current stages of awareness: magical thinking, fundamentalist religious thinking, me-first profit making, and heroic egocentricity, which separates us from the natural world and from groups in other stages, whose values seem insane to us. These stages of development have led to endless suffering, as well as to our inability to see the deeper nondual reality.

The warming climate is an urgent call, but it's not the cause; it's a symptom of our stage of awareness. It's impossible to imagine people who feel intimately interdependent with all living things who would treat the planet as an object to be used up for their own greed.

In 2020, we also can examine people's responses to the coronavirus epidemic as a reflection of their stage of awareness. That is, they will see the crisis through the worldview of their stage and respond accordingly.

In general, this kind of ongoing stress can cause people to regress to earlier stages of development, leading to feelings of helplessness, anxiety, and even paranoia, as we see and feel around us. Some will deny the danger; others will idealize it, focusing on silver linings. Each is a defense against a harsh, unthinkable reality.

People in egocentric awareness will be focused on their own safety and unaware of the survival needs of others. They may hoard food, hide in bunkers, and see others as dispensable because they feel no connection to the collective. (One man bought 17,000 bottles of sanitizer at the beginning of the pandemic.) In this stage, people will blame other groups for the danger and cling to the beliefs of their own group.

As people move into the ethnocentric stage during a crisis like this one, their sense of belonging will become primary. Whether it is their family, church, ethnic group, or political party, they will unconsciously identify with their tribe and project Other onto everyone else. ("Those Blue states won't get bailed out.")

If they continue to develop toward a more rational autonomy, people may seek a scientific solution to the crisis. They will analyze it, discriminate fact from fiction, apply critical thinking, and come up with solutions—more beds, more masks, more ventilators, vaccine. People in this stage can work together and innovate, but their focus is all external.

If our subjects take the great evolutionary leap into self-reflection, they begin to see themselves in context—and to see others in context. If each point of view results from early conditioning and life experience, who is right? Our subjects see that their beliefs are constructs and no longer trust true believers, whether religious, political, or scientific. But they are interested in others' inner experiences and in their own development.

As they evolve further, toward the worldcentric stage, they will see more clearly our global interconnectedness on every level, both its complexity and its shadow issues. They will continue to question rigid positions, as they see that we all create stories about everything, and these stories are not reality. They can then view the virus stories and conspiracy theories as mirrors of their own minds. For example, the voice of a shadow character may express denial: "The government can't tell me what to do." "I'm too young to be vulnerable." Or it may deny the darkness and romanticize the situation: "I see so many silver linings."

Moving toward the rare kosmocentric stage, people will experience pure awareness as the source of mind, and they will begin to identify with that, rather than with stories and beliefs that appear in the mind. The inner witness will arise as they observe how the mind works and how it separates them from all that is inherently interconnected.

With a taste of nondual reality, they will transcend and include the earlier stages that they experienced, now able to see them in others and to feel their unity with them.

Perhaps humanity as a whole is in late life. Perhaps, given the climate crisis and the virus pandemic, it's not just older people who need to wake up to *what is* and radically change our ways as individuals. Perhaps we, as a species, need to heed the call to let go deeply of the isolated ego's reign, move through a collective rite of passage, and emerge into alignment with a deeper spiritual reality to save our precious planet and its many exquisite life forms.

What Is Wisdom?

Wise + Elder often show up as a team in the vernacular. Does this mean that the beginning of wisdom appears only at the end of life?

Monika Ardelt, a sociology professor at University of Florida in Gainesville, wanted to expand research on late life satisfaction, which is typically linked only to physical and mental health, volunteering, and relationships. She found that with wisdom—defined as reduced self-centeredness, seeing life from multiple perspectives, and feeling tolerance for others—even people in nursing homes or with a terminal illness reported a greater sense of well-being, meaning, and contentment with the challenges of age. Her conclusion: "Wise people are able to accept reality as it is, with equanimity." (For details on Ardelt's work, see Phyllis Korkki's report, "The Science of Older and Wiser," in the *New York Times,* March 12, 2014.)

I found this interesting, but it left me with more questions: What is wisdom really? Is it an abstract, elusive concept? Or a set of skillful means to live daily life? Does wisdom trickle down into our daily choices, values, and actions? Can someone who is wise act immorally?

Does wisdom depend on genetics? Does it depend on a healthy brain or a particular brain region? Does it depend on a high IQ? Does it depend on psychological well-being and require emotional maturity?

Does wisdom depend on cultural transmission, such as Native wisdom about how we live in harmony with the Earth, or the wisdom of ancient sages and saints who passed down philosophy and religious doctrine about how we live in harmony with God or the gods?

Does wisdom depend on age, so that the measure of our days equals the measure of our wisdom? Does it depend on certain life experiences and how they are digested?

These questions led me to wonder: Does wisdom need to be intentionally cultivated? How can we pursue it? And for those of us who pursue spiritual development, can we age into awakening without wisdom? Or, conversely, how is wisdom distinct from enlightenment? How is wisdom different in different stages of awareness?

I came to realize that cognitive, emotional, moral, and relational development are necessary but not sufficient kinds of development to lead to what I mean by wisdom. I suggest that intellectual insight can result in *relative* wisdom, such as the growing body of knowledge demonstrated by the whole history of science, even climate science. Emotional insight, such as self-awareness from therapy and shadow-work, can result in relative wisdom. Moral insight, which leads us to increasingly ethical or altruistic action, can result in relative wisdom. Relational insight, such as how to treat loved ones or strangers with empathy, not blame, can result in relative wisdom. Even spiritual insight, which remains only knowledge or understanding about nondual reality, is relative wisdom. All of these are essential. But they are contents of awareness.

Only spiritual experience can result in *absolute* wisdom—defined in every contemplative tradition as an innate, culminating stage of spiritual development that involves a direct perception of the true nature of self and reality. This direct perception brings wisdom that is different from the relative forms. It is not content; it is beyond the mind, beyond thought, beyond image. It is wisdom of the transcendental, nondual, or divine reality—thus, absolute wisdom.

In *The World's Great Wisdom,* Roger Walsh gathers experts who review the timeless teachings and methods of diverse perennial traditions to cultivate the "art of wisdom." For example, the effort to attain *Chochmah,* the Jewish term for wisdom, as explained by Rabbi Rami Shapiro, is a lifelong project. To paraphrase him: We don't know wisdom; we awaken to it. "The point of wisdom is to reveal the true nature of reality as interdependent aspects of the singular God. One who realizes the nonduality of all things in, with, and as God, achieves a level of awareness that overcomes any sense of alienation." The result: "Compassion is how one lives Chochmah." And there are many Jewish practices for this purpose.

Wisdom in Christianity, as explained in Walsh's book by Luke Dysinger, is stated by Paul of Tarsus: "God made Christ Jesus our wisdom." Luke takes this to mean that wisdom is not an idea but a person. Christians are wise to the extent that their words and actions conform to the teaching and practice of Jesus. And there are many Christian practices for this purpose.

In Sufism, according to Reza Shah-Kazemi, the source of wisdom is spiritual submission to the Real, expansion of the heart, opening to the Light, and remembrance of God. The result: *fana,* a mystical state in which the lower self or ego is extinguished and "wherever you turn there is the face of God." And there are many Sufi practices for this purpose.

In Hinduism, as explained by Georg Feuerstein, wisdom progresses from relative insights to the direct realization of reality, or *jnana*. With this spontaneous knowing, things are seen as they really are, as pure consciousness, unfiltered through the mind or emotions. And the opposites of relative reality—subject/object, knower/known—disappear in a nondual truth. The mind is transcended; the practitioner no longer identifies with mind, body, or individual soul, and wisdom emerges. And there are many Hindu practices for this purpose.

In Buddhism, as explained by Ari Goldfield, "wisdom [*prajna*] is an innate awareness of our own true nature and the true nature of the outer world; is experientially spacious, blissful, and clear; imbued with love; and is inseparable from altruistic ethical conduct."

The Dalai Lama put it this way: "Wisdom involves seeing things as they are." For this reason, the Buddhist archetype of wisdom, Manjushri, waves a flaming sword to cut through the illusions of the mind. And there are many Buddhist practices for this purpose.

To ground this theory in human life, psychologist Drew Krafcik studied twenty people who were nominated by others as "wise," meaning deeply engaged in life and meaningful relationships, valuing service to others, being sought to counsel others, and able to reflect on their own internal experience. His subjects, as a whole, defined wisdom as arising from the unknown and also as practical.

Half of Drew's subjects said that they acquired wisdom through the role modeling of mentors and teachers who were ahead of them on the path, that they practiced what they learned, and that they were helped to find their own ways to turn within. Almost half of them spoke about wisdom as letting go, surrendering, and experiencing an emergence of something larger than their individuality. One-third of them described this process as breaking their identification with the thinking mind or getting the mind out of the way.

Finally, two-thirds of Drew's subjects reported that spiritual insight into being interconnected with the whole of life was key: "And finally it snapped. . . there isn't a spiritual and something else. . . . It's the all of everything, nothing is left out," as one put it. This led Drew to conclude that wisdom arises from a larger source, and we need to learn how to access that source. (You can read about his work "Words from the Wise," published in *Integral Review* in March 2015.)

So, the way to cultivate wisdom and become a Spiritual Elder becomes clearer: We need the ongoing, direct experience of pure awareness, the unconstructed, empty fabric of consciousness, to progress on the path to direct insight of nondual reality. It's our contemplative practices that lead to transient states of unity, which provide insights, and which potentially lead to stable higher stages and the experience of absolute wisdom.

Shadow formation and integration are also an intrinsic aspect of spiritual development. With shadow awareness, we can use our insights into the nature of our mind and see through the thought/obstacles that block our development when we either identify with them or repress them. Without shadow awareness, we cannot see that we are unconsciously identifying with a past identity or shadow character and becoming stuck, rather than moving toward letting it go. Or we cannot see that we are rejecting and repressing a character, forming new shadow material, rather than making it conscious.

With advanced shadow-work, we can view negative thoughts or feelings as objects of fear or desire, return to pure awareness, witness their construction by the mind, and see through them as transparent. We can use any thought, sound, or breath to return to nondual, pure awareness, witness the object of our attention, and let go of either identifying with it or repressing it.

Without examining the mind, we won't know that we are seeing reality only through a state of awareness (which is transitory, such as a dream or altered state) and a stage of awareness (such as egocentric or worldcentric). We will be blind to these filters that actually determine our experience.

Without mortality awareness, we cannot see the basic impermanence and interdependence of all things. The Buddha called the contemplation of impermanence "the king of all meditations."

Pure awareness, shadow awareness, and mortality awareness are portals to the direct experience of absolute wisdom, whether we call it God, Buddha nature, Christ nature, Atman, or the interconnectedness of all living things. Together, these qualities of awareness open us to a reality in which differences fall away, the alliance of opposites becomes apparent, and unity alone is. Yin/yang, birth/death, knower/known, seed/fruit, body/soul, One/Many—all are restored to their original unity.

Without opening these portals, we remain in some vital ways unwise, even ignorant. We refuse to let go deeply enough for the mind to rest in pure awareness, the ego to recede, and the idols of the past to be released. And the rite of passage fails.

But if, in fact, we are in a race between wisdom and catastrophe, we need it now more than ever. We are inundated by information, even relative wisdom, but starved for absolute wisdom.

As I said in the opening of the book, science has added years to life—but not life to years. Perhaps what we're missing is absolute wisdom.

Of course, inner work alone will not solve the climate crisis and other ongoing and imminent disasters. Certainly not. But if we heed the call to experience the reality of unity over duality, connection over separation, love over fear, perhaps humanity will take the leap in consciousness that is required of us now. If the insights of absolute wisdom lead naturally to skillful and compassionate action to relieve suffering, perhaps we will act in concert and in time.

For me, our ability to see the full truth of life and to uncover its hidden meaning depends on our reorienting to Spirit and experiencing the deeper and higher dimensions of life, dimensions beyond ego and its painful experience of separateness.

My conclusion: To perfectly realize wisdom is to gain the highest awakening, enlightenment, and liberation.

Transmitting Wisdom
to Future Generations

We can begin to see the further developmental tasks of becoming an Elder or a Spiritual Elder:

- cultivate absolute wisdom
- identify our own relative wisdom
- identify how to transmit both of them
- identify our receivers
- identify how to attune to our receivers

When we imagine transmitting wisdom, we typically think about sharing relative wisdom. We imagine a grandmother teaching a young one how to plant a garden, a grandfather teaching another how to read. We imagine a parent sharing existential insights with an older child in crisis or a teacher helping a student to master a field of study. These combinations of understanding and skill remain in the realm of relative wisdom, but, of course, they are essential exchanges.

Even depth therapies, such as shadow-work, explore the contents of the mind, conscious or unconscious. We may come to understand our wounds, recognize previously unconscious material, and develop greater self-acceptance at an ego level. All this self-knowledge leads to greater well-being and maturity; but it remains in the realm of relative wisdom.

If intuitive, transcendental wisdom is beyond concepts, beyond words, and beyond images, then how is it transmitted? It appears to depend upon direct internal experience. It requires training the mind through spiritual practice. So, how do we pass on That to others?

Each of the Spiritual Elders interviewed in this book have experienced different states of awareness and attained different stages of awareness. Each had a bit of wisdom that they wanted to pass on. If you look back at each interview, you may be able to detect their soul's mission, which compelled them to spend time in conversation with me, even at this late moment of their lives. Many of these Spiritual Elders continue to teach contemplative practices to those who follow them on the path, opening the way to others to experience absolute wisdom, as saints, yogis, and teachers have done throughout time.

For me, each book that I write has been an offering of my lifelong learning and of my soul's mission: to transmit information about consciousness. With this book, I have had particularly difficult hurdles to cross. But my soul's mission compelled me, day after day, hour after hour, to sit at the screen with the intention of transmitting my bit of wisdom to my fellow travelers in late life and to future generations as they age.

Throughout our days, we are surrounded by potential receivers of our wisdom. If we are unaware of them in the moment, the opportunity passes. The transmission is lost. So, I suggest that, as Spiritual Elders, we practice an awareness of this potential exchange from moment to moment. And we carefully attune to our receivers, listeners, and mentees and discover how to align with them so that they can receive the transmission, just as the rainmaker did. To do so, we may need to detect their felt sense of identity, stage of life, shadow issues, and stage of awareness so that we can alter our language to be heard.

At the same time, we too can continue to be receivers, especially as each moment becomes "grist for the mill" and we open our hearts in wider and wider circles, receiving life as it is, without right/wrong thinking, and with an intention to act for the greater good.

With each of my spiritual teachers, my receptor sites opened to a frictionless flow of transmission. If there is no "fit," then we can't "get" it, and allow it in to deeply change us.

But with one teacher two decades ago, I can recall listening and saying to myself, "I hear English words, but I don't have the translation program." It was as if he had changed each word's meaning into his own idiosyncratic language. His transmission to me was filled with static. And it failed to reach me. Be sure that your transmissions of wisdom are tuned and received.

An Interview with Integral Philosopher Ken Wilber

I first met Ken Wilber decades before he launched Integral Institute and it caught fire around the world. Standing next to him in a wooden A-frame house in Mendocino, California, I craned my neck up: He stood way over six feet tall, so, at five foot one, I felt dwarfed. At the time, I was avidly reading everything he wrote and reviewing it in the bulletin I helped produce. In the years since then, his writings have grown more complex and more inclusive, embracing all aspects of life in a grand "theory of everything." And my respect has grown more profound.

Several of his main concepts led to deep, lasting insights for me: states of awareness becoming stages, evolution through transcending and including earlier stages, separate lines of development, spiritual bypass, the Atman project. I feel deep gratitude to Ken.

When I reached out for an interview, he was available, as if no time had passed, despite a demanding writing and teaching schedule. He was then seventy, and I opened with this question: "Are you feeling old yet?"

"Parts of me feel old, other parts don't relate to my experience that way," he answered. "I feel better than ever."

How was he using the aging process for evolution? "Growing old is an opportunity to reset our priorities, a continuing chance to drop things that aren't important. If we continue to do that, then we will have left the world more whole than we found it. If every human could make that statement truthfully, then the planet would see a slow and consistent increase in those values."

Is his mortality affecting his choices? "There's an urgency now, no excuses. As the wisdom holders, we need to help people find what's important—to Grow Up by moving through the early stages of emotional maturing, Clean Up by doing shadow-work, Wake Up by doing spiritual practice, and Show Up by serving humanity in the world. Amidst the pain and the doctor's visits, these priorities give clarity to age. It's like an extended period of *sesshin,* or spiritual practice: We sit with the wisdom of a lifetime, the knowledge of what works and what doesn't, and reflect on how to help humanity."

Ken told me that his book *The Religion of Tomorrow* was like his last will and testament: "I've been studying the ingredients of self-improvement for fifty years. This book embodies the insights that made an impact on me for the future."

Any message for my readers? "Aging is a natural movement of the self if we let go again and again and move into higher and higher stages and an expanded sense of morality. In this way, we become a resource to others to bring deeper values and ideals into the world."

An Interview with Mystic Robert Atchley

When I met Bob Atchley, then seventy-nine, I was charmed by the quality of his presence, which pulled me into the moment with him. Bob taught gerontology for thirty years, was president of the American Society on Aging, and founded the journal *Contemporary Gerontology*. His pioneering book, *Spirituality and Aging*, made the case for late life as a stage for Elders to reach our spiritual potential of ego transcendence and connection to pure awareness.

Bob told me of a time when he realized that he had fulfilled society's prescriptions for a satisfying life, but he still felt a hole inside. Something was missing. So began his spiritual search. He studied with Alan Watts, attended meditation retreats, and went to India to see Swami Muktananda. While there in 1978 and 1979, he found his life teacher, Sri Nisargadatta Maharaj, an Advaita Vedanta guru and author of *I Am That*.

"Nisargadatta had a small loft in an out-of-the-way street in Mumbai," Bob told me. "I would climb a ladder and he would be there to give a blessing. The first time I entered, he said, 'So you have come.' After that, he greeted me, 'It's smiling Bob.'"

In his guru's presence, he said with a grin, "such love came through him that I was transported into a cosmic space. It changed my life, and a spiritual process took over that moved me from a rational, analytical guy to the heart."

Bob moved from Florida to Boulder, Colorado, and taught at Naropa University as chair of gerontology. In 1992, he attended a conscious aging conference with Ram Dass and Rabbi Zalman Schachter-Shalomi, who spoke about recovering the role of the wise Elder. Bob signed up for the training and, afterward, served Sage-ing International for many years, during which time he eventually became an honored Sage in the community.

Bob shared with me that, within the same few years, he found Nisargadatta, Ram Dass, and Rabbi Zalman. "I'm so grateful to the people who left tracks in the desert," he said.

When he retired, he went to a songwriter's school, and writing music became his passion. "I'm a conference bard now, transmitting love songs of spirit and social consciousness at public events."

"How has the evolution of your soul changed with age?" I asked. "I stay connected to that impersonal consciousness," Bob said. "It's an inner space as big as outer space. When stuff happens, I have that connection no matter what."

Bob died in 2018, shortly after this precious conversation.

❧ ❧

An Interview with Buddhist Teacher Anna Douglas

After three decades of teaching mindfulness at Spirit Rock in Northern California and in Tucson, Arizona, Anna, at the age of seventy-eight, turned her attention to Buddhist teachings about age and death. In our conversation, I asked her why.

"I used to live in New York and observe older people sitting on benches in the park. It would annoy me. I asked myself, "What's wrong with them? Why don't they *do* something? I had judgment. Now I'm one of them." (In other words, Anna discovered her inner ageist.)

She continued, "The changes in my own body, brain, and energy level are more noticeable now, and I don't want to do much. I don't want to multitask. I'm more easily satisfied with what's here, now. Also, many baby boomers over sixty are coming to Spirit Rock for retreats, motivated by their suffering about aging and seeking a practice and framework to deal with it. So, there's great consciousness raising when we're in the room together."

I asked her to explain how the Buddha's teachings might help with the physical, mental, and emotional changes of late life. She answered:

"We're finding the *dharma* now to be less remote and more profoundly useful. As an example, let's take the three marks or characteristics of existence: First, suffering is built into life. We want it to be different, we want a younger body. But our task is to accept that our physical aging is natural, not a failure.

"Next, impermanence: Everything is temporary. All physical and mental things are in flux, emerging and dissolving. Human life embodies this flux in the aging process of decaying and dying. But, again, we want it to be permanent, which creates a lot of suffering. So, our task is to see that it's all impermanent and work toward accepting that truth.

"Third, we are empty, without an essential self. But we constantly seek a permanent sense of self in our longings, our work, our creations, our children. With aging, our roles and self-images disappear. Our contributions may lessen. The solid sense of self can be seen through more easily as transparent, empty.

"With aging, our suffering, impermanence, and emptiness become more real, more obvious. The root of it is in our identification with the body. But if we experience unconditioned mind or pure awareness in meditation, then we're not so lost. Then we can find an opening to awakening.

"As the Buddha put it, 'Though the body is sick, let not the mind be sick.' That means, train the mind in well-being and just notice the passing forms in the world."

I wondered aloud how mindfulness practice changes as we age. "Mindfulness is an invitation to do one thing—breathe, be present, notice. In late life, it becomes easier because we're not so busy with our desires. Our longings have quieted down a bit. And our physical and mental activity slows naturally."

Anna spoke about how her experience of teaching mindfulness has changed over the decades. "It's taken a long time to find my voice as a woman in a patriarchal tradition. Now I have a sense of love and genuineness when I teach because my life experience and spiritual practice made me ripe. Aging settles us, makes us more authentic, which is what older people need—to become who we always were."

"Has your sense of time changed?" I asked.

"This time is a rich period of practice. The future is not visible; it doesn't exist. So, the work is not about the future. I'm feeling the gift of life, the blessing of experience," she told me.

"And the biggest surprise for you?"

"When I look back and review my life now, I can see all of the plans and agendas that I tried to force into happening. But my ego's agendas went nowhere. When I lived in Santa Monica and worked as a therapist, I just happened to see a flier for a talk by Joseph Goldstein. I walked into a small shed with ten people and heard the Four Noble Truths for the first time. I recognized it immediately as my path—and headed off to the center at Barre, Massachusetts. When I returned to California and opened Spirit Rock together with other teachers, it was a great adventure, and much better than anything I could have planned. I see now that things had to happen that way."

I asked if she wanted to add anything about the dharma of aging.

"Stay in your seat to develop stability of mind, to keep from getting swept away by thoughts. And reflect on ownership—*my* and *mine*. Practice letting go of thoughts, feelings, people, and things. Aging requires letting go, and meditation can help us cultivate that practice."

How does a spirituality of age force us to call into question our collective cultural values and priorities? How can our spiritual development serve the common good? As we saw in Wilber's stages, those with higher development move beyond ego concerns. As Roger Walsh told me, "Wisdom, benevolence, and ethics are strongly overlapping, interdependent virtues. The wiser people are, the greater the number of people and creatures they will seek to benefit, and the deeper the kind of benefit they will seek to offer."

So, as Roger put it, if development moves from *me* to *us* to *all of us,* Spiritual Elders will try to live their interconnection with all beings and act in service to the benefit of all beings. As one of the great Hindu sages, Ramana Maharshi, said, "All that you give, you give to yourself. If this truth is understood, who will not give to others?"

That's why the next summons is the call to sacred service.

Shadow-Work Practices

- Is a shadow character in you transmitting a belief or attitude to your children or grandchildren that does not align with your soul? Are you unknowingly transmitting ageism or any other prejudice to future generations?
- What are the consequences of obeying this shadow character?
- Can you begin shadow-work to root it out and stop the transmission?
- Which shadow character in you denies or resists the idea of spiritual awakening? Can you identify a shadow character that is skeptical of or even hostile toward your spiritual development? What is it telling you?
- What are the consequences of obeying this shadow character?
- Can you witness this shadow character and, instead, choose a contemplative practice now?
- Which outer obstacles distract you from a practice? How can you deal with them?
- What is your unique wisdom that will be lost when you're gone? What stops you from finding a way to transmit it?

Spiritual Practices

- How can you make the conditions of your aging conducive to the conditions needed for spiritual practice?
- Please practice forgiveness as a transmission.
- Please practice gratitude as a transmission.
- Can you detect your stage of awareness in Ken Wilber's map? How is it coloring your reality?
- Continue to practice: "I am not this mind." "I am not the Doer."

- How can you attune to the soul's longing for the source? Practice shifting your identity and your loyalty to Spirit or God?
- How can all people in late life join one another to accelerate the direct experience of expanded awareness in humanity?

🕊 Nondual Spiritual Practices to Age into Awakening

Nondual means "not two," in reference to the end of separation or duality. The mystical practices of all traditions aim to lead to pure awareness, transcendent states beyond thought and beyond image, which inevitably lead to higher stages of awareness. Despite their cultural and semantic differences, they all are about coming home to who we really are. Following are some examples.

◄ Neti Neti

The Hindu practice of *Neti Neti* (not this, not that) teaches us how to break our identification with all that is not Brahman or the divine One by seeing through it to its real nature. It is similar in concept to the practice of "I am not this body," "I am not this mind," "I am not this story," and so on, which we have seen throughout this book.

◄ Yoga

Yoga philosophy teaches that identification with body/mind is the root error that creates separation from source, or duality. As you release it, breath by breath, you realize that you are a spiritual being, a soul that is having experiences through a body/mind. In the context of age, you can extend this practice to meditation statements such as "I am not this age; I am that which lives and breathes through everything" and "I am not my name; I am that which lives and breathes through everything."

◄ Ram Dass

His primary practice was devotion to his teacher. But he taught us to break our identification with the body/mind and identify with loving awareness (or the witness): Concentrate on the heart, in the middle of the chest, and breathe in and out of the heart. Then keep repeating, "I am loving awareness." And become that awareness. Ram Dass taught that this will move us from ego to soul to the One.

◄ Dzogchen

The Tibetan Buddhist practice of Dzogchen, abiding in spontaneous open presence, follows earlier practices that prepare the mind for resting in its natural state.

◄ Vipassana

There are several stages of insight in the Vipassana tradition. After seeing mental and physical states as impermanent and unsatisfying, the desire for awakening arises. At each successive stage, the practitioner continues to notice and let go of whatever arises. After many insights, the mind extinguishes the fires of desire or grasping.

◄ Dharana

The Hindu practice of *dharana,* or concentration between the eyebrows on the sixth chakra, aims to bring deep concentration and *samadhi,* or nondual awareness. Later, the focus is on connecting the sixth to the seventh or crown chakra.

◄ Self-Inquiry

Popularized by Advaita teacher Ramana Maharshi, this practice explores *Who am I?* to uncover and detach from layers of identity. Instead of following each thought as if it were real, we return to the thinker—*Who am I?*—and finally see beyond the mind to unity or nondual reality.

◄ A Jewish Mystical Practice Offered by Rabbi Rami Shapiro

Look up the four Hebrew letters of God's name—*Yud Hay Vav Hay*—in Hebrew. Sitting in pure awareness, visualize the Hebrew letters stacked vertically, so that they look like a stick-figure human. Visualize the letters in this form, as an image of God, then dissolve them back into letters. Then repeat. This process is similar to the Tibetan Buddhist practice of deity yoga: sitting in emptiness, visualizing a god/goddess, then dissolving it back into emptiness.

◄ A Christian Mystical Practice from James Finley

Sit still, without an agenda, eyes closed, hands in your lap. Breathe in God's love, and breathe out love. Be present, open, awake, clinging to nothing, rejecting nothing. Any thought or feeling arises and passes away. God is the infinity of all arising and passing away. Give yourself over to love alone, with deep sincerity, in least resistance to being overtaken by God's oneness with us.

◄ Phowa

This Tibetan practice prepares us for liberation at death by cultivating the habit of moving consciousness through the top of the head (the crown chakra).

11

Elder Activism and the Call to Serve Something Larger than Ourselves

PARABLE

A Mitzvah: A Jewish Story

"When I was working in New York with elderly, poor orthodox Jews, I'd come upon a number of old synagogues—dirty, filthy, vandalized. I'd always had ambivalent feelings about synagogues—a kind of no-man's-land for me. If anything, they made me less sure of what it meant to be a Jew.

"But one day I came upon one that somehow caught me. That night I went to the service—very few people there, all down and out. And suddenly the thought came to me that I would clean the synagogue. Just that. And I did it.

"That's how it began. We'd bring in young people to clean these synagogues and in so doing get a sense of what they really meant—not a social club but a place where the entire life cycle of a people and their continuing relationship with God was to be celebrated.

"Myself, I found it hard to pray there. That was the stage I was at. But I helped bring a sense of order and beauty. You see, I had had an immense respect for that generation of Jews which had come to Palestine in the twenties

and thirties, who went back to the land not simply to rebuild the land but to be rebuilt by the land, by the work itself.

"That's what this became for me. This was a mitzvah, *an act of service, but it was also an act by which I myself was being rebuilt—rebuilt into a deeper relationship with my tradition and my people and that living faith."*

—As told in *How Can I Help?*
by Ram Dass and Paul Gorman

Those of us in any generation who were youth activists brought a missionary zeal to our idealistic activism. But we also were wounded, angry, self-righteous, and fighting inner demons, as well as outer injustices. Many of us, unconsciously identifying with an internal Savior, Helper, or Bodhisattva figure, thought we could save the world in some way. A few of us had a huge impact on a single issue. But for most of us, our idealistic efforts hit a wall of complex, interconnected vested interests, such as the military machine, fossil fuel industries, or big agriculture. Or we hit a wall of complex internal shadow issues, such as all-pervasive racism, sexism, and egocentricity.

As we do the inner work of age, we now can bring a more mature self-awareness and a more sophisticated sociopolitical awareness to activism and service. We can bring a long-term 360-degree view of life and a capacity for presence to listen without attachment. As Elder activists, we can bring our boons from our hero's journeys back to the larger world.

By aligning our late-life beliefs and moral values with our actions, we can bring our hard-won internal justice to the world of social justice. We can serve the common good by building bridges between the inner and outer worlds, fueling our activism more from grief than anger and more from compassion than self-righteousness. The result: less shadow projection and enemy making and more service as spiritual practice, or spiritual practice as service.

Today, fellow travelers in late life, we need to be those Elders for members of the youth uprisings. We need to bring our wisdom, knowledge, and skills to the issues of today by speaking boldly, marching alongside those brave kids, and mentoring them at school and on the streets. Perhaps if we create intergenerational collaborations, their efforts to protect the Earth, end income inequality, reduce gun violence, increase voting rights, and reform immigration and criminal justice policies will be written into law. And each generational legacy will be joined to the next.

As Jackson Browne sings, "I want to live in the world, not inside my head. I want to live in the world, I want to stand and be counted."

The Call to Sacred Service and Elder Activism

This chapter's opening story is a personal tale of a man who began serving others by repairing synagogues and discovered that, in the process, he was repairing himself. Like many of us who are called to serve—as teachers, therapists, social workers, activists, advocates, mentors, doctors, healers, mediators, philanthropists, grandparents, and more—he sensed the suffering of others, and it awakened in him a longing to help. A natural compassion rose up within him and urged him into action, and he reoriented to giving back.

He wasn't blocked by identification with feelings of isolation and powerlessness: "I can't do this alone." "I can't really make a difference."

He wasn't slowed by internal resistance: "Should I do this or not?" "Is it beneath me to clean?" "This is boring. I should do something else with my time."

He wasn't stopped by distraction: "I have better things to do." "They can find someone else." "It's an endless task."

And he wasn't blocked by his ego's agenda: "If I do this, maybe I'll get credit. Maybe they'll see how special I am."

He just saw something that needed to be done, and he spontaneously engaged in right action. He heard the call—and heeded the call.

Ultimately, to his surprise, he received as much as he gave. He was helped as much as he helped others. And the opposites—giver and receiver, helper and helped—disappeared in the sacred act of service.

This chapter explores the Elder's call to sacred service from the inside out: How do we hear the call to serve? Is it the ego/Doer, or is it a call of the soul?

How do we resist the call? Who are the shadow characters that block the natural outward flow of altruistic caring? What is the shadow side of helping? How can we shift our service from caring for ego to caring for soul?

And what is the evolution of the soul in service?

Today, the call to serve is alive and well among us. About 25 percent of current retirees aspire to volunteer. In the United States in 2016, people fifty-five and older formally volunteered 3.3 billion hours, making a huge social and economic contribution, according to the Corporation for National and Community Service.

Encore.org recently surveyed six community organizations to determine the impact of their Elder volunteers. They found that most volunteer Elders had contributed their skills and labor to the organizations, assisting them in taking action and creating community resilience. Many contributed new ideas, approaches, or tools to the organizations. Elders' work helped to scale up those organizations' actions, increase visibility to funders, cut operating costs or improve service, and launch new programs. Elder volunteers also coached, mentored, and built relationships with others.

People who volunteer report reduced stress, lower rates of depression, and better physical health than people who don't volunteer. In addition, from the perspective of the inner work of aging, people who resist the call to serve also resist the evolution of the soul.

As more and more Elders heed the call to serve, they are finding their tribes in groups like the Elders Action Network (formerly the Conscious Elders Network) and pledging to bring their unique gifts to the interconnected issues of this cultural moment. They are building networks of support around social justice, climate change, equal opportunity, and democratic governance. And they are finding "the moral voice of the Elder," as Lynne Iser, president of Elders Action Network, calls it.

The precept of service appears in every religious tradition: In Judaism, the practice of *tikkun olam,* "repairing the world," calls for gathering the holy sparks that are scattered across creation through generous acts of service. The performance of good deeds (or *mitzvoth* in the parable at the start of this chapter) is one way of repairing the world, along with Torah study and ritual commandments. In Christianity, service and good works are an attempt to imitate the life of Christ. In Sufism, service means serving the Beloved by serving others. In Buddhism, service and compassion for loved ones, teachers, and all living beings are part of the Eightfold Path and the Bodhisattva vow. Thich Nhat Hanh extended these teachings into "engaged Buddhism" by applying them to social, political, and environmental injustice.

In Hinduism, *karma yoga* is a path to the divine that purifies the mind and opens the heart. Its proponents teach that selfless right action is a kind of prayer because it's performed for the benefit of others, without the ego's attachment to outcomes. With karma yoga, we focus on the actions of daily life as spiritual practice by dedicating them to God, doing them impeccably, and letting go of attachment to outcomes.

Roger Walsh pointed out to me that these guidelines combine a transpersonal motive beyond ego, a commitment to impeccability that requires cutting through personal blocks and letting go of egocentric control. "We go into ourselves in spiritual practice to go more effectively out into the world," Roger told me. "And we go out into the world in order to go deeper into ourselves through the practice of *karma yoga* and awakening service. And we repeat this cycle until we realize that we and the world are one."

All the great traditions, then, teach about the evolution of the soul through service. By opening to the momentary circumstances of our lives and attuning to the inner call, reaching past our small self-preoccupations, letting go of our ego's agenda, and connecting with the soul of another, service becomes a spiritual path. It becomes the means of our evolution, as well as the natural result of our deepening and widening compassion due to spiritual practice.

In *Born to Serve,* Susan Trout, executive director of the Institute for the Advancement of Service, said: "The purpose of life, and thus of service, is to awaken knowledge of the soul. The process of using our experience to awaken the soul crafts our destiny, as surely as Michelangelo crafted a statue."

In this way, with our expanded awareness, we are reimagining service and activism—from the inside out.

The Shadow Side of Service

Like age, service is structured in consciousness. That is, the quality of our service depends on our connection to pure awareness and to shadow awareness. Our stage of awareness determines how and why we serve. It colors our hidden motivations to heed or deny the call.

If our ego's agenda is to gain value, recognition, or power and to fill an inner emptiness, we may unknowingly heed the call to serve in an effort to meet those needs. We will be outwardly directed, rather than self-reflective, and we won't be responsible for our own internal experience. Instead, we will most likely see the world in black/white, right/wrong terms, so we will serve others in a dualistic way, projecting onto them that which we cannot see in ourselves.

We may refuse to see our own helplessness: "You need help. I can help you."

We may deny our uncertainty, identifying with a rigid belief system: "I'm certain that I'm right. You don't know what's going on."

We may be blind to our own neediness or dependency: "You're a victim. I can save you."

This hidden motivation leads to an unconscious power shadow, an inferior/superior dynamic in which we will unconsciously identify with our role—the Doer, the Helper, the Fixer, the Savior. As we carry the Doer into the arena of service and seek validation for achieving goals, we may become identified with that power or influence and ignore our inner work, at our peril. Our ego needs may be met—to feel useful or superior. However, even as we believe we are on the right side of a cause, we will deny our own limits, perhaps one day acting out our own shadow issues around power, money, or sex.

In addition, we will not open to the depths of the receiver of our service, blinded to his or her beauty and talent. And we will not meet soul to soul.

Instead, stuck in a role-based dynamic, we will grow attached to the results of our actions (for example, "I succeeded" or "I failed") and to how others see them ("You're so generous" or "She doesn't know how lucky she is to have you"). In the shadow, we may unconsciously hope to maintain the original painful situation so that we can maintain our superior role of Helper to a Victim, Caregiver to a Patient, or powerful person to a disenfranchised person.

Many people who serve in this way suffer burnout or "compassion fatigue" from effortful overreaching and lack of self-care. They typically struggle with internal conflict, in much the same way as a workaholic—feeling fraudulent, fearing failure, disconnected from an internal source.

The same holds true for unconscious activism: When our ego needs to be right or superior, we project the shadow and create an Other, who carries those traits that we don't see in ourselves—ignorance, entitlement, anger, prejudice, and so on. When my generation raged against "the Establishment," we had valid critiques about war, materialism, and consumerism. But when we didn't trust all *those people,* we disowned our own needs for security and stability.

Whether in service or activism, when we are disconnected from an internal source and from the soul in others, we engage in scapegoating and enemy making, which we see in stark relief today. In fact, some world leaders are using this very weapon of shadow-projection to create a terror of Otherness with Islamophobia, anti-Semitism, and fear of immigrants. In the extreme, they justify war, slavery, and genocide to dehumanize or eliminate the Other. We have witnessed this phenomenon during the Crusades, the Inquisition, the decimation of Native populations around the world during the European colonial period, the slavery of Africans in the New World, and the Holocaust. Tragically, we see these same shadow projections turned into policies in our own times in the detention of immigrants in border camps.

Andrew Beath, founder of EarthWays Foundation, who has written about what he calls "conscious activism in the ecological epoch," told me that the same process of categorizing the world as us/them occurs in relation to nature. "We turn nature into an object and devalue its sacred beauty. Then we can rationalize our abuse of it and deny our interconnectedness, so that we can continue to pursue our self-interest."

A key attribute of conscious activism, Andrew said, is "no enemy." We need to move beyond the separate self-sense of ego and Other. "This is how we bring our spiritual development into activism."

When I asked him how he has persisted for decades in environmental activism in the face of our worsening crisis, he said, "My privilege brings responsibility. I live a life of purpose and meaning. Things may change, they may not. I'm positive, but not optimistic."

In the long term, if we wake up to our personal and collective shadow issues and do spiritual practice, we realize that what we seek is not "out there." As we take the time to recover and self-reflect, we can reimagine our beliefs and values and redesign our lives to include service in a healthier mode.

We can see the evolution of soul through service in three stages. In the first stage, service carries us from an activity that meets our own hidden needs into a larger arena of reconciliation and reparation. We experience life flowing through us, rather than the ego's need to control outcomes.

I learned, for example, during a course called "Waking Up to Our History" for the Elders Action Network, that some White residents of

Northern California are meeting with Native tribes to share their grief about how their own White ancestors treated Native Americans in the region. And they are seeking to make reparations by raising funds to buy land for native ceremonies.

Another White woman told us that, after training with Coming to the Table, whose mission is to heal the intergenerational wounds of racial injustice, she met and is working with a Black woman whose ancestors were enslaved by the White woman's ancestors. Together, these women are facing the truth of their family histories, expressing their shame and grief about it, and giving back their service into the community, ending the Us/Them division and closing the circle.

At the second stage, we start to see ourselves as part of a larger system in which we and the recipients of our service are both embedded, both giving and receiving care, energy, and love. We can receive, breathing in, and give, breathing out. We let go of the ego's hidden motives and feel held in a larger field that is both whole and broken, both perfect and in need of repair.

Now, we begin to see external circumstances as mirrors of our inner world. We see how our own shadow issues are shaping our service and can be accountable for them by doing shadow-work. As we center ourselves in silence and witness these inner voices, we can reclaim our projections onto others. Poor/wealthy, needy/helper, receiver/giver dissolve. And, ideally, we can attune to our own inner guidance, remembering that we are not the Doer. We are a soul in service.

At the third stage, the concepts of giver and receiver become a reflection of the collective unconscious, the soul of the world. I am serving another, and that person is serving me, within the larger field of consciousness, which is itself shaping us and being shaped by us. We are nodes in Indra's net, an image from Hindu myth that reflects findings from modern physics about the vast interdependence of all things. Indra's net, like a cosmic spider web, is an infinite network of interpenetrating points. At each node of the net, a jewel glimmers, holographically reflecting all the other jewels. This nondual stage of sacred service honors this vast interconnection of all living things.

My brother-in-law, Stephen Schuitevoerder, shared a startling personal experience of this interconnection. A psychologist, Stephen is a specialist in process-oriented psychology, which applies inner work to conflict situations around the world. He has brought it to the U.N., corporations, and educational settings.

Stephen's Jewish parents immigrated as children in the 1920s from Europe to South Africa. When he and my husband were growing up, the family did not speak of the Holocaust. But, in 1999, Stephen visited the Holocaust Museum in Washington, D.C., and was shocked to see page after page of people who had died in the camps with his unique last name—Schuitevoerder. In his rage and grief, Stephen began to study his genealogy and find more information about the men, women, and children in his lineage who were lost. He became furious with all of Europe for its participation in anti-Semitism and collusion with Nazism.

One day, Stephen was in a printing shop when he heard an older man speaking with a German accent. Stephen realized that the man could have been a soldier in WWII. He approached the man to challenge him about the war. The man replied that he was from Austria but had moved to Germany during the war (Stephen was holding his breath . . .), until they let him out of the concentration camp.

"I recall the blood draining from my face," Stephen said, "as I realized he was Jewish. It took a while for me realize what had happened. I had taken a specific quality, the man's accent, and generalized it to mean that he was a Nazi. I saw that this behavior of generalizing was what Hitler had done to the Jews. They had projected onto a whole group and persecuted them. I, too, had the ability to generalize and attack. It changed my perspective and refined my interaction with people. And this experience woke me up to the importance of doing inner work as a precursor to service."

Stephen shared this experience with a large group of his students. The next morning, David, a German man in the group, mentioned that Stephen's story was difficult for him. He spoke about the suffering of the German people during that time. Stephen approached David and they hugged. He told me that he felt a deep sensation in his heart as he realized that this was not only Stephen and David hugging each other but a Jew and a German embracing, reconciling the agonies of their history.

Afterward, Stephen sat down and began to sob, allowing the torment of his ancestors to move through him. Then this wave of sorrow expanded to include the agony of the German people, the splitting of their nation, and the violations done to them during the war. Then the wave expanded to all human beings as he realized that we all hold immense suffering in our bodies, in our DNA. We all hold the pain of our ancestors struggling to survive.

The next morning, a woman from the group approached Stephen. On the day that he had done this inner work in front of the group, she had received a message on her neighborhood Facebook page. A man had posted a photo of three commemorative stones that were laid in the street. Each one had a brass plate engraved with the name of a person killed in the Holocaust, their date of birth and death, and their place of death. The names on the plaques: Schuitevoerder. Three people, Stephen's ancestors. All connected by an invisible thread that bind us all.

Inner work/outer work. Individual soul/Soul of the world.

Heeding the Call or Denying the Call

Inner Work for Resistant Elders

The call to serve can be heard in many forms: to tithe money, volunteer, run for office, march in protest, feed the hungry, care for a loved one, give our wisdom, mentor the young, protect the Earth, and grandparent the kids. The call to serve is the call to love in action.

If we attune to ourselves and listen closely to our inner dialogue, it will pull us, like a magnet, reorienting us to give back. And love will show the way. Bruce Frankel, of Life Planning Network, felt deep concern for LGBTQ older people in New York. "They are some of the best educated, poorest, and loneliest people in the city," he told me. He dreamed of creating community with new technologies for this population and has built virtual villages to end isolation and increase access to care.

A therapist friend told me, following the California wildfires, "I want to work with firefighters and help them recover from trauma." She heard the call and found a training to do just that.

Another man had been to Liberia in the 1960s in the Peace Corps. When he retired, decades later, he heard the summons to return. He found that living conditions had worsened, so he committed to bring light to Liberia: He set up thousands of solar lights for homes, businesses, and hospitals.

An acquaintance left the corporate world and took a job teaching environmental classes at a community college. She told me, "I don't see anything more important than climate change now. I'm finding ways to contribute to this cause by training the next generation."

An insurance executive longed for more community and decided to become president of his synagogue, so that he could build his vision there. A neighbor teaches meditation in prisons once a month; he says that he receives as much as he gives.

Several women in my mountain town dreamed of supporting homeless families. They formed a group of thirty women who, in conjunction with the city, furnish free temporary housing for families in need and stock the apartments with furnishings and food each month.

The Raging Grannies, a grassroots network of "gaggles" of older women, urge us to "get off your fannies." They organize locally across North America around issues of social justice and sustainability. At their rallies and court hearings, they sing their protests.

The possibilities are endless. But we need to be able to tune in to the cries of the world without shutting them out. A shadow character will deny them: "What can I do about it?" "I'd rather not know." "I just want to enjoy my old age." If we deny them or distract ourselves and shut them out, we cannot heed the call.

On the other hand, we need to be able to tune in to the cries of the world without drowning in them, getting lost in the face of intolerable suffering and wallowing in sorrow, pity, helplessness, or guilt: "Everywhere I turn I see pain, hunger, illness, loss. I can only barely take care of myself."

This process is analogous to conscious aging. We must break through our denial to face the full truth about age and create the life we want now. In the same way, we must break through our denial of the call to serve and see the whole truth: the beauty *and* the terror of the world, the immense possibilities *and* the wretched hardships. We need to hold the tension of these opposites to live in the full spectrum of reality.

Then, in order to act, we need to attune to the inner world, to the voices within: "I'm drawn to that cause." "My passion is aroused here." "I can do something about that need." "This injustice is most important to me." "I have a gift for these people."

Instantly, for most of us, a shadow character can be heard. So, we center ourselves in silent meditation and witness the denial, resistance, and distraction that arise. We may, for example, witness the fear that we have nothing to give. Rory, a friend of mine, who works as a teacher, told me that he found himself struggling with this fear in the face of climate change. A decade ago, after training with Al Gore's Climate Reality Project, he had felt overwhelmed and impotent. He heard himself say, "That problem is so huge. I don't have the skills to have any impact."

But then, a year later, he discovered that his school district wanted to retrofit buildings and start offering classes about energy efficiency and renewable energy. He was there; he was qualified; he was ready.

Habitual feelings of powerlessness and invisibility may arise, especially in the face of ageism. So, we deny the call: "I'm too tired, too old, too powerless now." The inner ageist may collude with social ageism, resulting in paralysis. Stop, slow down, listen. Remember that this is a shadow character, not who you are. And you can decide if you want this part to stop you—or if you want to heed the summons, which arises from your soul, and move toward caring for something larger than yourself.

The fear of getting too close to suffering may come up. My friend Claire heard the call to help refugees. It kept returning, but she was terrified to get close to people in such distress, scared of being overwhelmed or even contaminated by their misery. As the immigration crisis reached our own borders and the federal administration separated children from their families, she found her unique response: to bring carloads of clothing and bathroom supplies to the children.

By using service as a mirror in this way, we are doing continuous, unbroken spiritual practice in daily life. And we are healing the split between activism and spirituality.

As Gandhi put it, "Those who say that religion has nothing to do with politics do not know what religion really means."

In our day, Buddhist teacher Jack Kornfield echoed this point: "Do not believe that meditation and contemplation are the fulfillment of the Buddhist Path. Inner peace, freedom and joy develop only when paired with the outer teachings of virtue, respect and mutual care," he wrote in a 2016 essay, "Now Is the Time to Stand Up."

"This is not about red or blue," Jack continued. "It is about standing up for the most basic of human principles, for moral action and the prevention of harm. It is embodying Dharma amidst the troubles of the world. . . . You have been training for this for a long time. With practice you have learned to quiet the mind and open the heart. You have learned emptiness and interdependence. Now it is time to step forward, bringing your equanimity and courage, wisdom and compassion to the world."

As we reorient from the ego's agenda to the soul's mission and heed this call to serve something larger than ourselves, we can ground ourselves in pure awareness. We can attune to the shadow voices within, deepening our self-knowledge and using shadow-work to move resistance out of the way. As a result, we can make a more conscious choice about when and how much to engage—and why.

An Interview with John Sorensen,
Founder of Elders Action Network

John, seventy-seven years old at the time of our interview, founded the Elders Action Network (EAN; formerly the Conscious Elders Network) after a long journey to find his late-life calling. He sold a technology company and felt "spiritually dead," he told me. He wanted to recapture the life force. He took classes and did psychotherapy to reignite his purpose.

Then, on a vision quest, he encountered his main shadow character, which told him, "You're not good enough." When he woke up to this message and how it was sabotaging him, he could stop obeying it. "I knew it wasn't true, and I wanted to spend these years giving back. But how?"

John heard an inner voice: "Teach leadership." He stopped and listened. "Organize the Elders of America."

He knew he had found his mission because he "felt the right fit."

When John heard his calling, he began to find people with the same zest to stand up in the public square. "We're not acting out of ego," he told me. "We don't need credit. We don't have all the answers. But we know we need a movement of Elders to tell it like it is."

Two kinds of Elder show up, John said: those who focus on outer work and those who focus on inner work. "We do outer work with the intention to grow in consciousness. We practice nonviolent communication, shadow-work, and sacred activism. We practice inner work in circles, so that we don't fall into enemy making."

Their growing special interest groups include Elder activists for social justice, climate change, and sustainable living. EAN teaches people in late life to get past the resistance to becoming an Elder so that we can become empowered in the world. "Inner and outer ageism are rampant," John said. "But I don't let it stop me. I'm so grateful to have energy and purpose. And EAN is building a foundation for future generations. It's a precious legacy."

An Interview with Roshi Wendy Egyoku Nakao, Former Abbot of the Zen Center of Los Angeles

Wendy embodies the union of activism and spirituality, or service and practice. She is a Zen Roshi, spiritual leader in a Zen Buddhist community, and her original teacher was Maezumi Roshi, who helped bring a renowned school of Zen, Soto Zen, to America. She also is a successor of the late Roshi Bernie Glassman, founder of the Zen Peacemakers Order, which gained fame for combining meditation and social action as a path. The order's spiritually based social engagement grew into the renowned Greyston Bakery, which provided jobs for people in need, whether homeless, HIV-positive, or former prisoners.

When I spoke with Roshi Wendy, she told me that her interest in spirituality grew out of her culturally diverse family and a need to find meaning in their differences. In 1975, a friend dared her to go sit in a silent Zen retreat for seven days, and she accepted the challenge. "There was no instruction. We would sit, the bell rang, we would unfold our legs, then sit again. We would practice walking meditation. Then sit again. I had no guidance. But something stirred in me. I went home and told my husband that I was leaving."

She had to follow this path alone, Wendy told me. She entered a longer training and met Maezumi Roshi. After five years, her mind still noisy, she learned mindfulness. "I was so surprised that I could sit the way I needed to. It was not rigorous, like Zen."

She began to build up inner silence and see how the mind works. On a longer retreat, she realized that she was trying to be an ideal person, an image in her mind. "I saw that I had to be simply me." She returned to Maezumi Roshi and was ordained as a Zen priest. Then she trained with Roshi Bernie in Zen Peacemakers.

When it was discovered that Maezumi Roshi was sexually involved with students and an active alcoholic, scandal rocked the Zen Center of Los Angeles, and most students left in despair. Roshi Wendy stepped up and, following a fire on the premises, decided to rebuild inside and out. She trained the remaining members in council to process their feelings about the devastating disillusionment with their teacher and to resolve disagreements. "In sitting, we face the wall," she told me. "In council, we face each other. It's the other arm of sitting."

She learned communication skills, such as speaking and listening from the heart. And she looked directly at the shadow issues of the community, the blind spots of spirituality. "We work now on our emotional integration and our discernment to detect potential conflict. I can read the energetic field and sense if something needs to be brought to the light."

She singled out a shadow of Buddhism: It has been filtered through a male monastic lens. "What would practice look like if the voices of women, such as Buddha's abandoned wife and his many early followers, had not been written out of his life story?"

At the Zen Center, Roshi Wendy broke up the traditional hierarchy and created a peer *sangha*, or community, for shared stewardship. Autonomous circles run the center and fit into the whole. All of this built a new container for an intentional spiritual community, and as problems arose, the container remained strong. "The old forms collapsed, but forty people came together to build a new structure, tell the truth about our history, and learn how to create another kind of community," Wendy told me.

She continued, "During the past twenty years, we've woven consciously the many threads of the Zen Center—including its light and shadows, its vertical and horizontal dimensions, and its feminine and masculine energies—into a resilient fabric with a newly emerging story and patterns. Stitch by stitch, we are sewing the robe of buddhas, the robe of awakened ones, which is the robe of liberation and service."

This orients us to a great vow, Wendy said. For Buddhists, the decision to take refuge means to commit to a life that is far larger than your own preoccupations. "Allow it to expand you and call you forth in new ways."

The Zen Peacemakers hold three tenets. The first is *not-knowing*, letting go of fixed ideas about yourself, others, and the universe. As Roshi Wendy put it, "Over the years I have discovered that this great field of not-knowing calls me to listen deeply to all that is arising. The limited sense of 'I' expands to include things strange and unfamiliar—things beyond my capacity to know, things that I may have considered 'not me'—all expanding and contracting in one seamless flow of interacting complexity."

"So," she continued, "I like to say, 'Know what you stand for.' We are all related and can never be separated. What are the everyday actions of my own hands, words, and heart that affirm this interconnected life that we are living all together?"

The second tenet, *bearing witness* to the joy and suffering of the world, asks us to face the conditions that are presented to us. "The present circumstances of your life are the perfect vehicle for your awakening. How can we use these very circumstances to forget the self, practice the precepts, and serve others?"

The third tenet, *taking action* that is caring and serves everyone and everything, includes action that is rooted in not-knowing and bearing witness. When the voice of a shadow says, "I can't," Wendy says, we must listen to what we tell ourselves and dialogue with the shadow.

These tenets orient members of the Zen Center to serve their community as spiritual practice: caring for local homeless people, creating food baskets for local churches, offering nonviolence training to teens, doing prison ministry, and planting trees locally. The Zen Center offers an apartment for a homeless youth to provide a stable circumstance for his transition to adulthood. They also assist formerly incarcerated people in reentering society and help feed youths who are transitioning from foster care to adulthood.

The call to serve is part of the Bodhisattva vow to liberate all beings by doing our spiritual practice to cultivate enlightenment for all beings, not merely for ourselves. "We move our intention from becoming enlightened for myself to the realization that we are all interconnected," Wendy said. "So, practice occurs in the environment of service. And service is practice."

Roshi Wendy stepped down as abbot of the Zen Center in May 2019.

Conscious Grandparenting

Caring for the Souls of Our Young Ones

When many of my women friends were either getting pregnant or longing to get pregnant, I used to think that I was missing a chip. I watched and waited for a maternal feeling, desire, or impulse of any kind—to no avail. As far as I was aware, during those years, I wanted only one thing: to become enlightened.

At nineteen, I was hooked on meditation and its promise. And when I saw the suffering all around me, near and far, I wanted only to be free of it.

My mother was devastated by this turn of events. She had flirted with early feminism and assumed that, unlike her, I would have both a career and kids. But neither called to me like the devotion to my spiritual vision.

Fast-forward two decades, past midnight on my biological clock: I met a man whose spiritual devotion was as fervent as my own—and he had kids. Another two decades later, they have kids—and I'm Grandma Connie.

Given that I had no experience as a parent and no positive grandparent to serve as an Elder for me, I'm making it up as I go, developing as a grandma while the kids develop as youths. And because I know that many of our early unconscious negative images of age stem from our grandparents, I feel acutely aware of my impact on them.

Today, when there are more Americans over fifty than under eighteen, many older people don't share this privilege of deep contact with grandkids. Our culture has shifted from multigenerational homes to rampant age segregation, with young people in school for long hours, middle-aged people at work for long hours, and older people in retirement communities or nursing homes. Age segregation is as widespread as racial segregation.

The result: Vast numbers of youth will grow old without close relationships to Elders and will default to stereotypes. (Beware the inner ageist!) And older people miss the vitality of relationships with youth and the opportunities to serve their families.

Despite this geographical or residential separation, we need to acknowledge the Elder wisdom that we want to transmit and pass it on. Great-grandfather Jerome Kerner, at the age of eighty-four, a board member of Sage-ing International, speaks and writes about grandparenting. He told me that, because his mother worked, his Nana was his primary caretaker, and her unconditional love provided him with emotional regulation. For kids, Jerome told me, grandparents can offset the pressure of parental authority, school performance, competitive sports, and other places where they feel the weight of high expectations. Without grandparents, he surmised, kids turn to social media, video games, and other even dangerous outlets, like drugs, to find this regulation.

Pat Hoertdoerfer, a grandmother of seven and a retired Unitarian Universalist minister, who is also a Sage-ing leader, described for me a unique family tradition to transmit values and a sense of belonging. In 2009, her family launched Cousins Camp to nurture the grandparent-grandchild relationship for a week each summer. "During Cousins Camp," Pat said, "we strive to live our core values, transmit family heritage, engage their imaginations, learn from each other, live close to the land, and play together. We enjoy waterfront activities, games, arts, and story time. Responsibilities are shared, privileges are shared, conflicts are resolved in camp council, and love is celebrated."

They begin the week, Pat told me, by defining their Cousin Camp promises: to act with kind words, helping hands, caring hearts, open minds, listening ears, and walking feet. They discuss these six promises and agree to practice them each day.

Sitting in council, they share how they could all do better. And they end council with an affirmation for each cousin: "You are a person, you are special, you are important. Not because of what you look like, not because of what you have, not because of what you can do. Just because you are You." (In terms of the themes of this book, this family is using communication to shift their relationships from ego to soul.)

I was deeply moved by Pat's story. But I realize that most families cannot meet this ideal. For some, there are conflicting values and distrust between generations. One client, a grandmother, told me that she deeply dislikes the materialistic, consumer-oriented values of her grandson's parents. She believes they supply him with stuff instead of supplying him with emotional support.

A grandfather told me that his adult children don't make time for imaginary play with his grandkids; they are so focused on perfectionistic performance that the young ones already show signs of anxiety.

And another grandmother told me that her grandkids are parked in front of their iPads or TV for hours each day. She cried as she described her powerlessness in this heartbreaking situation.

I share her concern. Research reported in *Virtual Child* by Cris Rowan confirms that the youth epidemics of attention disorders, aggressive behavior, lack of empathy, learning disorders, and obesity are correlated with overuse of technology. Kids are replacing parents and friends with virtual avatars. In some cases, online and gaming content is loud, violent, and sexual, which kids imitate on the schoolyard. According to Rowan, some 75 percent of kids today have tech in their bedrooms and may develop "video game brain," which hardwires them for a lack of impulse control.

The long-term result: They can become isolated from family members, lonely, depressed, and at risk for obesity and diabetes. The combination of being sedentary and overstimulated is perilous. The loss of normal brain development and human interaction has dire consequences.

The antidote: Time spent in nature reduces symptoms related to ADHD. Regular cardio exercise increases attention span. Physical touch calms the nervous system. Deep listening enables emotional regulation and empathy.

These findings provide guidelines for conscious parenting and grandparenting. We all can offer these antidotes. We can share the joys of play in the natural world and the rewards of exercise and exploring new things. We can talk about the fantasy of games versus the reality of life. We can teach them how to tune in to their own bodies, their feelings, their self-expression, so that, even as digital natives, they don't lose touch with themselves.

And how do we grandparent the kids' shadows—that is, the unconscious material that is inevitably formed by adults' communication styles or by the manner in which they make certain feelings, such as anger, or behaviors, such as crying, unacceptable?

One grandmother, a psychologist, told me that she observed how fear was transmitted from her adult son to her grandson. Then she watched her grandson develop an anxiety disorder. "But each weekend," she told me, "I made sure that little boy felt safe with me. He could feel the steadiness of my body and the calm of my mind. And he felt loved no matter what."

Clearly, each family has its own dynamic. Some will allow for open dialogue among generations, while others won't. Some will allow kids to express anger, fear, or sadness, while others won't. Some will allow for no-tech time, while others won't. But if we remember that we can be an antidote, we may find a way.

It also became clear to me through interviews that grandparenting can be a spiritual practice for Elders. While parents are absent or distracted, we can practice presence with our little ones. While parents are building ego identities and feeling concern about image, they may be critical of kids who don't meet their standards; we can practice acceptance and forgiveness. While parents are focused on performance, we can read them stories about heroes and heroines who find their unique gifts. All these experiences support the development of both Elders and youth.

Finally, I have found some indirect ways to share my values with grandkids, ways that don't challenge their parents. For instance, my grandson Jayden, age seven, and I play the question game when we're together. "Why does grass grow?" "Where do shoes come from?"

One day, he asked, "Where does water come from?"

As I began to describe how the rain falls on the mountaintops, freezes into snow, melts into rivers, and goes through pipes so that we can drink it, I watched his eyes light up. Something special was happening with this question and answer. I explored further how our bodies are made of water and how everything is interconnected, one living system, like a giant body. The excitement in his little body was palpable as he sensed a great truth, even for a moment. Clearly, this was not an intellectual understanding but a feeling of opening to all living things. He could feel less separate, less isolated, as he imagined water flowing through him and through his mom and dad as it flows from the sky into the rivers and back into him with each glass.

I felt such gratitude that, although I was never a mother, today I am a grandmother.

Climate Change

Collective Mortality Awareness

We have stretched ourselves to turn and face our individual mortality. Together, in this journey, we have twisted our bodies, hearts, and minds away from their habitual, seductive patterns of denial and compartmentalization to stare down this truth: *I too shall pass.*

Now, I'm asking you to stretch even further, to stare into the possibility of collective mortality: *Humanity too shall pass. All living things on Earth shall pass.*

I don't even want to write the words. I can hardly focus, let alone imagine this unthinkable truth. I get up and walk in circles to catch a breath.

But, as I sit down again, the mountain roads around my home are flooding, only weeks after we escaped wildfires. Climate change is here now. And all of it—human civilization, the animals, the Earth itself—is at risk.

We are in a collective rite of passage. Not at the threshold—but fully in it.

My friend Mitch Metzner, a longtime hospice midwife, says that, like a person in hospice care, the Earth is in liminal time, after life and before death—or reemergence.

So, I pose the same question I've asked throughout this book: How do we want to live now, given the whole truth?

And as we turn to face this truth for an instant, our rage, grief, and powerlessness break over us in a wave.

Listen to your shadow voices now: "Why did Connie have to go here?" "I don't want to read about this." "I bought a book about aging, not climate." "I recycle. What else can I do?"

We don't want to face this "inconvenient truth." We don't want to know what we can't tolerate knowing or what we can't change. "Yes, I should do something—but anything I do is useless. I can't really have any impact on this."

Yet doing nothing is also intolerable. It increases the anxiety, the guilt, and the dread. So, we stuff those intolerable feelings again and put down this book. And turn on the TV.

I understand. I do this myself. We can't stare too long at the sun.

But as we bury those daunting feelings and this certain knowledge in the shadow, as we repress them beneath awareness, something else happens: We numb out. And the unconscious fear and grief ripple through our bodies, eventually seeping up to the surface in other ways. People sense the disturbance in the Force, like an animal sensing danger. They report free-floating anxiety for unknown reasons and widespread depression because, as one high-school student told me, "There is no future for me."

This condition now has names—climate grief, climate trauma—and is an unprecedented, ever-present, ever-growing awareness.

Futurelessness—the people of my generation, the baby boomers, faced this at the peak of the Cold War and the buildup of the nuclear arms race. During those years, Joanna Macy wrote and taught about sharing our despair to carry us beyond our small, personal concerns and out into the world. Our despair, she taught, is a doorway to the realization of our mutual belonging in the web of life. Rather than bringing more isolation, our shared despair brings community and links us in solidarity—and in uncertainty—with all living things.

Now in her eighties, Joanna wrote in *World as Lover, World as Self,* "The loss of certainty that there will be a future is the pivotal psychological reality of our time."

We may not want to know. We may distract ourselves or even deny this truth. But we do know—with or without conscious awareness. And the animals know as extinctions spread. And the children know.

Deena Metzger has another name for it: extinction illness. She wrote recently, "It is possible that Extinction Illness is the root of all contemporary mental, physical, and spiritual diseases. Extinction Illness, the essential cellular knowledge and terror that one's life, one's people's lives, all life is threatened, that lineage is disappearing, that we, all, may well become extinct within a very short period time, that the future will be eradicated." (For Deena's full essay, see "Extinction Illness," published on the blog site of *Tikkun* magazine, January 3, 2019.)

When I first learned about climate change in the 1980s, I had a fantasy that it would bring humanity together under a common threat and a common purpose: to create a sustainable world. As Deena wrote, "In order to save our lives, we have to save everyone's life, human and non-human."

But despite the international conferences and national pacts, the necessary sweeping global action did not come to pass. Now, according to scientists, less than a decade remains to prevent the worst scenario.

Spiritual theologian Matthew Fox, founder of Creation Spirituality, calls this the "dark night of the species."

The great eco-theologian Thomas Berry put it this way in *Selected Writings on the Earth Community:* "In the 20th century, the glory of the human has become the desolation of the earth. The desolation of the earth has become the destiny of the human."

Today, the call to be an Elder *is* the call to be an Earth Elder.

Those of us in late life as I write this were the first generation to know about environmental disaster. In our youth, we became either vaguely or acutely aware of the consequences of our dependence on fossil fuels. Few of us did anything meaningful about it.

Today we know that what happens to each of us happens to all of us. Today, we are awakening from the trance of denial. We are called to bring the moral voice of the Elder to do our part for all living things.

Do you hear the call? It rises up from your soul and from the soul of the world. It may speak in your dreams, guide your intuition, rumble through your grief, or move through your love of nature.

This is an arena in which some Elder activists are highly engaged, writing investigative journalism, protesting fracking and pipelines, lobbying with Citizens' Climate Lobby, divesting retirement funds from fossil fuels, mobilizing climate voters, and marching with kids during school strikes. Many have taken the vow of the Order of the Sacred Earth: I promise to be the best lover and defender of Mother Earth that I can be.

As a Native American proverb says, "We do not inherit the Earth from our ancestors. We borrow it from our children."

What will you tell your grandchildren or great-grandchildren when they ask: What did you do when you found out about the climate crisis?

Shadow-Work Practices

- Do you hear the call to serve something larger than yourself?
- Can you identify the cause or issue that arouses the most passion in you and calls you toward it?
- Imagine yourself serving others or speaking up in the public arena about this. What stops you from getting engaged?
- What is your unique gift that only you can give? What stops you from giving it?
- Gandhi said, "My life is my message." What is your message?

Spiritual Practices

In Hindu myth, Hanuman, servant of the god Ram, tells Ram: "When I don't know who I am, I serve you. When I know who I am, I am you." Can you see the evolution of your soul through service? How can you be the change you long to see in the world?

🦋 The Ten Steps of Sacred Service through Karma Yoga

Roger Walsh outlines these steps, paraphrased here from his article "Karma Yoga and Awakening Service."

1. Before beginning any activity, stop, breathe, and become present to your purpose.
2. Offer the activity to God or the divine, however you understand it.
3. Choose an intention. Ask yourself, "What is this for?" Survival, comfort, awakening, the benefit of others, or some other motivation?
4. Do the activity as impeccably as you can.
5. Be mindful, observing your actions, intentions, and mental state.
6. Work with any reactions that arise, such as anxiety, anger, pride, hope, and disappointment, and use shadow-work here.
7. Release attachment to the outcome. Use the witness to let it go.
8. Stop at the end of the activity.
9. Reflect and learn about your action, its results, your ego, your mind, and your attachments.
10. Offer the benefits to the well-being of all.

🦋 The Six Perfections of Buddhism

In her book *Standing at the Edge,* Buddhist teacher Joan Halifax gives us a meditation prayer invoking the six *paramitas* or perfections—the qualities of compassion that embody the sacred service of a Bodhisattva:

❦

May I be generous.

May I cultivate integrity and respect.

May I be patient and see clearly the suffering of others.

May I be energetic, steadfast, and wholehearted.

May I cultivate a calm and inclusive mind and heart so I can compassionately serve all beings.

May I nurture wisdom and impart the benefit of any insights I may have to others.

PART 4

Life Completion

Carl Jung wrote that life is a luminous pause between two mysteries. Part 4 carries us further toward that final mystery, ushering us toward life completion and the encounter with the other world.

12

Moving toward
a Completed Life

PARABLE

Did Moses Die Fulfilled?
A Tale by Carol Orsborn

In a blog post called "Moses—Benched," Carol Orsborn suggests that the image of Moses, wandering in the wilderness for forty years but forbidden by God to enter the Promised Land at the end of his life, is like a Rorschach test for our stage of awareness. She asks, Did Moses die fulfilled?

Some people imagine Moses feeling angry and betrayed at the end of his life, shedding tears of despair. Others imagine him disappointed because he died before his task was complete. But perhaps that's how it is for everyone. We all leave some things, even important ones, unfinished.

Moses, at 120, died in the desert, not in the Promised Land. But God received his soul by kissing him on the mouth. Forgiven, complete.

Perhaps completion arises out of the knowledge that we have transmitted all that we have learned and have prepared the next generation to carry on our tasks. This Moses did. He had Joshua and a new generation of leaders to venture forth, and he sent them out with the hope that they would prosper and follow God or Spirit.

If we hold the view that Moses failed, we are judging him through a *goal-oriented lens: The only goal is entering the Promised Land. With this narrow view, we are bound for frustration and despair. (We are missing the 360-degree view of the soul's journey.)*

But through another lens, we can see Moses's life journey as invaluable but unfinished: He transmitted the Torah, while still wishing for more.

—To read Orsborn's complete post,
see "Moses—Benched," on CarolOrsborn.com, May 1, 2018

What is a completed life? Is it based on a feeling of gratitude, happiness, or forgiveness? Is it based on a belief of redemption, salvation, or reincarnation? Is it based on the achievement of an external goal? Is it based on the transmission of a legacy to a new generation? Is it based on an internal attainment of a spiritual stage of awareness?

If our evolution is blocked by an inability to overcome all the inner obstacles we have discussed in the preceding chapters, if we are unable to move through our denial and do the inner work of age, we cannot consciously do the work of life completion.

Many of us in late life have had the sense of wandering for years in a desert-like landscape and longing for home, at times shedding tears of despair, at times surrounded by loved ones and content. Like Moses, we have given precious gifts, and, like him, we sense that we have been denied entry to something, somewhere.

This image of the Promised Land has been out of sight in the shadow. Perhaps we have glimpsed it in our dreams or our art. For some people with a traditional religious orientation, it has been defined by others, conceived of as Heaven, or at the hand of God. For others with a more Eastern or mystical orientation, it has been conceived of as a level of consciousness, an awakening to the true nature of reality, a direct perception of the unity of all things.

In either case, conscious or unconscious, this image has acted as a lure, stimulating our soul's longing to reach what is just out of reach, to enter a promising new land. It has aroused our spiritual thirst and directed our wandering, orienting us in a direction, even unknowingly.

What is your own promised land? Who has forbidden entry?

Can life be perfect yet unfinished?

Each of us can live into these questions, carrying them like closed buds that open in time.

This exploration is not intended to be a bucket list of more doing or the ego's desire for a legacy of recognition. Rather it's about the longing of your soul that has guided your journey all along. It's about the soul's legacy.

As James Hillman put it in an essay on longing in *Loose Ends,* "Tell me what you yearn for, and I shall tell you who you are."

When she was sixty-eight, my dear friend Heather, who had never married, told me that her promised land was a loving relationship. Although she consciously yearned for it, she now understands that she unconsciously chose men who wouldn't commit so that she didn't have to commit. As she struggles with terminal illness, she mourns the romantic dream unfulfilled.

A client, Tom, at the age of eighty-one, reported that his promised land was a feeling of agelessness, a freedom from the limits of age. I pointed out that this was not so much about his pain at being seen as old by others, which is what he believed. It was about a spiritual longing, a yearning of his ageless soul. He decided to do a shamanic, psychedelic journey at the close of his life to break through the constructs of his separate sense of self.

Another client, Dinah, told me that her mother had been a practicing Catholic all her life. But as she lay dying, her mother pondered, "What if it's all a lie? What if I can't get into heaven—or there is no heaven?" She allowed the Doubter to surface only in her last few breaths, as she approached the final possibility of touching her beloved promised land.

Another friend, Tony, at the age of seventy-seven, told me that his promised land was seeing his grandchildren grow up. He imagined a time when they were mature and thriving, in part due to his loving presence. And that seemed like paradise to him, even as he knew that he wouldn't be there to enjoy it.

Lillian, a Holocaust survivor who escaped the Warsaw ghetto in Poland at age twelve, had survived by hiding in the woods alone. After being christened as "Alice" to disguise her from the Nazis, with her religious identity erased, she eventually immigrated to America, became a therapist, and had a family. She was now eighty-eight, and her promised land? "Giving the lie to Hitler" in the survival of her three grandchildren.

James, sixty-eight, had a successful career as an oncologist and faculty member at an acclaimed university. He dreamed for decades of making a scientific breakthrough that would end the epidemic of cancer. "I had every privilege," he told me. "I wanted to make the most of it. And I helped my patients, but I wanted to do something great, something life-changing in the world of cancer. So, now, at the end of my career, I feel grief. I feel failure."

James's promised land is out of reach. Was his ego so grandiose, his standard of success so high, that the feeling of failure was inevitable? Was his work a good enough contribution for James? Is an early shadow character sabotaging his sense of satisfaction and life completion? Was his soul's mission different from what he believed it to be?

These questions can apply to any of us in late life who had big dreams, who achieved something in any field, but who feel, now, that it's "not enough." We should have done more; we could have done more. But, somehow, we didn't.

A tall tale about Albert Einstein points to a precious legacy left incomplete: The day before he died, Einstein was observed scribbling on a yellow pad. It seems that his promised land, the theory of the unified field, was just out of reach. And yet his contribution to the world is undeniable.

As I contemplated this theme for myself, grief overcame me, and I quietly wept on and off for days. My heart ached with longing for something promised, something unattained that cannot, by nature, be attained. For me, the promised land was a unified or nondual level of consciousness that remains elusive. Although my fifty-year meditation practice has brought dramatic changes in my stage of awareness, it has not brought the promised land of enlightenment, as I understand it. So, I have lived, hand in hand, with gratitude for my teachers and practices and with grief for a receding dream.

Do I accept the limits of my evolution today and let go of the Seeker within, the part of me that's always striving for more awareness? I have been identified with this voice/feeling for as long as I can remember. I came to believe that it carries a vow made by my soul long ago.

But perhaps it is my ego that identified with the Seeker, co-opting it for its own agenda. Perhaps the Seeker in me now has become a shadow character, an obstacle to life completion. Can I release my identification with it, simply accept myself as is, and enjoy the life that remains?

These days, the twin threats to climate and democracy add further load to my grief. Perhaps the Activist in me also has become a shadow character, an obstacle to life completion. Can I release my identification with it and simply accept *what is,* trusting that life will unfold without my efforts?

As one of my teachers put it, "We must remain confident that the Earth is not set up for destruction. It's a soul purification planet."

Neurologist and author Oliver Sacks likened the seventh decade to the Sabbath, the seventh day. It's a time to rest, feel freedom, enjoy pleasure, appreciate beauty, and, perhaps, contemplate the sacred. Like Moses, Sacks's work had been transmitted, and so near the end he felt that he could deepen into a "time outside time."

But my mind resists: Sacks was not aware of the yearning for higher stages of awareness. And this promised land has been luring me for fifty years. How can rest be enough for my restless soul? Instead, is this the very time to fortify the Seeker, reclaim my inner divine image of a yogi, and intensify my practice, with less ego attachment to the outcome?

I sat with this dilemma for a while. Then it hit me: My soul's mission, to transmit information about consciousness, is part of the Doer's narrative. It's time to stop transmitting and *be* consciousness.

Deep breath . . .

Many members of the baby boomer generation, who came of age in the 1960s, desired lasting inner changes on a personal scale, but we also wanted, no, expected, lasting legacies on a collective scale. To return to our beginning: In 1967, we fervently believed that our vision of peace, human rights, freedom, self-expression, racial justice, and spiritual development would bend the arc of human history and become reality. Yet today, in 2020, we live with ongoing war and a constant erosion of human rights, even our basic rights to food, housing, health care, and economic opportunity. We live with ongoing political polarization and a constant erosion of democracy, even our basic right to vote and to have independent elected representatives. And we live with an acute awareness that most of humanity is operating from the limbic brain, reacting out of fear and projection, rather than from a rational, post-rational, or higher spiritual stage of awareness that includes the innate interconnection of all living things.

The new era that we envisioned when John Lennon sang "Imagine all the people sharing all the world" did not materialize. And, yes, people said we were dreamers. But even today, we're not the only ones.

We have our Joshuas, those in the next generations who carry the baton, as he did for Moses: We can stand with the high-school students who fight to end gun violence, the young people running for elected office, and the young meditators and yoga students everywhere who carry on the dream of awakening to Spirit. Most of all, we can stand with the youth movements that fight climate change: the Sunrise Movement, NextGen America, iMatter, Zero Hour, Generation Earth, and Our Children's Trust. They are the moral voice of our time.

And we can honor our own gifts and talents as we move inexorably toward trusting that they will no longer be needed by the whole.

An Interview with
Altered States Pioneer Stanislav Grof

I was thrilled when I tracked down Stan Grof in Europe and he agreed to speak with me. I had known Stan, a Czech psychiatrist and psychedelic Elder, at the high point of transpersonal psychology. He became a renowned researcher into altered states through holotropic breathwork, which changes awareness through deep, rapid breathing. His early research on perinatal life and birth trauma, and his later work (with his late wife Christina) on spiritual emergency, were profound influences on me. At eighty-six, Stan had just gotten married.

Stan began with two comments that I heard from so many others: He felt, from this vantage point, that he had lived several lifetimes in this one. And he had found his soul's mission early, so he never really felt that he worked. "I was surprised to be paid to do what I was interested in all my life."

After living in Prague until 1967, he moved to the United States and was delighted by the unrestricted freedom. He began to explore psychedelics—and they changed him. "Altered states opened me up to spirituality in an unexpected way. They gave me a direct connection with the cosmos. And, even now, I feel that connection without a mediator."

After a first marriage ended, Stan married Christina, and they taught together at the Esalen Institute, exploring altered states through breathwork. Holotropic breathwork continues to be taught around the world today as part of his legacy.

In addition, Stan founded the International Transpersonal Association and collaborated with Christina to form the Spiritual Emergence Network, which guides people who are having a spontaneous spiritual breakthrough that may appear to be a breakdown.

"This work was very rewarding. It saved me from psychiatry," Stan told me.

When Christina became seriously ill, he slowed down for years in order to accommodate her. After her death, he traveled the world again, doing trainings on breathwork. "I have lots of energy. I'm not tired, but I'm not the same driver either. Life is just not long enough for what I want to do."

Living with his new wife in Germany, Stan continues his mission to explore consciousness and leave behind a legacy. "There's a resurgence of psychedelic research now at fifteen universities. MDMA is being tested for vets with PTSD. It's very gratifying."

At the time of our conversation, he was moving toward life completion by living each moment to its fullest. And he had created two telecourses on the psychology of the future and a video series on holotropic altered states, so that his ideas have a digital afterlife.

An Interview with
Transpersonal Psychologist Frances Vaughan

I knew the late Frances Vaughan in the heyday of humanistic and transpersonal psychology. When I was working at Tarcher Publishing, we had released several of her pioneering books, including *Paths Beyond Ego,* coedited with her husband, Roger Walsh. Following a life-altering mystical experience on psychedelics, Frances had returned to school "so that her intellect could catch up with her experience," as she told me. We were all benefactors of that intention, as she worked tirelessly to build bridges between psychological and spiritual development beyond ego.

At eighty-two, at Roger's urging, Frances agreed to speak with me. She would die soon after.

"Life is a learning experience," she began. "As long as we're here, we're learning if we open to what shows up. As we age, we let go of the past and live more fully in the present. It's liberating to release our unfinished business and our preoccupations with what's gone. This is the last leg of the journey—no baggage needed. So, I urge people to stop clinging to how things were, release the guilt, fear, anger, and just experience love and joy in the present moment."

Frances went on to say that she was a divorced mother, a big planner, and a grandmother of five. Two years after she divorced, with two teenagers in tow, she met Roger—and couldn't have planned that. She spent forty years in private practice, teaching workshops on intuition, writing books, and integrating psychology with the spiritual practices of Zen, Vipassana, and the Course in Miracles.

Looking back, she saw that every decade was a big transition, but her life kept getting better. She found her way to work with heart and meaning and learned so much from clients and their holy longing. She saw how they created unnecessary suffering due to their fears, beliefs, and judgments about what should be, rather than *what is*. And she felt deeply blessed that she followed this call and found her soul's mission.

That mission continued after her formal work ended. "The call to service is everywhere," she told me, "to my husband, kids, neighbors. I have no energy for big causes now. But I have opportunities to relieve suffering all the time, wherever I find it, and to help others find peace."

At the time of Frances's death, Roger, a transpersonal and integral psychiatrist, wrote that deep wisdom and love flowed from her as a result of decades of contemplative practice. "But her primary focus was on daily life and relationships as places to offer love, service, and truth telling. Thus, she moved gracefully through life, offering insight and support to the many people who sought her wisdom."

On her last day, a friend asked about her current spiritual practice. Frances replied, "I'm practicing gratitude."

Shadow-Work Practices

- How do you imagine Moses's fate?
- What is your hidden image of the promised land? Is it achieving a goal, attaining a spiritual state, being forgiven for a trespass, or something else?
- Have you crossed over? Is that possible?
- What is your biggest incomplete? Can you accept it now? Or is a shadow character sabotaging your sense of life completion?
- Please return now to a moment in your inner work of age and see if you can loosen the grip of a past identity, belief, or feeling to move toward life completion.

Spiritual Practices

- What do you need to complete your life story so that you can live now as a soul?
- What transmissions of wisdom remain to be offered?
- Practice remembering who you are vs. your ideas of who you are.
- What do you need to complete so that you can die as a soul?
- Practice following your breath and letting go on the exhale, as if it were your last breath.
- Practice following the inner light as you let go of your fear of death and enter your next stage.

❦ Heart Sutra

The Buddhist Heart Sutra, chanted as a mantra, describes spiritual completion:

Gate, Gate, Paragate, Para Sam gate, Bodhi swaha.
Gone beyond, utterly beyond, everyone gone beyond to the
*   other shore,*
To the light, or awakening, hallelujah.

13

Reimagining Death as the Last Rite

PARABLE

An Appointment in Samarra: A Babylonian Tale

There was a merchant in Baghdad who sent his servant to market to buy provisions. In a little while, the servant came back, pale and trembling. He said, "Master, just now, when I was in the marketplace, I was jostled by a woman in the crowd. When I turned, I saw that it was Death that jostled me. She looked at me and made a threatening gesture. So, lend me your horse, and I will ride away from this city and avoid my fate. I will go to Samarra, and Death will not find me."

The merchant lent him the horse. The servant mounted it and dug his spurs into its flanks, and as fast as the horse could gallop, he went.

Then the merchant went down to the marketplace, saw Death in the crowd, and said to Her, "Why did you make a threatening gesture to my servant when you saw him this morning?"

"That was not a threatening gesture," Death said, "it was only a start of surprise. I was astonished to see him in Baghdad, for I have an appointment with him tonight in Samarra."

—"The Appointment in Samarra" is an ancient
Babylonian tale retold by W. Somerset Maugham

We all have an appointment with death. No matter who we are, what we believe, what we eat, and how much we've contributed, we as individuals will die. Having crossed the threshold from role to soul, from hero to Elder, we will be shepherded by Death across the threshold from Elder to ancestor.

We may deny it, compartmentalize it, or try to banish it entirely from our awareness. But no matter what, no matter where, no matter when, our death is scheduled on the cosmic calendar. The purpose of this chapter is to help us reorient to the whole truth of age: *I too shall pass.*

The mind can't conceive of our end; the ego can't tolerate its own annihilation. We imagine "my death," rather than Death as an archetype, a blueprint built into the cycles of every living thing. We imagine Death as intruder, Death as thief, Death as enemy, rather than an acorn falling, composting, and returning as an oak. Or a raindrop falling into the sea, rising again to form a cloud, and falling again to dissolve into its source.

When we identify with this separateness, this drop of "my-ness," our sense of isolation prevents us from seeing that death is as eternal as life. Without a portal to pure awareness, without a direct experience of unity, the interconnectedness of all, we personalize death—and try to overcome it.

Today, as I write, we are in the time of coronavirus. Our world has stopped spinning on its axis. We switch on the news or read the headlines and see death all around us. The count of precious lives lost continues to grow.

But even now, in this awful, eerie moment, some will continue to deny their vulnerability; they will resist restrictions and continue to live life as it was. However, others will wake up to mortality in this moment, more acutely aware of the tenuous thread of life, more acutely present to the gifts of love all around us and to the deeper truth that *all this shall pass.*

Denial also is peaking in the scientific community with efforts to vanquish death: Scientists are uploading minds into computers so that "we" live on without embodiment as post- or trans-humans. These materialists envision a future in which artificial, not human, intelligence makes bodies (and souls?) irrelevant.

Is this "progress"? Or is it death anxiety run amok?

In an unexamined life, youth is a spell. If it continues to grip us in late life, our inner ageist creates the agony of self-hate, and the treasures of late life cannot be found as we try desperately to overcome age.

Death, too, is a spell, cast by a force to be reckoned with, dragging us toward an end that we do not claim.

But if, as we age, we maintain mortality awareness in our peripheral vision, and it moves slowly into our sights, we may choose a different end. We may come to accept that to live in this world, we must love what is mortal. And painfully, but inevitably, we must let it go.

Those of us in late life are now observing our closest friends die. The obituaries fill with the writers, rockers, and inventors who are our age. No matter how reinforced our palace of denial, we are meeting the shadow of death a little each day. We are living on the verge of departure. That means that our known world is permeated with the unknown.

If we have not prepared with the three portals—shadow awareness, pure awareness, mortality awareness—intense feelings of fear, anxiety, anger, grief, and regret may erupt. This is natural. If we deny death, refusing to look at it, and if we identify with what does die, those fears will arise. For all of us.

Alternatively, to prepare, we can return to the root work: We can center in pure awareness by taking time to meditate, contemplate, or pray, breath by breath. We can use the practices that ground and open us, whether it's mantra, mindfulness, Zen, chanting, or devotion to a teacher or deity. We can connect with what lies behind our personality, beneath our roles. We can align with *what is* in presence and imagine, again and again, releasing our identification with our bodies, our thoughts, our feelings . . .

In *Walking Each Other Home,* Ram Dass put it this way: "Allowing ourselves to dissolve into the ocean of love is not just about leaving this body; it is also the route to Oneness and unity with our own inner being, the soul, while we are still here. If you know how to live and to love, you know how to die."

As the ego is leveled by aging consciously, completing its story to live as a soul, it opens to Mystery. Having released the spell of youth, the heroic myth of progress, the dreams of endless power, endless travel, endless hope, we can face the end gracefully. Having released the grip of opposites—youth and age, health and illness, independence and dependence, gain and loss, doing and being—we can release holding on and let go.

Ram Dass explains this further: "The art form in dying is that, at the moment of death, you are neither grabbing at life nor pushing it away. You are neither pushing nor pulling. It's the attraction [to life] and aversion [to death] that keeps you holding on" when it's time to let go.

We can reimagine dying from the inside out, moving inward again and again toward the soul. We can approach dying as a sacred passage, a final initiation.

The Shadow Knows

Its Secret Preparation for the End

One of my dearest friends, Sherry, is dying in this moment, now, as I write this page. I awoke weeping this morning and feel pulled to go to her, to be present with her . . . I await the call.

She is at home on hospice care. Before her lung cancer diagnosis eight months ago, she had a dream that she was caring for a dead body with dignity, learning to bathe it with gentle care. She was chanting and praying over it, then painting a casket with blessings.

"I'm the next body," Sherry told me firmly.

Following her dream's guidance, she planned her after-death care with a death midwife. After she passed away, she said, we would wash her body, wrap it in silk, and lie it on dry ice for three days. Friends and family, circling through the candlelit room, would meditate while wishing her spirit safe passage.

As an avid environmentalist, she had thought she would do green burial. But there is no more space left in this city. She considered cremation, but when she discovered the toxic environmental effects of it, she felt reluctant. She and her death midwife looked into green cremation, which is an emerging technology that uses water, rather than fire, and has less toxic impact. But it was not yet ready to go.

So she chose a sea burial. Her body would be taken to a marina, where a ship's captain agreed to return her to the water elements. With this vision, she was re-creating her death, just as she had re-created her life—from launching the first environmental company in the United States that sold nontoxic products to becoming a special education teacher, then a therapist and meditation teacher.

Now, it's reality. The phone rings, and I hear, "I can't give up. I need a miracle." She wants to try a new drug, one with horrific side effects. Yesterday, she was letting go. Today, she is holding on. Like so many, she is struggling against the loss of self-control, the loss of her capacity to have impact on what's happening to her. The loss of her dream of a long life of loving service.

In this moment, Sherry can't accept the truth that she is dying . . . and soon. The fighter in her is aroused and wrestles with another part of her that knows the harsh truth. She is swinging back and forth between living and dying, time and the timeless, certainty and mystery. And the tension between them is unbearable.

I realize then that hospice is a liminal space—a zone between the old world and the new one, between releasing not only our roles but life itself and embracing death. In hospice, the patient's body, mind, and heart are hanging between trapezes, in midair, without a net. No past. No future. Crossing a threshold, once again, but this time into a complete unknown.

Sherry had a moment of grasping on to the last trapeze bar—her identity as a cancer patient with hope of cure.

I bear witness to this sacred process in my dear friend. I, too, am holding on and letting go. I can feel my own desires to push her toward life, then again toward release. I watch others around her doing the same. My grief feels like a heavy weight on my chest that makes it hard to breathe, mirroring her breathing difficulties.

I do not want to project my own feelings and beliefs onto my dying friend. Then I will not be with her as she is. I will be with my idea of her and my idea of what she should do now. No, I tell myself with a breath, each of us has a right to choose how we die.

But I struggle with her lack of quietude, her need to surround herself with loved ones, constantly asking others' advice, rather than slowing, going within, and listening to the voice of her soul. I ask, softly and gently, about this. "You have a large, loving community," I say. "But can you listen to yourself with these murmuring voices around you day and night? Can you hear your inner voices?"

"No," she replied. "I can't hear my own intuition. I've spent sixty years learning how to attach to others, how to love them. Now I have to detach, let go of everyone. I'm not ready. And I'm afraid to be alone."

Sherry was so busy *doing* connection, from a lifetime of caring for others, that she was missing *being* connection—that is, recognizing the interconnected web of life that just *is*. And this emotional busyness was now, at this crucial moment, drowning out her inner guidance. "Who in you knows the truth about death?" I ask. "Who has guided you in the past and who is guiding you now?

"Oh, a white eagle came to me on a shamanic journey." She's smiling now. "It's a spirit guide I've been neglecting."

"Can you ask it for guidance now?"

"It tells me that dying is like a shamanic journey, traveling away from the body, past my fears and the images those fears generate, toward another realm. I've done that; I know how to do that."

"Anything else?" I ask.

"The eagle says that dying is safe," she tells me, as her body relaxes into the bed.

A few days later, the words ceased, and she began to pass in and out of awareness. I sat by the bed, joined my breathing pattern to hers, closed my eyes with hers, and entered silent presence. I felt closer to her then, dropping the roles of friend and colleague, simply loving her soul to soul.

I was not there at her death. But she took her last breath in peace, with her best friend holding her hand. Every detail of her vision was enacted. As the boat carried her body out to sea, dozens of dolphins circled and leapt into the air.

To my surprise, I discovered that Jung called death a goal that's being lived unconsciously in late life—that is, in the shadow. "If we listen to the quieter voices of our deeper nature we become aware of the fact that soon after the middle of our life the soul begins its secret work, getting ready for the departure," he wrote in "Memorial to J. S. (1927)."

In other words, the shadow knows. Sherry's dream was not unusual. A recent study of dreams in dying people confirms this observation. A team at Hospice Buffalo, a hospice and palliative care organization in New York State, conducted interviews with fifty-nine terminally ill patients to examine their dreams and visions and whether these could predict the timing of death. Their conclusion: As death neared, there was a dramatic increase in the frequency of these visions, particularly in seeing dead loved ones. And these incidents brought inner peace, in contrast to delirium.

The study, reported by Emily Gurnon in *Next Avenue,* found that 88 percent of the patients had at least one dream or vision of lost loved ones, and 99 percent believed they were real. Common themes included traveling, seeing loved ones, and being comforted by them.

Death is not a failure to the soul, then, as it is to the heroic ego. Rather, behind the ego's fortress of denial, something in the shadow is preparing us for the end. This something is separate from the conscious mind—but it's purposeful, helping us orient to the noble tasks of aging and death.

This something, I would add, is the soul's evolutionary impulse or holy longing, which is carrying us to the great return. This something is imagining Death not as an intruder, but as a homecoming. When we align with it, we are aligning not only with the cycles of nature but with evolution itself.

So, there is an intimate link between our relationship to shadow and our relationship to death. This link is embodied in Hades, Greek god of the underworld, sometimes known as the Good Counselor, who guides the dead across the threshold to the afterlife. Hades teaches us to be quiet and listen to the inner voices that direct us to the depths, to our own underworld.

When we resist the call, we deny the shadow of death. In denial, the ego does not open to the preparation occurring in the shadow. In denial, we live as if we will never die, and we fail to do life completion. We fail to become an Elder. We fail to cross over from role to soul. In denial, we die as if, in some ways, we never lived.

What if, instead, we were to open a channel of communication between ego and shadow so that the wall between them became more permeable? This, after all, has been our exploration throughout this book. We have allowed the ego to recede and the silenced voices from the darkness to be heard. We have coaxed them gently into awareness and discovered their precious gifts.

Now we meet the shadow of death, an impersonal force that is out of our control, with a purpose all its own. What messages might we hear in the whispers of Hades? What if we met Death as a counselor? What if we released our heroic strategies to defy it and, instead, coaxed Death to speak to us?

My dear, sweet friend heard the whisper of Death and heeded its call. An athlete only a few months ago, then a dying patient, Sherry also was an experienced meditator and student of Thich Nhat Hanh. She knew the deepest truth: Our individuality dies, our separateness dies.

But the spiritual essence of who we are cannot be annihilated. Whether we view that as atoms, genes, ecosystems, the web of life, a reincarnating soul, or transcendent Spirit, we are That. And It is eternal.

> *Going home, going home*
> *By the waterside I will rest my bones.*
> *Listen to the river sing sweet songs*
> *To rock my soul.*
>
> The Grateful Dead, "Brokedown Palace"

An Interview with Spiritual Teacher Mirabai Bush, Coauthor with Ram Dass

I spoke with Mirabai Bush, then seventy-eight, who was coauthor with Ram Dass of *Walking Each Other Home: Conversations on Loving and Dying* (2018). She had met him in India in 1970 and spent two years with him and their guru, Neem Karoli Baba. Both were radically transformed by Maharj-ji, as they call him. When they returned to the United States, Richard Alpert became Ram Dass and released *Be Here Now*, and the rest is history.

Mirabai founded the Center for Contemplative Mind in Society to bring spiritual practices to professionals in all fields, even to the Army and engineers at Google, she told me.

Ram Dass continued to teach by example, writing several books, including *Still Here* in 1997 to describe his journey in his '60s. When he was close to finishing the latter and looking for an ending, he had a massive stroke, which paralyzed him and caused aphasia. However, rather than give up his service and contribution, he continued to teach about his new limitations, focusing on our fears of aging and illness. He urged us to allow our own fears and limits to make us more real and to see them as "grace"—that is, a nudge to let go of everything false and limited and to identify with soul.

At eighty-seven, he told Mirabai that he wanted to continue to transmit what he was learning, even though he had aphasia. She would become his voice as he prepared to die and came to know this experience more intimately.

"I didn't know how we could capture that," Mirabai told me, "because he can't talk like he could before. So how does he transmit what he knows now? Through a series of conversations with me. And I decided that I would present him as he is now. It was a practice for me to simply listen, be present with whatever arose, and let go of my expectations," she said. "It required discipline on my part, but the love made it easy. I just wanted readers to feel that they were there with him, too."

A key theme: how to prepare for dying. "It's time to distance myself from the body," Ram Dass said, "to identify with the witness, with awareness, with the soul. The body is ending, but the soul will go on and on and on. I keep going inward to the soul."

He had studied with great teachers, read scriptures about death, faced symbolic death on psychedelics, and sat for years with the dying. But now it was his turn: "Death becomes simply the final stage of my practice," he said. "I've been shedding roles, like the role of 'strokee.' Letting go of regrets and loving the past for what it was and is: just thoughts. The key is to stay in your heart. Just keep loving."

Ram Dass wrote at length about the source of our fear of death: the feeling of separation, the ego's sense of "somebody-ness." "The ego is the steering mechanism for us as a separate entity functioning in the world. They installed the software into my computer, which is called the ego," he wrote. "I developed a model of who I am, who you are, and how to function so that I could survive."

But something happened along the way: "I forgot I was a soul. I began to think I was the computer program. Then I went from 'somebody' to 'somebody special.'" And the ego, a wonderful servant, became the master.

"The problem is not the ego itself but how identified we are with it, as I was," he said. "In spiritual evolution, you don't destroy the ego; rather, you stop identifying with it."

From my point of view, late life is an ideal opportunity to make this shift in awareness: The ego's identity of "somebody special" begins to crumble with the great levelers—age, illness, and death. If we are aware enough, that experience can open a vast space behind the mind and its self-concept.

"Aging is freeing," Ram Dass said. "Fewer attachments. I used to comb my hair, concerned about my baldness. Now I comb my hair with levity. Who cares about baldness!"

But fear can contract the internal space. "You need to find a place to stand in relation to change where you are not frightened by it. Be with the changes, work with the changes, but at the same time cultivate spacious awareness. This is what the deep spiritual work is about."

Ram Dass advised us to get close to our fear of death, the opposite of Western cultural patterns that banish all evidence of death into the shadow, beneath the shroud, behind the curtain. This reminded me of my visit to the holy Indian city of Varanasi, trying to get close to the cremation *ghats* on the Ganges by sitting in a small boat to watch as the fires consumed human flesh. Listening to the music and chanting as I breathed in the acrid air, I did not feel separate from those loving families or from those dead ones. I felt part of a communal sacred rite.

In those moments on the Ganges, I let my own mortality awareness penetrate deeply. *All things must pass. I too shall pass. My specialness shall pass. My legacy shall pass.*

How, then, do I want to live now? How do I choose to reimagine this time as I approach the end?

Yes, I have the privilege of being in conversation with Spiritual Elders. Yes, I have the gift of writing this book and passing on this wisdom. Yes, I adore my husband and my grandkids. I love my dancing and ukulele lessons. But all of that is doing. And all of that will end.

It is not really the answer to my question. I need to move from transmitting information about consciousness to *being* pure consciousness.

While speaking with Mirabai, I had the feeling that the exchange of loving presence is more primary than the words. The awareness is greater than the contents of awareness.

I felt joyful to have found yet another Elder who shares this insight. Grateful to have found another soul friend who is re-creating late life.

I asked what aging was like for Mirabai, who had flown back and forth from the East Coast to Maui many times for this project with Ram Dass. "My mother was old at seventy-five, quiet, withdrawn, disinterested in learning, and unable to be proactive. For me, this is a great age," she told me. "I'm engaged with young people, learning all the time, and in demand for my work teaching contemplative practices. At seventy-five, I got a titanium hip and got married!"

I asked Mirabai how her own spiritual practice has changed in late life. "Yoga has become more important for strength and flexibility. Meditation is now a part of who I am, not a discipline. And I've lived into Maharaj-ji's simple teachings—love everyone, serve everyone, and remember God—day by day."

I have not been a follower of Maharaj-ji. But I recognize that these are the teachings I want to live for the days that remain. I want to love not as a feeling but as a way of being, as Ram Dass put it. I want to shift from living as a role to live as a soul. I want to look at others as souls, so that my relationships shift from role to soul. If my ego is triggered by another, I want to remember that he or she is also a soul on a journey. I want to live from my spiritual center, which is connected to eternal Spirit.

"Being love is the best preparation for death," Ram Dass said. "Nowhere to go, nothing to fear, just loving awareness, unchanging, as everything around me changes, moment to moment. Being here right now, becoming immortality in the moment, now, and at the moment of death."

❋ ❋

And, for me, to love everyone, to serve everyone, and to remember God, I need to return to my meditation seat to dissolve into the ocean of pure awareness. Join me there.

In my end is my beginning.

T. S. Eliot

A Legacy Letter to the Grandchildren

You own my heart. This love has been a surprise—and the most precious gift of my late life. I was not a mommy. So, I did not expect to be a grandma. But I married Neil, and when you came into the world, I became Grandma Connie—and my heart swelled with the sight, sound, smell, and touch of each of you. This surprising love has forced me to grow, opening my heart wider and wider as you grow, too.

I see your radiance—and don't want to do anything to squash it. So, I try to meet it with my own diminishing energy, to stay up with you when you run and play and bike and scooter.

I see your beauty. Your value is in what you are, not what you do or what you own.

I see your curiosity about everything and your passion to learn letters, to recognize them and put together words. So, I try to be with you in your learning, as inspired and excited as you are. Your curiosity is a clue that can lead you on a lifelong treasure hunt.

I see your play—"The sun's up, it's time to play!"—and the joy in your faces when we go on our Sunday adventures, when we take our special family trips, when we celebrate your birthdays and holidays. And your joy stirs a joy in me that is youthful, innocent, and vibrant. For the child in us is alive at every age and can be rekindled with play.

And I see your one-of-a-kind-ness. No one has ever been like you before, and no one ever will be. No one has your smile or your voice or your fingerprint. And no one can take your place in the world, where you are wanted and needed to do your part. You are a light—and your job is to let it shine.

I want you to see in me that the full span of life is rich and meaningful, and that we never stop playing, learning, and loving. I want you to feel in me an unconditional loving presence, an embrace of all of who you are, a hand to hold to keep you safe, a lap that's warm and cozy.

As you continue to grow and become teens and adults, you will find a world that's not all safe, and people who are not all warm and cozy. You will face a planet in a climate crisis and a society with rich and poor people, who live very different lives. You will be disappointed, hurt, and angry sometimes, as all people are. You may have your heart broken; you will struggle with health problems or financial problems.

But my hope is that you will take my love with you. Like a locket next to your heart, you can carry my love as a feeling of your innate lovability. You can carry my positive gaze as a memory of your innate value.

As you find your way to a great education and a satisfying career, as you discover how to give and receive love, you will remember that there are boys and girls who are not as fortunate as you, not as loved or safe or happy as you are. And I hope that, when you're ready, you will turn and offer your hand, your love, and your positive gaze to them—and return all that you have received.

Don't let others define you and limit you. Some of you are being raised Jewish, others Christian, others agnostic—all right in one family. But the values that I'm sharing here transcend those differences; they are shared ideals that transcend religion, race, gender, geography, and age. And they can lead you to a life of meaning and purpose.

Don't let technology distract you from real human connection. Life does not happen via text or on Facebook, Instagram, Snapchat, WhatsApp, or whatever new platform comes along to mesmerize us; it happens face to face, eye to eye, skin to skin. It happens outdoors in the sun and rain, in the woods and wilds and oceans. So, remember to use your devices—your phones, tablets, computers, consoles—to serve you; don't serve them. Don't let your devices be the last thing you see before bed and the first thing you see when you wake up.

Always strive to connect to something greater than yourself—whatever form that takes for you. And you will find a meaningful life.

It may mean striving to understand how life began in order to unlock the mysteries of the universe, of human history, of our brains or cells. If this is your striving, then explore science—astrophysics, quantum physics, anthropology, neuroscience, physiology, or microbiology. And make your unique addition to the vast body of knowledge that science has built.

It may mean striving to understand why people do what they do, how they are motivated, why they hurt others, and how they recover from hurt. If this is your striving, then study psychology, like Neil, Cher, Sage, and me.

It may mean striving to understand the beauty of the natural world and to support the elegant web of life that connects us to plants, animals, and all living things. If this is your striving, then study botany, zoology, sustainability, and climate science.

It may mean striving to inspire people through creativity. If this is your striving, then explore the visual arts, performing arts, poetry, and music.

It may mean striving to make a difference to others, to ease their suffering and thereby contribute to the greater good. If this is your striving, then find a passionate cause—climate change, racism, sexism, homelessness, hunger, gun violence, poverty, education, refugees, animal welfare—and make it your own. Take the resources and gifts that you've been given and become an advocate, an activist, a teacher, a doctor, a volunteer, an attorney, a journalist, a candidate for office.

It may mean striving to figure out how your devices work. If this is your striving, then explore technology—robotics, artificial intelligence, social media—and steer them to be used for the common good.

It may mean striving to connect with the Great Mystery, something beyond your small self, behind the layers of life that we can see or touch. If this is your striving, then study religion, spirituality, and philosophy and find a contemplative practice that teaches you to sit quietly, alone, and hear the whisper of your soul. You may, like the great mystics before you, penetrate the veils covering our illusions and come to know your true source and destination.

As adults, and then Elders, strive to become your own ideal. Become the generous, compassionate role models you had or sought out. Become the grandparents whom Neil and I tried to be for you—or become even better than we were.

I had my shortcomings as a grandma. I ask for your forgiveness for my absence at important moments, my impatience with your anger or tears, my overeagerness to shape you to my own ideals. I was always imperfect, and I'm leaving you an imperfect world.

My generation's unfinished business falls to you. I fought for racial equality, watched moments of humanity waking up, then watched in sorrow as some in our nation went back to sleep. I fought for gender equality, watched moments of humanity waking up, then watched, heartbroken, as some in our nation went back to sleep. And I fought for environmental justice, watched moments of humanity waking up, then watched in horror as our nation, gripped in a stranglehold by oil companies, denied climate change and refused the call for a sustainable planet. So today, tragically, we hand down these fights to you, a challenging legacy but significant social causes that can offer you a purposeful life.

The future is being shaped now, as I write, in the hearts and minds of you children and in all children, everywhere, no matter their gender, race, culture, or class. The future lies in you—and whether you feel nurtured or abandoned, safe or afraid, confident or insecure, hungry or satiated.

The future lies in the role models you observe—your parents and elders, heroes and heroines. What do they strive for? What is the meaning of a successful life to them?

The future lies in the spiritual and moral values being transmitted to you—kindness, generosity, empathy, service, personal development, and caring for the Earth. How do your teachers and leaders live these values? Do they practice a lifestyle that embodies them?

The future lies in the vision we transmit to you. When I was a teen, long before you were born, I watched on TV as an astronaut sent back to us a photo of the Earth from space. We saw, for the first time, a tiny blue ball, floating in darkness, no borders, no labels. And I watched a moment of humanity waking up to the reality that we are all in the same boat, sharing the same small habitat and bound to the same fate. But all too quickly, many went back to sleep, remembering only their differences and their small self-interest. Today, climate change is a fierce reminder of that vision. The Earth is one living, breathing organism that feeds and sustains us, responds to our choices, and cries for your care.

So, the future is you: Each one of you is a fragile and powerful force for a more promising future for everyone.

I bless you, as you fill me with blessings.

Acknowledgments

To my parents, Tina and Mike Zweig, for the love and the wisdom that was transmitted every day. To my sister, Jane, for the growing and deepening loving friendship between us.

To SGR, for stimulating my holy longing; MMY, for directing my holy longing; Shankara, root teacher; Yogananda, for inspiration; and Ram Dass, for being our generation's scout, always lighting the way. Gratitude to RD for the phrase "from role to soul."

To Swamiji and Joan Harrigan, for the precious practices; Harri and the *satsang*, for spiritual family; Mevlana Rumi, for visiting my dreams; Hamid Ali, for inquiry practice; and integral philosopher Ken Wilber, for being the greatest mapper of the territory.

To Carl Jung, who took us by the hand, guided us into the Shadow, and charted the unknown; and to Marilyn Ferguson and Jeremy Tarcher, Bodhisattva mentors who are with me always. To Rabbi Zalman Schachter-Shalomi, whose legacy includes *From Age-ing to Sage-ing* and the organization Sage-ing International, which initiated me as an Elder and gave me a new orientation to late life. I especially want to thank my Sage-ing mentor, Charlotte Carlson, and Jeanne Marsh for their kind and wise presence. To Rick Moody, who offered me a lifetime of experience in this field with no strings. A deep bow of gratitude to all.

To my literary agent, Barbara Moulton, for her fierce persistence and loving support.

To the staff at Inner Traditions: my collaborative and generous editor Jamaica Burns Griffin, smart and vigilant copyeditor Nancy Ringer, cover designer extraordinaire Aaron Davis, Ehud Sperling, Jeanie Levitan, Jon Graham, Patricia Rydle, Eliza Homick, and enthusiastic publicist Ashley Kolesnik, who shepherded my baby into the world.

For the interviews: Thank you to Mirabai Bush, founder of Center for Contemplative Mind in Society, for your generous gift of conversation; the late Father Thomas Keating, founder of Centering Prayer; the late transpersonal psychologist Frances Vaughan; integral psychiatrist Roger Walsh; ageism activist Ashton Applewhite; transpersonal/ holotropic breath psychiatrist Stan Grof; novelist Deena Metzger; Roshi Wendy Egyoku Nakao of the Los Angeles Zen Center; Buddhist teacher Anna Douglas of Spirit Rock Meditation Center; kirtan master Krishna Das; Rabbi Laura Geller; Elder trainer Ron Pevny; Jungian analyst James Hollis; Rabbi Rami Shapiro; Jungian analyst Lionel Corbett; mythologist Michael Meade; the late honored Sage and mystic Robert Atchley; Jungian analyst Allen Koehn; author Carol Orsborn; humanistic psychology pioneer Tom Greening; therapist Lillian Trilling; environmental activist Andrew Beath; psychedelic Elder James Fadiman; therapist Howard Wallman; friends Ron Klepetar and Rick Weiss; and therapist Ray Anderson, now ninety-five.

During the writing of this book, three of them passed away: Father Thomas Keating, Frances Vaughan, and Robert Atchley. I'm so grateful to have received their sagacious words near the end of their lives.

To my dearest clients over many decades: Thank you for your courage and for the opportunity to serve. You, too, have been my teachers.

Thanks to Steve Wolf, soul friend, coauthor and coconspirator; Aaron Kipnis, dharma buddy and brother; and to Sherry Modell, who taught me what matters most at the end of life.

Gratitude to my giggle group: Neil, Steve, Paula, Rhoda, Riley, Linda, Malcolm, you are my circle of love, laughter, and support. We lost Linda, my soul sister, in November 2019, and I miss her every day. Then we lost Riley in 2020, after he modeled for all of us how to face death with equanimity. We are truly walking each other home.

Thanks to my consultation group: Neil, Patricia, Barbara, Bill, Gabrielle, your depth of insight and honesty continues to be an inspiration and source of great friendship.

My family with Neil: Sage and Leila, Cher and Brandon, you are a precious gift.

My grandkids: Jayden, Sienna, Kaleb, Eli, you are my little loves, and the surprise gift of late life.

A Shadow-Work Handbook for Aging Consciously

Dear fellow traveler in late life: You've now explored many of the shadow issues of age. But, as you've learned, our shadow characters continue to emerge, even as we begin to make them conscious, or romance them. The following steps give you a guide to continue the inner work of age by identifying the moment a shadow character appears, personifying it so that you can build a conscious relationship with it, and making different choices, so that you can find the treasures of late life.

1. Meet the shadow: Identify an attitude or behavior that leaves you feeling ashamed, anxious, immobilized, regretful, or depressed about your age. Here are a few possibilities: "Old is useless." "Old is ugly." "I can't do that anymore." "I feel invisible." "I have no voice." "I made so many mistakes." "I'm just waiting to die."
2. Describe that belief or attitude out loud to yourself, so that you take the inner voice and speak it out.
3. What are the feelings that arise with that inner voice? Do you feel sad, helpless, powerless, silenced, regret, lost, unattractive, or some other quality?
4. What are the bodily sensations that go with it? Do you feel a queasy belly, tight shoulders, a sunken chest, or some other symptom?
5. These are the mental, emotional, and physical early warning signs

that this ageist shadow character is emerging. Can you see an image of it? What is its age and gender?

6. Give this character a name. Then welcome it out loud into awareness. "I see you inner ageist." "I see you procrastinator." "I see you inner critic." "Welcome to my awareness."

7. Trace the roots of this character in your personal history and family patterns.

8. When you observe yourself experiencing those thoughts, feelings, or sensations identified above, repeat aloud the name of the shadow character to get your attention.

9. Romance the Shadow: Do your centering or meditation practice and breathe into your belly to witness the shadow.

10. Ask yourself, what are the consequences of obeying this shadow—for you and for others? (Will you hurt someone? Will you feel shame or regret? Will you sabotage yourself? How will it affect your health and behavior?)

11. Explore your choices: When you recognize that this shadow character is emerging, how can you respond differently to your life as it is?

12. Observe your resistances: If you choose not to respond differently, be aware of the internal and external results of your choice.

13. If you choose to respond in a new way, listen to a higher guidance, the voice of the soul.

14. Watch as the shadow character recedes, returns, and recedes again, with ever less power over you.

15. Remember who you really are, as you love and serve others.

Bibliography

Aaronson, Louise. *Elderhood: Redefining Aging, Transforming Medicine, Reimagining Life.* New York: Bloomsbury Publishing, 2019.

Adams, Susan. "How Daily Table Sells Healthy Food to the Poor at Junk Food Prices." Interview with Doug Rauch. *Forbes,* April 26, 2017.

Adelman, Marcy, et al. "LGBTQ Aging at the Golden Gate." San Francisco LGBTQ Aging Policy Task Force, March 2014.

Age Wave/Merrill Lynch. *Leisure in Retirement: Beyond the Bucket List.* Bank of America Corporation, 2016.

American Cancer Society. *Cancer Facts & Figures 2019.* "Facts and Figures Annual Report." Atlanta: American Cancer Society, 2019.

Anzick, Michael, and David A. Weaver. "Reducing Poverty among Elderly Women." Social Security Office of Policy report, January 2001.

Applewhite, Ashton. *This Chair Rocks: A Manifesto against Ageism.* New York: Celadon Books, 2020.

Arrien, Angeles. *The Second Half of Life: Opening the Eight Gates of Wisdom.* Boulder, Colo.: Sounds True, 2007.

Atchley, Robert. *Spirituality and Aging.* Baltimore, Md.: Johns Hopkins Press, 2009.

Au, Wilkie W., and Noreen Cannon Au. *Aging with Wisdom and Grace.* New York: Paulist Press, 2019.

Beath, Andrew. *Consciousness in Action.* New York: Lantern Books, 2005.

———. *New Creation Story,* vols. 1 and 2. Malibu, Calif.: New Epoch Books, 2014.

Becker, Ernest. *The Denial of Death.* New York: Free Press, 2007.

Berman, Phillip L., and Connie Goldman, eds. *The Ageless Spirit.* New York: Ballantine Books, 1992.

Berrin, Susan, ed. *A Heart of Wisdom: Making the Jewish Journey from Midlife through the Elder Years.* Woodstock, Vt.: Jewish Lights Publishing, 1997.

Berry, Thomas. *Selected Writings on the Earth Community.* Maryknoll, N.Y.: Orbis Books, 2014.

Blackburn, Elizabeth. "The Telomere Effect." *The Guardian,* January 29, 2017.

Blackman, Sushila. *Graceful Exits: How Great Beings Die.* Boston: Shambhala Publications, 2005.

Bly, Robert. *A Little Book on the Human Shadow.* New York: HarperCollins, 1988.

———. *The Sibling Society.* New York: Vintage Books, 1996.

Bolen, Jean Shinoda. *Crones Don't Whine.* York Beach, Maine: Red Wheel/Weiser, 2003.

Boyle, Patricia. A., et al. "Effect of Purpose in Life on Relation between Alzheimer's Pathological Changes on Cognitive Function in Advanced Age." *Archives of General Psychiatry* 69, no. 5 (May 2012).

Bredesen, Dale. *The End of Alzheimer's: The First Program to Prevent and Reverse the Cognitive Decline of Dementia.* New York: PenguinRandom, 2017.

Broadway, James M., and Brittiney Sandoval. "Why Time Seems to Go By More Quickly as We Get Older." *Scientific American,* July 1, 2016.

Bush, Mirabai, and George Kohlreiser. *Working with Mindfulness.* Florence, Mass.: More than Sound, 2013.

Butler, Robert. "An Interpretation of Reminiscence in the Aged." *Psychiatry: Interpersonal and Biological Processes* 26, no. 1 (1963): 65–76.

Campbell, Joseph. *The Hero with a Thousand Faces.* Princeton, N.J.: Princeton University Press, 1968.

Campbell, Todd. "9 Baby Boomer Retirement Facts That Will Knock Your Socks Off." *Motley Fool,* March 19, 2016.

Carstensen, Laura L. "Growing Old or Living Long." *Issues in Science and Technology* 23, no. 2 (Winter 2007).

———. "The Influence of the Sense of Time on Human Development." *Science* 312 (June 30, 2006): 1913–15.

Casteel, Beth. "Patients 80 and Older Would Benefit from Aggressive Treatment." *American College of Cardiology Journal,* March 16, 2015.

Chinen, Allan B. *In the Ever After: Fairy Tales and the Second Half of Life.* Wilmette, Ill.: Chiron Publications, 1989.

———. *Once Upon a Midlife: Classic Stories and Mythic Tales to Illuminate the Middle Years.* New York: Tarcher, 1992.

Chittister, Joan. *The Gift of Years: Growing Older Gracefully.* New York: Blue Bridge Publishing, 2008.

Clark, Maria. "22 Real-World Baby Boomer Health Care Statistics." Etactics (online), September 10, 2020.

Cohen, Gene D. *The Creative Age: Awakening Human Potential in the Second Half of Life.* New York: HarperCollins, 2000.

Cole, Thomas R. *The Journey of Life: A Cultural History of Aging in America.* Cambridge, U.K.: Cambridge University Press, 1992.

Conforti, Michael. "Intimations in the Night: The Journey toward New Meanings in Aging." In *Jung and Aging,* edited by Leslie Sawin, Lionel Corbett, and Michael Carbine. New Orleans: Spring Journal Books, 2014.

Corbett, Lionel. *Psyche and the Sacred.* New York: Routledge, 2020.

———. *The Religious Function of the Psyche.* New York: Routledge, 1996.

———. "Successful Aging: Jungian Contributions to Development in Later Life." *Psychological Perspectives* 56, no. 2 (2013): 149–67.

———. *Understanding Evil.* New York: Routledge, 2018.

Coughlin, Joseph. "Why 8,000 Is the Most Important Number for Your Retirement Plan." *Forbes* (online), April 13, 2019.

Cowan, Rabbi Rachel, and Lindal Thal. *Wise Aging.* Springfield, N.J.: Behrman House, 2015.

Dass, Ram. *Be Here Now.* San Cristobal, N.M.: Lama Foundation, 1978.

———. *Still Here: Embracing Aging, Changing, and Dying.* New York: Riverhead Books, 2000.

Dass, Ram, and Mirabai Bush. *Walking Each Other Home.* Boulder, Colo.: Sounds True, 2018.

Dass, Ram, and Paul Gorman. *How Can I Help? Stories and Reflections on Service.* New York: Knopf, 2005.

Davidson, Sara. *The December Project.* New York: HarperCollins, 2014.

Desbordes, Gaelle, et al. "Effects of Mindful Attention and Compassion Meditation on the Amygdala." *Frontiers of Human Neuroscience* 6 (November 2012): 292.

"The Economics of Longevity." *The Economist,* special report, July 8, 2017.

Eden, Jill, Katie Maslow, Mai Le, and Dan Blazer, eds, *Mental Health and Substance Use Workforce for Older Adults.* Washington, D.C.: The National Academies Press, 2012.

Eisenberg, Richard. "Why Isn't Business Preparing More for the Future of Aging?" *Next Avenue* (online), May 9, 2017.

Eitel, Barry. "The Rise of Baby Boomer Entrepreneurs." Lendio (online), May 27, 2019.

Ellin, Abby. "Finding Success, Well Past the Age of Wunderkind." *New York Times,* March 20, 2015.

Emerman, Jim. "New Stanford Research Demonstrates Power of Purposeful Adults 50+." Encore.org, March 13, 2018.

Emling, Shelley. "The Age at Which You Are Officially Old." AARP (online), June 14, 2017.

"Enterprising Oldies." *Schumpeter* (a blog of *The Economist*), February 25, 2012.

Erikson, Eric H., and Joan M. Erikson. *The Life Cycle Completed.* New York: Norton Books, 1997.

Eyre, Harris. A., Prabha Siddarth, Bianca Acevedo, Kathleen Van Dyk, Pattharee Paholpak, Linda Ecroli, Natalie St. Cyr, Hongyu Yang, Dharma S. Khalsa, and Helen Lavretsky. "A Randomized Controlled Trial of Kundalini Yoga in Mild Cognitive Impairment." *International Psychogeriatrics* 29, no. 4 (2017): 557–67

Ferguson, Marilyn. *Aquarian Conspiracy.* York Beach, Maine: Redwheel/Weiser Books, 2005.

Frank, Steven J. "In the Valley of the Shadow of Death." *Psychological Perspectives* 55, no. 3 (2012): 293–313.

Franz, Gilda. "Aging and Individuation." *Psychological Perspectives* 56, no. 2 (2013): 129–32.

Fredriksen-Goldsen, Karen, Charles Emlet, Hyun-Jun Kim, Anna Muraco, Elena Erosheva, Jayn Goldsen, and Charles Hoy-Ellis. "The Physical and Mental Health of Lesbian, Gay Male, and Bisexual (LGB) Older Adults: The Role of Key Health Indicators and Risk and Protective Factors." *The Gerontologist* 53, no. 4 (2013): 664–75.

Freed, Rachael. *Your Legacy Matters: Harvesting the Love and Lessons of Your Life.* Minneapolis, Minn.: Minerva Press, 2013.

Freedman, Marc. *Prime Time: How Baby Boomers Will Revolutionize Retirement and Transform America.* New York: Public Affairs, 2002.

Gawande, Atul. *Being Mortal: Medicine and What Matters at the End.* New York: Metropolitan Books, 2014.

Geronimus, Arline T., Margaret T. Hicken, Jay A. Pearson, Sarah J. Seashols, Kelly L. Brown, and Tracey Dawson Cruz. "Do U.S. Black Women Experience Stress-Related Acceleration of Biological Aging?" *Human Nature* 21, no. 1 (March 2010): 19–38.

Goldberg, Elkhonon. *The Wisdom Paradox: How Your Mind Can Grow Stronger as Your Brain Grows Older.* New York: Penguin, 2005.

Goleman, Daniel, and Richard J. Davidson. *Altered Traits.* New York: Avery, 2017.

Graham, Judith. "Learning to Advance the Positives of Aging." Interview with Kathy Greenlee. Kaiser Health News (online), November 2017.

Greenberg, Jeff, Sheldon Solomon, and Tom Pyszczynski. "How the Unrelenting Threat of Death Shapes Our Behavior." *The Atlantic,* May 4, 2012.

Grof, Stanislav. *Holotropic Breathwork.* New York: SUNY Press, 2012.

———. *The Way of the Psychonaut,* vols. 1 and 2. Santa Cruz, Calif.: MAPS, 2019.

Grof, Stanislav, and Christina Grof. *Spiritual Emergency.* New York: Tarcher/Putnam, 1989.

———. *Stormy Search for the Self.* New York: Tarcher/Putnam, 1992.

Gross, Daniel A. "This Is Your Brain on Silence." *Nautilus* 16, ch. 3, August 21, 2014.

Gruenewald, Tara, L. Arun S. Karlamangala, Gail A. Greendale, Burton H. Singer, and Teresa E. Seeman. "Feelings of Usefulness to Others, Disability, and Mortality in Older Adults." *Journals of Gerontology, Series B: Psychological Sciences and Social Sciences* 62, no. 1 (January 2007).

Guillen, Mauro F. "How Immigration Can Reverse America's Aging Population Problem." *Boundless,* September 23, 2020.

Gurnon, Emily. "What the Dreams of the Dying Teach Us about Death." *Next Avenue* (online), October 26, 2015.

Halifax, Joan. *Being with Dying.* Boston: Shambhala, 2008.

———. *Standing at the Edge.* New York: Flatiron Books, 2018.

Hanh, Thich Nhat. *The Blossoming of a Lotus.* Boston: Beacon Press, 2009.

Hanson, Rick. *Buddha's Brain.* Oakland, Calif.: New Harbinger, 2009.

———. *Neurodharma.* New York: Harmony Books, 2020.

Heilbrun, Carolyn G. *The Last Gift of Time: Life beyond Sixty.* New York: Ballantine Books, 1997.

Helburn, Judith. "Making Peace with Death and Dying." Spirituality & Practice e-course, October 2016.

Hesse, Hermann. *The Seasons of the Soul.* Berkeley, Calif.: North Atlantic Books, 2011.

Hillman, James. "Betrayal." In *Senex and Puer,* vol. 3 of *Uniform Edition of Writings of James Hillman.* Thompson, Conn.: Spring Publications, 2015.

———. *The Force of Character and the Lasting Life.* New York: Ballantine Books, 1999.

———. *Loose Ends: Primary Papers in Archetypal Psychology.* Thompson, Conn.: Spring Publications, 1975.

Hoblitzelle, Olivia Ames. *Aging with Wisdom.* Rhinebeck, N.Y.: Monkfish Publishing, 2017.

Hollis, James. "Amor Fati." *Parabola* 40, no. 4 (Winter 2015–2016): 10–15.

———. *Finding Meaning in the Second Half of Life.* New York: Gotham, 2006.

———. *Living an Examined Life: Wisdom for the Second Half of the Journey.* Boulder, Colo.: Sounds True Publishers, 2018.

Hu, Winnie. "Retire? These Graying Encore Entrepreneurs Are Just Starting Up." *New York Times,* September 17, 2018.

Intriago, Joy. "Older Americans Voting Patterns." Report on the website SeniorsMatter.com, February 20, 2016.

Jenkins, JoAnn. *Disrupt Aging.* New York: Public Affairs, 2016.

Josey, Alden. "The Last Renaissance: Individuation in the Ages 70–90." *Psychological Perspectives* 56, no. 2 (2013): 173–83.

Jung, Carl G. *Aion.* Vol. 9, part 2 of *The Collected Works of C. G. Jung.* Princeton, N.J.: Princeton University Press, 1969.

———. "Memorial to J. S. (1927)." In *The Symbolic Life: Miscellaneous Writings,* vol. 18 of *The Collected Works of C. G. Jung.* Princeton, N.J.: Princeton University Press, 1977.

———. *Mysterium Coniunctionis.* Vol. 14 of *The Collected Works of C. G. Jung.* Princeton, N.J.: Princeton University Press, 1970.

———. "The Personal and the Collective Unconscious." Vol. 7 of *The Collected Works of C.G. Jung.* Princeton, N.J.: Princeton University Press, 1977.

———. "The Stages of Life." In *Structure & Dynamics of the Psyche,* vol. 8 of *The Collected Works of C. G. Jung.* Princeton, N.J.: Princeton University Press, 1970.

Kadlec, Dan. "The Real Retirement Struggle: Defining Yourself as More than the Sum of a Long Career." *Time,* September 22, 2016.

Kalanithi, Paul. *When Breath Becomes Air.* New York: Random House, 2016.

Kanter, Rosabeth Moss, Peter Zimmerman, and Penelope Rossano. "Advanced Leadership Pathways: Doug Rauch and the Daily Table. Harvard Business School Case 316-105, March 2016.

Kaplan, Stephen. "The Restorative Benefits of Nature." *Journal of Environmental Psychology* 15, no. 3 (1995): 169–82.

Keating, Thomas. *Intimacy with God: Introduction to Centering Prayer.* New York: Crossroad Publishing, 2020.

———. *Invitation to Love: The Way of Christian Contemplation.* London: Bloomsbury Publishing, 2012.

Kerman, Sarah, and Colette Thayer. "Job Seeking among Workers Age 50+." AARP (online), October 2017.

Kita, Joe. "Workplace Age Discrimination Still Flourishes in America." AARP (online), December 30, 2019.

Kivipetto, Miia, and Krista Hakansson. "A Rare Success against Alzheimer's." *Scientific American,* April 2017.

Koontz, Katy. "Ram Dass On Being Infinite." *Unity* (September/October 2017). Reprinted on RamDass.org website.

Korkki, Phyllis. "The Science of Older and Wiser." *New York Times,* March 12, 2014.

Kornfield, Jack. *No Time Like the Present.* New York: Atria Books, 2017.

———. "Now Is the Time to Stand Up." *Lion's Roar* magazine, December 7, 2016.

Krafcik, Drew. "Words from the Wise." *Integral Review* 11, no. 2 (March 2015).

Kubler-Ross, Elisabeth. *On Death and Dying.* New York: Scribners, 1969.

Lamb, Erin, and Jim Gentry. "Denial of Aging in American Advertising." *International Journal of Aging and Society* 2, no. 4 (2013): 35–47.

Lee, Michelle. "Allure Magazine Will No Longer Use the Term 'Anti-Aging.'" *Allure,* August 2017.

Leider, Richard J. *The Power of Purpose: Find Meaning, Live Longer, Better.* Oakland, Calif.: Berrett-Koehler Publishers, 2015.

Leider, Richard J., and David A. Shapiro. *Claiming Your Place at the Fire: Living the Second Half of Life on Purpose.* Oakland, Calif.: Berrett-Koehler Publishers, 2004.

Leroy, Angie, S., Kyle W. Murdock, Lisa M. Jaremka, Asad Loya, and Christopher P. Fagundes. "Loneliness Predicts Self-Reported Cold Symptoms after a Viral Challenge." *Health Psychology* 36, no. 5 (2017): 512–20.

Levine, Stephen. *A Year to Live: How to Live This Year as If It Were Your Last.* Boston: Beacon Press, 1997.

Levy, Becca. "Improving Memory in Old Age through Implicit Self-Stereotyping." *Journal of Personality and Social Psychology* 71, no. 6 (1996): 1092–1107.

———. "Mind Matters: Cognitive and Physical Effects of Aging Self-Stereotypes." *Journal of Gerontology Series B 58,* no. 4 (July 2003): 203–11.

Levy, Becca, Luigi Ferrucci, Alan B. Zonderman, Martin D. Slade, Juan Troncoso, and Susan M. Resnick. "A Culture-Brain Link: Negative Age Stereotypes Predict Alzheimer's Disease Biomarkers." *Psychology and Aging* 31, no. 1 (2016): 82–88.

Levy, Becca, M. Slade, S. Kunkel, and S. Kasl. "Longevity Increased by Positive Self-Perceptions of Aging." *Journal of Personality and Social Psychology* 83, no. 2 (2002): 261–70.

Lief, Judith. *Making Friends with Death: A Buddhist Guide to Encountering Mortality.* Boston: Shambhala Publications, 2001.

Luders, Eileen, F. Kurth, E. Mayer, et al. "The Unique Brain Anatomy of Meditation Practitioners." *Frontiers in Human Neuroscience* 6 (February 29, 2012).

Luke, Helen. *Old Age.* Great Barrington, Mass.: Lindisfarne Books, 2010.

———. *Such Stuff as Dreams Are Made On.* New York: Parabola, 2000.

Lustbade, Wendy. *Life Gets Better: The Unexpected Pleasures of Growing Older.* New York: Tarcher, 2011.

Macy, Joanna. *World as Lover, World as Self.* Berkeley, Calif.: Parallax Press, 2007.

Marko, Eve Myonen, and Wendy Egyoku Nakao. *The Book of Householder Koans: Waking Up in the Land of Attachments.* Rhinebeck, N.Y.: Monkfish Books, 2015.

Martin, William. *The Sage's Tao Te Ching.* New York: The Experiment, LLC, 2000.

Maugham, W. Somerset. "The Appointment in Samarra," 1933.

McGreevey, Sue. "Eight Weeks to a Better Brain." *Harvard Gazette,* January 21, 2011.

Meade, Michael. *Awakening the Soul.* Vashon, Wash.: Greenfire Press, 2018.

———. *Fate and Destiny: The Two Agreements of the Soul.* Vashon, Wash.: Greenfire Press, 2010.

———. *The Genius Myth.* Vashon, Wash.: Greenfire Press, 2016.

———. *The Water of Life.* Vashon, Wash.: Greenfire Press, 2019.

———. "Where Have All the Wise Men Gone?" *HuffPost Contributor* (blog), September 11, 2011; updated November 10, 2011.

Menezes, Carolina Baptista, Maria Clara de Paulo Couto, Luciano G. Buratto, Fátima Erthal, Mirtes G. Pereira, and Lisiane Bizarro. "The Improvement of Emotion and Attention Regulation after a 6-Week Training of Focused Meditation." *Evidence-Based Complementary and Alternative Medicine* 2013 (2013): 984678.

Metzger, Deena. "Cancer Is the Answer." *The Sun* 110 (January 1985).

———. "Extinction Illness: Grave Affliction and Possibility." *Tikkun* magazine blog post, January 3, 2019.

———. *A Rain of Night Birds.* Topanga, Calif.: Hand to Hand, 2017.

———. *Writing for Your Life.* San Francisco: Harper, 1992.

Mogenson, Greg. "Dreaming the Father: A Son's Bereavement in Archetypal Perspective." *Quadrant* 27, no. 1 (Winter 1996–97): 35–59.

Montgomery, Kathleen, ed. *Landscapes of Aging and Spirituality*. Boston: Skinner House Books, 2015.

Moody, Harry R. "Baby Boomers: From Great Expectations to a Crisis of Meaning." *Generations: Journal of the American Society on Aging* 41, no. 2 (Summer 2017): 95–99.

———. "Dreams for the Second Half of Life." Unpublished manuscript.

Moody, Harry R., and David Carroll. *Five Stages of the Soul*. New York: Anchor Books, 1997.

Moore, Thomas. *Ageless Soul*. New York: St. Martin's Press, 2017.

Narboe, Nan, ed. *Aging: An Apprenticeship*. Portland, Ore.: Red Notebook Press, 2017.

National Institute on Drug Abuse. "Substance Use in Older Adults." Drug Facts report, July 2020.

National Institute on Retirement Security. "No Retirement Savings for Typical U.S. Households of Color." December 2013 press release.

National Institute on Retirement Security. "Shortchanged in Retirement: Continuing Challenges to Women's Financial Future." March 2016 press release.

Neumayer, Eric, and Thomas Plümper. "Inequalities of Income and Inequalities of Longevity." *American Journal of Public Health* 106, no. 1 (January 2016): 160–65.

Newberg, Andrew, and David Halpern. *The Rabbi's Brain*. Nashville, Tenn.: Turner Publishing, 2018.

Newhouse, Meg. *Legacies of the Heart*. N.p.: EBook Bakery Books, 2015.

Oakley, Diane. National Institute on Retirement Security, Report, March 2016.

O'Donohue, John. *To Bless the Space between Us: A Book of Blessings*. New York: Doubleday Press, 2008.

Officer, Alana. World Health Organization *Bulletin* 96 (March 9, 2018): 299–300.

Orsborn, Carol. *Fierce with Age* (newsletter), May 2018.

———. *Older, Wiser, Fiercer*. Nashville, Tenn.: Fierce with Age Press, 2019.

———. "Wondrous and Wild." *Quarterly Journal of Life Planning Network* 4, no. 2 (Spring 2017): 9–10.

Ostaseski, Frank. *The Five Invitations: Discovering What Death Can Teach Us about Living Fully*. New York: Flatiron Books, 2017.

Palmer, Parker. *On the Brink of Everything*. Oakland, Calif.: Berrett-Koehler Publishers, 2018.

Penick, Douglas. "Taken Away and Given." *Tricycle,* Fall 2015.

Perera, Sylvia. "Circling, Dreaming, Aging." *Psychological Perspectives* 56, no. 2 (2013): 137–48.

Pevny, Ron. *Conscious Living, Conscious Aging.* New York: Atria Books, 2014.

———. "Navigating Life's Transitions." *Spirituality & Practice,* 2017.

Pillemer, Karl. *30 Lessons for Living.* New York: PlumePenguin, 2011.

———. *30 Lessons for Loving.* New York: Penguin RandomHouse, 2015.

Plotkin, Bill. *Soulcraft.* Novato, Calif.: New World Library, 2003.

Ramana Maharshi. *The Spiritual Teachings of Ramana Maharshi.* Boston: Shambhala, 1988.

Ramirez-Valles, Jesus. *Queer Aging.* New York: Oxford University Press, 2018.

Remen, Rachel Naomi. "Seeing with New Eyes." *Institute of Noetic Sciences Review* 44 (Winter 1997).

Remington, Katie, and Matt Bendick. "An Encore for Purpose," Stanford University, *Cardinal at Work,* September 21, 2016.

Rhee, Nari. National Institute on Retirement Security, Report, December 2013.

Richmond, Lewis. *Aging as a Spiritual Practice.* New York: Gotham Penguin, 2012.

———. *Every Breath, New Chances: How to Age with Honor and Dignity, A Guide for Men.* Berkeley, Calif.: North Atlantic Books, 2020.

Rinpoche, Soygal. *The Tibetan Book of Living and Dying.* New York: Harper Collins, 1992.

Robinson, John C. *The Three Secrets of Aging.* U.K.: O-Books, 2011.

———. *What Aging Men Want: The Odyssey as a Parable of Male Aging.* U.K.: Psyche Books, 2013.

Rohr, Richard. *Falling Upward: A Spirituality for the Two Halves of Life.* San Francisco: Jossey-Bass, 2000.

———. *Immortal Diamond: Search for Our True Self.* San Francisco: Jossey-Bass, 2013.

Rosenberg, Larry. *Living in the Light of Death.* Boston: Shambhala Publications, 2013.

Roszak, Theodore. *The Making of an Elder Culture.* British Columbia, Canada: New Society Publishers, 2009.

Rothe, Cydny. "Musings on Death." *Psychological Perspectives* 56, no. 2 (2013): 184–99.

Rowan, Cris. *Virtual Child: The Terrifying Truth about What Technology Is Doing to Children.* Sechelt, British Columbia: Sunshine Coast Occupational, 2010.

Russell, Bertrand. *Portraits from Memory and Other Essays.* New York: Routledge, 2021.

Sacks, Oliver. "My Own Life." *New York Times,* February 19, 2015.

———. "Sabbath." *New York Times,* August 14, 2015.

Sarton, May. *At Seventy: A Journal.* New York: Norton Books, 1984.

Sawin, Leslie, Lionel Corbett, and Michael Carbine, eds. *C. G. Jung and Aging: Possibilities and Potentials for the Second Half of Life.* Washington, D.C.: Spring Publications, 2014.

Schachter-Shalomi, Zalman, and Ronald S. Miller. *From Age-ing to Sage-ing: A Revolutionary Approach to Growing Older.* New York: Warner Books, 1995.

Scott-Maxwell, Florida. *The Measure of My Days.* New York: Penguin Books, 1968.

Shah, Idries. *Fatima: The Spinner and the Tent.* Los Altos, Calif.: Hoopoekids Press, 2006.

———. *Tales of the Dervishes.* London: Idries Shah Publishing, 1967.

Shapiro, Rabbi Rami. *Hasidic Tales.* Woodstock, Vt.: Skylight Paths Publishing, 2011.

———. *Holy Rascals.* Boulder, Colo.: Sounds True, 2017.

———. *Perennial Wisdom for the Spiritually Independent.* Woodstock, Vt.: Skylight Paths Publishing, 2013.

———. *Surrendered.* Woodstock, Vt.: Skylight Paths Publishing, 2019.

Shapiro, Rabbi Rami, and Marcia Ford. *Sacred Art of Lovingkindness.* Woodstock, Vt.: Skylight Paths Publishing, 2006.

Sherman, Edmund. *Contemplative Aging.* New York: Guardian Knot Books, 2019.

Sinclair, David A. *Lifespan.* New York: Simon & Schuster, 2019.

Singh, Kathleen Dowling. *The Grace in Aging.* Somerville, Mass.: Wisdom Publications, 2014.

———. *The Grace in Dying.* New York: Harper Collins, 1998.

Smith, J. Walker, and Anne Clurman. *Generation Ageless: How Baby Boomers Are Changing the Way We Live Today.* New York: Harper Collins, 2007.

Smith, Stacey L., Marc Choueiti, and Katherine Pieper. *Over 60, Underestimated: A Look at Aging on the Silver Screen.* University of Southern California Annenberg School for Communications and Journalism, February 2017.

———. *Seniors on the Small Screen: Aging in Popular Television Content.* University of Southern California Annenberg School for Communications and Journalism, 2017.

———. *Still Rare, Still Ridiculed.* University of Southern California Annenberg School for Communications and Journalism, January 2018.

Soeng, Mu, Gloria Ambrosia, and Andrew Olendzki. *Older and Wiser: Classic Buddhist Teachings on Aging, Sickness, and Death.* Barre, Mass.: Barre Center for Buddhist Studies, 2017.

Soffer, Kim. "To Reduce Suicides, Look at Guns." *Washington Post,* July 13, 2016.

Steindl-Rast, Brother David. "Learning to Die." *Parabola* 2, no. 1 (Winter 1977): 22–31.

Terrell, Jessica. "Make Early Retirement Enticing to Teachers." Direct Administration (online) March 16, 2016.

Terry, Sabrina. "Poor Old People: The Graying of Racial and Gender Wealth Inequality." Report from National Community Reinvestment Coalition, November 20, 2019.

Thomas, Bill. *Second Wind: Navigating the Passage to a Slower, Deeper, More Connected Life.* New York: Simon & Schuster, 2007.

Tornstam, Lars. *Gerotranscendence: A Developmental Theory of Positive Aging.* New York: Springer, 2005.

Trout, Susan. *Born to Serve: The Evolution of the Soul through Service.* Alexandria, Va.: Three Roses Press, 1997.

Turrell, Kenneth. "Age Discrimination Goes Online." *AARP Bulletin,* Nov. 7, 2017.

Ulanov, Ann. *Religion and the Unconscious.* Philadelphia: Westminster Press, 1975.

Vaillant, George E. *Aging Well.* New York: Little Brown, 2002.

Vaughn, Frances. *Awakening Intuition.* New York: Anchor Books, 1979.

———. *Shadows of the Sacred.* Wheaton, Ill.: Quest Books, 1995.

Walsh, Roger. *Essential Spirituality: 7 Central Practices to Awaken Heart and Mind.* New York: Wiley, 1999.

———. "Karma Yoga and Awakening Service." *Journal of Transpersonal Research* 5, no. 1 (2013): 2–6.

———. "Wisdom: An Integral View." *Journal of Integral Theory and Practice* 7, no. 1 (2012): 1–21.

———, ed. *The World's Great Wisdom.* Albany: State University of New York Press, 2014.

Walsh, Roger, and Frances Vaughn, ed. *Paths Beyond Ego.* Los Angeles: Tarcher, 1993.

Weber, Robert, and Carol Orsborn. *The Spirituality of Age.* Rochester, Vt.: Park Street Press, 2015.

Weller, Francis. *The Wild Edge of Sorrow: Rituals of Renewal and the Sacred Work of Grief.* Berkeley, Calif.: North Atlantic Books, 2015.

Wheeler, Mark. "Memory Loss Associated with Alzheimer's Reversed for First Time." UCLA Newsroom, October 2, 2014.

Wheelwright, Jane Hollister. "Old Age and Death." *Quadrant* 16, no. 1 (1983): 5–27.

Wight, Richard, et al. "Internalized Gay Ageism, Mattering, and Depressive Symptoms among Midlife and Older Gay Men." *Social Science and Medicine* 147 (December 2015): 200–208.

Wilber, Ken. *The Atman Project.* Wheaton, Ill.: Quest Books, 1990.

———. *Integral Meditation: Mindfulness as a Path to Grow Up, Wake Up, and Show Up in Your Life.* Boston: Shambhala Publications, 2016.

———. *Integral Psychology.* Boston: Shambhala Publications, 2000.

———. *Integral Spirituality.* Boston: Shambhala Publications, 2006.

———. *The Religion of Tomorrow: A Vision of the Future of the Great Traditions.* Boston: Shambhala Publications, 2017.

———. *Sex, Ecology, Spirituality.* Boston: Shambhala Publications, 2001.

Wilber, Ken, Terry Patten, Adam Leonard, and Marco Morelli. *Integral Life Practice.* Boston: Shambhala Publications, 2012.

World Health Organization. "Dementia." World Health Organization (online), September 21, 2020.

Yalom, Irvin D. *Staring at the Sun: Overcoming the Terror of Death.* San Francisco: Jossey-Bass, 2009.

Yogananda, Paramahansa. *Autobiography of a Yogi.* Los Angeles: Self-Realization Fellowship, 1998.

Zweig, Connie. *Meeting the Shadow of Spirituality.* Bloomington, Ind.: iUniverse, 2017.

———. *A Moth to the Flame: The Life of the Sufi Poet Rumi.* Lanham, Md.: Rowman & Littlefield, 2006.

Zweig, Connie, and Jeremiah Abrams. *Meeting the Shadow.* New York: Tarcher, 1990.

Zweig, Connie, and Steve Wolf. *Romancing the Shadow.* New York: Ballantine Books, 1997.

Index

AARP, 33, 80, 85–86

absolute wisdom, 293

acceptance
 as spiritual practice, 36–37
 as stage of grief, 207, 208

activism
 Elders involved in, 247, 311, 319, 322, 333
 unconscious vs. conscious, 314–15

addiction problems, 4

age. *See also* old age
 archetypes of, 34–35
 three portals of, 40–65

ageism
 collective shadow of, 78–83, 88
 inner form of, xv, 68–78
 late-life creativity and, 212
 movement against, 84–87
 shadow-work on, 44, 87–88

aging
 consequences of beliefs about, 75–78
 creativity linked to, 211–12
 as fate of everyone, 34–36
 ideals of successful, 28–30
 identity crisis related to, 14–16, 30–31, 116

individual perceptions about, 32–34, 36

late-life treasures of, 6–7

memory loss related to, 148–53

opposites characteristic of, 31–32

statistics about age and, 2–5

Alpert, Richard. *See* Ram Dass

Altered Traits (Goleman and Davidson), 286

Alzheimer's disease, 148–52, 153, 156

anger stage of grief, 206

annihilation, fear of, 60, 61

anxiety, 21, 60, 135, 331

Applewhite, Ashton, 84–85

Aquarian Conspiracy, The (Ferguson), 179, 214

archetypes
 of age, 34–35
 projection of, 219
 of shadow, 10, 108

Ardelt, Monika, 291–92

Atchley, Robert, 61, 284, 300–301

Atman project, 63

attention restoration theory, 155

Atwood, Margaret, 213

awareness
  loving, 6, 50, 305–6
  mortality, 59–65, 66, 67, 252, 295
  pure, 11–12, 49–59, 66–67, 295
  shadow, 40–49, 65, 212, 295
  stages of, 285–91

Baddie Winkle, 27
bag lady shadow figure, 70–75
bargaining stage of grief, 206–7
Beath, Andrew, 315
Becker, Ernest, 59
beliefs
  ageist, 75–78
  reclaiming, 227–29, 238
  religious, 28, 62, 175, 221–22
  secular, 62
  seeing through, 236–37
Berry, Thomas, 332
betrayal
  primal trust and, 194–95, 202, 224
  shadow-work related to, 198, 204
"Betrayal" (Hillman), 194
Blackburn, Elizabeth, 52
Blooming of a Lotus, The (Hanh), 36,
  234
Bly, Robert, 42, 114
Boyle, Patricia, 156
brain health
  age-related stereotypes and, 77
  enhancing plasticity and, 153–57
  meditation and, 155, 157, 286
  memory loss and, 148–53
Bredesen, Dale, 153–54
Broadway, James M., 251
Browne, Jackson, 310

Buddha
  divine messengers of, 16–19, 283
  meditation on death, 62, 295–96
Buddhism, 58–59, 62, 243, 294, 312,
  334–35
Bush, Mirabai, 232, 235, 356–59
Butler, Robert, 165

Cameron, Julia, 103
Campbell, Joseph, 177, 244, 245, 248
cancer
  life-altering power of, 124, 131–35,
  274
  metaphors for dealing with, 128–31
"Cancer Is the Answer" (Metzger),
  124, 130
caregiving
  emotional repair and, 198–99
  need to give or receive, 140–41
  sacred service of, 143–45
  shadow-work related to, 141–42
Carstensen, Laura, 81, 192
Carter, Jimmy, 222
Casteel, Beth, 82
Chinen, Allan, 246
Christianity, 224, 293, 307, 312
Christmas Carol, A (Dickens), 170
climate change
  age-related issues and, 4–5
  collective mortality and, 330–32
  Elder activism on, 333
  stages of awareness and, 288–89
Cohen, Gene, 138–39, 213
Cohen, Leonard, 124, 213
Colby, Anne, 100
completed life, 338–47

Conforti, Michael, 93

Conscious Living, Conscious Aging
(Pevny), 20, 257

Corbett, Lionel, 230, 276–77

Coughlin, Joseph, 96

COVID-19 pandemic, 65, 290

Creative Age, The (Cohen), 138, 213

Creative Elders, 247

creativity
examples of late-life, 212–13
link between aging and, 211–12
reclaiming your lost, 209–16,
217
as spiritual practice, 213–15

Critic shadow character, 43, 134, 168,
264

cultural shadow, 47, 69, 78

Dalai Lama, 236, 294

Damon, William, 100

Davidson, Richard J., 286

death, 348–59. *See also* mortality
awareness
awareness of, 58–65
denial of, 59–60, 349–50, 355
fear of, 60, 61–62
personal process of, 351–54
preparing for, 350–51, 354–55,
359

dementia, 148, 149

denial
of life repair, 193
of mortality, 59–60, 65, 206
as stage of grief, 205–6

Denial of Death, The (Becker), 59

dependency, fear of, 31

depression
disillusionment vs., 146–47
medical model view of, 145
as stage of grief, 207

depth, portal to, 40–49

dharana practice, 306

Dickens, Charles, 170

disillusionment
depression vs., 146–47
spiritual, 219–26

divine messengers, 16–19
life-changing illness, 122, 131
retirement, 90, 96
shadow-work practice, 36

Douglas, Anna, 301–3

dreams
divine messengers in, 16–19
dying people with visions and, 354
life review occurring in, 169–70
shadow explored through, xiv,
107–8, 261

Dylan, Bob, 70, 213, 231

Dysinger, Luke, 293

Dzogchen practice, 306

Earth Elders, 247, 332

ego
identification with, 39
life review of, 172–81, 189
releasing the agenda of, 255
transcendence of, 243–45, 246, 288

egocentric awareness, 287, 288, 290

Einstein, Albert, 341

Elders
activism of, 247, 311, 319, 322, 333
characteristics of, 245–54

conscious grandparenting by, 326–30

crown of age metaphor, 277–78

friendship between, 138

inner work for becoming, 259–65, 278

interviews with, 257–58, 271–77

meeting our Inner, 266–69, 280

reimagining the meaning of, 269–71, 280

rite of passage for, 255–56

sacred service by, 310–30, 333

shadow-work for, 256, 260, 278–80

shift from heroes to, 7, 244, 255, 259

Spiritual, 247, 254, 282, 283–84, 297–98

types and examples of, 247

wisdom of, 291, 297

Emling, Shelley, 33

emotional repair, 192, 194–201

caregiving as context for, 198–99

shadow-work related to, 198, 216–17

Encore.org, 101–2, 311

entrepreneurs, 101–2

ethnocentric awareness, 287, 288–89, 290

extinction illness, 332

extroverts, 27–28

Eyre, Harris A., 155

fate, aging as, 34–36

Fatima parable, 164–65

fear

of aging, 44

of death, 60, 61–62

of dependency, 31

Ferguson, Marilyn, 179, 213–14

Feuerstein, Georg, 294

Forbes, Marjorie, 212

forgiveness, 204

Foster, Jeff, 208

Fox, Matthew, 332

Frank, Steven J., 132–34

Frankel, Bruce, 318

From Age-ing to Sage-ing (Schachter-Shalomi and Miller), 22, 63, 248, 268

Gandhi, Mahatma, 321

gay ageism, 3, 81–82

Geller, Laura, 97–98

gender inequality, 2

gerontology, 83

Goldfield, Ari, 294

Goldman, Ari L., 212

Goleman, Dan, 286

Gorman, Paul, 144, 309

grandchildren, legacy letter to, 361–65

grandparenting, conscious, 326–30

Greenlee, Kathy, 83

grief

emotional repair related to, 204–5

reimagining the stages of, 205–8

Grof, Stanislav, 344–45

Gross, Daniel, 155

Gurnon, Emily, 354

Hakansson, Krista, 153

Halifax, Joan, 11, 334

Hanh, Thich Nhat, 36–37, 234, 236, 312

Hanson, Rick, 156–57

Harrison, George, 53

health. *See also* illness

   ageist beliefs and, 75–78, 82

Heart Sutra of Buddhism, 347

Hemingway, Ernest, 89

Hero

   archetypal journey of, 177–78

   shift to Elder from, 7, 244, 255, 259

Hero with a Thousand Faces

   (Campbell), 248

Hillman, James, 194–95, 223,

   340

Hinduism, 35, 49, 56, 57, 117, 284,

   294, 312

Hockney, David, 249

Hoertdoerfer, Pat, 327

Hollis, James, 60, 169, 199–200

Houston, Jean, 286

How Can I Help? (Ram Dass and

   Gorman), 144, 309

Hu, Winnie, 101

identity crisis, 14–16, 30–31, 116

illness, 121–61

   cancer as, 127–35

   caregiving related to, 140–45

   as divine messenger, 122, 131

   life-altering power of, 121–23,

     131–35

   memory loss as, 148–53

   mental health and, 145–47

   metaphors for describing, 128–30

   mind/body split and, 125–27

   sacred wound of, 123–25, 131

   shadow-work for, 135–40, 160

   as spiritual practice, 158–61

implicit ageism, 76

income inequality, 2

inequality, age-related, 2–3

initiations, 170–72, 201

inner ageist, xv, 68–78

   dramatic consequences of, 75–78

   late-life creativity and, 212

   meeting your own, 70–75, 87–88

   resistance to life review by, 168

   shadow-work practice, 87–88

Inner Elder, 260, 266–69, 272, 280

Inner or Divine Child, 266

inner voices, 9, 41–42, 92, 206

Integral Spirituality (Wilber), 254, 287

integral stages, 288

introverts, 27–28

Iser, Lynne, 312

Jacobson, Dorrie, 27

Jagger, Mick, 181

Jobs, Steve, 64, 102

Judaism, 54, 243, 306–7, 312

Jung, Carl

   on ego transcendence, 243

   on personal shadow, xiv, 9

   on root of post-midlife problems, 22

   on secret work of death, 354

   on significance of aging, 44–45

   on spiritual projection, 218, 230

   on tension of opposites, 32

karma yoga, 143, 209, 312, 334

Keating, Thomas, 54, 60–61, 185–88

Kerman, Sarah, 80

Kerner, Jerome, 327

Key in the Darkness parable, 38

Kierkegaard, Søren, 165
Kirste, Imke, 155
Kivipetto, Mila, 153
Kornfield, Jack, 321
kosmocentric awareness, 288, 289, 291
Krafcik, Drew, 294–95
Krishna Das, 56–59
Kroc, Ray, 102
Kübler-Ross, Elisabeth, 205

Lennon, John, 343
Leroy, Angie, 127
letting go, 20, 207, 259, 278–79
Levy, Becca, 75–77, 78, 97, 149
life repair, 163, 190–239
    emotional repair as, 192, 194–201
    following life review, 191–94
    lost creativity found through,
        209–16, 217
    mortality awareness and, 192, 200
    obstacles to, 193, 200
    shadow-work for, 198, 201–4, 216–17
    spiritual repair as, 218–39
    stages of grief and, 204–8
life review, 163, 164–89
    descriptions of, 172–81
    dreams and, 169–70
    framework for, 178
    initiations and, 170–72
    life repair following, 191–94
    national or collective, 177
    purpose of, 165–68
    resistance to, 168–69
    shadow-work and, 181–85, 189
    spiritual, 189
light, reclaiming, 226–27, 238

liminal space, 103, 147, 158, 352
liminal time, 20, 115, 116, 279
Little Book on the Human Shadow, A
    (Bly), 42
loneliness, 127
longevity
    age-related beliefs and, 77
    dementia risk related to, 148
loving awareness, 6, 50, 305–6
Luders, Eileen, 53
Luke, Helen, 260–61

Macy, Joanna, 331–32
Maharishi Mahesh Yogi, 178
master and butler parable, 242–43
Matisse, Henri, 122
McGreevey, Sue, 155
Meade, Michael, 148, 245, 271–73
medical model, 113, 145
meditation
    age and practice of, 28, 33–34, 55
    brain health related to, 155, 157, 286
    grief processed through, 209
    life-changing illness and, 133
    physiological benefits of, 52–53
    pure awareness practice of, 66–67, 88
    shadow-work and, 49–51, 52, 53
Meeting the Shadow of Spirituality
    (Zweig), 57, 224
memory
    aging and loss of, 148–53
    delaying the loss of, 153–57
    self-stereotypes and, 76
mental health
    depression and, 145–47
    suicide and, 3–4

messengers. *See* divine messengers

Metzger, Deena, 124, 130–31, 273–75, 332

Metzner, Mitch, 331

Milarepa and Marpa story, 214–15

Miller, Ronald S., 22, 268

Milligan, Patricia, 80

mind/body split, 125–27

mindfulness practices, 36–37, 62, 234, 302. *See also* meditation

Mirren, Helen, 86

Mitchell, Joni, 268

mitzvah parable, 308–9

Monet, Claude, 122

Moody, Harry (Rick), xiii–xv, 83, 92, 107, 146, 170

Moore, Robert, 254

mortality awareness, 59–65. *See also* death

anger and, 206

collective, 330–33

denial vs., 59–60, 65, 206

life repair and, 192, 200

practices for, 66, 67

sense of time and, 252

spiritual progress and, 295–96

Moses, Grandma, 212

Nakao, Wendy Egyoku, 323–25

narrative self, 185

near-death experiences, 124, 169

neediness, 136–38

Neem Karoli Baba, 56, 356

Neti Neti practice, 305

new beginnings, 20

Newberg, Andrew, 286

Nisargadatta Maharaj, 300

noise vs. silence, 155

non-doing principle, 282

nondual spiritual practices, 305–7

Oakley, Diane, 99

Officer, Alana, 85

O'Keeffe, Georgia, 212

old age

consequences of beliefs about, 75–78

as fate of everyone, 34–36

individual experience of, 25–28

opposites characteristic of, 31–32

perceptions and meaning of, 32–34, 36

successful aging ideal and, 28–30

Old Man and the Sea (Hemingway), 89–90, 93

Orsborn, Carol, 22–23, 117, 251, 338

Pasternak, Boris, 212

peak-and-decline narrative, 212

Pei, I. M., 213

Pevny, Ron, 20, 257–58, 279

phowa practice, 307

physical abuse, 203

Pillemer, Karl, 213

Plotkin, Bill, 108

portals of age, 38–65

to depth, 40–49

to presence, 59–65

to silent vastness, 49–59

post-traumatic growth, 203

presence, portal to, 59–65

primal trust, 194–95, 202

projection, 33, 219

promised land, 339–42

pure awareness, 11–12, 49–59

   meditation practice, 66–67, 88

   shadow-work practice, 66

   spiritual progress and, 295

purpose

   beyond the self, 100–101

   cognitive health related to, 155–56

Queer Aging (Ramirez-Valles), 82

racial inequality, 2–3

rainmaker parable, 281–82

Rajneesh (Osho), 254

Ramana Maharshi, 54, 304

Ram Dass

   on caregiving, 140, 144–45

   on death and dying, 351, 357–58, 359

   devotional path of, 56, 305

   meditation practices of, 66–67, 305–6

   post-stroke experience of, 159, 285

   teachings of, 5–6, 24, 26, 39, 50

Ramirez-Valles, Jesus, 82

Rauch, Doug, 103–4

reinvention

   creativity and, 212

   retirement as, 100–104

relative wisdom, 292–93

Religion of Tomorrow, The (Wilber), 300

religious beliefs, 28, 62, 175, 221–22

Remen, Rachel Naomi, 170–72

reminiscence, 165

renewal process, 208

retirement, 89–120

   author's story about, 110–15

   as divine messenger, 90, 96

   personal meaning of, 90–92

   as reinvention, 100–104

   rite of passage for, 115

   shadow-work for, 92–96, 98–99, 104–10, 119

   social context of, 96–100

   as spiritual practice, 116–20

Rhee, Nari, 99

Rilke, Rainer Maria, 10

rites of passage, 19–25, 115, 255–56

roles, shift to soul from, 5–6, 116

Romancing the Shadow (Zweig and Wolf), 145, 179, 207

Rowan, Cris, 328

Rule of Saint Benedict, 62

Russell, Bertrand, 250–51

Sacks, Oliver, 167, 342

Sage-ing International, 22

Sanders, Colonel, 102

Sandoval, Brittiney, 251

Schachter-Shalomi, Zalman, 22, 54, 63, 180, 204, 248, 268

Schuitevoerder, Stephen, 317–18

self-blame, 125, 133, 207

self-care, 128, 143, 159

self-expression, 210–11

self-inquiry practice, 54, 306

self-reflection, 11, 47, 169, 290

service, 308–35

   call to sacred, 310–13, 318–21

   conscious grandparenting as, 326–30

interviews about, 322–25
shadow-work and, 313–18, 320–21, 333
spiritual practices and, 334–35
severe teachers, 180–81, 191
sexual abuse, 203, 224
shadow
    archetypes representing, 10, 108
    awareness of, 40–49, 65, 212, 295
    death process linked to, 355
    dreams exploring, xiv, 107–8, 261
    Jung's description of, xiv, 9
shadow-work
    ageism and, 44, 87–88
    caregiving and, 141–42
    completed life and, 341, 342, 346
    Elder transition and, 256, 260, 278–80
    how to engage in, 9–10
    illness and, 135–40, 160
    life repair and, 198, 201–4, 216–17
    life review and, 181–85, 189
    meditation and, 49–51, 52, 53
    retirement and, 92–96, 98–99, 104–10, 119
    sacred service and, 313–18, 320–21, 333
    spiritual development and, 295, 304
    steps for aging consciously, 369–70
Shah-Kazemi, Reza, 293
Shapiro, Rami, 54–55, 293, 306
Siddhartha, 13, 17–18, 19, 44, 283. See also Buddha
silence vs. noise, 155
silent vastness, 49–59
Sisyphus, 46, 47, 48–49
social isolation, 127

Sorensen, John, 322
soul
    as deeper identity, 39
    forgiveness arising from, 204
    life review and, 184, 185, 203
    shift from role to, 5–6, 116
spiritual bypass, 183, 234
spiritual disillusionment, 219–26
Spiritual Elders, 247, 254, 282, 283–85, 297–98
spiritual practice, 10, 28
    acceptance as, 36–37
    choosing for late life, 233–36
    completed life as, 347
    creativity as, 213–15
    illness as, 158–61
    life review as, 189
    mortality awareness as, 67
    nondual forms of, 305–7
    pure awareness meditation as, 66–67
    reinventing the Elder as, 280
    retirement as, 116–20
    shadow-work as, 295, 304
spiritual repair, 218–39
    disillusionment and, 219–26
    questions to contemplate for, 237–39
    reclamation process in, 226–37
stages of life (ashramas), 117–18
"Stages of Life, The" (Jung), 44–45
Steindl-Rast, David, 236
stereotypes, ageist, 76–77
Still Here (Ram Dass), 159, 356
stress, 52–53, 155, 157
Sufism, 243, 293, 312
suicide, 3–4, 145

Tarcher, Jeremy, 179
Tegn, Nicolai, 82
telomeres, 52–53
Terrell, Jessica, 81
Thayer, Colette, 80
Thomas, Bill, 21
360-degree view, 113, 182, 184, 203, 251
time affluence, 26
Tiresias myth, 121, 122
Tornstam, Lars, 243
transcendence, 21, 243–45, 246, 288
transitions, 21, 255
treasures of late life, 6–8
Trout, Susan, 313
trust, betrayal of, 194–95, 202, 224
Turrell, Kenneth, 80

unconscious, personal, 40–41
unfinished business, 61, 199, 216
unlived life, 182, 210

Vaughan, Frances, 61, 209, 345–46
victim perspective, 196, 202
Vipassana practice, 306
volunteering, 311
voter participation, 3

Walking Each Other Home
    (Ram Dass and Bush), 351, 356
Walsh, Roger, 208–9, 293, 303, 312, 334, 345
Wilber, Ken
    on contemplative practice, 235
    on human development, 21–22, 63, 254
    interview with, 299–300
    on spiritual bypass, 183, 234
    on stages of awareness, 20, 286–88
wisdom
    meaning and cultivation of, 291–96
    transmitting to future generations, 297–98
Wolf, Steve, 105, 179
"Wondrous and Wild" (Orsborn), 251
Wood, Beatrice, 68–69, 74
Woodman, Marion, 277–78
worldcentric awareness, 287, 289, 290–91
Wright, Frank Lloyd, 213

Yoga philosophy, 305

Books of Related Interest

Change Your Story, Change Your Life
Using Shamanic and Jungian Tools to Achieve Personal Transformation
by Carl Greer, Ph.D., Psy.D.

The Spirituality of Age
A Seeker's Guide to Growing Older
by Robert L. Weber, Ph.D., and Carol Orsborn, Ph.D.

An Energy Healer's Book of Dying
For Caregivers and Those in Transition
by Suzanne Worthley

Your Symphony of Selves
Discover and Understand More of Who We Are
by James Fadiman, Ph.D., and Jordan Gruber, J.D.

Herbs for Healthy Aging
Natural Prescriptions for Vibrant Health
by David Hoffmann, FNIMH, AHG

Before I Go
The Essential Guide to Creating a Good End of Life Plan
by Jane Duncan Rogers

Walking Your Blues Away
How to Heal the Mind and Create Emotional Well-Being
by Thom Hartmann

An End to Ageing?
Remedies for Life Extension
by Stephen Fulder, Ph.D.

INNER TRADITIONS • BEAR & COMPANY
P.O. Box 388
Rochester, VT 05767
1-800-246-8648
www.InnerTraditions.com

Or contact your local bookseller